BRIGHAM YOUNG UNIVERSITY
Church History Symposium

The WORLDWIDE CHURCH

MORMONISM *as a* GLOBAL RELIGION

EDITED BY MICHAEL A. GOODMAN
AND MAURO PROPERZI

RSC BYU
DESERET BOOK

Published by the Religious Studies Center, Brigham Young University, Provo, Utah, in cooperation with Deseret Book Company, Salt Lake City.

Visit us at rsc.byu.edu.

Printed in the United States of America by Sheridan Books, Inc.

Visit us at DeseretBook.com.

Cover design by Carmen Cole and interior layout by Madison Swapp.

ISBN: 978-0-8425-2973-0

US Retail: $31.99

Library of Congress Cataloging-in-Publication Data

Names: Brigham Young University Church History Symposium (2014 : Provo, Utah; Salt Lake City, Utah), author. | Goodman, Michael A., 1963- editor. |
Properzi, Mauro, editor.
Title: The worldwide church : Mormonism as a global religion / edited by Michael A. Goodman and Mauro Properzi.
Description: Provo : BYU Religious Studies Center, 2016. | Includes index.
Identifiers: LCCN 2015035472 | ISBN 9780842529730 (alk. paper)
Subjects: LCSH: Church of Jesus Christ of Latter-day Saints--Congresses. |
Mormon Church--Congresses.
Classification: LCC BX8605 .B75 2014 | DDC 289.3/32--dc23 LC record available at http://lccn.loc.gov/2015035472

Contents

South and Central America

Worldwide

Introduction

The Worldwide Reach of Mormonism

Michael A. Goodman

From Samuel Smith's first missionary efforts in June of 1830 to the newest missionary joining the now more than 88,000 missionaries worldwide, the Church continues the modern-day effort to fulfill the Lord's mandate: "Go ye therefore, and teach all nations, baptizing them in the name of the Father, and of the Son, and of the Holy Ghost" (Matthew 28:19). Though the first formal missionary effort outside the borders of the United States occurred only a few months after the official organization of the Church in April 1830, the Church remained largely a North American institution through the next 130 years.[1] As of 1960, only 3 percent of the 290 stakes of the Church existed internationally, and almost all of those were stakes that combined areas within the United States with contiguous areas of Canada and Mexico.[2] Suffice it to say, things have changed from those largely American beginnings.

A quick look at the last thirty years shows how dramatically the Church has transformed. Numbers never tell the whole story, but they can illuminate trends and point to important issues. This is certainly

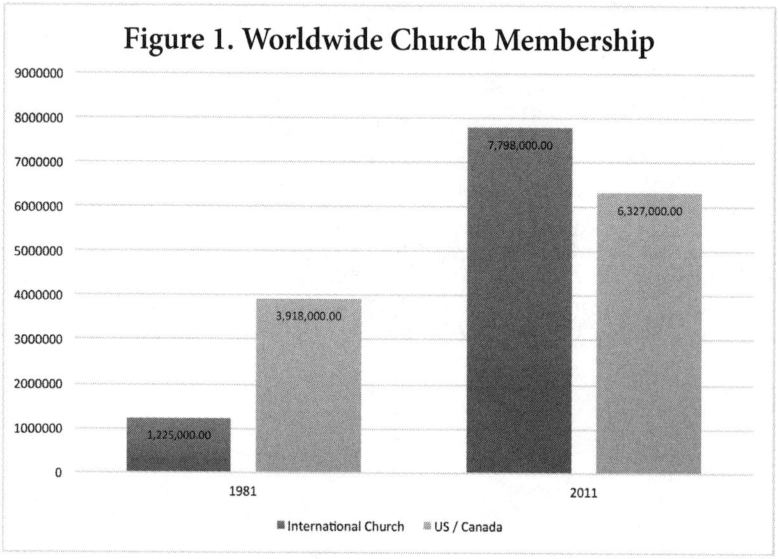

true regarding the internationalization of the Church. Figure 1 illustrates the demographic change that has taken place:

In thirty years, the international membership has grown from less than a quarter of the total Church population to over 55 percent. While U.S. and Canadian growth came in at 61 percent over that thirty-year period, international growth came in at a staggering 537 percent. And the trend shows no sign of changing. In 2013, the Church announced fifty-eight new missions, with over forty of them located in international areas.

Though international growth has far surpassed U.S. and Canadian growth in the last 30 years, as might be expected, that growth has varied widely by area. For example, though European growth has been almost three times that of U.S. and Canadian growth by percentage, it pales in comparison to Central American growth (which was over 18 times larger by percentage) or African growth (which was almost 44 times larger by percentage). Figure 2 gives detailed growth statistics by area worldwide:

Figure 2. Percent Growth From 1981 to 2011

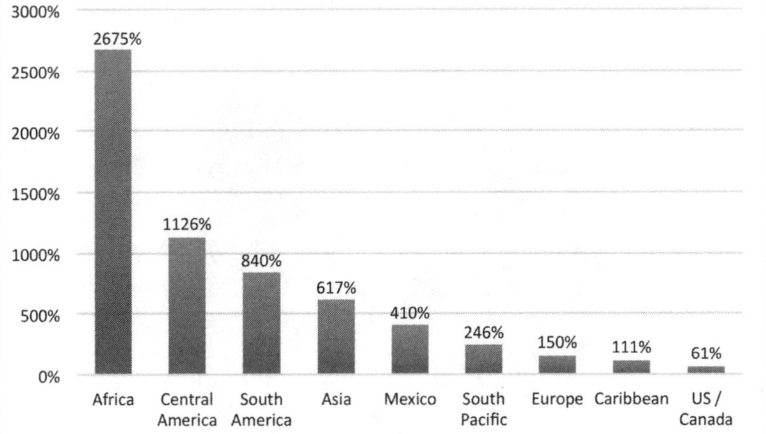

As a result of international growth, the current demographic makeup of the worldwide church is vastly different than it was fifty years ago when less than 3 percent of stakes included international areas. As of 2011, 48 percent of all stakes were located in international areas with total international membership at 55 percent. As the figure 3 shows, the international Church has a strong Latin American flavor. Mexico and the countries of Central and South America combine to include 39 percent of total Church membership. However, Asian growth over the last ten years has almost equaled Latin American growth, and African growth has more than doubled it. With growth in Africa, Asia, and Latin America, each far outstripping growth in the United States and Canada, the Church will become less and less an American church and more and more an international church as time passes. This reality will require a much greater emphasis on the study of the international Church than has previously been undertaken.

One step in that direction came in March 2014 when Brigham Young University and the Church History Department jointly sponsored the Church History Symposium entitled *The Worldwide Church:*

Figure 3. Worldwide Church Population - 2011

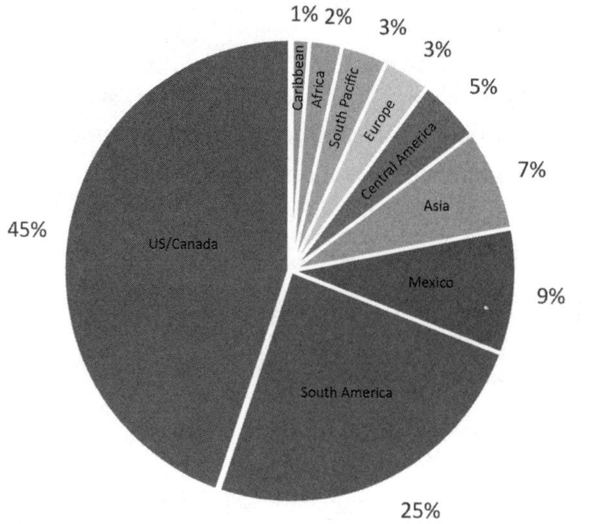

The Global Reach of Mormonism. One highlight of the symposium was President Dieter F. Uchtdorf's powerful keynote address entitled "Seeing Beyond the Leaf." Emphasizing the importance of learning our history, President Uchtdorf took his title from a remark made by Michael Crichton in which he stated, "If you don't know history, then you don't know anything. You are a leaf that doesn't know it is part of a tree." President Uchtdorf went on to encourage us to be more diligent in our study and work in Church history and challenged us to take the lessons learned and make a difference both in our personal life and in the Church as a whole. Terryl Givens provided another keynote address in which he highlighted the universal nature of the gospel of Jesus Christ. The symposium included fifty-eight total presenters who shared research that covered dozens of countries and numerous important topics regarding the international Church.

As a result of this symposium, many scholars—some who had not worked in the area of international Church history before, as well as others who had—made several important contributions to our understanding. Over fifty presentations were made at the conference covering subjects or presenters from six continents. Presenters were invited to submit their work in the form of scholarly papers, and this volume is the result of that effort. Knowing that there were many more quality presentations than we would be able to include in this volume, we encourage presenters to submit their work for publication in other possible venues.

As we continue to investigate the internationalization of the Church, it is crucial that we study the international Church in context. We must continually seek to understand the Church within the larger context of other cultural, political, and religious influences. For example, it is important to understand how local culture and traditions influence the growth of the Church in each land. We must also look at how local politics and legal realities influence the spread of the Church internationally, especially how these factors affect the religious freedoms of different countries and cultures. The intersection between the LDS Church and other faith traditions will continue to be a fruitful ground for investigation. Social issues and structures often differ across cultures. These social issues, such as gender and family relations, will need to be included as scholars seek to understand the international Church.

Besides understanding how external context influences the growth of the Church, another important facet that needs to be examined is how the internationalization of the Church impacts culture and administration within the Church. For example, how does the internationalization of the Church impact curricular issues? What impact will the increased demand for translation of Church materials and the need to make them quickly accessible to an ever-broader worldwide membership have on the Church? How does the continued growth of the Church in less-affluent areas impact Church finances, not to mention the ever increasing and diverse physical facility needs? How will the administrative structure of the Church need to adjust to effectively teach and train leaders and members worldwide? These are only some of the ways the internationalization of the Church will impact culture and administrative reality within the Church.

Elder Neal A. Maxwell once said, "The Church has done many difficult things, and from these achievements one would not wish to detract. But all the easy things the Church has had to do have been done. From now on it is high adventure!"[3] That statement was made in 1979. Though true at the time, that statement seems even more appropriate today. As the Church moves forward in the twenty-first century, it will face unique challenges made all the more daunting because of the worldwide scope of the work. In his address at the Church History Symposium mentioned earlier, Terryl Givens asked, "How do you export and disseminate the gospel in all its purity and goodness to myriad peoples, nationalities, ethnic groups and societies, without the cultural trappings and accretions it has acquired? The problem is as old as Christianity." Just as the Lord's Church in former times learned to operate globally after starting on a far more local scale, the Lord's Church in the latter days must also learn to thrive on a worldwide scale after starting with similarly local origins. Ours will be the task of not only helping with that work but documenting it for all to see and understand.

Notes

1. The mission of Joseph Smith Sr. and Don Carlos Smith to Canada in September 1830 began international missionary work in the latter days.
2. This statistic and all of the statistics in this article were taken from *Deseret News Church Almanacs* for the respective years.
3. Neal A. Maxwell, "The Old Testament: Relevancy within Antiquity," in *A Symposium on the Old Testament* (Salt Lake City: The Church of Jesus Christ of Latter-day Saints, 1979), 12.

1

Seeing Beyond the Leaf

President Dieter F. Uchtdorf

When I received the invitation to participate in this symposium, I felt like it was something close to my heart. I'm not entirely sure of all the reasons why, but I do know this: history is important. And keeping ourselves anchored to the lessons learned from history will enable us to emulate the best of what it means to be human. It can also help us avoid the worst. Georg Wilhelm Friedrich Hegel, the German philosopher and idealist, said, "We learn from history that we do not learn from history," which is supported by George Santayana, who said, "Those who cannot remember the past are condemned to repeat it."[1]

The late novelist Michael Crichton is reported to have said, "If you don't know history, then you don't know anything. You are a leaf that doesn't know it is part of a tree."[2] History teaches us not only

President Dieter F. Uchtdorf is a member of the First Presidency of The Church of Jesus Christ of Latter-day Saints.

about the leaves of existence; it also teaches about the twigs, branches, trunks, and roots of life. And these lessons are important.

One of the weaknesses we have as mortals is to assume that our "leaf" is all there is—that our experience encompasses everyone else's, that our truth is complete and universal. As I considered what I wanted to speak about today, it seemed that the metaphor of the leaf needed to be at the heart. But I also ran across an old Yiddish expression that goes, "To a worm in horseradish, the world is horseradish." I want to emphasize that the truth embraced by The Church of Jesus Christ of Latter-day Saints extends beyond leaves and certainly beyond horseradish. It extends beyond time and space and encompasses all truth—from the mysteries of the tiniest atoms to the vast and incomprehensible secrets that the universe holds so tantalizingly before us.

The gospel of Jesus Christ encompasses not only the truth of what was and what is but the truth of what can and will be. It is the most practical of all truths. It teaches the way of the disciple—a path that can take ordinary, flawed mortals and transform them into glorious, immortal, and limitless beings whose divine potential is beyond our meager capacity to imagine.

Now, that is practical truth. It is priceless beyond imagination. It is truth of the highest order. The pursuit, discovery, and application of truth are what we are on this earth to discover. The gospel of Jesus Christ not only encompasses all truth, but it specializes in the knowledge that will be of greatest worth to us in this life and throughout the eternities to come.

Seeing Beyond Our Leaf

As mentioned before, one of the traits we share as human beings is that we assume that our own experience is a true and proper base from which to view the rest of the world. For example, when we are healthy, we presume that those we meet are healthy and judge them by that standard. When we are sick, we are more likely to wonder if others are sick as well. We assume that the leaf of our existence defines the world.

Tolkien began his famous novel *The Hobbit* with these words: "In a hole in the ground there lived a hobbit." If you remember, Bilbo Baggins lived in a comfortable home in the Shire, a small, peaceful village that celebrated gardening, community gatherings, and a meal schedule that included breakfast, second breakfast, elevensies, lunch, afternoon tea, supper, and dinner.

Bilbo was quite content with the leaf of his life. And it was beautiful for all that. But little did he know of the twigs, branches, trunks, and roots that were all around him. Little did he know of distant towers, trolls, and talking trees. The farther he went from the comforts of the Shire, the more remarkable and strange the world became.

While Tolkien's world was one of fiction, it can serve as a metaphor for our own experience. I grew up in a small branch of the Church in Zwickau, East Germany. Our little meetinghouse was a beautiful building with an old air-driven organ. It was my privilege to sometimes have the assignment to work the bellows that supplied air to the pipe organ. While the congregation sang our beloved hymns of the Restoration, I pumped with all my strength so the organ would not run out of wind. The eyes of the organist unmistakably indicated whether I was doing fine or needed to increase my efforts quickly.

I loved our little meetinghouse with its stained-glass window that showed Joseph Smith kneeling in the Sacred Grove. When I was young, I supposed that this was what the Church looked like—that what I was seeing in Zwickau was what every other member of the Church saw during their Sunday experience throughout the world—that the little leaf of my experience was the same as everyone else's.

As I grew older, our family moved to Frankfurt, where the Church was a little larger. There were more members there. The meetinghouse looked different.

The older I got, the more exposure I had to the Church in its many forms throughout the world. I have worshipped with the Saints of God in congregations throughout the world, from the most humble of homes to the great Conference Center in Salt Lake City.

Now it is approaching seven decades since that small child sat behind the organ pumping wildly, trying to force enough air through its pipes so that the congregation could hear the beautiful music. I have seen the Church—leaf, twig, branch, trunk, and root. And though outwardly the Church appears different in the various areas of the world, I can affirm that it is of the same spirit and the same essence wherever you go. It rests upon the foundation of the blessed Redeemer, and it is guided by the rock of revelation. No matter how different the Church may appear in its outer form, wherever you travel the inner Spirit of Christ is the same in every congregation, and that is how it should be.

I stand in awe of how the Holy Spirit transforms the lives of individuals, regardless of their cultural, economic, or social background, and leads all mankind to forsake the natural man and cleave to the light, to feel the mighty change that comes to those who seek God's truth. I have met men, women, and children on every continent who have experienced this transformative rebirth in their hearts, causing them to "have no more disposition to do evil, but to do good continually."[3]

Humility Leads to Spiritual Knowledge

Oftentimes it is not the wise nor the great who respond to the words of the prophets, but the poor in heart, the humble, and those who suffer. Frequently, these are they who approach their own Hill Onidah, open their hearts to the word of God, and arouse their faculties to "exercise a particle of faith"—even if they can only muster "no more than [a] desire to believe."[4] Sometimes all it takes is the smallest seed—merely a desire to believe—for faith to sprout, blossom, and become good.[5] Sometimes we must go to the Father in earnest prayer, tears wetting our cheeks, as we repeat the words the distraught father offered to the gentle Christ, "Lord, I [do] believe; help thou mine unbelief."[6]

From small seeds, great trees grow.

From small beginnings, the Lord can work miracles in our lives.

From Humble Beginnings

Our Heavenly Father is able to make great things come from small beginnings. In fact, this is often His preferred strategy.

Case in point, I invite you to consider the small Galilean town of Nazareth. Why do you suppose our Heavenly Father chose to have His Only Begotten Son raised in this relatively insignificant town in Galilee? Why Nazareth? Why not Jerusalem? Or Rome, for that matter?

The Jewish convert to Christianity Alfred Edersheim wrote of this area that "there was a general contempt in Rabbinic circles for all that was Galilean." And that "Galilean—Fool!" was a common expression.[7]

The town of Nazareth is not mentioned in the Old Testament, nor does Josephus speak of it. I understand that the Talmud lists sixty-three Galilean towns but does not mention the city of Christ's youth. When Nathanael first heard of Jesus, he voiced a question that must have been on many an inquirer's lips: "Can there any good thing come out of Nazareth?"[8] And yet from this small, out-of-the-way town came the Light of the World, the Savior of mankind, the Redeemer.

Eighteen centuries later, in another small, out-of-the-way town, lived a young man who walked into a grove of trees near his home with a question in his heart. He knelt in prayer to ask God for direction in his life. Palmyra was nestled in upstate New York, far from the intellectual and cultural centers of the United States (let alone the world). Why would our Heavenly Father choose such an out-of-the-way place to reveal Himself to man?

From these two unlikely and disregarded places—Nazareth and Palmyra—emerged two figures who would change the world.

"The Foolishness of God"

Throughout the record of sacred history, we find that our Heavenly Father teaches His children over and again not to place their trust in the wisdom of the world—not to overvalue what the world holds in high regard. He teaches us that "the foolishness of God is wiser than men; and the weakness of God is stronger than men."[9] And yet we have an almost irresistible desire to assume that the leaf of information we have in our possession is a representation of all there is to know. We assume that the horseradish that we see all around us is proof that the world is made of the substance.

We do the best we can with the information at our disposal to make assumptions and increase the body of knowledge—and this is a noble pursuit. However, when we assume that what we know is all there is to know, we miss the mark and our philosophies and theories fall short of the rich truths that populate heaven and earth.

In the words of Orson F. Whitney, an early Apostle of the Church, the gospel "embraces all truth, whether known or unknown. It incorporates all intelligence, both past and prospective. No righteous principle will ever be revealed, no truth can possibly be discovered, either in time or in eternity, that does not in some manner, directly or indirectly, pertain to the Gospel of Jesus Christ."[10]

Our Heavenly Father teaches this lesson to His children over and again—He warns against setting aside the knowledge of God or dismissing its importance. He teaches us that we should not assume that what we know—what we can prove and test and verify—is all that there is. "We believe all that God has revealed, all that He does now reveal, and we believe that He will yet reveal many great and important things pertaining to the Kingdom of God."[11]

God sees infinitely more than we do. His perspective is infinitely more complete and profound than ours, "for as the heavens are higher than the earth, so are [His] ways higher than [ours], and [His] thoughts than [ours]."[12] He has more information than we do. And a little more information can make all the difference in the world.

Since English is not my native language, I enjoy looking into the meaning of individual words—even plain ones. Take the word *plane* and another word *plane* spelled exactly the same way. Both words have the same amount of letters, and they sound just the same. Nevertheless, there are huge differences between them. One is a handy tool for smoothing planks of uneven wood. The other is an infinitely better choice for transoceanic travel.

A small amount of additional information—and perhaps a bit of context—makes a wondrous difference in our capacity to understand the meaning of words and the meaning of life's circumstances.

God Chooses the "Foolish Things of the World"

In our world today, we seek out the wise, wealthy, and well-known. We honor their opinions and follow their research. Compare that with how our Heavenly Father operates. He often chooses "the foolish things of the world to confound the wise; and God hath chosen the weak things of the world to confound the things which are mighty."[13]

"And if men come unto me I will show unto them their weakness. I give unto men weakness that they may be humble; and my grace is sufficient for all men that humble themselves before me; for if they humble themselves before me, and have faith in me, then will I make weak things become strong unto them.

"Behold, I will show unto the Gentiles their weakness, and I will show unto them that faith, hope and charity bringeth unto me—the fountain of all righteousness."[14]

He uses the weak and insignificant to bring to pass His work. He gently reminds us that the "things which are despised, hath God chosen, . . . that no flesh should glory in his presence."[15]

His knowledge of truth is so infinitely greater than ours that He looks upon the wisdom of the world as perhaps we might look upon the dogmatic assertions of a pedantic fool. Though the fool may speak words with passion and conviction, he may lack essential information.

The Need for Faith

We must not abandon God's revealed truth—which comes from the roots and source of all righteousness and truth. For what we see, in contrast, is the truth of our leaf.

Frederick the Great, the eighteenth-century king of Prussia, was one of the most innovative and successful military strategists in history. But he was not always successful. After his defeat at Kunersdorf, many of his soldiers widely scattered in confusion. The story is told that "one [soldier] was brought before the king, who asked him why he had run away. 'Because things were going badly for Your Majesty.'

"Frederick reflected for a moment, then said mildly, 'I suggest that you wait a week. Then, if things are still going badly, we will quit together.'"[16]

There will be times when it may appear that things are going badly for the truth of God—that the evidence of the world contradicts God's utterances. For my part, I have learned to be patient, knowing that in the end things will work out. God's kingdom will continue to grow. The truth will continue to flourish and spread throughout the earth. Sometimes all it takes is a little faith and a little patience. Things which may appear impossible now may become matter-of-fact in years to come.

The Freiberg Temple

May I offer you a personal experience that illustrates this? You are all well aware that in 1961 the Soviet Union permitted the building a wall that would cut off the city of West Berlin from the surrounding area. This wall was a symbol of the Cold War and served as a metaphor for the separation and division of the communist world and the democratic Western world. One of the resulting side effects of this increased isolation was that it became increasingly difficult for members of the Church in East Germany to visit the Swiss Temple—the only temple in Europe at that time.

Seven years later, in 1968, Elder Thomas S. Monson, an Apostle of the Lord Jesus Christ, visited the Saints in the German Democratic Republic (DDR). President Monson said of that visit:

> On a cloudy and rain-filled day I journeyed to the city of Görlitz, situated deep in the [DDR] near the Polish and Czech borders. I attended my first meeting with the Saints. We assembled in a small and ancient building. As the members sang the hymns of Zion, they literally filled the hall with their faith and devotion.

> My heart was filled with sorrow when I realized the members had no patriarch, no wards or stakes—just branches. They could not receive temple blessings—either endowment or sealing. No official visitor had come from Church headquarters in a long time. The members could not leave their country. Yet they trusted in the Lord with all their hearts.
>
> I stood at the pulpit, and with tear-filled eyes and a voice choked with emotion, I made a promise to the people: "If you will remain true and faithful to the commandments of God, every blessing any member of the Church enjoys in any other country will be yours." Then I realized what I had said. That night, I dropped to my knees and pleaded with my Heavenly Father, "Father, I'm on Thy errand; this is Thy Church. I have spoken words that came not from me but from Thee and Thy Son. Wilt Thou fulfill the promise in the lives of this noble people."[17]

In 1975, six years after President Monson's first visit to the German Democratic Republic, he came again, went to a beautiful place high above the Elbe River near Dresden and Meissen, and rededicated the East German Mission for the advancement of God's work. I quote from his prayer:

> Grant, Heavenly Father, that the membership here may receive their patriarchal blessings and live in such a way as to bring the promises to fulfillment.
>
> Heavenly Father, wilt Thou open up the way that the faithful may be accorded the privilege of going to Thy holy temple, there to receive their holy endowments and to be sealed as families for time and all eternity.

The dedicatory prayer continues with the most wondrous pronouncements. If you haven't read it yet, I recommend it warmly. President Monson concludes:

> Amidst the ringing of church bells this morning, and the singing of birds in this, the forest which Thou hast created, music fills our souls and gratitude fills our hearts as we humbly acknowledge before Thee that Thou art our

> Father, that with Thee all things are possible, and that Thy Gospel has been restored upon the earth. . . .
>
> Grant that the way may be cleared for the program of the Church in its fulness to come to this people, for they, through their faith, have merited such blessings.
>
> As Thy humble servant, acknowledging the divine revelation and inspiration of this day, I therefore invoke Thy holy blessings upon Thy work and upon Thy people in the Dresden Mission of The Church of Jesus Christ of Latter-day Saints.[18]

When I first learned about these wonderful promises by a prophet of God, my heart filled with gratitude to the Lord but at the same time with an encroaching feeling of uncertainty, almost unbelief. There seemed no possible way that these beautiful promises to our people could happen in their lifetime, if ever. How could a temple be built and operated in East Germany? I had faith in the Lord, and I loved and acknowledged President Monson as a prophet, seer, and revelator. I wanted the Saints in that country to have the full blessings of the gospel, but at the moment I just couldn't see a way in which this could be accomplished.

I grew up in East Germany; that's where my family joined the Church. Harriet's ancestors came from the same part of Germany. We wished these promises to be fulfilled. But we knew firsthand of the challenges in our country. Was it possible to receive these promised blessings at a time of great political and societal division and isolation, at the time of the Cold War? I felt somehow like the man who cried out, "Lord, I believe; help thou mine unbelief." It was clear to me that the evidence of the world contradicted the word of an Apostle of the Lord.

Almost a decade later, Harriet and I had all but forgotten this prophetic promise. We were attending the Swiss Temple one day when Harriet overheard a conversation between two elderly sisters

The construction of the Freiberg Germany Temple is one of the great miracles in the history of the Church in Europe. It is a wonderful example of how God can make the impossible possible in any part of the world.

from East Germany. The elderly at the time were the only ones in the DDR who were allowed to travel to the Swiss Temple, as the regime felt sure that they were not a flight risk.

One of these elderly sisters was talking to her friend about a very strange message she had received the same morning. Her son had informed her that soon a temple would be built in the DDR, the German Democratic Republic!

Harriet told me that this poor sister must have been very confused or lost her mind over the continuous wishful thinking to have a temple in East Germany. We felt sorry for these sisters but also a little amused at the same time when we shared the episode with our friends. There wasn't even a temple in West Germany. How could the Church build one in the DDR?

A few days later, the Freiberg Temple was announced.

In June of 1985, President Gordon B. Hinckley dedicated in East Germany the Freiberg Germany Temple as a house of the Lord. It was the first temple behind the Iron Curtain. A temple in a communist land that almost everyone (including me) had said would never be possible in our lifetime.

The construction of the Freiberg Temple is one of the great miracles in the history of the Church in Europe. It is a wonderful example of how God can make the impossible possible in any part of the world.

The lesson here is an important one: God knows what we do not. What may seem impossible for us is not impossible to Him. What we mortals may write off as foolishness may be entered into the book of heaven as fact.

God is good and faithful, and He performs His work in ways that sometimes are not comprehensible to our mortal minds. He asks that we have a little faith, a little patience, that we believe. He asks us to seek after Him and believe in His word.

It is my conviction that those who disregard the reality of heaven will ultimately find themselves on the wrong side of history.

The Importance of Keeping Records

I assume that all of you love to study history. Talking to you about the importance of history or the keeping of records would appear almost like "taking owls to Athens," "carrying coal to Newcastle," or "selling snow to Eskimos."

As a slight variation of what I said at the beginning, let me add, "Those who *don't* study history are doomed to repeat it, and those *who do* study history stand by helplessly *while everyone else* repeats it."

On April 6, 1830, a revelation was given to Joseph Smith the Prophet at Fayette, New York. The revelation was given at the organization of the Church in the home of Peter Whitmer Sr. Six men, who had previously been baptized, participated. By unanimous vote these persons expressed their desire and determination to officially organize the Church. In this revelation, one half-sentence has great significance for our consideration today. It reads, "Behold, there shall be a record kept among you."[19]

Almost five years later, in February of 1835, Joseph Smith met with nine members of the Twelve and placed before the council an item that would be of importance. He told them that he had learned something from experience that gave him deep sorrow. Then he said:

> It is a fact [that] if I now had in my possession, every decision [we] had [made] upon important items of doctrine and duties, since the commencement of this work, I would not part with them for any sum of money; but we have neglected to take minutes of such things, thinking, perhaps, that they would never benefit us afterwards; which, [if we] had them now, would decide almost every point of doctrine which might be agitated. But this has been neglected, and now we cannot bear record, to the Church and to the world, of the great and glorious manifestations which have been made to us, with that degree of power and authority we otherwise could, if we now had these things to publish abroad.

Joseph Smith then urged the members of the Twelve to keep records of events and decisions. He said if they would do this, even with items that may seem to have little or no worth, that later they would "find [them] of infinite worth, not only to your brethren, but [they] will be a feast to your own souls."[20]

With this being emphasized by the Prophet Joseph, I thank you for the efforts you are making to record the history of the Church and its people.

At the organization of the Church, in the home of Peter Whitmer Sr., a revelation was given that contained these words of great significance: "Behold, there shall be a record kept among you."

Sometimes we feel that our lives are mundane and trivial. "Of what interest would my life be to anyone?" we might say. Those of you who are deeply involved in the recording and teaching of history can answer that question far better than I. You understand the worth of records that may have seemed trivial and mundane to the people who wrote them at the time but are cherished and treasured years later.

I commend you for all you do to keep a history of the Church and for your efforts in encouraging others to keep a record of their lives and their families. This is a cause that is of great importance to God's work and to His Church.

I am grateful for the marvelous work that is being done to prepare and publish *The Joseph Smith Papers*. Learning about the real struggles and real successes of early Church leaders and members is a very faith-promoting process for me. We always need to remember that transparency and openness keep us clear of the negative side effects of secrecy or the cliché of faith-promoting rumors. Jesus taught the Jews, "And ye shall know the truth, and the truth shall make you free."[21] Truth and transparency complement each other. "The glory of God is intelligence, or, in other words, light and truth."[22]

A Religion of Learning

My dear brothers and sisters, one of the most fascinating things about this mortal experience is that there is so much to learn. Isn't it a remarkable feeling to belong to a Church that not only embraces truth—no matter the source—but that teaches there is much more to come, that God "will yet reveal many great and important things pertaining to the Kingdom of God."[23] As a result, we are humble about the truth we have. We understand our knowledge is a work in progress, that the leaf we have before us is simply one microscopic snapshot—part of an infinitely vast forest of fascinating knowledge.

Our little world—our small section of experience—may be an accurate and true reflection of our reality. But, it is only an infinitesimal atom in the vast universe of what we eventually will know. Isn't that a glorious concept!

Isn't it wondrous to belong to a Church that teaches that infinite progress and eternal knowledge await those who set foot upon the path of discipleship of Jesus Christ and follow it in faithfulness and dedication?

I wish you the best in this noble effort as you pursue the great adventure of recording and bringing more light to history. The roads we travel are certainly not guaranteed to be easy or ever pleasant, but if we keep traveling in the pursuit of truth, they will always lead back to the ultimate truth: they will lead us to our Heavenly Father, who is the great historian, the great record keeper, the great Creator, mentor, and friend. Of this I testify and leave you my blessing as an Apostle of the Lord, in the name of Jesus Christ, amen.

Notes

1. George Santayana, *Reason in Common Sense*, vol. 1 of *Life of Reason; Or, The Phases of Human Progress* (New York: Charles Scribner's Sons, 1905), 284.
2. Michael Crichton, *Timeline* (New York: Knopf, 1999), 73.
3. Mosiah 5:2.
4. Alma 32:27.
5. See Alma 32.
6. Mark 9:24.
7. Alfred Edersheim, *The Life and Times of Jesus the Messiah* (McLean, VA: Macdonald, 1988), 225–26.
8. John 1:46.
9. 1 Corinthians 1:25.
10. *Elders' Journal*, October 15, 1906, 26, as quoted in Spencer W. Palmer, "World Religions (Non-Christian) and Mormonism: Overview," in *Encyclopedia of Mormonism*, ed. Daniel H. Ludlow (New York: Macmillan, 1992), 4:1589.
11. Articles of Faith 1:9.
12. See Isaiah 55:9.
13. 1 Corinthians 1:27.
14. Ether 12:27–28.
15. 1 Corinthians 1:28–29.
16. Clifton Fadiman and Andre Bernard, *Bartlett's Book of Anecdotes* (Boston: Little Brown and Company, 2000), 218.
17. Thomas S. Monson, "Thanks Be to God," *Ensign*, May 1989, 51.
18. Dedication and rededication prayer for the German Democratic Republic, given by Elder Thomas S. Monson near Radebeul, between Dresden and Meissen, April 27, 1975; see http://www.mission.net/germany/berlin/history/prayer.htm.

19. Doctrine and Covenants 21:1.
20. "History of Joseph Smith," *Millennial Star*, April 2, 1853, 212–13.
21. John 8:32.
22. Doctrine and Covenants 93:36.
23. Articles of Faith 1:9.

Africa

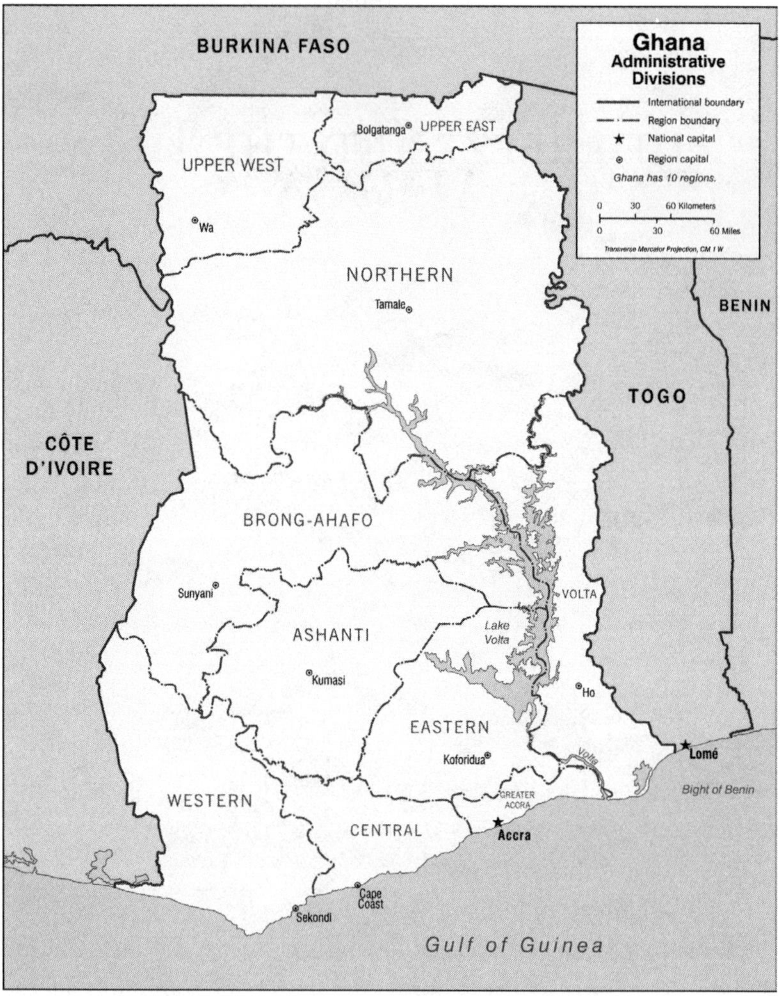

Ghana is often recognized as the first sub-Saharan colony (depending on how that is defined) to achieve independence from its European colonizers. That independence came in 1957.

2

The Freeze and the Thaw

The LDS Church and the State in Ghana of the 1980s

J. B. Haws

In the middle of June 1989, the government of Ghana suspended all activities of The Church of Jesus Christ of Latter-day Saints in that nation.[1] While there had been rumblings of trouble in the months previous to the suspension, nearly all Ghanaian Mormons only found out about "the freeze" when it was announced on the radio. The suspension was as severe as it was sudden. Military and paramilitary groups occupied the Church's buildings and farm. All LDS Church meetings were discontinued. Foreign Church missionaries and leaders were forced to leave the country—and they were given one week to do so. The future was uncertain, to say the least.

After eighteen months of tight restrictions, the suspension was lifted. Ironically, in the years following the freeze, the LDS Church in Ghana grew as never before. A noteworthy side effect of the

J. B. Haws is an assistant professor of Church history and doctrine at Brigham Young University.

government's action against the Latter-day Saints was that the Church received unprecedented attention in that country. The government inquiries into Mormon activities and beliefs fueled widespread interest when full Church activities resumed.

It is a fantastic story—a story of intrigue (the CIA—or at least the specter of the CIA—even played a role), of tension, of diplomacy, of patience, of perseverance. And it is a story that has been told really well in other places—by Emmanuel Kissi, for example, in his book *Walking in the Sand*, as well as by those who have recorded and analyzed a number of oral histories with Ghanaian Latter-day Saints: Dale LeBaron, Matthew Heiss, and former mission and temple president in Ghana John Riding, to name a few. This paper is indebted to their work.

What this article hopes to do is to take its bearings from an analogy that Melissa Inouye recently presented to the Mormon History Association and then published in the *Mormon Studies Review*. Her analogy centers on the banyan tree. Unlike an oak tree, whose branches all grow from one central trunk, the banyan tree's branches send down "prop roots" that become, in a sense, trunks in their own right—roots that become indistinguishable from the central trunk. Inouye proposed that this is a way to think about the history of the LDS Church in various locales around the world, where central trunk *and* prop root are both nourishing the growth of the tree.[2]

In this case, Inouye's analogy at the very least calls for a clearer understanding about what was happening on the ground in Ghana—a clearer understanding of what the soil was like into which this specific prop root planted itself and drew out nutrients and strength. A view from that ground level raises some questions: What was it about the LDS Church in Ghana, and specifically the Ghana of 1989, that aroused suspicion? What was life during the freeze like for Ghanaian Mormons—Mormons like a newly married branch clerk, or a sister missionary whose service was cut short by the freeze, or a Church employee whose brother led the Ghanaian government? And what changed during and after the freeze? All of this—and more—was part of the mix, so these are the questions to be considered in turn here.

Trying to tackle these questions does at least three things. First, it can help outsiders (of which I am one) appreciate that the freeze in Ghana was not as arbitrary or as capricious or as vindictive as it might initially appear. It is worth being cautious about making assumptions about the story of the freeze as a simple or formulaic persecution narrative when the reality is much more complex. Second, it heightens our appreciation for the real people who walked a very tight rope of faith under fire—and came out more committed than ever. Finally, this paper also aims to offer new information about the resolution of the ban on the Church because of recently released oral-history archival material.

Trying to Hold on to the "Revolution"

Ghana stands out in African history as the first sub-Saharan colony to achieve independence from its European colonizers. Independence came in 1957, but stability did not.

By late 1981, three "republic" governments had come and gone, each one terminated by a military coup of some kind. And by 1981, the most recent such transition had been the shortest lived. Flight lieutenant Jerry Rawlings, a junior military officer, led in 1979 what has been called "the mutiny" against his military superiors who were running the country. Rawlings's group then turned governmental control to elected officials—this was the "third republic." But only two years later, Rawlings and his Provisional National Defense Council (the PNDC) retook control from President Hilla Limann's government because of widely reported accusations of government corruption and mismanagement. Rawlings announced to the nation that this was not a coup but a revolution, a chance to change the status

In 1981, flight lieutenant Jerry John Rawlings (shown here in 2009) retook control of the Ghanaian government as leader of the Provisional National Defense Council (PNDC). (© Pruneau / Wikimedia Commons / CC-BY-SA-3.0.)

quo in Ghanaian government. He spoke about giving the people the chance to govern by wresting control from the old establishment of Ghana's upper class.[3] It almost goes without saying that this unsettled traditional power structures in Ghana, and a number of Ghanaian conservatives saw the PNDC as modeling itself after Communist regimes—although in the end these assumptions proved too simplistic, based more on rhetoric than realities.[4]

Still, the PNDC's initial foreign policy course did send a strong anti-establishment message. Rawlings's government felt that Ghana was too beholden to the West—to the United States and Western Europe. Rawlings therefore distanced his government from those traditional trading partners and made visible overtures to a number of nations; some of those overtures created diplomatic waves. The PNDC quickly forged strong ties with Gaddafi's Libya. Rawlings also invited investment and advisement from Cuba, from Bulgaria, from East Germany, and from the Soviet Union. While Rawlings may have simply envisioned a course of economic independence from the powerful nations that had long held sway in Ghana, as well as the chance to learn from other revolutionary regimes with staying power, western observers worried that Ghana was aligning itself with the Soviet bloc.[5]

Already by 1984, there were repeated assertions by PNDC officials that the CIA sought to oust the revolutionary government and reinstate the old political elite that the PNDC had displaced. What might have seemed to be only propaganda-type conspiracy theories instead found credibility in 1985, when an American operative named Sharon Scranage "[leaked] information about the CIA network to her Ghanaian boyfriend," himself an intelligence operative in Ghana and cousin to PNDC head Jerry Rawlings. This boyfriend, Mike Soussoudis, was arrested by U.S. officials when he visited Scranage—and he was later only released as part of a prisoner exchange. This web of intrigue and repeated talk of a "revolutionary government" threw fuel on global fires that created heat, paradoxically, in the Cold War world.[6]

The irony is that by the mid-1980s, Rawlings's government did something of an about-face and sought to reestablish stronger economic ties with the United States, Canada, and Western Europe. Soviet diplomats had candidly told Rawlings that the USSR's internal problems meant that the Soviets were not in a position to provide the infusion of investment that the PNDC sought. Ghana's relationship with the West, therefore, was necessary but shaky, tainted by distrust on both sides.[7]

The PNDC's foreign-policy troubles were not simply overseas, however. Ghana's neighbors felt that Rawlings's revolution was a destabilizing threat in the region. After a coup in Burkina Faso, that nation's new leader, Captain Thomas Sankara, openly thanked Jerry Rawlings for supporting his cause. For their part, Togo and the Ivory Coast created bad blood with the PNDC when they harbored Ghanaian expatriates and became, in essence, staging grounds for anti-PNDC groups.[8]

Feeling the threat of outside interference, the PNDC government also sought to curb internal dissent. In 1987, in response to student protests about the PNDC, Rawlings's administration completely closed three prominent college campuses. And by the mid-1980s, it was widely understood that for "all intents and purposes, an independent press had ceased to exist"; in March 1989, only three months before the freeze on the LDS Church, the "government revoked the licenses of all publications and required their editors to re-apply for registration." The ostensible reason for the re-registration was to "[protect] moral standards" and "restore basic standards of decency in journalism and . . . conserve scarce paper for essential educational publications." Critics, however, noted that the assertion of these kinds of controls seemed undeniably aimed at silencing any opposition.[9]

One such prominent spokesman for the opposition, Professor Albert Adu Boahen, put it this way in February 1988: "We have not protested or staged riots because we trust the PNDC, but because we fear the PNDC! We are afraid of being detained, liquidated or dragged before the CVC [Citizens' Vetting Committees] of NIC [National Investigations Committee] or being subjected to all sorts of molestation. And in any case have Ghanaians not been protesting at all as the Head of State thinks? They have been in a very subtle and quiet way—hence the culture of silence."[10]

At the same time, this picture of an overly totalitarian regime calls for some nuance. It should be noted that the Rawlings government seemed sincere in its self-perception that it was warring against endemic corruption. The availability and reliability of civil services in Ghana did improve during the 1980s.[11] And, importantly, when the PNDC did give way to the "fourth republic" and open elections in 1992, Jerry Rawlings won the majority vote for president—and he was reelected in 1996. That says something, in the very least, about a public divided in its appraisal of PNDC efforts.

Plus, it seems safe to say that, for this author and for most readers, it would be difficult to understand the shadow of imperialism that Ghanaians still felt keenly in the 1980s—being, as they were, only one generation removed from their declared independence in 1957. Centuries of exploitation created psychic wounds that still were understandably raw in the 1980s. "What probably made the West edgy" about Ghana in the early 1980s, one historian proposed, was the "hysterical, vituperative, anti-American, anti-imperialist propaganda which became the hallmark of the nation's media at this time."[12]

Who Are These Mormons? CIA Operatives or "God Makers"?

In that climate, Mormons—especially the American Mormon missionaries—seemed doubly suspicious.[13] As early as 1983, the *People's Daily Graphic*, a Ghanaian newspaper, listed "the Mormons (the Church of Jesus Christ of Latter Day Saints)" as one of the "identifiable organisations, which have been implicated in CIA activities elsewhere, [and] should be viewed with some suspicion and close and vigilant watch in Ghana." (The article also included the Peace Corps, the Unification Church, the "Hare Krishnas," and the International Catholic Youth Federation, among others, in this list of "identifiable" CIA affiliates.)[14] The potency of such accusations during a volatile time—and especially the pressure of public sentiment against the CIA—led one African Studies professor to tell the *New York Times* in 1985 that "Rawlings cannot appear to be soft on the C.I.A." given the mood in Ghana.[15] And rumors about the Mormons persisted. "Who knows," a Ghanaian newspaper asked in December 1986, "whether [Latter-day Saints] are an offshoot of the C.I.A.?"[16]

By the time of the freeze, Mormons had two decades of history in Ghana, even though the Church had only been in the country officially for one decade. Pioneers like Joseph W. B. ("Billy") Johnson had organized groups of hundreds of believers even before missionaries arrived in 1978 on the heels of the revelation extending the priesthood to all worthy males and temple blessings to all worthy Saints. Billy Johnson's pre-1978 success was a foretaste of the growth that would come after 1978. In the Church's first official decade in Ghana, missionaries baptized 8,500 new converts.

But apart from sheer numeric growth, there were other signs of Mormon success—and that made other Ghanaian religionists uneasy. Mormons were securing properties and constructing buildings. And Mormon missionaries drove cars, a sure sign of affluence. Plus the general religious terrain of 1980s Ghana was undergoing some plate-tectonic shifts. New churches were popping up everywhere. Enthusiastic converts were leaving more traditional and long-tenured denominations and flocking to these new groups; in that, the Mormons were only one of many new religious sects. This membership movement was not lost on the mainline churches of Ghana's Christian Council, who raised their defenses, too, and wondered aloud if these new religious movements had designs to destabilize Ghana, or at least extract wealth from her citizens.[17] With Mormonism at least, they found some potent ammunition for a counter-attack.

One of the significant blows to Mormonism's public reputation in the 1980s came in the form of a movie called *The God Makers*. This movie, spearheaded by former Mormon Ed Decker and his Saints Alive in Jesus, painted the LDS Church in ominous, even Satanic, hues. The movie connected Mormonism with suicide and with forced family breakups, and lumped the Church's theology and temple rites with paganism and the occult.[18]

The movie's producers said the movie was being shown to 1,000 groups—often church groups—and 250,000 viewers a month in the United States in 1983 and 1984.[19] And with that kind of potency, Saints Alive, or Ex-Mormons for Jesus, took the film abroad. The film and its purveyors first created a stir in Israel, where BYU was building its Jerusalem Center.[20] Then Ed Decker's group and its pamphlets and film played a significant role in precipitating the Ghana freeze. *The God Makers* aired on national television on a couple of occasions in Ghana, and Saints Alive held a special screening for Ghanaian state officials.[21] Latter-day Saints in Ghana at the time felt that both government and religious leaders who were suspicious—and perhaps grudging—of Mormon growth were all too receptive when these anti-Mormon materials made their way into Ghanaian hands.[22]

Saints Alive leveled two charges against the Latter-day Saints that seemed especially damning. Their first charge was that Mormons carried out bizarre rituals in their temples, rituals that were reenacted on screen in *The God Makers*. One supposed Ghanaian Mormon published in the newspaper an account of what he said he had witnessed in the temple, including the ceremonial washing of initiates in the bodily fluids of corpses.[23] The second charge was that Mormonism allegedly positioned blacks as eternally inferior to whites. Statements from nineteenth-century LDS leaders about priesthood restrictions or the curse of Cain and skins of blackness understandably grated on Ghanaian ears.

These allegations of Mormon deviance offended Ghanaians on a number of fronts: national sovereignty, patriotism, race, and religion. With all of this in the air, it is not difficult to see why some officials turned chilly—and in this light, the freeze seems less reactionary and less outrageous than it otherwise might seem. On the same day in June 1989 when the freeze was imposed on Mormons, the government likewise froze the activities and assets of the Jehovah's Witnesses and two smaller, homegrown religious sects. These additional targets of sanctions raised the same types of public apprehension; after all, Jehovah's Witnesses abstained from signs of national patriotism, a troubling stance in the eyes of a revolutionary government already feeling the dissatisfaction of a number of constituencies.

A View of the Freeze from Ghanaian Saints

It's worth stating the obvious here: even if this contextualizing of the freeze makes it more understandable, none of this made the freeze any less painful for those who were so deeply affected by it. Isaac Addy, the Church's director for temporal affairs at the time, described the seven days after the announcement of the freeze as "the most hectic times in my life in Ghana." Addy had to arrange for the quick departure of all foreign missionaries from the country. He said that they had to "rub the name of the Church off the vehicles to enable them to go through the angry crowds." So much of the anxiety for Ghanaian Church members was caused simply by the unknown. "Why were they angry? I don't know," Isaac Addy reflected in an oral history years later. Why were the mission president and his wife thoroughly searched at the airport before leaving Ghana? What were government officials looking for? "This," Addy said, "is exactly what no one knows." But Church members consistently saw the anecdotal evidence pointing to anti-CIA, *God Makers*–type propaganda as the underlying trouble.[24]

Another source of significant distress for Church members was the abrupt loss of control over the Church's properties. William Sowah was a recently married branch clerk at the time of the freeze. When he heard the government's announcement, he rushed to the branch office to retrieve as many of the Church records as he could before the lockdown. "After that," Sowah said, "the meeting house was taken over by military men. They would sleep there, they would do everything. They would live there like their home."[25] Two weeks

William Sowah spent a night in jail after being arrested during a sacrament meeting in a neighbor's home. (Photograph by Greg W. Haws.)

after the sweeping sanctions, Stephen Apeaning Abu, the Church's district president in Abomosu, watched as a military convoy "ransacked all the rooms" of the Church's meetinghouse, "looking for evidence of subversive activities against the state to justify placing the permanent ban on the Church." The "only useful thing they could take away was money that had been locked up in the cabinet." They "warned [President Abu] never again to set foot there"—and then the convoy drove to a Church welfare farm nearby and auctioned off the Church's three hundred chickens. They "warned President Abu to keep off the farm," too.[26]

The freeze also left native Ghanaian missionaries in limbo for several days. Jessie Nyaconor Boafo, one of Ghana's first sister missionaries, was only three weeks away from finishing her mission in her home country when the freeze was announced. She and her companion were immediately placed under house arrest by the police in Kumasi as the officers awaited instructions from their superiors in Accra. Although the sister missionaries were uncomfortable with these officers who were stationed at their living quarters essentially day and night, the close contact with these policemen gave the missionaries opportunities to talk about the gospel message they had been preaching. One by one, Jessie Boafo remembered, they gave away two boxes' worth of copies of the Book of Mormon to policemen who were curious about this church that had been singled out by the government, and the officers would tuck the books quietly in their shirts. Finally, word came that the Ghanaian missionaries were to be returned to their homes. In front of a crowd of people who had gathered to witness their departure, the senior officer searched the two sisters' luggage item by item and showed each item to the crowd. When the officer found Sister Boafo's journal—marked where she had just finished writing—he opened it, and then read what Sister Boafo had recently written about his subordinates' interest in the Book of Mormon. Furious, he tore out those pages from Sister Boafo's journal before returning it to her. Her mission thus came to a brusque end.[27]

Because of the forced departure of foreign missionaries, Church officials immediately put an emergency local leadership plan into place. Priesthood holders were authorized to administer the sacrament in their own homes. Branch presidents made regular visits to each home. Emmanuel Abu Kissi, the district president in Accra, became the acting president of the Ghana Accra Mission. And Joseph W. B. Johnson and his wife became "silent missionaries," changing "their mode of operation from missionary work to strengthening the Saints."[28]

Ghanaian Church member Priscilla Sampson-Davis noted that most of the Saints dealt with the awkwardness of the freeze with quiet resolve. There were no protests against the government, no riots. There were simply home meetings and visits to strengthen one another. The Church took very seriously the government's mandate.

Sampson-Davis adamantly noted to an interviewer during the freeze that the Church respected the law and did not even perform baptisms during the freeze.[29] Incidentally, the *Deseret News Church Almanac* published in the year of the freeze did not even list Ghana in its directory of countries where the Church was established.[30]

But while the Saints were very strict about honoring the law against using Church facilities, sometimes even home meetings incurred the displeasure of the authorities. William Sowah remembered an occasion when he joined in a sacrament service at the home of the Larbie family. William had picked up two other men who had not been very active in the Church before the freeze, but who accepted his invitation to join in the sacrament that day. Unfortunately, during the course of that home meeting, just as the men were giving a blessing to Brother Larbie's sick nephew, the Church members "heard gun shots" and "these military people came, they came to the house." William said that the Mormons were accused of "worshipping secretly," even though small home gatherings had been ostensibly allowed. All of the Mormon men at the home were arrested.

When asked how the authorities were alerted to the meeting, William Sowah offered this speculation: "Larbie was an ex-military man. He had retired from the military, he retired right before he joined the church. When he was in the military, it appeared that . . . when he comes in contact with the young boys in the neighborhood . . . he was the one who typically disciplined them. So some people thought it was the right time to pay him back." When the men were locked in the already-crowded jail cell, the self-appointed "cell captain" asked the new arrivals, "What brings you here?" William said, "We told him that we were in a house having a prayer and they arrested us for breaking the law." The cell captain came back with, "Since you are pastors, you are going to preach to us this evening."

"That night," William recalled, "they wanted us to preach, so we shared the story of the restoration, of Joseph Smith."

> We didn't have the Book of Mormon with us, but we shared it and we asked them to look for the Book of Mormon any time they come out of the cell, any time they get the opportunity and read it. And I bore my testimony that I know that this is the true church of Jesus Christ of Latter-day Saints, and nothing will shake my faith. . . . I bore that testimony, then Brother Larbie bore his testimony, and the two [less active brothers also bore their testimonies]. By the time we finished bearing testimony, the place became quiet. It was total quiet. Everybody else drifted to sleep, but we were so quiet and we had a very blissful night. All the noise ceased. My thought was that they were all probably pondering, and then they fell asleep. Typically when the cell captain asks you, it is just ridicule, just to make fun. That is what it was intended, really. After they received the message, I believe the Spirit touched their hearts. The next morning, about 8:30, the officers opened the cell and asked us to come out."[31]

William Sowah and his fellow Mormons had been rescued by Isaac Addy, the Church's very busy temporal affairs manager. What makes the story even more interesting is that Isaac Addy was also the older half-brother of Jerry Rawlings, Ghana's head of state.[32] That personal dynamic proved beneficial in a number of cases, but it also put Isaac Addy in an awkward spot. Yet as much as any other factor, it was Isaac Addy's presence and influence that precipitated the end of the freeze.

Addy related that when he heard the announcement of the freeze, he went to his (and Jerry Rawlings's) uncle, Kojo Tsikata,

> the second in command . . . in charge of all security. . . . I said, "Do you realize I'm a member of this church." He said, "Yes, I know you are a member of the Church." "Why did you do this to me? Why didn't you tell me what was going to happen?" He said, "Someone came to the cabinet and showed us a film." And he said, "When we are trying to help South Africa get out of apartheid, you'll bring apartheid into this country. You have some buildings that you call a temple, and blacks can't enter." I said, "Are you sure? . . . Why didn't you talk to me: You know I'm a member. Why didn't you ask me these questions? Can you give me forty-five

> minutes: I want to go home and come back and defuse this instantly. . . . I want to bring you some evidence." I went home. I brought my temple sealing certificate and brought my temple recommend. [Isaac Addy had joined the Church in England in 1976, and he and his wife had been sealed in the London Temple in the summer of 1978]. I said, "Have a look at this document. I have been to the building you say no blacks have been to. I didn't go through because I'm related to the president of this country. When I went into the temple, by then you [had] not even come into power, so there was no political connotation here." He looked at it. "Are you sure, Isaac?" I said, "Yes. I'm telling you this." Then he relaxed. And the words that came out of his mouth always ring in my ears: "We have been misled."
>
> I said, "Now that you have been misled, what are going to do about it?" "We have set certain things in motion. Please allow the dust to settle." Those were his words. The dust settling took eighteen months. So from day one I knew what was going to happen.[33]

"The Thaw"

In large measure, that vignette is emblematic of just what changed in national temperature, so to speak, that brought the freeze to an end: personal encounters between government officials and Church members—especially Ghanaian members—that changed minds, and hearts, about the Mormons. "Thaw" therefore seems a fitting metaphor to describe what was a gradual process, effected by a number of key actors. Isaac Addy worked, early on, to get permission for the Church's Area Presidency and legal advisers to enter Ghana and meet with government officials. These Church representatives surprised Ghana state officers because, in Isaac Addy's words, "no one of the General Authorities talked about property." The Church's message was, "When the time comes, if we are not able to come back, we will donate all our property to the appropriate charitable organization." The government authorities "were shocked," Addy remembered, especially considering widespread fears that new churches in Ghana were bilking their members. Emmanuel Kissi, in his role as acting mission president, wrote numerous reports to answer the charges circulating about the Church. As the dust was settling, Isaac Addy pushed for Church members to have access to the Church's buildings to maintain and clean them for some time before they were allowed to worship there. The government also allowed some mission staff to return to office work, although Priscilla Sampson-Davis noted in July 1990 that the staff often could not get much work done because there were so many interested parties showing up at the office to ask for more information about this mysterious church that the government had banned.[34]

When there were signs in late 1990 that the government was about to lift the ban, the Church even asked Catherine Stokes and Bob Stevenson, two African-American Latter-day Saints, to travel to Ghana to meet with the media there. Church officials told Stokes that the Ghanaian government wanted the media to meet with African-American Mormons to "assure the people that [they] were, in fact, doing the right thing" in ending the freeze. After the press conference, Ghana's minister of culture told Latter-day Saint officials to "file the papers" for government recognition.[35]

The thaw was thus partly due to Latter-day Saint efforts, but also due, ironically, to the lobbying strength of Ghana's mainline churches. In a twist that the PNDC likely did not foresee, it was the government's requirement that *all* churches be "registered" (analogous to what had been required of media outlets—listing assets, beliefs, etc.) that may have proved to be the PNDC's very undoing. The mainline churches, some of whom had supported sanctions against the new sects, protested that this government incursion was too much to ask, since it treaded on precious religious liberties. (Emmanuel Kissi saw this as many churches realizing that they were forced to take a bitter pill that they had hoped to administer to others.)[36] Historian Paul Nugent noted that "the greatest mistake of the Rawlings regime was to provoke the churches, since the latter were particularly well organized and wielded an influence over substantial sections of the population." In the prefatory material to his book about the PNDC, Nugent even listed the freeze on Mormonism as one of three dozen significant mileposts in his timeline of the rise and demise of Rawlings's revolutionary government.[37]

This was the paradox of Law 221, the Religious Bodies (Registration) Law, as it proved unexpectedly beneficial for the Latter-day Saint cause from two directions. On the one hand, the law prompted a national discussion about freedom of religion. Only four months after the law (and the simultaneous freeze) was announced, in October 1989, Ghana's major churches "submitted a 'pastoral letter' to the government" saying, in no uncertain terms, "We cannot in conscience register under PNDC Law 221 as it stands."[38] When these powerful churches refused to register, the government knew that public opinion would side with the churches on this issue. This Ghanaian "Christian Council" then leveraged that clout even further by calling for a return to democratic elections. "In October and November of 1990 the country as a whole debated the subject of democracy. Sunday, October 25, was designated the beginning of a week of prayer for the nation."[39] One month after the freeze was lifted, in a December 1990 memorandum to the government, the Christian Council outlined "steps towards restoration of civilian rule," urging that "the independence of the Church and other religious bodies be guaranteed in the Constitution to ensure the freedom of worship envisaged in the United Nations Declaration on Human Rights."[40] The tide of public opinion would carry the day; democratic elections were set for late 1992, Law 221 was repealed that same year, and freedom of worship was one of the rallying cries for the new republic.

In the meantime, though, the government's religious registration requirement also seemed to benefit the LDS Church in another way. Latter-day Saints involved in negotiations with the PNDC sensed early on that government officials recognized they had acted against the Mormons based on misinformation. Thus the registration process appeared to provide a way for government officials to save face in reinstating the Church's official standing when they announced that they had found the LDS Church *fit* to register. "The Mormons," it was reported, "had undertaken to observe the nation's laws and respect its cultural dignity."[41] With that, the freeze was over.

As regular Church operations resumed, Ghanaian Mormons noted some fallout. Some Latter-day Saint converts returned to their former denominations during the freeze; it was understandably hard not to have a church in which to worship. But overall, the thaw resulted in expansion rather than contraction—and because of that, seeing the freeze in retrospect, Ghanaian Latter-day Saints took a providential perspective. "In the whole of Ghana," Emmanuel Kissi realized, "wherever there is an Akasanoma Preset Radio, and whatever language is spoken in Ghana has been fully exposed to the name of the Church. Also, now that everyone knows that we have been through the mill and have come out clean, those who would not have liked to be seen associating with the church for various reasons will now feel very free to search for knowledge and judge for themselves whether or not to become Latter-day Saints."[42]

Nicholas Ofosu-Hene Opare was just such an investigator. He was a young constable who was assigned a weeklong, all-night guard duty of the Tema Branch LDS building as part of the government's lockout of Mormon facilities. He said that he saw "in the midst of the debris" of that "turned outside down" building "a cover of the Book of Mormon staring at me"—which he tried to ignore, "because of the stories . . . that the book was demonic." But, he remembered, "despite my effort not to look at the direction where the book was, it still stared at me." He finally picked up the book and "read throughout the night." He hid the book in the building so that the book would not be vandalized, and each night of his duty tour he read the book—and soon felt that this "was the most correct among all the book of scripture I had ever read." When his police assignment at the branch building ended, the fact that Latter-day Saints "all had gone underground" meant that he "did not get any [Church] member to talk to." But after the freeze ended, and after he had been transferred to Kumasi, he saw LDS missionaries walking through his barracks. He "chased them and invited them to come and start teaching me"—and he and his wife and sons all joined the Church.[43]

Elder Freebody Mensah reflected on a post-freeze prayer he offered when a member of the Area Presidency visited them. At the time, he was a district president for the Church in Kumasi.

> "In the prayer I expressed what had actually happened to us during the freeze. I started the prayer by thanking the Lord for the freeze on the Church activity in Ghana. And I was to learn later that this really surprised the Saints including President Sackley. Why thank the Lord for the freeze? But as I went on with the prayer all became clear and understandable. That for one and half years during the freeze we have witnessed fathers taking the roles of branch presidents in the family and sons of priesthood bearers blessing and passing the sacrament, mothers playing the role of Relief Society presidents and also the daughters and everyone together for the eternal goal. There was the family, first basic unit of the Church in action. Hitherto we have known this as a principle. We grew close to our families, we loved our wives and our children more, the adversity and ridicule turned into blessings. We have been made better people for what we have endured. And we really thank the Lord for the freeze."[44]

"During the freeze," William Sowah reflected, "there were a lot of questions asked about the church. People didn't really know about the church, but the freeze made them know that they should investigate this church." That curiosity led to what William Sowah called a "boom in baptisms"—less than a year after the freeze officially was lifted in November 1990, two stakes were organized in Ghana. Remarkably, when the Cape Coast Stake was organized in April 1991, 2,673 Saints

In 1998, President Gordon B. Hinckley announced plans to build a temple in Accra, Ghana. The temple was dedicated in 2004. The Church News *reported that "the first person to hear the news [about the temple] was Ghanaian President Jerry Rawlings, who met with President Hinckley . . . at the presidential home in Accra." (Photograph by Greg W. Haws.)*

were in attendance—93 percent of the membership in the area. Another striking evidence of the Ghanaian Saints' resilience came in the post-freeze service of native Ghanaian missionaries. Seventy-six such missionaries had been in the field at the time of the freeze. Fifty-seven returned to finish their full-time missions after the freeze.[45]

One last milestone in Ghanaian LDS Church history has bearing here. By 1998, Church membership in the nation had doubled, as had the number of stakes.[46] That year—1998—saw Church President Gordon B. Hinckley in Accra, announcing to a crowd of over 6,500 Latter-day Saints that he had, that very morning, "approved the purchase of a beautiful piece of ground" for the construction of a temple. The spontaneous outburst of cheers from the crowd spoke to just how far the Church had come in that country.[47]

It is also telling that the *Church News* reported that "the first person to hear the news [about the temple] was Ghanaian President Jerry Rawlings, who met with President Hinckley shortly after noon at the presidential home in Accra." The conversation between the two leaders turned, perhaps inevitably, to 1989. Significantly, President Rawlings offered this conciliation: "I must take back some of the conflicting signals."[48]

If the announcement of temple plans was the close of one chapter and the opening of another for Ghanaian Latter-day Saints, "conflicting signals" seems to strike the right note about the complexity of the previous decade. And President Rawlings's public admission of a change of heart speaks to the efforts of so many who worked to keep geopolitical and cultural and religious forces from uprooting the Mormon seedling—what he and other initially suspicious compatriots came to see as a truly "Ghanaian Mormon seedling"—that now, twenty-five years later, is flourishing in West African soil.

Notes

Special thanks to the following for their insightful perspectives and research help: Clint Christensen; Michael Cosgrave; Greg and Debi Haws; Matt Heiss; Daniel Judd; Barbara Morgan; Nicholas Ofosu-Hene Opare; John C. Riding; Melissa Ring; and William and Jocelyn Sowah.

1. Importantly, the activities of the Jehovah's Witnesses were also suspended at the same time, but for different reasons. Mostly the Jehovah's Witnesses aroused suspicions in their resistance to expressions of national allegiance.
2. Melissa Wei-Tsing Inouye, "The Oak and the Banyan: The 'Glocalization' of Mormon Studies," *Mormon Studies Review* 1 (2014): 78–79.

3. For the history of the PNDC government years, see Paul Nugent, *Big Men, Small Boys and Politics in Ghana: Power, Ideology, and the Burden of History, 1982–1994* (London and New York: Pinter Publishing, 1995).
4. See Nugent, *Big Men, Small Boys and Politics in Ghana*, 46–48, for a discussion of what Rawlings called "sham democracy." Compare Kwame Boafo-Arthur, "Ghana's External Relations since 31 December 1981," chapter 8 in *Ghana Under PNDC Rule*, ed. E. Gyimah-Boadi (Oxford: Codesria, 1993), 138, for the statement of Brigadier Nunoo-Mensah of the PNDC: "We are making friends with everyone. We do not intend to take part in big power politics. We are too small and weak to get involved in that. We have stretched out our hands to make friends with everyone regardless of his ideological thinking or his political persuasion." See also Stephen Engelberg, "Officials Think Spying Led to Death of C.I.A. Informant in Ghana," *New York Times*, July 13, 1985, 6: "The State Department issued a statement today which said relations with Ghana were good and added, 'We assume they will continue to be.' The Department took issue with some news reports it said characterized Ghana as a Marxist state. Reports linking its foreign policy to the Soviet Union of Libya were 'quite inaccurate,' the State Department said."
5. See Boafo-Arthur, "Ghana's External Relations since 31 December 1981," 137–39, 143–44.
6. Nugent, *Big Men, Small Boys and Politics in Ghana*, 123–14. For reporting on the story in the United States, see Stephen Engelberg, "C.I.A. Clerk and Ghanaian Charged in Espionage Case," *New York Times*, July 12, 1985, A13; and "Swap in Spy Cases Made with Ghana," *New York Times*, November 26, 1985, B6. See also Boafo-Arthur, "Ghana's External Relations since 31 December 1981," 149: "Paradoxically, while Ghana was seriously working towards normalization of relations, the US intensified its efforts at destabilization. . . . The most serious incident was the exposure of a local CIA network in Accra in July 1985."
7. See Engelberg, "Officials Think Spying Led to Death of C.I.A. Informant in Ghana," 6: "Mr. Rawlings, who came to power in a coup in 1981, has been recently seeking a rapprochement with the West." See also Boafo-Arthur, "Ghana's External Relations since 31 December 1981," 145–46.

8. See Boafo-Arthur, "Ghana's External Relations since 31 December 1981," 142–43; see also Nugent, *Big Men, Small Boys and Politics in Ghana*, 108–9.
9. Nugent, *Big Men, Small Boys and Politics in Ghana*, 179, 190.
10. Nugent, *Big Men, Small Boys and Politics in Ghana*, 163.
11. Nugent, *Big Men, Small Boys and Politics in Ghana*, 190–91.
12. Boafo-Arthur, "Ghana's External Relations since 31 December 1981," 148.
13. William Sowah, interview by author, October 16, 2013, 6, transcript in author's possession.
14. "The United States CIA: Enemy of People's Power," *People's Daily Graphic* (Accra, Ghana), April 1, 1983, 3.
15. Zaki Ergas, professor of African Studies at Georgetown University, quoted in Engelberg, "Officials Think Spying Led to Death of C.I.A. Informant in Ghana," 6.
16. Quoted in Emmanuel Abu Kissi, *Walking in the Sand: A History of The Church of Jesus Christ of Latter-day Saints in Ghana*, ed. Matthew K. Heiss (Provo, UT: Brigham Young University Press, 2004), 174.
17. Charges about Mormon bizarreness took on new believability when a number of new religious movements proved to be in the business of bilking congregants of their money—"at one point, for example, members of the Christ Apostolic Church actually demonstrated against their own leaders and requested a probe of church finances by the National Investigation Committee." Nugent, *Big Men, Small Boys and Politics in Ghana*, 188. See also this excerpt from an article that appeared in a December 1986 newspaper in Ghana, quoted in Kissi, *Walking in the Sand*, 174: "Today, years after independence, these missionaries are still interested in our minerals and natural resources. And to further exploit us, they have again resorted to the use of the Bible to cover up their true colours. They have come in many forms and the latest edition is the Church of Jesus Christ of Later Day Saints [*sic*]."
18. For an overview of the organization and evolving emphasis of Ex-Mormons for Jesus, see Sara M. Patterson, "'A P.O. Box and a Desire to Witness for Jesus': Identity and Mission in the Ex-Mormons for Jesus/Saints Alive in Jesus, 1975–1990," *Journal of Mormon History* 36, no. 3 (Summer 2010): 54–81.
19. Bob Keeper, "Ex-Mormons' Film Sparks Controversy," *Register-Guard* (Eugene, OR), January 14, 1984, photocopy in possession of the author; Janet Barker,

"Anti-Mormon Film Makes Impact on South Bay," *South Bay Breeze* (Torrance, CA), January 21, 1984, B2.

20. In the summer of 1985, Mormon leaders charged "Decker and his group, Saints Alive" with "fomenting protests by orthodox Jews in Israel." That summer, "Saints Alive showed the 'God Makers' . . . to a committee of the Israeli Knesset" and "[helped] organize a letter-writing protest campaign" directed at Mayor Kolleck. See "Mormon Project Under Fire," *Seattle Times*, August 9, 1985, B4. See also Thomas A. Indinopulos, "Mormon-Jewish Turmoil in Zion," *Christian Century*, December 4, 1985, 1123: "Added voices of opposition come from Protestant, evangelical, Catholic and Eastern Orthodox officials who fear the proven success of Mormon missionaries will entice the predominantly Arab laity of churches in the Holy Land into their fold. The battle line was drawn in early July when local Christian leaders challenged the Mormons' right to call themselves Christian."
21. See Priscilla Sampson-Davis and John Equain Sampson-Davis, interview by E. Dale Lebaron, July 12, 1990, MSS 1937, box 5, folder 10, 16, L. Tom Perry Special Collections, Harold B. Lee Library, Brigham Young University, Provo, Utah. See also Daniel C. Peterson, "P. T. Barnum *Redivivus*: Review of Ed Decker, *Decker's Complete Handbook on Mormonism* (1995)," *Review of Books on the Book of Mormon* 7, no. 2 (1995): 64: "In the West African nation of Ghana, he [Ed Decker] helped to persuade the dictatorial government of Jerry Rawlins [*sic*] to suspend the activities of the Church in June 1989; one week before the official edict was issued, *The God Makers* was shown on Ghanaian television. 'That, I'm sure, cemented some attitudes,' [Decker] remarked."
22. See Kissi, *Walking in the Sand*, 183, 218, 220, 235n12. For more on *The God Makers*' reach in the United States, see Tammy Tanaka, "Ex-Church Members Employ Mormon Techniques against the Church," *Religious News Service*, February 21, 1984, 4. By early 1984, "filmmakers . . . estimate[d] it [was] seen by up to 250,000 a month nationally." Janet Barker, "Anti-Mormon Film Makes Impact on South Bay," B2.
23. Kissi, *Walking in the Sand*, 190. It should be noted that Emmanuel Kissi emphatically wrote that no Ghanaian Church member by the name of the article's author was ever was found.

24. Isaac Addy, interview by Matthew K. Heiss, September 15, 1998, 7, James Moyle Oral History Program, OH 1837, Church History Library, Salt Lake City, Utah.
25. Sowah, interview, 6.
26. Kissi, *Walking in the Sand*, 131–32.
27. Jessie Nyanconor Boafo, interview by Barbara Morgan, November 2013, copy in possession of author. I am indebted to Professor Morgan for making this interview available.
28. Kissi, *Walking in the Sand*, 207–8.
29. Priscilla Sampson-Davis, interview, 6–7.
30. See *Deseret News 1991–1992 Church Almanac* (Salt Lake City: Deseret News, 1990), 132–33; see the notice of the freeze on page 9.
31. Sowah, interview, 7–9.
32. Isaac Addy died in November 2014. For a news report announcing Addy's death, as well as his connections to both Jerry Rawlings and The Church of Jesus Christ of Latter-day Saints, see Isaac Yeboah, "Anlo Chiefs Console Rawlings," *Daily Graphic*, November 20, 2014, http://graphic.com.gh/news/general-news/34099-anlo-chiefs-console-rawlings.html.
33. Addy, interview, 8.
34. Priscilla Sampson-Davis, interview, 6–7. See also Thomas Kwamena Appiah, interview by Dale LeBaron, December 6, 1990, MSS 1937, box 2, folder 1, 17, L. Tom Perry Special Collections, Harold B. Lee Library, Brigham Young University, Provo, Utah, where Thomas Appiah described visiting the mission office in Ghana in December 1989 after he returned from him mission in London. He said, "Here was a case that the Church was closed down and the only contact with the Church was just my family and the mission home where there were a few other members there doing Church paper work."
35. Catherine M. Stokes, interview by Matthew K. Heiss, November 11, 2009, James Moyle Oral History Program, OH 4364, Church History Library, 16–21, 23–24.
36. See Kissi, *Walking in the Sand*, 208–16.
37. Nugent, *Big Men, Small Boys and Politics in Ghana*, 187. For Nugent's timeline, see page x.

38. Casely B. Essamuah, *Genuinely Ghanaian: A History of the Methodist Church Ghana, 1961–2000* (Trenton, NJ, and Asmara, Eritrea: Africa World Press, 2010), 91–92.
39. Essamuah, *Genuinely Ghanaian*, 90.
40. Kwame A. Ninsin, *Ghana's Political Transition, 1990–1993: Selected Documents* (Accra: Freedom Publications, 1996), 33–35.
41. "Ghana Lifts Ban," *Washington Post*, February 2, 1991, G1. See also Kissi, *Walking in the Sand*, 239–40.
42. Kissi, *Walking in the Sand*, 245.
43. Nicholas Ofosu-Hene Opare, email correspondence with author, October 20, 2015. As of 2015, Opare was the president of the Church's district in Tamale, Ghana.
44. Ghana Mission Files, box 1, folder 15, Church History Library. See also Kissi, *Walking in the Sand*, 243–53. Freebody Mensah was sustained as an Area Seventy of the Church in 2009 and released in 2013.
45. See "Ghana Accra Mission Following the Lifting of the Freeze," in Ghana Mission Files, box 1, folder 15, Church History Library.
46. Sowah, interview, 10.
47. Steve Fidel, "A Temple to Be Built in Ghana," *Church News*, February 21, 1998.
48. Fidel, "A Temple to Be Built in Ghana."

Asia

The Afghanistan coat of arms.

3

Organizing the Church in Afghanistan

Kenneth L. Alford

Roughly the size of Texas, with a population of thirty-one million people, Afghanistan has suffered almost four decades of continuous warfare. The mountainous terrain and forbidding weather can be harsh. War has destroyed much of the country's infrastructure, making it one of the poorest nations on earth. Ninety-nine percent of the country is Muslim—predominantly Sunni. With a 75 percent illiteracy rate, life expectancy is only forty-three years, and the infant mortality rate is the highest in the world. Almost half of the country is over six thousand feet in altitude. Only 12 percent of the land can support agriculture, and water is scarce. Poverty, drug trafficking, and other criminal enterprises are widespread.[1] It has been said, only partly in jest, that the only measure in which Afghanistan leads the other nations of the

---

Kenneth L. Alford is an associate professor of Church history and doctrine at Brigham Young University.

world is alphabetically. Afghanistan is challenging—geographically and culturally.

Getting Organized: 2001–2007

The limited introduction of the gospel in Afghanistan is directly connected to the Al-Qaeda-orchestrated attack unleashed at the World Trade Center and the Pentagon on September 11, 2001. The first Latter-day Saint combatants arrived during the earliest days of Operation Enduring Freedom—the designation given to military operations there. As numerous military units, mostly American, stormed into Afghanistan in the following months, many of them brought LDS servicemen group leaders who were called and set apart by stake presidents in the United States who assumed they had authority to call priesthood leaders to serve in Afghanistan.[2] While well intentioned, this practice sometimes led to confusion as multiple military units, each with their own Latter-day Saint group leader, arrived at the same location in Afghanistan.

Initially, there was no centralized or formal Church organization or authority within the country. Rather, LDS soldiers and civilians organized and met independently, which was similar to what had taken place during previous military conflicts. The major difference this time was the fact that the military was operating within a Muslim country where open proselyting was forbidden. Military service member groups quickly formed across the country, though. The nature of conflict meant that travel between Church groups was difficult and often dangerous. One of the biggest initial challenges was that no one knew where organized Church groups were meeting within the country.

In mid-2003, Church headquarters in Salt Lake City determined that Afghanistan would fall under the Asia Area headquartered in Hong Kong. Area Seventy William K. Jackson—a physician working

Chaplain Mark Allison, U.S. Army, and Elder William Jackson, who served as an Area Seventy for Afghanistan, helped to organize some of the initial Church units in Afghanistan. (Courtesy of Mark Allison.)

for the U.S. State Department in New Delhi, India—whose position enabled him to travel throughout Afghanistan—was given the responsibility to organize the Church within Afghanistan. Things were disjointed at first. As Elder Jackson noted, "We just sort of felt our way the first few months."[3] In the fall of that year, LDS chaplain (Major) Mark L. Allison, who was stationed in-country, was invited to work closely with scattered LDS group leaders across the country to create and maintain a "shepherd's list"—a weekly by-name roster of Latter-day Saints in Afghanistan.

The first Church conference, with approximately seventy members attending, was held at Bagram Air Base in December 2003. Elder Jackson, who presided, said it was interesting to see "a stack of rifles along the back instead of strollers."[4] Two additional Church conferences were held in Afghanistan during the following year.

The first baptism recorded in Afghanistan took place in 2004. Alexandro Rangel, a twenty-one-year-old United States Marine, was baptized in "an improvised wading pool made by U.S. Marines near the flight line at the Coalition Forces Base at Bagram and surrounded on all sides by weapons and munitions of war." Chaplain Allison noted, "As I made preparations for this battlefield baptism and knowing we lacked any white clothing, I spoke up at a meeting of fellow military chaplains and asked if any of them had white clothing I could borrow for a Latter-day Saint baptism. My request was met with awkward silence, until suddenly Father Hubbs, a Roman Catholic priest and army chaplain, said, 'Yes, I have two white cleric robes you are welcome to use . . . if you don't mind using Catholic priest robes.'" One of the other attendees chided Father Hubbs, stating "You don't want to do that. The water will be dirty and will stain your white robes." To which Father Hubbs answered, "If that happens it will be for a good cause." Chaplain Allison commented, "I will always be grateful to this colleague, priest and friend for his kindness shown on this occasion to Latter-day Saints military personnel."[5]

By 2005, Elder Jackson reported that "we were feeling a little more organized."[6] Latter-day Saints were meeting in small groups that varied widely in size. Captain Jon Petty, U.S. Army, shared one example of how church services were conducted during this period:

> When I arrived in Kandahar, Afghanistan, the LDS servicemembers' group met twice a week: Sunday mornings for church and Thursdays for FHE. . . . We met in . . . our makeshift chapel, an old mud building built to house the generators that ran the Kandahar Airfield during Taliban rule. It was also the chaplain's quarters. There was free food on the table next to us during our meetings. It was not uncommon to be giving a talk on Sunday and have half of the group munching on something at the same time. . . . I suggested we meet together more often. No one objected. . . . Some of these same men patrolled daily outside the wire in Afghanistan. They knew that

District President Gene Wikle renders a final salute at a memorial service for Sergeant First Class Glen J. Whetten on March 19, 2010 at Camp Blackhorse, east of Kabul, Afghanistan. (Courtesy of Gene Wikle.)

> they could be taken at any time. . . . Our motto was "you put on your garments, put on your body armor, say a prayer and go."[7]

In 2006, when Eugene "Gene" J. Wikle, a retired U.S. Air Force officer who served as a senior civilian advisor to the Afghan Air Force, arrived in Afghanistan there were six Church members who met for Church each week at Camp Eggers in Kabul, Afghanistan's capital. By February 2007 there were twenty-one members, and Wikle was called as the Camp Eggers servicemen's group leader. Two months later, Elder William K. Jackson set him apart as the senior servicemen's group leader for the entire country. Discussions began in December with the

Church Military Relations Office in Salt Lake City regarding "the possibility of creating a military district in Afghanistan."[8]

Kabul Afghanistan Military District: 2008–2014

The Kabul Afghanistan Military District of the Church of Jesus Christ of Latter-day Saints was officially organized on July 1, 2008—"the only combat district in the Church."[9] Gene Wikle was called as the district president—possibly "the only district president in the Church who [did] not have his eternal companion with him."[10] According to President Wikle, "The primary purpose of creating a military district was to provide a judge in Israel and to have the ecclesiastical authority that was needed in Afghanistan."[11] He received a special letter of "expanded priesthood authority" from the First Presidency

Kabul Afghanistan Military District Leadership (July 2009). Left to right: John Oravis, District Clerk; Winn Noyes, First Counselor; Gene Wikle, District President; Robert Horner, Second Counselor; Carol Thompson, District Relief Society President. (Courtesy of Gene Wikle.)

An Easter morning Latter-day Saint baptismal service in Afghanistan. Note that several attendees are carrying weapons. (Courtesy of Mark Allison.)

and the Quorum of the Twelve authorizing him to "issue temple recommends, handle Church disciplinary matters, ordain Melchizedek Priesthood holders, recommend and release missionaries, and undertake other such priesthood work as may be necessary." He was told, "With specific review and approval of the headquarters-based General Authorities directing your work, you are given authority to oversee the baptism and confirmation of converts in the few locations where such activities are permissible and approved." Creation of a new Middle East/Africa North Area, that included oversight responsibility for Afghanistan, followed on August 1.[12]

There were approximately 400 members in the Kabul Afghanistan District when it was created—soldiers, sailors, Marines, government employees, contractors, visiting university professors, nongovernmental organization employees, and humanitarian workers from more than a dozen countries. The Kabul Military Branch at Camp

Eggers was the first branch established in Afghanistan (organized on Friday, August 29, 2008). The branch consisted of U.S. embassy personnel, military servicemembers, civilian and contractor military advisers, university faculty, general contractors, and others. A total of four branches were initially established at coalition military bases that had larger numbers of Latter-day Saints. Servicemen's groups, varying in size from several dozen people to a single member, were created wherever Latter-day Saints were stationed throughout the country. The district organization was extremely fluid, with dozens of servicemen's groups. Between troop rotations and work reassignments, there was seldom a week in which one or more servicemen's groups were not either organized or closed.

The Church in a War Zone

Organizationally, administratively, and procedurally, the Church in Afghanistan was unique. Thursday and Friday is the Islamic weekend, and the U.S. embassy in Kabul is closed on Fridays, so the Kabul Branch, which had a higher percentage of civilian and nonmilitary Latter-day Saints than other Church units in the district, held its weekly church meetings on Fridays. The other branches and servicemen's groups all met on Sundays on "U.S. military or coalition force bases."[13] Some Church meetings were held in base or camp chapels; others met anywhere available space could be found. Church meetings were held in tents or even outside at some of the smaller forward-operating bases. Most units held weekly two-hour meetings, as work requirements permitted few of the Church members to attend an entire three-hour block of meetings. Many branches and groups held two separate sacrament meetings every week in an attempt to accommodate the varied schedules of their members.[14] Every Church unit within the district was asked to report membership and meeting attendance weekly. For some isolated Church members, the only real

This small chapel at Camp Leatherneck in Helmand Province is an example of the varied facilities where Latter-day Saint congregations held religious services in Afghanistan. (Courtesy of Gene Wikle.)

contact with the Church each week came in the form of an inspirational email message sent by one of the members of the district presidency.

Church meetings, "to put it in a wartime perspective," were clearly different. "You have men and women who come in there who are fully armed with their issued weapons—sitting in sacrament meeting—be it a nine-millimeter [pistol] on their hip or an M-16 [rifle] slung over their shoulder, and we have priesthood brethren who kneel down and bless the sacrament who have a weapon on them." During a branch sacrament meeting at Kandahar Air Base, while the "sacrament is being blessed, you can hear rockets impacting around you. The siren is going off. [Branch] President Cox looked up in the middle of the prayer to see what the other members were doing. Nobody moved. There was not a word of hesitation in saying the sacramental prayer. The members just continued on as if nothing was going on around them. There was a sense of peace and calm in that chapel that they were able to have, and they continued on to bless that sacrament while they were under a rocket attack."[15]

The fact that the Kabul Afghanistan Military District functioned in a war zone influenced the way that many Church leaders received callings and were set apart to serve in those callings. Because at any given time there were several dozen to over seventy separate Church units within the district, the administrative demands on the district presidency were significant. The fact that Afghanistan was an active war zone and the district presidency was unable to visit many—if not most—of the member locations, added a unique challenge regarding calling new branch and servicemen group leaders. Out of necessity, email and phone calls replaced face-to-face interviews. As President Wikle observed, "Because we're in a war zone, as a district presidency, we cannot freely travel around a country that's the size of Texas. For obvious security reasons, we cannot just get in a car and drive down the road to visit another branch or service member's group. So everything that we do in administering the affairs of the Church throughout this country is done primarily by email, occasionally by cell phone, rarely in person because of the security situation." He explained how the process worked: "When I'm extending a call, be it to a branch president, a counselor in a branch presidency, an elders quorum president, or a district council member . . . [I] send them a set of personal priesthood interview questions and ask them to please respond to those questions and then for the district presidency to prayerfully consider the response and prayerfully consider calling this individual. And then when we feel so inspired and directed by the Lord . . . [we] email a response back to that individual and extend a call to them via email."[16] He further explained, "I have called men to be branch presidents, group leaders, and elders quorum presidents that I have never met, and I probably will never meet in this lifetime."

Setting apart new leaders was equally problematic. "The majority of the people who will serve as a servicemen's group leader will never actually have hands laid on [them] and be set apart," said Wikle.[17] LDS military chaplains and district high councilors were authorized to set leaders apart whenever possible. The Church Military Relations Committee, through the approval of the First Presidency and Area Presidency, sent an official letter of appointment to servicemen group leaders, district council members, and members of the district presidency signifying that they had been set apart to function in their new positions. To help train new leaders, the district presidency developed seven in-country, in-service lessons that were distributed by email. It was significant that they were "in the middle of a war zone," but the goal of the district presidency was, as far as possible, "to function the same way as a [regular] stake and a ward would."[18]

Relief Society offered another distinctive challenge. Unlike earlier military conflicts in which the participants were exclusively men, recent conflicts have had an increasing number of women serving in the ranks, and the district presidency felt keenly the responsibility to help meet their needs. The conflict in Afghanistan is the first time in Church history that district and local Relief Society units have been organized within an active war zone. Carol Wilson Thompson—originally from Provo, Utah, and teaching with her husband at a university in Kabul—was called as the first Relief Society president for the newly created Kabul Branch and then as the first district Relief Society president. Commenting on her unique callings, Thompson stated, "I

A Friday, July 10, 2009, meeting of the Kabul Afghanistan Branch Relief Society. Left to right: Daffney Scherer, Margaret Owens, Bonnie Anderson, Libby Brown, Kyoko Wilson, Carol Wilson Thompson, and Barbara Thompson. (Courtesy of Gene Wikle.)

received an email from President Wikle. I had received emails before from him . . . so I didn't think anything about it. I clicked on it to open it and noticed that it said 'Called to Serve.' I thought, 'Hmmm. Another message. Some inspirational thing.' I read it, and it was asking me to serve as the district Relief Society president." She was "flabbergasted but very honored and very humbled. . . . After I had picked myself up off the floor, I thought, 'I wonder what that's going to be like. What will I do? How will I accomplish this?' . . . It was very frustrating. Most of the sisters in the Kabul Branch were not able to move around the city. They couldn't freely go to visit someone. The only contact they had was at church or through email."[19]

Missionary work was also different. When the Kabul Afghanistan Military District was created in 2008, President Wikle was "called and set apart, to not only serve as a district president, but as a mission president" as well.[20] Shortly after the Middle East/Africa North Area was organized, the new area presidency, in coordination with the Afghanistan district presidency, released guidelines for sharing the gospel in Afghanistan. Their directive stated that "the following guidelines for sharing the gospel should be followed by all LDS military and civilian members stationed in Afghanistan:"

> One: *Sharing the gospel.* Sharing the gospel with non-Muslim members of the coalition forces is permitted provided they express an interest in learning more about the Church and the gospel. Proselyting of any kind among Muslims is strictly prohibited. Please be respectful of their beliefs and be an example of the gospel and the way you live your life.
>
> Two: *Church attendance.* Non-Muslim friends or acquaintances who express an interest in learning more about the Church may be invited to attend church services and activities. You should not invite Muslims to attend. Their mere association with Christian faith groups may result in harm or death to them or their family members.
>
> Three: *Gospel teaching.* A non-Muslim person who has expressed a desire to learn more about the gospel and has attended church services

may receive the missionary lessons with prior approval of the district president of the Kabul Afghanistan Military District. . . .

If we follow these simple guidelines, we will all receive great blessings in accomplishing the Lord's will in this part of his vineyard.[21]

Additional Challenges

Living the Word of Wisdom in Afghanistan could also be challenging. Only six percent of the available water within the country is safe to drink, so Afghans boil their water before drinking it, and boiled water can easily be made into tea. Afghan tea, known as chai, plays a major role in Afghan society. One American military veteran explained the important social role that chai fills this way: "A Talib[an] will not kill you while offering you hospitality. It just isn't done. They may have been shooting at you an hour before, and they will be planning their next ambush even as you sit there with them, but they won't kill you during chai or while you are leaving immediately afterwards. A mile up the road is a different story, but not during chai." The website *Afghan Lessons Learned for Soldiers* counsels service members that "more often [than not], the offer of chai was not an obligatory gesture but a genuine expression of friendship and a desire to have relaxed conversation with another. Either way, refusal of an invitation is a delicate thing. . . . Chai is more than the tea. If an Afghan ever offers you chai, take him up on it."[22] Advice and military counsel such as this certainly placed Latter-day Saint service members in a potentially difficult position as almost everyone in Afghanistan is frequently invited to drink chai.

President Wikle emailed counsel to the members in his district regarding living the Word of Wisdom in Afghanistan. On January 1, 2010, he counseled:

I received inquiries from members who are recently arrived in Afghanistan asking about the Afghan custom of drinking tea in the

> appropriate responses when offered tea to drink. You should not drink the tea. The Afghans as part of their custom will always offer you tea to drink. I counsel all of our members to always take a bottle of water with you when you meet with the Afghans. You'll have an Afghan translator with you. Prior to meeting with the Afghans, you need to explain to your translator you do not drink tea for religious purposes. You can explain that you have made covenants with God not to drink the tea.
>
> When you meet with the Afghans and are invited to drink tea, you can then politely explain to your translator you do not drink tea. You can further explain you had brought the bottled water to drink instead of the tea. Kindly thank the Afghans for their hospitality. I have always found that the Afghans will respect your religious beliefs. . . . Your example of living the gospel including the Word of Wisdom is the best example we can give the Afghans. The Lord will bless you for observing the Word of Wisdom and for your positive example of living the gospel of Jesus Christ.[23]

Home teaching and visiting teaching programs were likewise adapted to wartime conditions in Afghanistan. As one LDS soldier stated, "Home teaching and visiting teaching means a lot over there when you're in a war zone."[24] In addition to standard home and visiting teaching assignments, the district presidency "by inspiration . . . implemented what we call Mormon Battle Buddies: . . . combat home teaching and combat visiting teaching." The program was instigated because "more and more of our members [were] serving their second, third, fourth, or even fifth combat tour." District leadership noticed increasing "signs of stress among our LDS members" and "felt that we needed to do more than just assign people to be a 'home teacher' or a 'visiting teacher.'" When members arrived in a new area, the presiding authorities assigned him or her "a Mormon battle buddy that they can actually meet. The purpose being that if you run into a stressful situation, if you need somebody to just talk to, if you need help in any form or fashion, the first Latter-day Saint you can turn to is your Mormon battle buddy."[25]

Establishing the Church in Afghanistan often required ingenuity and creativity. The first semiannual district conference was no exception. Operating within a war zone, it was impossible for the entire district to meet together. In April 2009, President Wikle suggested to his area presidency that "if you want to be able to reach one hundred percent of all the members [in the Kabul Afghanistan Military District], we need to do a conference and record it on a DVD . . . and they could watch the district conference."[26] Church headquarters in Salt Lake City, with the assistance of Elder Jeffrey R. Holland, Sister Julie Beck (Relief Society general president), and members of the area presidency videotaped district conference talks. Talks were similarly recorded in Kabul by Eugene Wikle, district president, and Carol Thompson, the district Relief Society president. Their talks were added to the "virtual district conference" DVD produced in Salt Lake City. The district had five hundred members at that time, but one thousand copies of the DVD were shipped to

On Friday, March 5, 2010, members of the Kabul Afghanistan Branch participated in a country-wide "virtual district conference" on recorded video. (Courtesy of Gene Wikle.)

Kabul so that a copy could be given to current as well as future members. Copies of the DVD were distributed throughout the district and viewed by Latter-day Saints across Afghanistan in June 2009. Copies of the district conference DVD were also distributed to many family members, which provided much-needed comfort and assurance.

Tender Mercies

In 1 Nephi 1:20, Nephi wrote, "But behold, I, Nephi, will show unto you that the tender mercies of the Lord are over all those whom he hath chosen, because of their faith." During a general conference address in 2005, Elder David A. Bednar explained that "the tender mercies of the Lord are real and that they do not occur randomly or merely by coincidence. . . . Truly, the Lord suits 'his mercies according to the conditions of the children of men' (D&C 46:15)."[27] Many Latter-day Saints serving in Afghanistan felt they received the Lord's tender mercies. Two examples of the many tender mercies experienced in Afghanistan illustrate the Lord's watchful eye over Latter-day Saints serving there. The first is from Area Seventy William K. Jackson, and the second is from Apostle Jeffrey R. Holland.

On November 16, 2005, Elder Jackson was in Kandahar, Afghanistan, to complete State Department responsibilities, take care of medical patients, and conduct Church business. He was traveling down a narrow road through the city center in an armored six-ton SUV, the third in a six-vehicle convoy led by a Toyota Hilux brimming with Afghan soldiers and a fifty-caliber machine gun mounted on the open truck bed. Between a large cement median in the middle of the road and storefronts built up to the very edge of the road, there was little maneuver room for drivers. The convoy's fourth and fifth vehicles were empty flatbed trucks going to Kabul Airport to pick up supplies. The driver of the vehicle immediately behind Elder Jackson's SUV stopped briefly "to pick up his fifteen-year-old nephew who had skipped school that day to go out to the American air force base."[28]

As their convoy passed the city market, a green sedan abruptly squeezed into the middle of the convoy in front of Elder Jackson's vehicle. At a point where the road widened slightly, the embassy SUV driver attempted to pass the green car, but "he kind of took up residence in the middle of the road, so we were unable to get past him." A few moments later, the SUV driver was able to pull alongside of the green sedan. Elder Jackson looked into the car and saw a "young Afghan man with a beard like every other man on the street. As we were just getting by him . . . I knew he was going to hit us . . . I consciously sort of tensed my muscles [and] leaned over in the seat." But instead of "hearing the grinding metallic destruction of his vehicle, what I heard instead was a deafening explosion. He was a suicide bomber, first one in the history of Kandahar. And he had swung back over to broadside us and detonated. There was this big explosion. And then everything went black, and I felt weightless." His twelve-thousand-pound vehicle came "crashing to the ground forty meters down the road. We landed on our roof, and we spun around in the road and rolled over on the passenger side of the street." His security detail yelled at him to exit the vehicle, which he did through a hole where the windshield had been a few seconds before.

What greeted his view was "something out of Hollywood, but it was real. There were people screaming and yelling everywhere. Down the road where we were facing was a big black mushroom cloud going up where the bomber's car had exploded. . . . There were people crying, I could see cars that had been blown into buildings. I could see pieces of people. There had been a motorcycle right next to us when this guy detonated; I can't imagine that he stood any kind of chance at all. Even the fifteen-year-old boy who was joyriding with his uncle was killed instantly. It was surreal." He started to return to the vehicle to retrieve his briefcase when one of his protective detail shouted at him, "Doc, are you crazy. There's no way you're going back over there." At that split second, "Almost on cue, the diesel tank erupted and blew up. And there was a second deafening explosion as our car just disappeared inside of a bright orange mushroom cloud." Miraculously, they quickly discovered that "other than a singe on one of the soldiers and a little cut, none of us were injured, no broken bones, no eardrum injuries, no loss of consciousness. Our car, as I would see later in pictures, was destroyed completely; [it] was just torn to pieces, . . . [and] the bomber's car was completely atomized. The only recognizable part of his car that was left was the front bumper. And it was a football field farther down the road. . . . And yet we walked away."[29]

The second tender mercy had the power to affect every Latter-day Saint serving in Afghanistan. In 2009, Elder Jeffrey R. Holland was the last speaker on the first district conference DVD for the Kabul Afghanistan Military District. As he reached the end of his conference address, he stated, "Brethren and sisters, we've had a wonderful district conference with you. As I said at the beginning, I only wish we could see your faces. I wish we could have stood with you to sing as we stood here to sing, wish we could shake your hand. More than that, I wish we could lay our hands on the head of each one of you, and give you a blessing. So, in lieu of being able to do that personally, I'm going to do it apostolically. I'm going to do it by the authority that is mine, through this telecast, and onto this DVD." Elder Holland then announced that "by the power of the holy priesthood that I hold, and the authority that I've been given, I pronounce a blessing on each one of you within the sound of my voice, and the reach of this telecast. I do it as if indeed my hands were upon your head, and with the power of the priesthood upon you just that efficaciously." He blessed "each one of you, that although you are in harm's way daily, that you will have the power of heaven upon you, including the attendance of angels, on your right hand, and on your left. I bless you that you will know that you are being prayed for at home and abroad, and especially by the leaders of the Church here at headquarters, all of us. And we pray for your loved ones, wherever they may be, wherever home is." He also blessed the district members to "be men and women on a mission, and that you'll strive to help others to embrace the gospel, and live their religion. I bless you that such a time of war, and such a period away from home, will be a strengthening time, not a debilitating time in your life, in the formation of your character, and in the strengthening of your faith. I bless you that you will draw nearer to God, and that you will know how much all of us need Him, in good times or bad, in war time, or in peace." He then extended his apostolic blessing, stating, "I bless you that you will not worry about your loved ones, and . . . I pronounce in this blessing, a blessing on them, as if they were in this congregation."[30]

In December 2014, President Barack Obama announced that active combat operations in Afghanistan would cease at the end of that month.[31] In response to the president's announcement, the Kabul Afghanistan Military District was disbanded on December 21, 2014. The Kabul Military Branch continued, though, to function with oversight responsibility for the few remaining Church groups in Afghanistan.[32]

Several valuable lessons were learned during the six-year life of the Kabul Afghanistan Military District that can be applied to future military deployments. First, in order to avoid or reduce confusion and conflicting lines of authority, it is important to provide organizational guidance to ecclesiastical leaders as close to the beginning of a military deployment as possible. Second, military districts can provide needed priesthood keys to members while deployed. And third, the Church is extremely adaptable and can organize anywhere under almost any conditions to effectively meet the needs of its members.[33]

Service in Afghanistan was difficult, but Latter-day Saints serving there found that if they would "pray always, and be believing" then "all things shall work together for your good" as the Lord has promised

(D&C 90:24). As President Wikle observed, "I have yet to ever hear the testimony or receive an email from a Latter-day Saint who has said that their experience in Afghanistan has not uplifted them, has not strengthened their testimony of the gospel of Jesus Christ."[34]

Notes

1. Central Intelligence Agency, "Afghanistan," The World Factbook, https://www.cia.gov/library/publications/the-world-factbook/geos/af.html.
2. William K. Jackson, interview by Kenneth L. Alford, May 6, 2014, in "Elder William K. Jackson," DVDC 5015 2014 Jac, L. Tom Perry Special Collections, Harold B. Lee Library, Brigham Young University, Provo, UT.
3. William K. Jackson, interview.
4. William K. Jackson, interview.
5. Mark L. Allison, interview, November 22, 2004, Brigham Young University Saints at War Project.
6. William K. Jackson, interview.
7. Jon Petty, interview, 2005, Brigham Young University Saints at War Project.
8. Eugene J. Wikle, interview, April 3, 2009, 2, OH 4258, Church History Library, Salt Lake City.
9. Eugene J. Wikle, interview, April 6, 2010, 112. The military district in Afghanistan worked so well that in 2009 a similarly organized military district was established within Iraq to meet the needs of Latter-day Saints serving there.
10. Eugene J. Wikle, interview, April 3, 2009, 6.
11. Eugene J. Wikle, interview, April 3, 2009, 3.
12. Eugene J. Wikle, interview, April 3, 2009, 16.
13. Eugene J. Wikle, interview, April 3, 2009, 1–2; April 6, 2010, 84. The Kabul Branch had the most diverse membership. President Wikle explained, "You have diplomats serving at the U.S. embassy in Kabul in a variety of different positions. We have a number of members who are serving with the United States Agency for International Development—USAID—who are doing a great

deal of capacity building within the country. We have DOD—Department of Defense—contractors—such as myself,—civilians, who are working there. We have educators. We've had college professors advising at Kabul University and at other private institutions. We have non-government aid workers, who are working for different UN or private agencies providing relief to the people of Afghanistan." Eugene J. Wikle, interview, April 6, 2010, 84–85.

14. Eugene J. Wikle, interview, April 6, 2010, 84.
15. Eugene J. Wikle, interview, August 28, 2009, 34–35.
16. Eugene J. Wikle, interview by Kenneth L. Alford, August 29, 2009, Brigham Young University Saints at War Project.
17. Eugene J. Wikle, interview, April 3, 2009, 4.
18. Eugene J. Wikle, interview, April 3, 2009, 17–18.
19. Carol Wilson Thompson, interview by Kenneth L. Alford, February 11, 2010, Brigham Young University Saints at War Project.
20. Eugene J. Wikle, interview, April 3, 2009, 3.
21. Middle East/Africa North Area Presidency, The Church of Jesus Christ of Latter-day Saints, letter, October 7, 2008.
22. "Chapter 3: Culture (Lesson 3A: Chai and the Pashtunwali)," *A.L.L.=Afghan Lessons Learned for Soldiers* (blog), afghanlessons.blogspot.com/2009/05/chapter-3-culture-lesson-3a-chai-and.html.
23. Eugene J. Wikle, email, January 1, 2010.
24. Eugene J. Wikle, interview, April 3, 2009, 17.
25. Eugene J. Wikle, interview, April 6, 2010, 86.
26. Eugene J. Wikle, interview, April 6, 2010, 95.
27. David A. Bednar, "The Tender Mercies of the Lord," *Ensign*, May 2005, 99.
28. William K. Jackson, interview.
29. William K. Jackson, interview.
30. Jeffrey R. Holland, Kabul Afghanistan Military District Conference DVD, 2009.
31. Dave Phillips, "Mission Ends in Afghanistan, but Sacrifices Are Not Over for U.S. Soldiers," *New York Times*, December 31, 2014, www.nytimes.com/2015/01/01/us/mission-ends-but-sacrifices-are-not-over-for-us-soldiers.html.
32. Eugene J. Wikle, email to author, December 24, 2014.

33. The organizational lessons learned in Afghanistan were put into practice a little over a year later when Elder Paul B. Pieper of the Seventy formed the similarly organized Baghdad Iraq Military District on November 9, 2009. See "LDS Military District," www.mormonwiki.com/LDS_Military_District.
34. Eugene J. Wikle, interview, April 6, 2010, 104.

4

Shifting Focus to Global Mormonism

The LDS Church in India

Taunalyn Rutherford

A central concern in the study of any religious tradition is the attempt to situate it in a broader world religion framework. The attempt to categorize and define Mormonism, or The Church of Jesus Christ of Latter-day Saints, has proven to be a challenge to scholars throughout the Church's history. Mormonism has been called "the first major faith to appear on the earth since the prophet Muhammed rode out of the desert,"[1] a "new religious tradition,"[2] an "American world religion,"[3] a "fourth way in world Christianity alongside Protestantism, Catholicism, and Orthodoxy,"[4] and a "global Christ-centered faith."[5]

A further demonstration of this difficulty in defining the LDS Church is Sydney E. Ahlstrom's expression in his religious history of America. Of Mormonism he said, "One cannot even be sure if the object of our consideration is a sect, a mystery cult, a new religion, a

Taunalyn Rutherford is an adjunct instructor of religion at Brigham Young University and a PhD candidate at Claremont Graduate University writing her dissertation on the Church in India.

church, a people, a nation, or an American subculture; indeed at different times and places it is all of these."[6] As Ahlstrom opined and as is the case with any subject, Mormonism looks different and can be defined differently depending on the theoretical lens that is applied, the time period examined, and the geographical area studied. The problem of defining the Church of Jesus Christ becomes even more challenging in an age of globalization. Scholars have noted the "shifted shape of world Christianity." As Mark Noll observes, "it is as if the globe had been turned upside down and sideways. A few short decades ago, Christian believers were concentrated in the global north and west, but now a rapidly swelling majority lives in the global south and east."[7] This phenomenon is evident in the LDS Church as well. The LDS Church is like a multifaceted gem that will look differently and reflect the surrounding culture differently depending on when it is viewed, who is viewing it, and from what angle and location it is viewed. I suggest that we cannot begin to truly understand the Church of Jesus Christ, define Mormonism, or write the history of the Latter-day Saints until we look at facets of the global Church that have been overlooked. The aim of this study is to demonstrate how shifting the focus of Mormon history to the "global south and east," in this case India, can open new understanding and reinvigorate the study of LDS Church history. The LDS Church in India is a facet of Mormonism that is in need of examination and can reflect important understanding to Mormon studies and religious studies in general.

India is a country with 1.2 billion people and an LDS population of 12,257.[8] Scholars project that by 2025 the population of India will surpass that of China, causing it to be the most populated country in the world. Growth for the Church in India has occurred slowly and often without the aid of the traditional structures of organized missionary work that have been common in other countries. The first official mission in India spanned a brief period in the mid-nineteenth century, and the efforts of the first missionaries to India earned the acclaim of historian and Church authority B. H. Roberts, who stated that "there is nothing more heroic in our Church annals than the labors and sufferings of these brethren of the mission to India."[9] The second wave of LDS missionary work included periods of organic growth within the subcontinent as Indians were introduced to the Church or its literature through member missionary influences. Any official missionary work was done under the leadership of either the Singapore or the International Mission presidents during the second half of the twentieth century. Work in India was facilitated mainly through senior couples initially and then eventually a meager number of foreign and native Indian missionaries called to the Singapore mission. In 1993, Gurcharan Singh Gill became the first mission president to India, and the India Bangalore Mission was established. Gill makes an interesting case study because he came from a Sikh background, converted to the Church in the United States, and attended and eventually taught at Brigham Young University. He is a reminder that as the Church grows in India, the engagement with the religions of India will bring new challenges as well as new insights from traditions such as Hinduism, Jainism, and Sikhism—not to mention unique indigenized forms of Christianity, Islam, and Buddhism.[10]

The age of the LDS Church as an organized entity with a local mission is therefore relatively young in India, and its twentieth-century narrative barely even falls into the category of history. The first (and currently the only) stake on the subcontinent of India was formed in Hyderabad in May 2012. The age of the Church thus necessitates the use of anthropological lenses and qualitative methods of oral history and ethnography to try to understand the Church, record the history of the Church, and move forward in our understanding of the Church's needs in India. In addition to secondary sources and archival research, my work in recording and analyzing the history of the Church in India draws from over 150 oral history

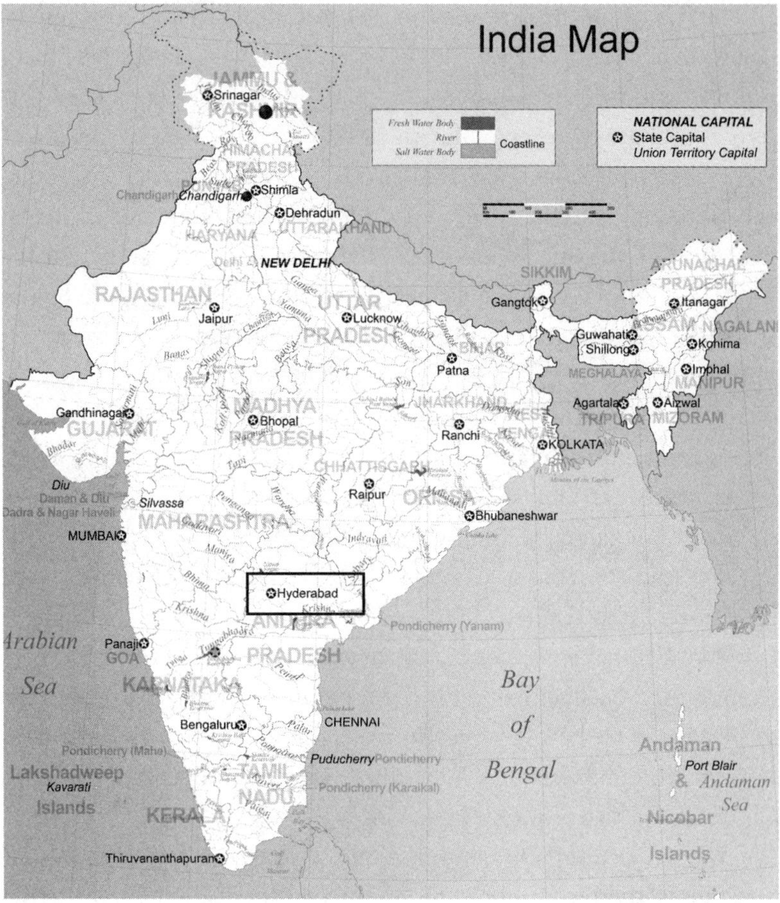

Map of India showing the location of Hyderabad, where the first LDS stake was organized.

interviews of Latter-day Saints conducted during a month of ethnographic participant-observation fieldwork in India in the spring of 2014 with follow-up work during the fall of 2015. I have not even begun to scratch the surface of what can and should be done in this vast area of LDS Church history. My work adds to the historical narrative while pointing to potential work to be done on the Church in India in the fields of sociology, anthropology, missiology, gender studies, and narratology. This work demonstrates that focusing on the history of the Church in the global south, particularly the emerging Church in India, reveals the richness of Mormonism as a focus of study in the broader interdisciplinary field of religious studies while breathing new life into the work of Mormon history.

History of the Church in Hyderabad

I will focus on the Church in Hyderabad as a case study. In spite of the organic and unorganized origins of the Church in India, one much-anticipated stake located in the city of Hyderabad was finally organized in May 2012. The narratives of the origins and the lives of the pioneer members in Hyderabad are instructive in demonstrating the issues that the Church faces in India. The history of the Church of Jesus Christ in Hyderabad is not a traditional mission narrative in which Western missionaries travel to a new land and open the work. It begins in Apia, Samoa, where Elsie and Edwin Dharmaraju, natives of Hyderabad, met the Richard and Lillian Ashby family, Latter-day Saints who were in Samoa serving under extremely unique circumstances. The Ashbys, along with their five children, were called to Samoa in spite of the fact that Lilly was in advanced stages of breast cancer. She was called to work as much as possible with the sister missionaries, and her husband to work in more of a humanitarian role to assist the work in hospitals in Samoa. Nine months into their mission, Lilly passed away. Although their mission seemed to be a tragedy, their service contributed to Church history in India. In addition to the influence of missionaries and members in Samoa, the Ashbys' friendship and example, and the gift of Lilly's Book of Mormon with her testimony written inside, influenced Elsie and Edwin Dharmaraju, who investigated and joined the Church three months after Lilly's death.[11]

The Dharmarajus, who still had strong ties to Hyderabad, felt compelled to share the gospel with their own family back in India. They were

Hyderabad Stake Center. (Courtesy of author.)

set apart as special missionaries for three months in 1978 to travel to their relatives and friends in Hyderabad and teach them the gospel. The perspective from those family members who were present on the day that eighteen relatives of Darmahraju were baptized carries a common theme: Edwin was the patriarch of the family; therefore, the family followed him. Edwin Dharmaraju's nephew John Santosh Murala, who is now a pediatric heart surgeon, and at the time of our interview was serving as a counselor in the Bangalore Mission presidency, was the youngest person to be baptized on December 27, 1978, being age eight at the time. He shared candidly, "I'll be very honest, most of the family joined the Church because [Edwin] was like the patriarch of the family, and he said, 'I've joined the church, it's the true church, and I want you all to join,' and everyone said OK, and we all took baptism."[12]

Familial and even larger group conversions, such as tribe and caste conversions, have been common in the broader history of Christian missions in India.[13] The LDS Church, however, has emphasized individual conversion and growth in "centers of strength" and has thus resisted the route to mass conversions. On the other hand, the RLDS Church in the 1960s saw tremendous growth among an indigenous tribal group (the Sora people in Orissa) through mass conversions, and today the Community of Christ claims higher numbers of members in India than the LDS Church claims to have there. On any given Sunday, there can be up to 15,000 Sora members of the Community of Christ in attendance at meetings. Unfortunately, they have also been targets of violence in anticonversion riots by right-wing Hindu groups. Comparing these "Mormonisms" and their differing missiological approaches in India is fascinating and instructive and another important site for future research.[14] Furthermore, it underscores the importance of understanding anti-conversion politics in India and their effect on the LDS Church, an important topic that will be addressed later in this paper.

At this point in the narrative it is important to note that the organization of the Church as an institution in Hyderabad, India, even though it began with an instantaneous extended family baptism, did not happen all at once. The Church in these early years was somewhat comical in the mind of John Murala, who recalls with laughter:

> We didn't have any missionaries in those days. As an eight-year-old boy I used to set up the sacrament. My sister, brother and me used to clean up and I used to give talks. Everyone went to their church in the morning—to the Baptist church or to the Protestant church—and we used to come back in the evening and have the church, our church, and it was just a social gathering. The TV came into Hyderabad for the first time at that time, and everybody was so interested . . . in television in those days, and on Sunday at 7:00 in the evening they used to have a movie on TV. So we used to have the church from 5:30 to 6:30, and sometimes it used to start late at 6, and so my uncle as the branch president used to say, 'Come on, let's finish

> fast—the movie time, movie time, movie time! I just look back and I just laugh at what all we did in those days.[15]

The Edwin Dharmaraju family is representative of the many families who have come into the LDS Church from other Christian denominations in India. This again demonstrates the need to understand the broader history of Christian missions in India. Methuselah Leonard Wilson, another relative of Dharmaraju who also joined the Church in 1978, was then responsible for establishing the Church of Jesus Christ in Rajahmundry, a city east of Hyderabad. Brother Wilson proudly traces his ancestry back to members of the Christian community said to have been established by the Apostle Thomas in Tamil Nadu in the first century AD. Indian Latter-day Saints who come from a Christian background are recognizable by their "Christianized" names and by the traditions they bring to their membership in the LDS Church from other Christian denominations. For example, the Katuka family, who were among the first converts to the Church in Rajahmundry from the missionary efforts of Leonard Wilson, came from a strong Lutheran family.

A member of the Katuka family, Suvarna, was one of the first native Mormon missionaries to be called to serve in India in 1986. While in the home of Suvarna Katuka with his wife Swarupa and son Joshua for a family home evening, I noted how his family was very accustomed to singing all verses of both an opening and closing hymn at their weekly family nights as well as their daily scripture study. I credited this practice to the senior LDS missionaries who must have taught them this, until I visited Suvarna's brother's home—a brother who has chosen to return to Lutheranism. At the conclusion of an extended family dinner, the family opened Lutheran hymnbooks and began to sing the hymns that had been translated into Telugu. Hymns common to both the Andhra Evangelical Lutheran Church (AELC) and the LDS Church were chosen, like "How Great Thou Art," and everyone young and old sang together. It was evident that at least in part, the Suvarna Katuka family's enthusiasm for singing hymns came from the AELC's efforts in the twentieth century to translate Lutheran hymns into Telugu and to "come out as a Native Church in the context of Telugu Culture."[16] Hymn singing in the LDS Church in India is done in English. One aspect of the "centers of strength" policy in India is administering the Church in English while it is being established and while translation work is still in progress. This presents a challenge for members who struggle with English, and yet members from Christian backgrounds often carry a strong tradition of hymn singing from their Christian past and show an enthusiasm for Protestant hymnody that has permeated the culture of the Church. This suggests an additional field of research for Church history in musicology.

The transition for new members from other sects of Christianity to the LDS Church would seem to be an easier process than that of a member coming from a Hindu background. Yet the narratives of Church members who have roots in Hinduism reveal no greater difficulty than is normally experienced by a new member. One characteristic that seems to come from the Hindu culture is a strong devotion to God. Understanding how past experiences with Hindu religious traditions informs the life of a Latter-day Saints in India reveals insights and implications for the study of missiology and indigenization in the LDS Church in India and the international Church as whole. The theory of intertextuality can also be put to use in looking at historical narratives. The idea that every "text" is fundamentally intertextual, or in other words, "a tissue of quotations drawn from innumerable other texts, cultural assumptions and vested interests," is helpful in asking how the experiences of Indian converts from Hinduism or Sikhism influence their lives as Latter-day Saints.[17]

In India, the word "conversion" is charged with meaning and carries the baggage of colonialism and anti-Christian politics. There is a growing literature tracing the history of political and legal debates on religious conversion in India.[18] The issue of religious liberty in this nascent yet most populous democracy is instructive to similar struggles in the United States.[19] The debates over religious conversion in India gained momentum during the first half of the nineteenth century under the British Raj when those involved in the nationalist movement promoted the concept of a common religious identity of Hindus. Gandhi, while emerging as a leading figure in the nationalist movement, was an important voice for indigenous Indian religions in this debate. Gandhi argued, "Every nation considers its own faith to be as good as that of any other. Certainly the great faiths held by the people of India are adequate for her people. India stands in no need of conversion from one faith to another."[20] In addition to this principle of self-reliance, referred to as *swadeshi,* Gandhi also "considered that religion was embodied in the religious heritage of one's forefathers—thus a person was born into it."[21] In other words Gandhi saw religion not in the Western sense of the word as something that one had the right to choose but rather as one's *dharma* or the karma-laden path of duty one was to follow, and "therefore conversion to another religion was not only religious apostasy but also a denial of the self."[22] Because of limits on the number of foreign missionaries allowed into India, the number of missionaries with North American backgrounds has been relatively low. And yet the native missionary force has consistently carried the added weight. There has been a tempering of Americanization in the Church in India as local leaders and missionaries have taken the helm. One could even wonder if the slower growth of the Church has been a blessing to allow for equal parts of indigenization and correlation.

The leaders of the Church are sensitive to the issues of Hindu nationalism in India and cognizant of the problems of the use of terms like "conversion." The Asia Area Presidency, mission presidents, and local Church leaders are careful to respect the laws of the land in India. Missionary work was initially limited to Indian Christians, and there are strict measures that the Church takes to ensure that "conversion" from another religion complies with the law of the land and is not by force or coercion. (This has been the policy the Church followed in India since its first missionary work in the mid-nineteenth century.) Although not in overwhelming numbers, in a country where Hindus represent over 80 percent of the population, there are Hindus who join the Church and experience strong opposition in the process. One example is the narrative of an early member in Hyderabad that ties into the Dharmaraju history. Her story illustrates some of the challenges of those Latter-day Saints who come from Hindu backgrounds.

Annapurna Guru was raised in a Hindu home and was fourteen years old when her brother Murthy found the missionaries at the local bus stop in Hyderabad, not far from where the local LDS meetinghouse was located. Murthy eventually joined the Church even though his parents were opposed to his doing so. Annapurna, as the only daughter, was not allowed to leave the home on Sunday to accompany her brother to church. Converting to Christianity was out of the question even though her parents sent her to a Catholic school; she would be unmarriageable unless she remained a Hindu. Her brother brought her all the literature that he could from the Church. Annapurna was an English literature student, so she was a voracious reader and quickly read through the Book of Mormon and was convinced that it was true. She then read all the missionary literature that Murthy brought to her and in no time was on to *Jesus the Christ* and *A Marvelous Work and a Wonder*. Finally, after five years of investigating the Church on her own, rarely meeting another member besides her brother and never having stepped foot inside the church building, she reached the age where she could legally join the Church without the permission of her parents. She was finally allowed to have the missionary discussions secretly in the home of a member, but when it came time for her to be interviewed for baptism, mission president Neil Twitchell felt a strong impression that it was too dangerous for Annapurna to be baptized at that time because her parents were so against it. For the next two years, Annapurna pled with the Lord and with President Twitchell to be baptized.

After Annapurna, who was determined to join the Church and serve a mission, turned down three proposals of marriage to Hindu prospects, her parents insisted that she marry the next person they chose for her. Murthy, like many older brothers in India, felt a responsibility to find a suitable husband for his younger sister, and with the help of friends in the Church arranged for her to meet someone who was a member of the Church. Annapurna was introduced to John Santosh Murala, the nephew of Edwin Dharmaraju, whose story we told earlier. John was on vacation from Chandigarh where he was doing his surgical residency and visiting family in Hyderabad when he was introduced to Annapurna during a meeting that her brother arranged. After talking with her for fifteen minutes, John was convinced that Annapurna was the woman he wanted to marry and had a strong confirmation of this through the Spirit. (When Annapurna tells the story, she claims they met and talked for only ten minutes and she felt nothing. She was under the impression that she was asked to come to a nearby Church member's home to await a call from the mission president.)

The next day, Murthy came to Annapurna with a proposal from John. Because her parents sensed that something was going on, they moved the date for the wedding up. With one week to go before her wedding, Annapurna decided that this was her only chance to join the Church of Jesus Christ. Annapurna chose to run away and marry John secretly, because with the permission and protection of a husband she could join the Church and someday be sealed in the temple. Through tears she explained to me:

> I was totally heartbroken. I never ever thought I had to do something like that. I knew it was a wrong thing to do. Whatever said and done they are

> my parents. They really love me, they really took care of me. . . . But I didn't know anything else to do. . . . I felt really bad, even now I feel bad. But for everybody's salvation I had to take that step. I had to take that step for my posterity and also for my parents' ancestors to do their temple work and all that. I had to take that step. If not in this life, in the next life they will know why I have done that.[24]

Annapurna's sacrifice for her faith and her mental anguish over having to choose to turn against the faith of her father is still something she lives with. Although John's devotion to Annapurna, his success as a heart surgeon, and their three beautiful children have helped patch things with her immediate family, her extended family and friends still look down on her. She says she is disgraced and that "even now people when they see me some of them even don't talk with me properly because of the thing I have done, left my house and married a Christian."[25] The cost of membership for Latter-day Saints in India cannot be underestimated, and the reasons they choose to stay in spite of these costs should be understood and heard.[26] (See picture of Murala family.)

Murala family in 2011. John and Annapurna with their children Neil, Keith, and Abish.

Furthermore, the story of the origins of the

Church in Hyderabad cannot be properly viewed without addressing the issues of patriarchy in Indian culture. The story of the first baptisms in the Darmahraju family was a story of patriarchy. The narratives of women like Annapurna reflect the dominant patriarchal structures in India. Latter-day Saint historians and scholars need to make use of feminist theology in order to understand the dueling patriarchies within a Church that honors and encourages righteous patriarchal structures yet is in conflict with a culture that is imbued with patriarchies that limit women's agency. The majority of the Latter-day Saints that I interviewed in India used the word "patriarchy" in a pejorative manner to talk about something they were overcoming, and "priesthood" or "gospel culture" was used most often as a highly positive alternative to this patriarchy. Scholars of Mormon history need to address issues of patriarchy head-on and use growing literature from feminist scholars who argue for the merit and agency of women who chose to work within patriarchal religions and together with male authority that they consider benevolent and ultimately a source of greater freedom for them.[27]

Another "pioneer" family from Hyderabad is the Gutty family. They demonstrate how members are navigating between their Mormon and Indian identities as they help establish the Church from a small branch to the first stake in the country. The four Gutty siblings come from a strong Baptist heritage, and their maternal grandfather was a pastor in the Baptist Church. Although neither father nor mother chose to join the LDS Church, they allowed their children the freedom to pursue their own path, which, as one of the Gutty children states, "does not really happen in Indian families."[28] All four of the Gutty children eventually joined the Church, although the eldest brother and his wife are no longer actively affiliated with the Church.

In 1987 missionaries came to the Gutty home at Christmastime. Seeing a star decoration on their home, the missionaries knew they were Christians and felt secure in knocking on the door. Victor invited

President John Gutty with his extended family.

them in, listened to their message, and began to attend church. It was the fellowship that appealed to Victor when he first attended the Church in Hyderabad. There were only fifteen to twenty members, and the congregation was still just a home group, but Victor says he was drawn in by the warmth he felt from the members and the activities that they had. It is difficult to imagine how a church that was so small and new and conducted completely in English would be more appealing to Victor than the well-established and indigenized Baptist Church that he was attending with his family; however, he was drawn to the "fellowship" in the Church and was baptized in May of 1988. The appeal of the fellowship in the Church was a common theme that ran through all of the interviews I conducted. Victor, in talking about what he has seen in the history of the Church in Hyderabad, said, "Well some people call me a pioneer, and that makes me feel very old actually. I'm not a pioneer." He acknowledges that he has seen

Choir singing at the organization of the Hyderabad India Stake led by Madhura Gutty.

many people come into the Church and some of them leave and has experienced a tremendous amount of persecution from his Christian friends. "But through all of this opposition, one thing that I observed is God is working in the gospel. And the gospel will go forward no matter how much opposition is there," states Victor.[29]

Some of the first people Victor invited to come into the Church were his siblings. His sister Madhura joined in 1988. She helped organize the first stake choir in Hyderabad to sing at the organization of the stake in May 2012 and was still leading the stake choir with sari-clad women and men in what they refer to as "priesthood attire" when I attended stake conference on May 4, 2014. (See picture of Madhura leading stake choir.) After Madhura and Victor had joined the church they went to work on their youngest brother, John, who Madhura says "was a very shy guy" and would never come out to listen to the missionaries. Even after being baptized, John was inactive for a time. He said that while in the process of preparing for a difficult exam in school, one of the women in the Church told him, "You're not going to get through unless you get into the Gospel and listen to what the Lord says. You're actually missing a lot of blessings." John said that her words "prick[ed] his heart and mind" and he decided to return to church. He said that as he interacted with the other youth in the small branch, he was "activated by the game of volleyball." (The volleyball games that took place in the yard of the church building and in conjunction with seminary in Begumpet, a neighborhood in Hyderabad, were mentioned in many of the oral history interviews.) John Gutty's first calling in the Church was branch librarian, and six months later, at the age of sixteen, he was called as the Young Men president. He is now serving in the Hyderabad Stake as India's first stake president.[30]

The Guttys led out in balancing the culture of India with "gospel culture." President Gutty has emphasized the need to understand where Indian cultural traditions are in conflict with the teachings of the gospel. For instance, dating and marriage in a culture where dating is considered to be a Western practice with strong ties to a culture of promiscuity and where arranged marriages, or at least "love-cum-arranged" marriages, prevail presents serious questions about what is "gospel" and what is just culture. In a love-cum-arranged marriage, a couple may fall in love and decide to work to convince the parents to come to an arrangement on the marriage. There is still a strong submission to the will of parents and extended family in these cases, and at times the issue of a dowry arises—a practice that is actually illegal but still persists. This can even be a challenge among Church members. President Gutty said that he often counsels parents to use any money that would have been transferred for dowry or used for an elaborate wedding to help pay for a couple's trip to the temple in Hong Kong to be sealed.

Another difficulty that is unique to India is the caste system. The majority of the individuals that I interviewed said that they have not experienced any issues within the Church over caste. Caste is not taught or encouraged in the Church, however it is still very prevalent in Indian

Members of the stake presidency and their wives in Hyderabad India. Back, left to right: Suresh Natarajan (first counselor), President John Gutty, Monohar Mekala (second counseler). Front, left to right: Sowmya Natarajan, Sudha Gutty, and Josephine Mekala. (© Keeler Photography.)

culture and so intersects with the lives of members. When members did talk of negative experiences with caste it often centered on marriage. In the broader Indian culture, there have been efforts to abolish the caste system; however, in the case of marriage, caste boundaries tend to be valued, particularly within the older generation. There is increased possibility as youth interact in Church programs that they will fall in love with someone from another caste. Some have left the Church because a son or daughter has married below their caste, and this causes resistance from some parents against the culture of dating or even socializing within the Church. The dating guidelines in *For the Strength of Youth* pamphlet, which seem extremely conservative to the Western mind, can be a major stretch for those accustomed to Indian culture.

One of the institute classes that I attended in Hyderabad was a marriage and family class taught by the country's Church Educational

System director and his wife. Much care was taken to define "dating" according to the gospel. There is a need for leaders in the Church to emphasize the fact that the Hollywood portrayal of dating is not what is meant in *For the Strength of Youth*, but rather dating in groups with high standards of moral conduct. Young single adult conferences are seen as crucial opportunities to associate with others and get to know the other active LDS youth in the area and sometimes the entire country. After a mission, which most often follows the completion of a bachelor's degree in Indian culture, young single adults take opportunities when they are gathered with other Church members to "propose." The term "propose" in Indian parlance means to express the desire to seriously and prayerfully pursue the option of marriage and begin the process of helping parents get on board. There was even a lesson in the marriage and family course where the instructor had students role-play how to "propose." In an important example of LDS Indian indigenization, or what the Church handbook would refer to as "local adaptation," Church leaders in India have officially suggested that the age of sixteen is too early to begin dating and that in India the age to begin dating should be after eighteen. Additionally, leaders are proactively interpreting the term "dating" for youth in India in ways that work within the broader Indian culture.

One conflict in the literature of how to define Mormonism and whether it is truly a world religion or a still just an American religion is the argument over the requirement of "indigenization," an anthropological term used to describe the process of local or indigenous people who take a new thing and make it their own. This concept is articulated by Matthew Bowman, author of *The Mormon People: The Making of an American Faith.* Bowman identifies Mormonism as a global religion because "it is present on every continent," but not a world religion because unlike Islam or Catholicism, Mormonism has not "found a way to adapt its forms to share its meaning in a panoply of cultures."[31] I think the issue, however, is not that Mormonism hasn't found a way to "adapt its forms and share its meaning," but rather that when Bowman says "Mormonism" he is referring to the institutional Church in Salt Lake City, Utah. "Mormonism" is not what will ultimately do the work—it is the local members who will do and are right now doing the work. The process of indigenization happens from the bottom up, and although it occurs at a slower pace in the centralized structure of the LDS Church, it has always been present. With greater encouragement in the handbook for local units to adapt to local needs and as the Church becomes more established with local, native leadership, the process will continue in ways that are sure to surprise scholars. For instance, Douglas Davies concurs with Bowman and maintains that to qualify as a world religion, Mormonism would need to be "established in many different cultures and adapt itself to local patterns of ritual and of thought as have Buddhism, Christianity and Islam," which he argues it is not likely to do.[32] There are, however, compelling arguments by Mormon studies scholars that suggest otherwise. For instance, at the 2014 Brigham Young University Church History Symposium, Richard E. Bennett made a case that "Mormon indigenization is not a contradiction in terms," and Terryl L. Givens argued for "the portability and ceaseless transmutations of Zion."[33]

Jehu Hanciles has argued, "Globalization implies quite complex interaction and interdependence between the global and the local. It incorporates dominant processes, to be sure, but its dynamic renders the constructs of 'margin' and 'center' fluid and interchangeable."[34] Hanciles's work, as he demonstrated in his 2014 Tanner Lecture address to the Mormon History Association, has important implications for Mormon history and understanding The Church of Jesus Christ of Latter-day Saints. Mormon studies scholar Melissa Wei-Tsing Inouye has argued along the same lines that we should question our assumptions about center and periphery in examining the LDS Church. She asks, for instance, "Where is Mormonism's charismatic center?" and suggests that it is in the global south. As demonstrated in the narrative of this paper, there is an invigorating power in the stories of non–North American Mormons. Inouye calls attention to the increase in miraculous stories recounted in Mormon sources in the twenty-first century that come from the "peripheries" of Mormonism and wonders insightfully "if charismatic resources in Mormonism's Global South might be harvested and redistributed to the church at large as a sort of 'charismatic welfare' for those less fortunate Mormons in parts of the world affected by the modern famine."[35] As we shift the focus of Church history to examine facets of the Church in places like India, we will not only better understand how to define Mormonism but also see how the history of The Church of Jesus Christ of Latter-day Saints is being written by and for the whole world.

Notes

1. Rodney Stark, *The Rise of Mormonism*, ed. Reid L. Neilson (New York: Columbia University Press, 2005), 139.
2. See Jan Shipps, *Mormonism: The Story of a New Religious Tradition* (Urbana and Chicago: University of Illinois Press, 1987), x, 149.
3. See Eric A. Eliason, ed., *Mormons and Mormonism: An Introduction to an American World Religion* (Urbana: University of Illinois Press, 2001), 1–15.
4. Stephen Prothero, *God is Not One: The Eight Rival Religions that Run the World* (New York: HarperCollins, 2010), 12.
5. Mormon Newsroom, "Mormonism Is a Christ-Centered, Global Faith," video, 2:25, http://www.mormonnewsroom.org/article/mormonism-christ-centered-faith.
6. Sydney E. Ahlstrom, *A Religious History of the American People*, 2nd ed. (New Haven and London: Yale University Press, 2004), 508.
7. Mark A. Noll, *The New Shape of World Christianity: How American Experience Reflects Global Faith* (Downers Grove, IL: IVP Academic, 2009), 19–20.

8. Mormon Newsroom, "Facts and Statistics: India," http://www.mormonnewsroom.org/facts-and-statistics/country/india.
9. B. H. Roberts, *A Comprehensive History of the Church*, 6 vols. (Provo, UT: Brigham Young University Press, 1965), 4:72.
10. For the most detailed account of the history of the Church in India, see R. Lanier Britsch, *From the East: The History of the Latter-day Saints in Asia* (Salt Lake City: Deseret Book, 1998).
11. John Santosh Murala, oral history, interview by Taunalyn Rutherford, May 4, 2014, in author's possession. See also William Kesler Jackson, "Lillian Ashby and the Dharmarajus: How One Woman Helped Plant the Church in India," Church History, June 11, 2014, https://history.lds.org/article/lillian-ashby-india-dharmaraju?lang=eng.
12. John Murala, oral history.
13. The literature on Christian missionaries in India is vast, but some of the most helpful sources include Robert Eric Frykenberg, ed., *Christians and Missionaries in India: Cross-Cultural Communication since 1500* (Grand Rapids, MI: Eerdmans, 2003); Rowena Robinson and Sathianathan Clarke, eds., *Religious Conversion in India: Modes, Motivations, and Meanings* (New Delhi: Oxford University Press, 2003); and David Mosse, *The Saint in the Banyan Tree: Christianity and Caste Society in India* (Berkeley: University of California Press, 2012).
14. Currently the best accounts of RLDS/Community of Christ history in India can be found in Matthew Bolton, *Apostle of the Poor: The Life and Work of Missionary and Humanitarian Charles D. Neff* (Independence, MO: John Whitmer Books, 2008), 60–63; and in Steven L. Shields, "Community of Christ's Encounter with Asia: Challenges of Relevance, Pluralism, and Indigenization," *John Whitmer Historical Association Journal* 33, no. 1 (Spring/Summer 2013): 30. In 2014 David Howlett conducted research in India for a forthcoming fiftieth-anniversary history of the Community of Christ in India. See also Taunalyn Rutherford, "Claiming Stakes of Zion in Modern India: Comparative Mormon Missiology," unpublished paper presented at JWHA, Lamoni, Iowa, September 2014.

15. John Murala, oral history.
16. K. L. Richardson, "The Church and Native Culture: A Telugu Lutheran Perspective," in *Indian Journal of Theology* 35, no. 2 (1993): 80–86.
17. See Roland Barthes, *Image, Music, Text* (New York: Hill and Wang, 1977).
18. See for example Sebastian C. H. Kim, *In Search of Identity: Debates on Religious Conversion in India* (New Delhi: Oxford University Press, 2003); Robinson and Clarke, *Religious Conversion in India.*
19. See Goldie Osuri, *Religious Conversion in India: Sovereignty and (Anti) Conversion*, Routledge Contemporary South Asia Series: (New York: Routledge, 2013); Kim, *In Search of Identity*; Gauri Viswanathan, "Literacy in the Eye of India's Conversion Storm," in *Conversion: Old Worlds and New*, ed. Kenneth Mills and Anthony Grafton (Rochester: University of Rochester Press, 2003).
20. Mahatma Gandhi, *Young India*, 23 April 1931, quoted in Kim, *In Search of Identity*, 12.
21. Gandhi, quoted in Kim, *In Search of Identity*, 12.
22. Kim, *In Search of Identity*, 29.
23. Kim, *In Search of Identity*, 29.
24. Annapurna Guru Murala, oral history, interview by Taunalyn Rutherford, May 5, 2014, in author's possession.
25. Annapurna Murala, oral history.
26. A part of Annapurna's story was published in the *Ensign*. See Rochelle Welty and Jan Pinborough, "God Had His Own Plans for Me," *Ensign*, April 2003, 54–56.
27. See Anne M. Clifford, *Introducing Feminist Theology* (Maryknoll, NY: Orbis Books, 2001); Gerda Lerner, *The Creation of Patriarchy* (New York: Oxford University Press, 1986); Andrea Radke Moss, "Mormon Studies in the Classroom: Mormon Women, Patriarchy and Equality," *Juvenile Instructor*, May 8, 2014.
28. Madura Gutty, oral history, interview by Taunalyn Rutherford, May 8, 2014, in author's possession.
29. Victor Gutty, oral history, interview by Taunalyn Rutherford, May 15, 2014; in author's possession.

30. Madura Gutty, oral history.
31. Matthew Bowman, *The Mormon People: The Making of an American Faith* (New York: Random House, 2012), 221–22.
32. Douglas J. Davies, *The Mormon Culture of Salvation: Force, Grace and Glory* (Burlington, VT: Ashgate, 2002), 5.
33. See Terryl L. Givens, "The Global Church," in this volume. See also Richard E. Bennett, "Pentecostals and Mormons in Africa," paper presented at the 2014 Church History Symposium, March 6, 2014.
34. Jehu J. Hanciles, *Beyond Christendom: Globalization, African Migration, and the Transformation of the West* (Maryknoll, NY: Orbis Books, 2008), 386.
35. Melissa Wei-Tsing Inouye, "The Oak and the Banyan: The 'Glocalization' of Mormon Studies," *Mormon Studies Review* 1 (2014): 70–79.

5

Religious and Cultural Influences Faced by the First LDS Missionary in Thailand

Michael A. Goodman

To understand a religion's reception into a country and culture, it is necessary to understand the historical, cultural, and religious milieu into which it enters. The Church of Jesus Christ of Latter-day Saints first entered ancient Siam through the efforts of Elam Luddington on April 6, 1854. Luddington spent 129 days introducing Mormonism in Siam with no apparent success. On August 12, 1854, he left Siam on the barque *Serious*, captained by the same man who brought him to the country four months prior. This man, Captain James Trail, and his wife were the only baptisms Elam Luddington would have in Siam. In his official mission report he stated, "After making every exertion in my honor to establish a church, I found it entirely useless and left them to enjoy their own religion."[1] This would be the only formal attempt to introduce Mormonism to Siam for over one

Michael A. Goodman is an associate professor of Church history and doctrine at Brigham Young University.

A French map of ancient Siam dating to 1686.

hundred years. Luddington's experience was anything but unique for those who sought to introduce Christianity to Siam prior to the nineteenth century. Unknown to Luddington, Christianity had a 350-year history in Siam with little to show for the effort. The cultural, political, and religious realities of Siam created several challenges, which, if not totally unique, were in some ways unequaled throughout Southeast Asia. Almost no other country which allowed Christian proselyting appears to have been as resilient to the spread of Christianity. Too often, Mormon international history is presented somewhat in isolation from the context into which it went. The following study is an attempt to understand some of the reasons behind Siam's incredible resilience to the spread of Christianity in general, and to Mormonism specifically through the first half of the nineteenth century.[2]

Buddhist Foundations

The beginnings of Siam (modern-day Thailand) lay in the migration of the Tai people over a thousand years ago. These migrants, with some intermingling of Mon and Kmer indigenous inhabitants, form the foundation of ancient Siam.[3] The Tai (ไท) were united more by culture and language than geography. Though they spread from the Yunnan province of South China to small groups in northern India, the largest grouping settled in the areas now known as Laos and Thailand.[4] Even before their coming, Buddhism was a powerful influence in the lands the Tai people would come to inhabit. Between the sixth and the ninth century, a strong Buddhist foundation had been laid in central Southeast Asia and came to be associated with the name Dvaravati (ทวารวดี).[5] Known as more of a civilization than a state, Dvaravati, with its ancient Buddhist underpinnings, became a dominant influence throughout the area.

One of the other major civilizations that inhabited the area before the Tais came were the Khmers. The Khmer empire was largely

Buddhist, with infusions of Brahman culture. The archaeological evidence throughout the area points to an extensive and powerful Buddhist civilization and culture.[6] In short, before the Tai established their first state, Buddhism was already intricately associated with the political powers throughout the area. Besides providing meaning and purpose to individual lives, Buddhism became central in binding the people to their rulers. The Tai people became strongly integrated with the "universal, institutionalized religious tradition" of Theravada Buddhism by the end of the tenth century.[7] The following narrative will show how the Buddhist connection between the common people and their rulers was established and how it becomes a primary reason for Thailand's resilience to Christian and Mormon proselyting.

Though some sources claim that the Nan Chao dynasty who ruled in South China in the eighth and ninth century were the first Tai state, documentary evidence linking the Nan Chao with the Tai is weak. By the thirteenth century, however, the Tai would definitely create their own state. The kingdom of Sukhothai was founded in 1238 by the father of King Ramkhamhaeng. However, it was King Ramkhamhaeng (พ่อขุนรามคำแหงมหาราช, 1239–98) who is credited with expanding the borders and creating diplomatic relationships with the other kingdoms of the day.[8] Closely associated with the rise of the first Tai state was "the revivification of the Buddhism already professed by the Tai through contact with Singhalese (Theravada) Buddhism and the foundation of strong, well supported Buddhist monastic institutions throughout the region."[9] Ramkhamhaeng was a devout Buddhist who staunchly supported not only Buddhism in general but the formal monastic community which oversaw it. He gave official royal support to the Buddhist establishment in 1277 and went as far as sharing his own throne with the Buddhist monks once a week so that they could teach Dhamma (ธรรม, righteousness) to the people. From the very beginnings of the Tai state, Buddhism became inextricably connected to national identity. As Wyatt states, "That state was Buddhist, but the religion was also

Relief of King Ramkhamhaeng the Great.

political, certainly to the extent that political unity and identity were founded upon a religious basis."[10]

This royal connection between the state and Buddhism would continue when the next Tai kingdom supplanted Sukhothai. The Kingdom of Ayudhya (อยุธยา) was established in 1351 by King Ramathibodi (สมเด็จพระรามาธิบดีที่, 1314–69). He and his successor kings would provide state support and construct many important Buddhist monuments. One of the greatest kings of Ayudhya, King Naresuan (สมเด็จพระนเรศวรมหาราช, 1555–1605), who reclaimed Ayudhya for the Tais from Burmese subjugation, was known as a staunch supporter of Buddhism and its connection to the state. He maintained close ties to the Sangha, the religious leadership of the Buddhist monastic community. Each successor king maintained or strengthened this connection. In fact, during the reign of one of the final kings of Ayudhya, King Borommakot (สมเด็จพระเจ้าอยู่หัวบรมโกศ,

Sukhothai-style Buddha from the temple at Sri Chum.

reigned 1733–58), the strength of Siamese Buddhism under royal patronage hit what might be considered an apex.

Ceylon (modern-day Sri Lanka) was considered by many to be the center of Theraveda Buddhism for centuries. It was from Singhalese Buddhists monks that Siam looked for guidance through much of its history. However, due to a perceived decline in Theravada Buddhism in Ceylon as a result of Portuguese and Dutch rule, a delegation was sent to Siam in 1751 requesting help to revitalize Singhalese Buddhism. King Borommakot sent a delegation of 18 Siamese monks to reordain Singhalese monks and reestablish a purer form of Theravada Buddhism.[11] Wyatt speculated that in some ways this actually made Siam the preeminent center of Theravada Buddhism in the world.[12]

In accordance with the tradition formalized by King Ramkhamhaeng, the kings of the next (and current) major Tai kingdom, Rattanakosin (อาณาจักรรัตนโกสินทร์), continued the strong relationship between the royal house and Buddhism.[13] The Chakri (ราชวงศ์จักรี) dynasty began with King Phra Phutthayotfa Chulalok

(พระพุทธยอดฟ้าจุฬาโลก, 1737–1809), afterwards known as Rama I. One of his first actions as king was to further solidify the state's connection with the Sangha or Buddhist leadership, even going so far as issuing ecclesiastic laws to bring greater discipline to the monkhood. He further organized a grand council to establish an authoritative version of the Tipitaka, the Buddhist scripture. His patronage and support of Buddhism went beyond most, if not all, of his predecessors'. More and more, the monarchy and Buddhism became inextricably connected. One author went as far as to say that "the pre-1767 trend towards Buddhist kingship was now realized."[14]

This trend continued with Rama II (พระพุทธเลิศหล้านภาลัย, 1767–1824) and Rama III (พระนั่งเกล้าเจ้าอยู่หัว, 1787–1851, respectively). Both considered themselves defenders of Buddhism.[15] By the time Mormonism first appeared in Siam, the fourth king of the Chakri dynasty was on the throne, Rama IV (พระบาทสมเด็จพระปรเมนทรมหามงกุฎ, 1804–68), otherwise known as King Mongkut. King Mongkut was a renowned Buddhist monk for twenty-seven years before ascending to the throne. Before becoming king, he became head of the board responsible for Pali examinations (the official language of the Buddhist scripture Tipitaka) and, as a result, exercised a certain amount of control over instructions for the whole Buddhist monkhood in Siam.[16] He was famous for his efforts to restore Siamese Buddhism to its purest form both before and after his coronation as king and even was responsible for the creation of a major sect (Thammayut, ธรรมยุติกนิกาย) within Thai Buddhism.[17] As can be seen, from the foundations of Tai statehood, the monarchy has been intimately connected with Buddhism and it was a very symbiotic relationship. The close relationship gave legitimacy to both the Siamese royalty and to the ruling Buddhist council—the Sangha specifically, and Siamese Buddhism in general.

However, it was not only the Siamese royalty which became intimately associated with Buddhism, but the Tai people themselves. By

King Mongkut (Rama IV) in European-style dress.

combining the powerful transcendental influence of the religion itself with the patriotic allegiance the Siamese felt to their kings, the Buddhism of ancient Siam became a powerful national identity for the common Siamese. To be Siamese was to be a Buddhist, and to be a loyal Siamese was to be a loyal Buddhist. As a result, Buddhism, which has been a part of the Siamese identity for over millennia, became even more important in the lives of everyday Siamese. As one author put it, Buddhism "spread like wildfire on a wave of popular enthusiasm" with the support of the king and rulers again and again throughout their history.[18]

Christian Beginnings

As central as Buddhism has been to Siamese leadership and society in general, Siam has been remarkably open to other religions. Though Mormonism didn't appear in Siam until the mid-nineteenth century, Christianity has had an official presence, and there has been Christian proselytizing in Siam, since the early sixteenth century.

Except for a few isolated cases, officially sponsored or widespread persecution of other religions in Siam has rarely existed. From the earliest entry of Christianity to Siam, Christians have not only been free to proselyte, they have repeatedly been provided with lands and other resources to share their faith.

Catholicism in Siam

The first Catholic presence in Thailand came from Portuguese delegations headed by Duarte Fernandez, who was sent by Alfonso de Albuquerque, the Portuguese Viceroy of India.[19] After the Portuguese captured Malacca in 1511, Fernandez was sent to the Siamese capital of Ayudhya, because they considered Malacca a vassal of Ayudhya. King Ramathibodi II (สมเด็จพระรามาธิบดีที่ II) exchanged several delegations with the Portuguese, and these delegations culminated in the first "treaty" between Siam and a European nation in 1516.[20] The earliest Catholic missionaries came to Thailand in 1555.[21] Jeronimon de la Cruz and Sebastian de Canto actively proselyted and both died as martyrs, de la Cruz at the hands of Muslims and de Canto at the hands of Burmese invaders. Though these missionaries attempted to work with the Siamese, they found that they were not easily converted and spent much of their time among the Portuguese and the Chinese.

Alfonso de Albuquerque served as the governor of India.

King Ramathibodi monument, Ayutthaya, Thailand.

This same pattern continued for the next three hundred years. Spanish Franciscans came in 1582 but abandoned Siam two years later.[22] The two main Catholic missionary bodies who would work among the Siamese were the Jesuits (largely from Portugal) and the Society of Foreign Missions of Paris (MEP from France).[23] These two groups often did not see eye to eye, which caused further challenges for Christian proselyting.[24] For the most part, these Christian missionaries had good relations with the Siamese royalty. King Songtham (สมเด็จพระเจ้าทรงธรรม, reigned 1611–28) continued to grant foreigners the right to practice their religion.[25] The Society of Foreign Missions took over the main responsibility for proselyting not only in Siam but much of Asia. By 1669 Siam became a formal apostolic vicariate, the organizational step before a diocese is organized.[26]

King Ramathibodi III, also known as King Narai the Great (สมเด็จพระนารายณ์มหาราช, 1633–88), established a school taught by Catholic missionaries to help educate the young Siamese royals and nobles.[27] In 1685, as part of a formal treaty with France, the king again gave royal permission for Christian missionaries to proselyte throughout the kingdom. He further gave permission to operate a seminary to train Catholic missionaries for all of Asia. King Louis XIV of France even sent emissaries to King Ramathibodi III in hopes

Portrait of King Louis XIV.

of converting him to Christianity.[28] However, despite tremendous royal support and the presence of over 2,000 foreign Christians in Ayutthaya at this time, there were few, if any, Siamese converts. Sources put the number of Siamese converts up through 1690 from zero to a handful.[29] While approximately a thousand Catholics were living in Siam by 1770, almost all were of a foreign background.[30]

In 1680 King Ramathibodi III engaged as his foreign minister Constantine Phaulkon, a Greek who worked closely with the

Portuguese and then the French. Both the influence of Phaulkon on the king and the fear that the French were becoming too aggressive in their attempts to affect Siamese politics led to one of the only periods of systematic persecution that Christians ever experienced in Thailand, though to some extent it was aimed at the French more than at Christians in general. Phaulkon was assassinated, and the French were largely excluded from public life for several decades. There were also periodic persecutions from 1730 through 1760, but these persecutions came as often as not from the invading Burmese or other foreign sources, not the Siamese.

The Catholic Church continued to labor in Siam as the nineteenth century began. Though they had small success among the rank and file of the Siamese, they maintained close personal ties to the royalty and continued to play an active role in education and social services in the kingdom. Possibly the most renowned Catholic father to labor in Siam was Bishop Jean-Baptiste Pallegoix (1805–62). He was intimately associated with King Mongkut, because Pallegoix taught the king Latin, mathematics, and astronomy.[31] King Mongkut even spoke at Pallegoix's funeral. Not only did these missionaries associate and have influence with the king, they also had influence with a wide range of other Thai royals and highly influential people.[32] In some ways, it seems astounding that the Catholic Church could have so much influence with the highest levels of Thai society and yet have such little success in spreading Christianity among the Thai people in general. However, on close examination, the strong influence these Christian leaders and missionaries had was always in conjunction with secular issues such as science, medicine, and technology. Furthermore, the Protestant missionaries experienced this same pattern of strong influence in secular subjects but little influence in religious ones.

Protestantism in Siam

Catholicism was not the only branch of Christianity to enter Thailand before the Latter-day Saint faith; protestants began work in Thailand almost thirty years before the first Mormon effort. In 1828 two Protestant missionaries began working in Siam: Reverend Carl Gutzlaff, a German physician who worked for the Netherland Missionary Society, and Reverend Jacob Tomlin, an Englishman who worked with the London Missionary Society.[33] They were welcomed by the Portuguese (Catholic) consulate and provided with a house on the consulate grounds.[34] They translated the Gospels and the book of Romans into Thai and had some success among the Chinese, but little among the Siamese. These two missionaries also made a mistake that would be repeated by many future missionaries. In their attempt to promote Christianity, they at times denigrated Buddhism. As a result, they were almost forcibly removed from the country.[35] But Protestant missionaries were still able to establish a church. Along with William Dean, Reverend and Mrs. John Jones from the American Baptist Mission established the first Protestant church in Siam with eleven members, all Chinese. The Baptists would labor for thirty-eight years among the Siamese but ultimately refocus their work on the Chinese, with whom they experienced much greater success.[36]

One reason Catholic and Protestant missionaries might have had some success with Chinese and other immigrants was the fact that they were not always connected to the Siamese nobility through the corvée system. Corvée was a system of forced labor in which common Thai people were under obligation to provide labor in the form of public works or military service to the nobility. This service could range from three to six months of the year. The system gave strong control over the common people to the nobility, and the nobility used the Buddhist establishment to help administer the system. However, foreign immigrants such as the Chinese were not always held to the same requirement. In fact, by the last part of the nineteenth century, immigrants began seeking protection from Christian priests to avoid the abuses which at times happened at the hands of Thai nobles. For this reason, as well as others, immigrants were more free and motivated to experiment with other forms of religion. Also for these reasons, Thai nobility at times seemed more averse to Christian influence than were Thai royalty, as they had more to lose from the conversion of those under their authority.

Other notable missionaries arrived during this time. Another physician, Reverend David Abeel from the American Board of Commissioners for Foreign Missions (ABCFM, largely Congregationalists), arrived in Bangkok in June 1831. A third physician, Reverend Dan Bradley, MD, arrived from the ABCFM in 1835, and labored in Siam for almost thirty-eight years.[37] Besides missionary work, Reverend Bradley was responsible for several firsts in Siam. He performed the first surgery (to save the life of a Buddhist monk), performed the first inoculations at the request of the king, and brought the first printing press to Siam.[38] He printed the first newspaper and the first official government publication in Siam.[39] Bradley served in Thailand until his death in 1873. He was well known by King Mongkut and had a fairly tumultuous relationship with him. Several times he tried to convert the king and at other times condemned him for polygamy or idolatry.[40] In 1840 another ABCFM missionary, Reverend Jesse Caswell, would arrive. He was a close friend to Prince Mongkut and tutored him in English and science before Prince Mongkut became king.

By 1840 there were twenty-four Congregational and Baptist missionaries in Bangkok. Within twenty years, only three couples were left, along with the Bradleys. The next major missionary push came from the Presbyterian Church. The first Presbyterian missionaries had a profound impact in Thailand but, once again, mostly among

๏หนังสือจดหมายเหตุฯ

THE BANGKOK RECORDER.

Vol.II เล่ม ๑ บางกอก เดือน หก ขึ้นเจ็ดค่ำ จุลศักราช ๑๒๒๗ March 1st 1865. คริศศักราช ๑๘๖๕ ใบ ๑ No. 1.

หนังสือ หลวง

First Thai newspaper printed in Thailand—March 1, 1865, by Protestant missionary Dan Beach Bradley.

foreign nationals and in areas outside of missionary work. The first Presbyterian missionary, Reverend William Buell, started his work in 1840. However, he stayed for only three years because of his wife's illness. He was replaced by Reverend and Mrs. Stephen Mattoon and Reverend Samuel House (also a physician) in 1847. Reverend Mattoon would become the first American consul to Siam in 1856. Dr. House became known as "the man with a gentle heart" for the great medical service he offered. He became the first surgeon to use anesthesia (ether) in Thailand and would serve over three thousand patients in his first year and a half in the country.[41] He would later be invited to live at the palace and serve as a teacher to King Mongkut's children. Furthermore, several of the missionaries' wives taught English to the women in the palace at King Mongkut's request.

As can be seen, many of the Christian missionaries, both Catholic and Protestant, had remarkable access and at times close relationships with the rulers of Siam. For three hundred years, Christians missionaries had remarkable freedom to proselyte.[42] Many served the leaders at the highest levels of Thai society. They had translated the Bible into Thai by the early 1840s and had several church buildings both in Bangkok and in the north. And yet there were precious few Thai converts. Kenneth Wells's *History of Protestant Work in Thailand* lists the converts as of the mid-1860s as follows:

- First two missionaries from 1828 to 1831: zero Thai converts
- Twenty-two missionaries affiliated with the ABCFM from 1831 to 1839: zero Thai converts
- Numerous Presbyterian missionaries from 1840 to 1859: one Thai convert
- Numerous American Baptist missionaries from 1833 to 1863: forty-five total converts (all or almost all Chinese).[43]

In 1855 a British diplomat claimed that there were fewer than ten practicing Protestant Thais in the country.[44] A veteran missionary published the following statement in 1871: "There is scarcely another field in which modern missions have been established where the introduction of the gospel has met so little opposition as in Siam proper. . . . It is equally just to say that there is scarcely any other field which has been so barren of results."[45]

Mormonism in Siam

It was into this religious and cultural environment that Elam Luddington entered as the first missionary of The Church of Jesus Christ of Latter-day Saints in Siam. Luddington was born November 23, 1806, in Harwinton, Litchfield County, Connecticut.[46] He was baptized by Joseph Smith, the Church's founder, on May 16, 1840. His descendants noted the close relationship Luddington shared with the Prophet Joseph, with many hours spent together eating and sleeping under the same roof, as well as working together.[47] Luddington served as a missionary for the Church in different parts of the United States for the first five years of his membership. He spent the next seven years serving in different capacities as an officer for various church and civic organizations. However, his life would change forever at a meeting held on August 27–28, 1852. At this meeting the leaders of the Church called 108 missionaries to serve throughout the world. Missionaries were called to Africa, Australia, China, Denmark, France, Germany, Great Britain, India, Norway, Prussia, and Siam.[48] Four missionaries were called to Siam; however, only Luddington would end up serving there.

Luddington's reaction was typical of his past willingness to serve: "Being unexpectedly called upon at the fall conference of 1852, . . . we all acquiesced by saying Amen, it being an almost unknown part of the world, where but few white men ever tread the soil, so we were all anxious to fill this important mission."[49] After arranging their affairs, the missionaries took leave of their families—almost all of the missionaries were married—on October 21, 1852. By January 9, they arrived in San Francisco and began raising money to buy ship passage. They set sail on January 29 on the clipper ship *Monsoon*. This was one of the few ocean journeys of Luddington's entire mission that was not fraught with life-and-death danger. The missionaries arrived in Calcutta, India, on April 26 after a journey of 10,936 miles in eighty-six days. The missionaries met with the American consul, Mr. Hoofnicle, who treated them with kindness and made numerous inquiries for them. Mr. Hoofnicle informed the Siam-bound missionaries that it would be impossible to travel overland to Thailand, because the second Anglo-Burmese war blocked their route. He further explained that it would be impossible to go by ship until after the fall monsoon season had passed. Luddington and Levi Savage, another missionary called to Siam, were assigned to labor in Burma until it became possible to travel to Siam.

Luddington wrote in a letter, "A few Sabbaths ago, I preached on the government wharf to a company representing most of the nations and peoples under heaven—Burmese, Bengalese, Malays, Brahmins of different casts, Mussulman, Armenians, Jews, and Gentiles. . . . I believe this service has opened the blind eyes or hearts of some."[50] In Burma, Luddington worked largely with Europeans. They baptized two men by January 1854, bringing the total baptisms in Rangoon to ten. By the beginning of 1854, Luddington was determined to make it to his assigned field of labor in Siam. After a perilous ocean journey, he arrived in Singapore on March 6.

Clipper Ship Monsoon, *on which Elam Luddington sailed in January of 1853.*

While in Singapore, Elder Luddington called on Colonel W. J. Butterwort, governor of Singapore and Malacca from 1843 to 1855, and preached to him but was rejected. On March 25, Elder Luddington boarded the barque *Serious* on the final leg of his journey to Siam. Elder

Luddington said he "preached the first Mormon sermon . . . in the Gulf of Siam" and that even though "the Lord was with him" and "they paid good attention," none of the passengers were receptive. In fact, he said, the other preachers contended against him—a harbinger of coming events. Luddington finally reached Siam on April 6, 1854, over a year and a half after leaving his home in Utah. Three days after his arrival, Elder Luddington taught the first Mormon sermon in Siam proper at the residence of Captain James Trail and his wife. That night, April 9, 1854, Elder Luddington baptized Captain Trail and his wife at their request. These two would be his only converts while laboring in Siam.

A few weeks after arriving in Siam, Luddington wrote a letter in which he stated, "I am following my calling at this time in the jungles of Siam, far from a civilized nation and surrounded on the one hand by wild savages, and by wild beasts of prey on the other."[51] Luddington felt persecuted the majority of the time he was in Siam. However, he felt that the abuse was largely brought on not by the Siamese but by the Catholic and Protestant clergy.[52] As mentioned earlier, there was a history of infighting among the Christian missionaries in Siam, and Luddington seems to have experienced some of it. Luddington preached at least one sermon every Sunday he was in Siam, usually to an audience of eight to ten Europeans. He made an effort to preach to the Siamese as well, but language and culture were near insurmountable barriers. He stated that he attempted to learn the language, though he was discouraged by the reports from other Christian missionaries. One missionary reported he had tried to learn the language for seven years and still couldn't preach a sermon in Siamese.[53]

Luddington attempted to preach not only to the Europeans and common Siamese but also to the highest officials of the kingdom. He reported, "Since I have been here I have visited the minister of Foreign affairs, a native of Siam. I preached nearly one hour to him, through an interpreter. He wanted to know much about the Book of Mormon, and if the Prophet would not come to his country."[54] Elder Luddington also wrote a letter to King Mongkut. He later explained: "I have written a long letter to the king . . . at his request. He being desirous to know something about gold plates, I gave him a brief synopsis of the same."[55] He complained that the letter to the king had to pass through a dragoman (translator) and that "every sentence was misconstrued by the dragoman." He sought to personally meet with King Mongkut as well as the second king, Phra Pin Clau, the brother to King Mongkut. In a letter, he wrote that he had just received word that the second king wished to see him. Both King Mongkut and King Pin Clau spoke enough English that if Luddington had been granted an audience, they could have conversed together. There is no evidence, however, that he was ever granted a personal audience with either of them, although he did attend two festivals at the invitation of King Mongkut and at which the king was present. But having received no training in culture, Luddington made several errors. At one of the festivals, he reported, "I took my seat on a mat, with my feet towards the king for which I was very much censured, my guide told me the cause of the excitement saying it is very improper to put your feet towards the king."[56]

While attempting to preach the gospel, Luddington continually encountered opposition. "I was surrounded several times by the natives and twice I was stoned, once I was turned out of the palace and once out of the cathedral and poison was administered to me."[57] He never gave any explanation for this persecution from the Thai natives, and again, he laid the blame for it mainly at the feet of the other Christian ministers. At the end of a letter Elder Luddington wrote after fleeing Siam, he stated, "I was rejected, and I washed my feet as a testimony against my foes—American missionaries and Europeans." Ultimately, Elder Luddington felt he had done everything in his power to fulfill his mission in Siam, but to no avail. "After making every exertion in my honor to establish a church, I found it entirely useless and left them to enjoy their own religion."[58] On August 12, 1854, Elder Luddington took passage again with Captain

James Trail on the *Serious* bound for Singapore. He had spent 129 days in Siam.

Thus ended the first attempt to introduce Mormonism to the Siamese. As was the experience of every other Christian missionary to make the attempt, there was little, if any, evidence of success. In Thailand, just as throughout Southeast Asia, the Christian missionaries had the usual cultural and linguistic challenges. However, the fruits of success in Siam were markedly fewer than in the other countries, even other countries which were predominantly Theravada Buddhist.

One author noted three reasons why Christianity has struggled to find converts in Thailand. The failure of Christianity to convert significant numbers of the Thais could be partly explained by the fundamental differences in the basic world views of Christianity and Theravada Buddhism, partly explained by the salience of Buddhism in the Thai identity and way of life, and partly explained by the often uncompromising attitudes of both Catholic and Protestant missionaries toward the "heathen" beliefs and customs of the natives whom they have sought to convert.[59] As this paper has shown, the second reason most definitely had a profound impact.

Perhaps one reason the Siamese royalty allowed so much freedom to Christian missionaries was the reality that their influence was seen as negligible despite the freedom to proselyte. The powerful combination of Buddhism's deep historical tie to the area and people, the unique way in which Siamese royalty intermingled their influence with their religion, and the loyalty of the Siamese people to their leaders and traditions created a powerful bulwark against the spread of every type of Christianity in the ancient kingdom of Siam.

Notes

1. Elam Luddington, report, October 16, 1845, Missionary Reports 1831–1900, MS 6104, folder 10, item 9, Church History Library, Salt Lake City.

2. For a more detailed account of Elam Luddington's missionary efforts rather than the milieu in which he labored, see Michael A. Goodman, "Elam Luddington: First Latter-day Saint Missionary to Thailand," in *Go Ye into All the World: The Growth and Development of Mormon Missionary Work*, ed. Reid L. Neilson and Fred E. Woods (Provo, UT: Religious Studies Center; Salt Lake City: Deseret Book, 2012), 241–60.
3. Abha Bhamorabutr, *Short History of Thailand* (Bangkok: BMA, 1982), 2.
4. Chris Baker and Pasuk Phongpaichit, *A History of Thailand* (Cambridge: Cambridge University Press, 2005), 3.
5. David K. Wyatt, *Thailand, A Short History* (New Haven: Yale University Press, 1984), 21.
6. Kurt Behrendt, "The Mon-Dvaravati Tradition of Early North–Central Thailand," *The Metropolitan Museum of Art*, http://www.metmuseum.org/toah/hd/mond/hd_mond.htm.
7. Wyatt, *Thailand, A Short History*, 31.
8. Bhamorabutr, *Short History of Thailand*, 3.
9. Wyatt, *Thailand, A Short History*, 38.
10. Wyatt, *Thailand, A Short History*, 55.
11. Ronald Smith, *Siam; or, the History of the Thais from 1569 A.D. to 1824 A.D.* (Bethesda, MD: Decatur Press, 1967), 84.
12. Wyatt, *Thailand, A Short History*, 129.
13. James Basche, *Thailand: Land of the Free* (New York: Caplinger, 1971), 25.
14. Baker and Phongpaichit, *A History of Thailand*, 31.
15. Walter Vella, *Siam under Rama III, 1824–1851* (New York: J. J. Augustin, 1957), 28.
16. A. B. Griswold, *King Mongkut of Siam* (New York: The Asia Society, 1961), 15.
17. Basche, *Thailand: Land of the Free*, 51.
18. Baker and Phongpaichit, *A History of Thailand*, 7.
19. Dirk Van der Cruysse, *Siam and the West, 1500–1700* (Chiang Mai: Silkworm Books, 1991), 7.
20. Noel Busch, *Thailand: An Introduction to Modern Siam* (New York: Van Nostrand, 1959), 51.

21. Saad Chaiwan, "A Study of Christian Mission in Thailand," *East Asia Journal of Theology* 2, no. 1 (1984): 62–74.
22. Van der Cruysse, *Siam and the West*, 13.
23. Peter C. Phan, *Christianities in Asia* (West Sussex: Wiley-Blackwell, 2011), 143.
24. Kenneth S. Latourette, *A History of the Expansion of Christianity* (Grand Rapids: Zondervan, 1971), 3:297.
25. Van der Cruysse, *Siam and the West*, 118.
26. Samuel Hugh Moffett, *A History of Christianity in Asia* (New York: Orbis Books, 2005), 2:51.
27. Van der Cruysse, *Siam and the West*, 165.
28. Smith, *Siam*, 56, and Bhamorabutr, *Short History of Thailand*, 48.
29. See Wyatt, *Thailand, A Short History*; Van der Cruysse, *Siam and the West*; and Moffett, *A History of Christianity in Asia*.
30. Marten Visser, *Conversion Growth of Protestant Churches in Thailand* (Netherlands: Uitgeverij Boekencentrum, Zoetermeer, 2008), 61.
31. Abbot Low Moffat, *Mongkut, the King of Siam* (Ithaca, NY: Cornell University Press, 1961), 14.
32. Wyatt, *Thailand, A Short History*, 177.
33. Moffett, *A History of Christianity in Asia*, 2:350.
34. Kenneth Wells, *History of Protestant Work in Thailand, 1828–1958* (Bangkok: Church of Christ in Thailand, 1958), 6.
35. Barend Terwiel, *A History of Modern Thailand, 1767–1942* (St. Lucia: University of Queensland Press, 1983), 134.
36. Moffett, *A History of Christianity in Asia*, 2:351.
37. Moffett, *A History of Christianity in Asia*, 2:350–51.
38. Terwiel, *A History of Modern Thailand*, 169, and Wells, *History of Protestant Work in Thailand*, 10–11.
39. Moffett, *A History of Christianity in Asia*, 2:351.
40. Moffat, *Mongkut, the King of Siam*, 157.
41. Wells, *History of Protestant Work in Thailand*, 23.
42. Likhit Dhiravegin, *Siam and Colonialism, 1855–1909: An Analysis of Diplomatic Relations* (Bangkok: Thai Watana Panich, 1974), 44.

43. Wells, *History of Protestant Work in Thailand*, 2.
44. Visser, *Conversion Growth of Protestant Churches in Thailand*, 62.
45. Moffett, *A History of Christianity in Asia*, 350.
46. Details of Elam Luddington's early life come from Elam Luddington, "Luddington Family and All Existing Portions of an Autobiographical Sketch," folios I and IV, Family History Library, Salt Lake City.
47. Ancestral records kept by Karen Bush, a descendant of Elam Luddington. Copy in author's possession.
48. Andrew Jenson, *Church Chronology*, 2nd ed. (Salt Lake City: Deseret News, 1914), 46.
49. Elam Luddington, letter to *Deseret News* editor, circa October 1855, MS 6104, Folder 14, Church History Library.
50. Elam Luddington, "The Burma Mission," *Millennial Star*, January 1, 1854, 190.
51. Elam Luddington, "The Siam Mission," *Millennial Star*, May 1, 1854, 540.
52. R. Lanier Britsch, "The East India Mission of 1851–56: Crossing the Boundaries of Culture, Religion, and Law," *Journal of Mormon History* 27, no. 2 (Spring 2001): 158.
53. Elam Luddington, "Siam," *Deseret News*, November 16, 1854, 132.
54. Luddington, "The Siam Mission," 540.
55. Luddington, "The Siam Mission," 541.
56. Luddington, letter.
57. Luddington, letter.
58. Elam Luddington, "India-China," *Deseret News*, June 20, 1855, 120.
59. Erik Cohen, *Indigenous Responses to Western Christianity*, ed. Steven Kaplan (New York: New York University Press, 1995), 36.

6

History of the Church in Taiwan in the 1970s

Po Nien (Felipe) Chou

How did the political and religious dynamics in Taiwan affect the development of The Church of Jesus Christ of Latter-day Saints (LDS Church) in Taiwan during the 1970s? How did the first mission, first area conference, and first stake in Taiwan affect the Church in the 1970s? This article examines important insights to the significant events of the 1970s history of the LDS Church in Taiwan, placed within the context of the political and religious climate in Taiwan during this period (see appendix). By adhering to its position of political neutrality, the LDS Church avoided difficulties experienced by the Presbyterian Church in Taiwan (PCT) and U.S. officials in the tense political environment of the 1970s, thus allowing the LDS Church to organize its first stake and first three missions in Taiwan.

Po Nien (Felipe) Chou is a religious educator and manager of the Office of Research for the Seminaries and Institutes (S&I) of The Church of Jesus Christ of Latter-day Saints.

Political and Religious Background prior to the 1970s

Taiwan is an island located off the east coast of the People's Republic of China (PRC). In the seventeenth century, Christianity was introduced by Catholic and Protestant missionaries. The Han Chinese conquered Taiwan and brought Buddhism and Taoism in 1683, driving out Christian missionaries until the nineteenth century. When these missionaries returned, the island was filled with Buddhist temples.[1] Efforts to establish Christianity were limited when the Japanese controlled the island from 1895 until the end of World War II in 1945. By 1949, Mao Zedong's Communist army established the PRC in China after defeating Chiang Kai-shek's Kuomingtang (KMT) government, which relocated to Taiwan.[2] Refugees from mainland China brought a combination of Buddhism, Taoism, and Confucianism to Taiwan.[3] Chinese Catholics and other Christians were also among the refugees.[4] The government imposed martial law and regulated free speech and religious freedom in Taiwan but also welcomed Western Christian missionaries following the U.S. military and economic aid.[5] This facilitated the entry of American LDS missionaries. The Presbyterian Church in Taiwan, which had arrived in the nineteenth century, was very vocal and critical of the government's restriction to religious freedom and called for local autonomy.[6] The Presbyterian Church's confrontation with the government resulted in the expulsion of some of their church leaders, a situation the LDS Church avoided as a result of their policy of political neutrality.[7]

With a small group of American LDS servicemen stationed in the region, the Southern Far East Mission was established in 1955 and the first four LDS missionaries were sent to Taiwan in 1956.[8] Elder Mark E. Petersen visited and dedicated Taiwan for the preaching of the gospel in 1959,[9] the first edition of the Chinese Book of Mormon was published in 1965, and the Hong Kong–Taiwan Mission was created in 1969.[10]

Taiwan Loses UN Seat but Gains Its First Mission and CES Programs

During the 1960s and 1970s, the financial support from the United States and others led to dramatic economic growth in Taiwan. In 1970 the Hong Kong–Taiwan Mission had 9,442 total members, including between 153 and 159 missionaries. By 1971, Taiwan became its own mission with over 4,500 members and 90 missionaries serving. W. Brent Hardy, who was serving as the president of the Southern Far East Mission, became the president of the Hong Kong–Taiwan Mission in 1969. On January 1, 1971, this mission was divided, and Malan R. Jackson was called to preside over the newly created Taiwan Mission.[11] President Harold B. Lee, then First Counselor in the First Presidency, visited Taiwan and challenged the members "to prepare themselves . . . to receive the greater blessings of the Lord."[12] The establishment of the

1971, President Harold B. Lee, then counselor in the First Presidency, visits Taiwan. Pictured from left to right: Elder and Sister Komatsu, President and Sister Lee, President and Sister Jackson (Taiwan Mission).

Taiwan Mission was important to further the growth of the Church in Taiwan. Since the 1950s, the missionaries and members in Taiwan lacked local supervision from the distant Southern Far East or Hong Kong–Taiwan Missions. Lanier Britsch, an LDS scholar, noted that supervising the work in Taiwan from a distance was challenging and limited in its ability to move the work forward.

> The Church did not take hold in Taiwan quite as quickly as it did in Hong Kong. . . . [The mission president] could not visit Taiwan very often. . . . This led to feelings of separateness among many of the Taiwan workers. When Heaton or his counselors visited Taiwan, . . . the missionaries treated them coolly, and when the leaders were gone, the Taiwan elders disregarded some mission rules and directions. But during the last part of 1958, President Heaton assigned his counselor, W. Brent Hardy, to live in Taiwan and act as president. This change brought the desired effect, and from then on the work progressed at a faster pace.[13]

If having a counselor in the mission presidency living in Taiwan was important for the work to progress in 1958, imagine the effect of having a mission president presiding and living in Taiwan. The prior feelings of neglect from a distant Church leader were quickly forgotten, and the Saints in Taiwan moved forward with renewed commitment. Local Taiwanese converts served as full-time missionaries in the 1970s. Wang Li-Ching, for example, was a convert and a twenty-year-old college student in 1971. She was going home after her final exams and felt impressed to get off the bus to stop by the Taiwan Mission office. She was met by Malan Jackson, the mission president, as she entered the mission office, and he was prompted to call her on a mission. Wang readily accepted and served as Jackson's secretary and translator.[14] She was among the many young adults in Taiwan who accepted calls to serve and assist in the 1970s. There were 28 local Chinese missionaries by 1971.[15]

About a month after the United Nations formally changed China's seat from the government in Taiwan to the one in mainland China,

Elder Marvin J. Ashton, then an Assistant to the Twelve, was sent to visit the Saints in Taiwan in November 1971.[16] The Presbyterian Church in Taiwan issued three public statements critical of the government in Taiwan in the 1970s including "Public Statement on Our National Fate" in 1971.[17] The LDS Church maintained a neutral position and avoided making political statements. Feng Xi noted the impact of this policy on the LDS Church:

> There was increased tension between the government and the Christian churches in Taiwan. . . . The Presbyterian Church had been in conflict with the Kuomintang. In the early 1970s, it sharply criticized the regime's authoritarian structure. . . .
>
> President Jackson instructed his missionaries to stay away from politics and refrain from sensitive comments. As a result, there never occurred a harsh confrontation between the Mormon Church and the Taiwan government. Problems like a rejection of visas to foreign missionaries never happened to the Mormons. This cautious and neutral political position of the Church, well observed by all later mission presidents, laid a good foundation for developing future relations between the Church and top Taiwan government officials in the 1980s.[18]

In 1972, U.S. president Richard Nixon visited mainland China to help normalize relations.[19] Although the United States continued to support and recognize the government in Taiwan, there was increased concern and uncertainty among those living in Taiwan. As the world turned its attention to China, the Church remained interested in and committed to its missionary efforts in Taiwan.[20] The establishment of the Taiwan Mission in 1971 helped to instill faith and hope among the Saints in Taiwan. While the people of Taiwan felt abandoned by the world, the Saints in Taiwan appreciated the care and interest of the Church leaders in Salt Lake. In 1972 regional representatives visited mission districts to provide training and leadership opportunities as they had been doing with stakes. Mission representatives helped to train and increase effectiveness of

Alan Hassell, Michele Hassell, Wan Ng Suk-Yi (Alice), and Wan Kon-Leung (Joseph), December 1974. Hassell served as the first CES coordinator in Taiwan, followed by Wan. (Courtesy of Alan Hassell.)

missionaries.[21] Additionally the first health missionaries were sent to Taiwan to help teach disease prevention,[22] evaluate health resources, and address health issues.[23]

In 1973, Alan R. Hassell and his family were sent from the United States to Taiwan to help establish Church Educational System (CES) programs. Hassell set up the first CES office in Taiwan and visited branches throughout the island to help coordinate seminary and institute programs.[24] Before Hassell and his family returned to the United States in 1974, he had hired local CES coordinators to continue the program. By the late 1970s, there were over 350 seminary and over 400 institute students in Taiwan. Yang Tsung-ting was baptized in 1973 and was among the first institute graduates in 1977. Juan Jui-Chang was baptized in 1974 and recalls making the decision to serve a mission because of a seminary teacher. Both Elders Yang and Juan would later serve as stake presidents and Area Authority Seventies in Asia.[25] They have both talked about the importance of the seminary and institute programs of the Church in their lives and the lives of other members of the Church throughout Taiwan.[26] Their experiences illustrate the importance of the CES programs in preparing local missionaries and future Church leaders in Taiwan.

Missionary Lessons Adapted to Local Culture and Customs

On June 20, 1974, the Taiwan Mission was renamed the Taiwan Taipei Mission. Thomas P. Nielson served as the Taiwan Taipei Mission president from 1974 to 1977. At the time Nielson received his call, he was a professor of Chinese literature at Arizona State University. His experience and understanding of the Chinese culture was critical to the growth of the Church in Taiwan. Nielson used the uniform lesson plan implemented by the Church Missionary Department but also implemented critical adaptations based on the local culture and customs which helped increase the harvest of new converts in Taiwan.[27] Feng Xi credited Nielson for the immediate results:

> Nielson succeeded Jackson as the president of the Taiwan Mission. . . . Nielson, with a Ph.D. in Chinese language and literature, was a dynamic and culturally oriented mission president. . . . Nielson stressed the importance of missionary cultural awareness in order to make them carry out their proselyting in a Chinese way, which he believed would make proselyting more effective in the long run. Quite often he read poems of the Chinese Tang dynasty to his missionaries and did many other things to increase their cultural awareness. Not long after his arrival, the Church held a meeting in Asia and asked its mission presidents to focus more on the increase of baptisms. After that, Nielson changed his style to more practical methods that would produce immediate results.[28]

While many Western countries were established with basic Judeo-Christian beliefs, this was not the case for most of Asia. The Taiwanese were influenced by the tenets of Buddhism, Taoism, and Confucius. These tenets coupled with the deep sense of duty to honor their ancestors led to challenges in teaching the Taiwanese. Adaptations made by Nielson included a series of filmstrips developed during this period to help investigators with a Buddhist background understand the value the LDS Church placed on families, the need to search after one's ancestors, and the essential role of temple ordinances for their salvation. [29]

Yang Tsung-ting, who grew up in a Buddhist home before he was baptized in 1973,[30] explained that "most Taiwanese parents expect that when they die, their children will burn paper money and incense for them and offer food. Otherwise, they fear they will be hungry and poor in the next life. That is why older people sometimes panic when they see their young people join the Church." Yang continues by noting an adaptation that helps minimize the fear from the elderly as follows: "Church members emphasize ancestors but in a different way. . . . We do family history work, submit names to the temple, and perform ordinances for their eternal benefit."[31] A 1975 *Friend* article noted that "one reason the gospel has been so well accepted in Taiwan and other Oriental countries is because of the Church's emphasis on genealogy work. Great honor and respect are given to ancestors in these countries."[32]

The adaption of the missionary lessons benefited the Church in Taiwan, and by 1975 there were about 7,000 members in 30 branches, with 200 full-time missionaries serving in Taiwan.[33] There are various examples of how the missionary efforts in the 1970s would bless the growth and development of the Church in Taiwan, both the immediate as well as distant future. Wang Wei was converted in 1973, and twenty years later he and his wife, Wang Hsiao-Feng, would serve as the first Chinese temple president and matron. Wang served as the Taipei Taiwan temple president from 1993 to 1997[34] and regularly taught the importance of searching out one's ancestors and then bringing those names to the temple to perform the necessary saving ordinances in their behalf. Juan Jui-Chang joined the Church in 1974 and served as a missionary in the Taiwan Taipei Mission, as a stake president, and as an Area Seventy in Asia. He recounted the following experience in the temple:

> I felt the Spirit more strongly than ever while performing the work for my parents. In the sealing room, I represented my father and my wife represented my mother, and we knelt together at the altar. We felt it was the greatest thing we could do for our parents. . . . We need to help people see that the gospel is not something foreign to Taiwanese culture but something we already know pieces of.[35]

The experiences of these converts from the 1970s illustrate the significance of understanding the culture and the impact of the adaptation made to take the gospel to the Chinese people in Taiwan. Understanding the culture and helping investigators understand the importance of families and the work in behalf of their ancestors within the context of the restored gospel were key concepts in helping many join the Church through the waters of baptism.

Publication of Remaining LDS Scriptures

After Hu Wei-I completed the Chinese translation of the Book of Mormon in 1965, Ch'e Tsai-Tien was asked to be the principal translator for the Doctrine and Covenants and the Pearl of Great Price. Other people participated in the review and revision process in Hong Kong before it was finally ready for printing in 1973.[36] There were challenges due to differences between Cantonese and Mandarin (Chinese dialects used in Hong Kong and Taiwan, respectively), as well as personal preferences of mission presidents and various reviewers or translators.

> The translation of the Doctrine and Covenants into Chinese was an unhappy experience for all concerned. In August 1966 President Garner called his counselor in Taiwan, President Ch'e Tsai Tien, to translate the Doctrine and Covenants and the Pearl of Great Price into Chinese. . . . A year or two later Ch'e sent his translation of the Doctrine and Covenants to Hong Kong for review by Brothers Ng Kat Hing (head of translation projects in Hong Kong for almost a decade by this time) and Liu Nga Sang. In Hong Kong a number of other people became involved in the review and revision process. . . . The basic difficulty involved in completing a suitable translation grew out of two problems: too much nit-picking and too many personal preferences on the part of mission presidents and other reviewers and basic differences in structural preference between Cantonese and Mandarin speakers. The official version of the Doctrine and Covenants was published by Brother Ng in Hong Kong. However, the Taiwan Mission, under Malan R. Jackson, published its own version.[37]

There were challenges between the two versions published, particularly due to significant differences in the text. Browning notes that "the great genius of the Chinese writing system, which has served to unify that nation for three thousand years, seems on the verge of being frustrated by competing versions of the same material by the Hong Kong and Taiwan translation offices."[38] Despite these difficulties, the Chinese translations of the Doctrine and Covenants and of the Pearl of Great Price were officially published in 1975 and 1976, respectively.[39] This was a significant milestone in the history of the Church among the Chinese. Twenty years after the first four missionaries arrived in Taiwan, the Chinese translation of all latter-day scripture was finally completed. This allowed missionaries to use these new scriptures in proclaiming the gospel and helped members to deepen their doctrinal knowledge and understanding of the restored gospel. The translated scriptures were welcomed by the Saints, and their full impact cannot be adequately measured or appropriately quantified.

Taiwan's First Area Conference and Visit by the President of the Church

During this period, the general conferences of the Church originating from Salt Lake City were not easily accessible to members of the Church in various locations around the globe, including Taiwan. Area conferences helped to provide an opportunity for Church leaders from Salt Lake to visit with members in various areas of the world, providing these members with the opportunity to hear General Authorities teach and train them in person.[40] When President Spencer W. Kimball visited Taiwan in 1975, he was the first President of the Church to visit Taiwan, and the area conference held on August 14, 1975, was the first one of its kind in Taiwan.[41]

The announcement in May 1975 that President Kimball was coming to Taiwan in August to preside over the first area conference in Taiwan was very timely. It came shortly after Chiang Kai-shek, the president of Taiwan, had passed away in April 1975.[42] This transition left concerns and uncertainty concerning the political future of Taiwan and its relationship with China.[43] President Nielson published "In Remembrance of President Chiang" in *The Voice of the Saints*, noting that Chiang was a good man and president who was a spiritual leader and loved by everyone. Nielson urged the people to have courage and pray for the Spirit to lead this country to freedom in a time of uncertainty.[44] The Saints' respect for the government facilitated President Kimball's visit with the new president of Taiwan.

Prior to the arrival of President Kimball, there was much planning and preparation. No effort was spared to invite every Church member and to reach out to the general public. President Nielson credited the members and local leaders for the success of President Kimball's visit. The area conference was held in the Dr. Sun Yat-sen Memorial Hall in Taipei with about 2,500 Church members and friends in attendance. Many saw and heard a living prophet of God in person, and many more were able to hear President Kimball by means of the radio and television. Elder Kevin Moss, who attended the conference, recorded the following:

> President Spencer W. Kimball arrived from Hong Kong with other General Authorities. They were joyously received by a large crowd of Chinese members—"a gracious and respectful mobbing," as one elder put it. After a press conference at the Grand Hotel, President Kimball, President Benson, and Brother David Kennedy were taken to meet Yen Chia-Kan, president of the Republic of China. Together they spent forty-five minutes discussing genealogy and the role of the family. President Kimball also explained the Church Welfare System, which impressed President Yen, who pointed out similarities between it and the operation of some of the ancient family clans. President Yen was presented with a beautiful, white, leather-bound edition of the Book of Mormon.[45]

During the general session of the area conference, President Kimball talked about temples and announced the plans to build a temple in Tokyo, Japan. He also emphasized the importance of service and missionary work, while sharing his vision of carrying the restored gospel to the whole world.[46]

> Thursday night, August 14, the Sun Yat-sen Memorial Hall was an enormous fusion reactor of people and anticipation. All eyes were fixed on President Spencer W. Kimball as he arose to speak. He spoke as a prophet. . . . He explained the purpose of the temple to be built in Japan. "You, too, can have one," he said. He elaborated on his theme of missionary work. "We expect hundreds of your local young men" to serve on missions, . . . then said in closing, "We leave the blessings of the Lord upon you, your posterity, and upon this land."[47]

The members were excited to hear the prophet speak and recognized the importance of preparing for a temple and answering the call to serve missions. They rejoiced for the rare and unique opportunity to hear the President of the Church speak to them in person.

Their faith and testimony of the gospel were strengthened, along with their desire to serve the Lord and help build up the Church in Taiwan. Following President Kimball's visit and promise, members and missionaries in Taiwan worked hard to increase the number of baptisms and worthy members, and by November 1984, the Taipei Taiwan Temple was dedicated by President Gordon B. Hinckley.[48]

First Stake and Second Mission Organized

In 1975, there were 30 branches and over 7,000 members found in three member districts in the mission and an American servicemen's district. Even though it was very difficult to get permission from the government to leave the country to enable them to do temple work, the members in Taiwan were tracing their genealogy back thousands of years and preparing for the blessings of the temple.[49] After the area conference, President Nielson submitted a proposal to the First Presidency to create the first stake in Taiwan. On January 13, 1976, he was notified that his request was approved. Several weeks later he also received word that the Taiwan Taipei mission was to be divided to create the Taiwan Kaohsiung Mission. Nielson and other Church leaders were excited. Elder Gordon B. Hinckley arrived in Taipei on April 19, 1976, and selected Chang I-Ch'ing to be the first Chinese stake president. Chang became the first Chinese stake president when the Taipei Taiwan Stake was created on April 22, 1976, with six wards, five branches, and 4,497 members.[50] The *Ensign* reported these milestones as follows:

> Two major milestones in the history of the Church in the Far East were reached April 22 and April 25 when the first stakes were organized in Taiwan and Hong Kong, representing the first stakes among the Chinese peoples. . . .
>
> The new stakes were organized under the direction of Elder Gordon B. Hinckley of the Council of the Twelve, assisted by Elder Adney Y. Komatsu, Assistant to the Council of the Twelve and the area supervisor for the Far East.[51]

Twenty years after the first missionaries arrived in Taiwan, the first stake in Taiwan was organized. This was a significant milestone in the history, development, and growth of the Church in Taiwan. Wang Ping-Huang was among the first to be ordained to the office of a bishop. Hu Wei-I, who translated the Book of Mormon into Chinese, became the first stake patriarch for the Church in Taiwan.[52] While a district is supervised by a mission president, a stake is independent of the mission and supervised by a stake president. The establishment of the first stake of Zion in Taiwan is an indication of the strength and maturity of the local leadership.

Efforts in the 1960s and early 1970s to help members go to the Laie Hawaii Temple were met with difficulties due to the financial cost and government restrictions.[53] During this period, it was difficult to get permission to leave the country in order to attend a temple.[54] But following the creation of the first stake in Taiwan, the First Presidency sent an invitation to the newly called stake presidency and bishops to travel to Church headquarters for general conference. This letter of invitation allowed these Taiwanese leaders to get a visa from the Taiwanese government, which was a rare and unique blessing. Wang Ping-Huang's daughter remembers the excitement her father had in receiving permission from the government to travel with others to Utah in 1977. Because the Salt Lake Temple was closed during general conference, these leaders went to the Provo Utah Temple to receive their temple blessings.[55]

On July 1, 1976, the Taiwan Kaohsiung Mission was created, and P. Boyd Hales served as its president. The new Taiwan Kaohsiung Mission had 3,600 members, while the Taiwan Taipei Mission had 4,600 after they were divided.[56] The creation of this second mission is a significant event, because it reflects the growth and development of the Church in Taiwan. Across the Taiwan Straits, Mao Zedong had passed away on September 9, 1976, and Deng Xiaoping emerged as his successor.[57] With the passing of Mao in China in 1976 after the passing of Chiang Kai-shek in Taiwan the previous year, it was unclear how the relationship between Taiwan and mainland China might change with their political successors. Notwithstanding the uncertainty and changing political dynamics in the region, the Church continued to progress. The creation of the first stake and second mission was the highlight of the growth experienced in 1976.[58] By 1977, when Frederick W. Crook replaced Thomas P. Nielson as the mission president for the Taiwan Taipei Mission, membership in Taiwan had surpassed membership in Hong Kong. In 1977 there were 7,933 members in Taiwan compared to 4,256 in Hong Kong.[59]

United States Transfers Recognition of ROC to PRC, and Taiwan's Third Mission Is Created

The political situation between mainland China and Taiwan has always been delicate, with martial law in place in Taiwan throughout the 1970s and into the 1980s. As noted earlier, the UN had already transferred China's seat from Taiwan or the Republic of China (ROC) to mainland China or the People's Republic of China (PRC) in 1971. The United States continued to recognize the government in Taiwan as the legitimate Chinese government until December 1978. A telegram from the U.S. Pacific Command reported the following situation:

> On January 1, 1979, the United States changed its diplomatic recognition of Chinese government from the ROC to the PRC . . . and acknowledged the PRC position that there is but one China and Taiwan is part of China. . . . On December 28 and 29, 1978, . . . a U.S. representative was sent to the ROC for negotiations with ROC President Chiang Ching-Kuo. . . . Upon arrival to Taipei, ROC's capital, there was a great disturbance with the presence of the Americans. Understandably so, the Taiwanese people were angered by the "betrayal" of the U.S. Government. There were several

> protests and the Americans, only with heavy security precautions, were able to navigate the city safely to and from meetings . . . to negotiate four principal objectives that would, hopefully, provide a sort of compromise between the two nations.[60]

The conflict between the Presbyterian Church in Taiwan and the Taiwanese government intensified in 1979 after U.S. president Jimmy Carter's emphasis on human rights and the diplomatic recognition of mainland China by the United States. The 1979 Kaohsiung Incident started as a peaceful demonstration by advocates of Taiwan's independence but turned into a confrontation with the local riot police. The Taiwanese government blamed the Presbyterians for the unrest and arrested its leadership.[61] Reverend K'ao Chun-ming, the general secretary of the Presbyterian Church, was imprisoned.[62] Although the LDS Church remained politically neutral, the Kaohsiung Incident and this change in U.S. policy slowed missionary work in Taiwan temporarily for a few months, as some became suspicious of religious groups as well as Americans. The animosity towards American missionaries due to the political situation became less evident by the time Douglas H. Powelson became the new mission president for the Taiwan Taipei Mission in 1979.[63] China's "open door policy" allowed for the first group of Brigham Young University's Young Ambassadors performing group to visit mainland China in 1979. This period of openness for China was an important step in providing stability in the region, lowering the tension between mainland China and Taiwan and allowing the Church to continue to flourish in Taiwan. In 1979 the Church in Taiwan included fifty-one wards and branches when new mission presidents arrived and mission boundaries were reorganized.[64]

In 1979, George A. Baker Jr. replaced Hales as the mission president for the Taiwan Kaohsiung Mission, and Douglas H. Powelson replaced Crook as the mission president over the Taiwan Taipei Mission when Crook became the mission president for the newly formed Taiwan Taichung Mission (consolidated into the Taiwan Kaohsiung Mission in

1982). "The Taiwan T'aichung Mission was created from the Taiwan Taipei and Taiwan Kaohsiung Missions. No stakes were in this new mission, located in an area of 5.4 million nonmembers and 1,882 members."[65] The Church continued to grow despite the political challenges.

Concluding Remarks

The early missionary efforts during the 1950s and 1960s were important in laying a foundation for the expansion of the Church in Taiwan. However, there were significant events in the 1970s that helped to cement the initial foundation and further expand the work during this period as well as the future of the growth of the Church in Taiwan. While Taiwan lost diplomatic recognition from the UN and the US, and other Christian religions like the Presbyterian Church in Taiwan would struggle with the Taiwanese government, the LDS Church was able to expand and support the Saints in Taiwan.

Major Church historical events in Taiwan in the 1970s included the creation of the Taiwan Mission in 1971, the establishment of CES programs, the adaptation of the missionary lessons, the Chinese translation of the remaining LDS scriptures, the first area conference and visit by President Kimball, the organization of the first stake in Taiwan, and additional missions in Taiwan (Kaohsiung Mission and Taichung Mission). These important events and developments in the 1970s helped to expand missionary efforts as well as develop and prepare local leadership in Taiwan. New converts from the 1970s would include future stake presidents, Area Seventies, and the first Chinese temple president.

Notes

1. Murray A. Rubinstein, "Taiwanese Protestantism in Time and Space, 1865-1988," in *Taiwan: Economy, Society and History*, ed. E. K. Y. Chen, Jack F. Williams, and Joseph Wong, (Hong Kong: Centre of Asian Studies, 1991).

2. Ian Skoggard, "Taiwan," Countries and Their Cultures, http://www.everyculture.com/Sa-Th/Taiwan.html.
3. Charles B. Jones, *Buddhism in Taiwan: Religion and the State, 1660–1990* (Honolulu: University of Hawaii Press, 1999).
4. Chen-Tian Kuo, *Religion and Democracy in Taiwan* (Albany, NY: State University of New York Press, 2008), 53–54.
5. Yunfeng Lu, Byron Johnson, and Rodney Stark, "Deregulation and the Religious Market in Taiwan: A Research Note," *Sociological Quarterly* 49, no. 1 (Winter 2008): 139–53.
6. Murray A. Rubinstein, *The Protestant Community on Modern Taiwan: Mission, Seminary, and Church* (Armonk, NY: M. E. Sharpe, 1991).
7. Feng Xi, "A History of Mormon-Chinese Relations: 1849–1993" (PhD diss., Brigham Young University, 1994), 176–77.
8. "Facts and Statistics: Taiwan," *Newsroom*, http://www.mormonnewsroom.org/facts-and-statistics/country/taiwan/.
9. John Hilton III and Po Nien (Felipe) Chou, "The History of LDS Seminaries and Institutes in Taiwan," *Mormon Historical Studies*, 14, no. 2 (Fall 2013): 83–106.
10. R. Lanier Britsch, *From the East: The History of the Latter-day Saints in Asia, 1851–1996* (Salt Lake City: Deseret Book, 1998).
11. Britsch, *From the East,* 259.
12. "Taiwan Saints Eager for Temple Blessings," *Ensign*, November 1984, 107–9.
13. Britsch, *From the East,* 254.
14. Wang Li-Ching (Sandy Lee), phone interview by Po Nien (Felipe) Chou, Cedar Hills, Utah, November 18, 2013.
15. Paul Hyer, "Taiwan," in *Encyclopedia of Latter-day Saint History*, ed. Arnold K. Garr, Donald Q. Cannon, and Richard O. Cowan (Salt Lake City: Deseret Book, 2000), 1216–17.
16. Ng Shee-Nan and Chin Ching-Man, *The Church of Jesus Christ of Latter-day Saints: History in Hong Kong, 1949–1997*, trans. Anita Chin (Hong Kong: Printforce Printing, 1997).

17. Christine L. Lin, "The Presbyterian Church in Taiwan and the Advocacy of Local Autonomy," *Sino-Platonic Papers* 92 (January 1999).
18. Feng Xi, "Mormon-Chinese Relations," 176–77.
19. Harry Harding, *A fragile relationship: the United States and China since 1972* (Washington DC: The Brookings Institution, 1992).
20. William Heaton, "China and the Restored Church," *Ensign*, August 1972, 14–18.
21. "New Supervisory Program for Missions and Regions," *Ensign*, September 1972, 87–89.
22. "Church's Health Team Teaches Maternal Care," *Church News*, March 3, 1979, 13.
23. Margaret R. J. Kitterman, oral history, interviewed by Richard L. Jensen, Salt Lake City, Utah, May–September 1975, Historical Department (1972–2000), History Division (1972–80).
24. Alan Hassell, unpublished personal history of work in Seminaries and Institutes, copy in possession of the author.
25. John Hilton III and Po Nien (Felipe) Chou, "The History of LDS Seminaries and Institutes in Taiwan," *Mormon Historical Studies* 14, no. 2 (Fall 2013): 83–106.
26. Po Nien (Felipe) Chou, personal history and journal entries, 2000–2005.
27. Britsch, *From the East*, 265.
28. Feng Xi, "Mormon-Chinese Relations," 177.
29. Taiwan Taipei Mission Historical Reports, March 31, 1976, Church History Library.
30. Richard Stamps and Wendy Shamo, *The Taiwan Saints* (self-published book commemorating the fortieth anniversary of the Church in Taiwan, 1996), 23–25.
31. Christopher K. Bigelow, "Taiwan: Four Decades of Faith," *Liahona*, May 1999, 29.
32. "Friends in Taiwan," *Friend*, November 1975, 13.
33. "Country Information: Taiwan," *Church News*, February 1, 2010, online at http://www.ldschurchnews.com/articles/58663/Country-information-Taiwan.html.
34. Britsch, *From the East*, 294.

35. Bigelow, "Taiwan: Four Decades of Faith," 29.
36. Ng and Chin, *History in Hong Kong*, 102.
37. Britsch, *From the East,* 267–68.
38. Diane E. Browning, "The Translation of Mormon Scriptures into Chinese" (unpublished paper, Brigham Young University, 1977), 21–22.
39. Britsch, *From the East,* 268.
40. Ng and Chin, *History in Hong Kong.*
41. Britsch, *From the East,* 271–77.
42. Harry Harding, *A Fragile Relationship: The United States and China since 1972* (Washington DC: The Brookings Institution, 1992).
43. Janice Clark, "Taiwan: Steep Peaks and Towering Faith," *Ensign*, August 1975, 55–58.
44. Thomas P. Nielson, "In Remembrance of President Chiang," *The Voice of the Saints*, May 1975, 46.
45. Kevin Moss, "Conference in Taiwan," *Ensign,* October 5, 1975, 91–93.
46. Spencer W. Kimball, "When the World Will Be Converted," *Ensign*, October 1974, 2–14.
47. Moss, "Conference in Taiwan," 91–93.
48. Britsch, *From the East,* 291–94.
49. Clark, "Taiwan: Steep Peaks and Towering Faith," 55–58.
50. Britsch, *From the East,* 277.
51. "Two New Stakes for the Far East," *Ensign*, June 1976, 87.
52. Wang Li-Ching (Sandy Lee), interview.
53. "Taiwan Saints Eager for Temple Blessings," 107–9.
54. Clark, "Taiwan: Steep Peaks and Towering Faith."
55. Wang Li-Ching (Sandy Lee), interview.
56. "Eleven New Missions Formed This Year," *Ensign,* June 1976, 87–88.
57. Harry Harding, *A Fragile Relationship.*
58. "Taiwan Saints Eager for Temple Blessings," 107–9.
59. Britsch, *From the East,* 262–65.

60. "Telegram from the U.S. Pacific Command to the Department of State and the White House," in *Foreign Relations of the United States, 1977–80* (Washington, DC: U.S. Government Printing Office, 1991), 13:680–86.
61. Rubinstein, *Protestant Community on Modern Taiwan*, 3–5.
62. Feng Xi, "Mormon-Chinese Relations," 176.
63. Britsch, *From the East,* 263–66.
64. Britsch, *From the East,* 277–78.
65. "Nine New Missions Announced," *Ensign*, June 1979, 76.

Appendix—Chinese & LDS Historical Events

Year	Chinese Historical Events	LDS Church Historical Events
1971	UN changes China's seat from Taiwan to mainland China. Presbyterian Church issues a series of political statements.	Taiwan Mission created with Malan R. Jackson as president, followed by visit by President Harold B. Lee, First Counselor in the First Presidency. Jackson maintains Church's political neutrality. Elder Marvin J. Ashton, Assistant to the Twelve, visits Taiwan.
1972	U.S. president Richard Nixon visits mainland China.	
1973		CES programs established in Taiwan.
1974		Thomas P. Nielson replaces Jackson as president of the Taiwan Mission. Taiwan Mission renamed Taiwan Taipei Mission, and missionary lessons adapted.

Year	Chinese Historical Events	LDS Church Historical Events
1975	Chiang Kai-shek, president of Taiwan, passes away. Yen Chia-Kan becomes president of Taiwan.	Nielson writes "In Remembrance of President Chiang." President Spencer W. Kimball meets Yen Chia-Kan, and presides at the first area conference in Taiwan. Chinese edition of the Doctrine and Covenants is published.
1976	Mao Zedong, chairman of the People's Republic of China, passes away.	Chinese edition of the Pearl of Great Price is published. Taiwan Taipei Stake is created with Chang I-Ch'ing as president. Taiwan Kaohsiung Mission is created with P. Boyd Hales as president.
1977		Frederick W. Crook replaces Nielson as president of the Taiwan Taipei Mission.
1979	U.S. changes diplomatic recognition from Taiwan to mainland China. Kaohsiung Incident occurs: clash between Presbyterian Church and Taiwanese government.	Taiwan Taichung Mission is created with Frederick W. Crook as president. Douglas H. Powelson replaces Crook as mission president for the Taiwan Taipei Mission. George A. Baker Jr. replaces Hales as mission president for the Taiwan Kaohsiung Mission.

7

Is the LDS Church a Japanese New Religion?

Greg Wilkinson

The concept of Japanese "new religions," or *shinshūkyō* (新宗教), formalized after World War II and eventually became a common and self-referential religious category. New religious movements based on a syncretism of several religious influences began to emerge at the end of the Tokugawa period (early nineteenth century). Today, academic studies, legal recognitions, public perceptions, and some religious organizations themselves have created the category and traditions of new religions.[1] In the twenty-first century, the Mormon image in the Japanese mind[2] is a new religion (*shinshūkyō*) image. A survey of contemporary literature in both English and Japanese provides ample evidence for the predominance of this new religion image for The Church of Jesus Christ of Latter-day Saints. An analysis of Japanese history, characteristics, and worldview can explain

---

Greg Wilkinson is an assistant professor of Church history and doctrine at Brigham Young University.

why the LDS Church, in both its historical and its current traits, is perceived and categorized as a new religion. Sydney Ahlstrom has written about Mormonism generally, "One cannot even be sure if the object of our consideration is a sect, a mystery cult, a new religion, a church, a people, a nation, or an American subculture."[3]

Categorization as a new religion could have significant organizational and evangelical detriments. Often, new religions are not seen positively, and this view has increased since the terrorist violence of Aum Shinrikyō, a Japanese new religious movement once led by Asahara Shōkō, in 1995.[4] For many Japanese, the term "new religion" has become synonymous with "cult."[5] However, we shall see that averting religious categorization, as Ahlstrom suggests about the LDS Church, can also have serious implications. Nevertheless, LDS leaders, missionaries, and members in Japan should be aware of new religions and the serious consequences that links to new religions can have for their church.

The LDS Church in Literature on Japanese New Religions

Commonly, the term "new religion" is applied to religious organizations founded or formed after a determined date or period of time. Religious organizations formalized within the last two hundred years are often categorized as new religions, though the time frame can vary. However, definitions of new religions by characteristics rather than chronology can be challenging and even problematic. Often the "new" in new religions is determined by context rather than the chronological age of the religion itself. As traditional religions internationalize, they are often interpreted as "new" within the countries in which they expand; this is often the case for Asian religions that migrate to Europe or America. Often alternatives to traditional religious institutions are labeled as "new" even though these alternatives were founded several hundred years ago. These alternatives are constantly changing in order to stay vital and relevant to contemporary peoples and situations. All these factors lead to not one definition, but several diverse definitions for new religion.[6] In Japan, the definition of new religion (*shinshūkyō*) is more exact and consistent, representing a category of religion with political recognition and widespread public identification. Japanese new religion or *shinshūkyō* is more than an academic term or general description; it is a religious category that is used precisely to reference specific groups by the media, in government statistical reports, within laws and regulations, and by established religions, as well as the general public. *Shinshūkyō* has also become a self-referential term for many religious groups.[7] A broad and yet admittedly unscientific sampling of how the LDS Church is described in both Japanese and English sources provides strong evidence for the perception that the LDS Church is a Japanese new religious movement.

The initial arrival of LDS missionaries to Japan in 1901 brought a variety of opinions and even criticisms by the Japanese media and populace. Some Japanese who were trying to eliminate Japan's concubine laws and traditions saw polygamy-practicing Mormons as an affront to that effort. Some newspapers even called for banning Mormonism from Japan. As part of ongoing debates on Mormonism between several newspaper editors, an editorial in the Osaka *Mainichi* on August 21, 1901 (just weeks after the arrival of Elder Heber J. Grant) included the following: "As long as it is not prejudicial to public peace, any religion is permissible, be it Buddhism or Christianity. Among the ignorant public, even Tenrikyo or Renmonkyo is allowed to exist. Then, what in the world should prevent the coming of Mormonism?"[8] The connection between the LDS Church and Tenrikyō or Renmonkyō, both prominent new religions at the time, is certainly not intended to be complimentary, but does make the argument that certain characteristics of the LDS Church align it more

Perfect Liberty Church, Osaka, Japan.

Salt Lake Temple, Utah, USA. (Photo by David Iliff.)

with Japan's new religions than with Protestant Christianity, especially due to public controversies and media scrutiny.[9]

This study focuses attention on contemporary general reference and academic books in both Japanese and English on Japanese new religions. Japan's new religions are a consistently popular topic for researchers and publishers. Dozens of reference books and academic monographs have focused on Japan's new religions, and a sampling of such works reveals a few interesting things.

There are two types of books that include a discussion of new religions: books that focus on religion in modern Japan, and books that focus on the new religions specifically. The LDS Church is often mentioned in academic works on modern Japanese religions written in English. Mark Mullins discusses Mormonism in his article "Christianity as a New Religion" in *Religion and Society in Modern Japan.*[10] Shimazono Susumu includes Mormonism in his study of modern Japan's religions in *From Salvation to Spirituality,*[11] both as an example of a new religion generally[12] and as a new religious movement within Japan.[13] Interestingly, Shimazono never references Mormonism independently, but always as an example of imported Christian new religions, along with Jehovah's Witnesses and the Unification Church.[14] Ian Reader, in *Religion in Contemporary Japan*, also mentions Mormonism. The first mention discusses whether a Mormon convert can still participate in explicitly Buddhist or Shinto traditions like *obon* or New Year's observances while being true to their Mormon conversion and convictions. When Reader analyzes the new religions, he reports, "It is common for Japanese academics to treat non-mainstream Christianity (for example the Jehovah's Witnesses, the Mormons and the Unification Church (the Moonies), all of which proselytize in Japan) as new religions."[15] However, many books in English on religion in modern Japan do not mention Mormonism at all, much less categorize them with the new religions.[16]

Within works on Japan's new religions specifically, mentions of Mormonism are common. This is surprising because many monographs focus on a case study of a single organization.[17] In Japanese, there are several works that are marketed toward a much larger audience than most academic monographs, and the LDS Church is often mentioned within these trade or reference publications. While not all books of this type include Mormonism, some of these works do include the LDS Church as a Japanese new religion.

A guidebook of new religions published in 2000[18] includes a short description of the LDS Church. Estimates of membership both in Japan (about 110,000) and worldwide (10,300,000) are provided. Joseph Smith is listed as the founder of the Church, but Gordon B. Hinckley (Church President in 2000) is not listed as the current leader; that distinction is given to Kitamura Masataka. In 2000, Kitamura "Eugene" Masataka was director of temporal affairs for the LDS Church's Asia North Area with headquarters in Tokyo. Kitamura has also served as the president of an LDS stake and as the president of one of several LDS missions in Japan.[19] Kitamura is recorded as the Church's legal representative on government documents establishing the Church as a legal corporation, or *shūkyō hōjin* (宗教法人). The choice of Kitamura as the current leader is a good indication that this guidebook defines the LDS Church more as a Japanese new religious movement than a global religious organization. The LDS Church is given the moniker "the Christian Church that emphasizes family."[20] A very brief description of the Church's founding, the Book of Mormon, and Heber J. Grant's founding of missionary work in Japan is provided, along with the entire first article of faith and some of the thirteenth article of faith. The entry finishes by noting that the members of the Church do not drink alcohol and then provides the address and phone number for the Presiding Bishop's office or area headquarters in Tokyo.

The Illustrated New Religions Guide[21] from 2006 also included the LDS Church. This guide divides the new religions into four types: Buddhist, Shinto, Christian, and Another (*shokyōkei*/諸教系).[22] The Christian new religions are listed in the final section, and the LDS Church is the last of four organizations included. Along with the LDS Church, the Unification Church, Jehovah's Witnesses, and The Spirit of Jesus Church[23] also have profiles. Similar to the guidebook published in 2000, the profile on the LDS Church includes membership estimates (123,000 in Japan and 10,300,000 worldwide) and also uses the moniker "the Christian Church that emphasizes family." Joseph Smith is listed as the founder, and Doniel Gordon Rich[24] is listed as the current Church leader and representative. By 2006 Eugene Kitamura had been replaced by Don Rich as director of temporal affairs in Tokyo. The guide includes certain aspects of Church history, including its founding in New York by Joseph Smith as one of six founding members, the move to Utah for religious freedom, the end of polygamy in 1890, and the 1901 start of missionary work in Japan by Heber J. Grant. A special section also gives important dates in Joseph Smith's life, including his birth in Vermont (1805), the first angelic visit of Moroni (1823), his receiving the gold plates (1827), the publication of the Book of Mormon, and the establishment of the Church (1830). The number of Church buildings in Japan (308) and the number of teachers or *kyōshi*/教師 (814, with 584 of those foreign born) are also included in the profile. For most new religions, teachers or *kyōshi* would refer to full-time or professional clergy, but in the LDS case, this refers to full-time missionaries. The profile also includes unique features of the LDS Church, including the prohibition of alcohol, tobacco, and coffee; the paying of tithing; and the missionary service of members between the ages of nineteen and twenty-five (two years for men and eighteen months for women).

The LDS Church is very briefly mentioned in another recent book on Japan's new religious movements called *Japan's New Religions*.[25] No information about the LDS Church is provided besides its name and a membership figure of 123,321.[26] The other Christian organizations listed in the book include the Unification Church (560,000), Jehovah's Witnesses (217,400), The Spirit of Jesus (28,990), and Seventh-Day Adventist (15,317).

These examples of books on Japanese new religions show that while the LDS Church is considered a Japanese new religion, it is not a very significant one where significance is measured by membership statistics. In books where profiles of about 100 new religions are provided, the over 100,000 members of the LDS Church in Japan warrant inclusion.[27] In works where fewer groups are profiled or analyzed, the LDS Church is not included or specifically analyzed. In *Japan's New Religions*, profiles of twenty new religions are provided. While the Unification Church and Jehovah's Witnesses have membership numbers to warrant profiles, the LDS Church does not. It can be safely concluded that in Japan, the LDS Church would be categorized as a new religion before it would be included in the category of Christianity, like most other Protestant or Catholic organizations.

Chronology of New Religions

In order to further analyze the inclusion of the LDS Church as a Japanese new religion, the first issue that needs to be addressed is how old a religion can be before it is no longer considered "new." Academic studies have provided a periodization of Japanese new religion development starting in the early nineteenth century and continuing through several stages of growth and stasis up until the closing of the twentieth century.[28] The 1830 founding of the LDS Church would make it one of the oldest of Japan's new religions, but well within the earliest period of development. Inoue Masakane (1790–1849) and Nakayama Miki (1798–1887), the founders of Misogikyō and Tenrikyō, respectively, are older than both Joseph Smith and Brigham Young, and their movements are still labeled as "new" in Japan. Other new religions from the earliest stage of development include Kurozumikyō (founded in 1814) and Nyoraikyō (founded in 1802).[29] This places the LDS Church within the same period of development as some of the best-known new religious movements in Japan. Specifically as a Japanese movement, the LDS Church started at the beginning of the twentieth century (1901). Both Sōka Gakkai and Ōmoto, two of the largest Japanese new religions, have similar histories of development. Sōka Gakkai was founded in 1930, survived years of persecution during World War II, and then began impressive postwar growth and development.[30] Ōmoto was founded in 1899, had a good prewar following that resulted in persecution and state suppression, and then continued to grow and develop postwar.[31] As either a global organization starting in 1830 or a Japanese religious movement beginning in 1901, the LDS Church would certainly share time periods of development with several firmly established Japanese new religions.

Characteristics of New Religions

The most common way of classifying Japan's new religions is through identifying similar traits or characteristics. Two of the first monographs in English to specifically study the new religions both analyzed these movements through identifying key characteristics.[32] These studies by H. Neill McFarland and Harry Thomsen have influenced subsequent research on Japan's new religions, which have also analyzed these groups through identifying and comparing similar characteristics.[33] There are many commonalities among the characteristics identified by McFarland and Thomsen; a combined list from their studies would include:

1. charismatic leadership (established through theophany and divine communication);
2. concrete goals (especially in evangelism and growth);
3. community identification;
4. highly centralized organizations;
5. massive construction projects resulting in large gathering places and architectural icons;
6. mass activities and conferences;
7. establishment of a religious center (like Mecca);
8. Millennialism with doctrines and designs to build a kingdom of God on earth;
9. syncretism, mysticism, and novelty in teachings and doctrines;
10. structures and principles that are easy to understand, enter, and follow; and
11. a critical optimism where the movement provides necessary hope to a deteriorating world society.

Both McFarland and Thomsen would argue that it is not so much each individual characteristic but the influence that these characteristics have together that shapes and identifies new religions. The LDS Church includes every characteristic identified by McFarland and Thomsen in one way or another.

Analyzing the LDS Church in comparison to this list of characteristics presents some interesting parallels. The biography of Joseph Smith is certainly a story of charismatic religious leadership through theophanies. LDS Church headquarters in Salt Lake City, often called Temple Square, provides ample evidence for the characteristics of massive construction projects as gathering places or architectural icons, mass activities or conferences, and the establishment of religious center or Mecca. Studies on Mormon history have often focused on their unique blend of millenarian beliefs and teachings of critical optimism.[34] While some arguments could be made as to how well the LDS Church does represent or illustrate each trait, surely Mormonism would not be disqualified from the Japan new religion category based on an analysis of characteristics.

Worldviews of the New Religions

In her monograph on Kurozumikyō, Helen Hardacre includes a theory of understanding new religions which goes beyond simply a list of common traits to a more holistic approach based on worldview.[35] Hardacre argues that an analysis of worldview, rather than doctrine or practice, can reveal commonalities among the new religions. While related to cosmology, Hardacre defines *worldview* as a "set of relations believed to link the self, the body, the social order, and the universe as a whole."[36] Within this argument, she attempts to move beyond simply explaining the new religions as reactions to a series of crises (resulting in the label "crisis cults") and reducing the new religions to a select number of common elements (shamanism, faith healing, ancestor worship, and so forth). Hardacre explains, "The collection of elements that has been called constitutive of the new religions is in fact derived from a more basic source: worldview."[37] It is not discrete trait elements that define new religions as a category or the inclusion of any specific organization within the category, but rather how these traits work together to create a worldview. Discrete characteristics become both elements and expressions of worldview. This is an important qualification of research on new religions through analysis of characteristics or traits. Both humans and horses have several similar characteristics, but that does not necessarily mean the categories which include both humans and horses are academically useful, or that such categories make a compelling argument that humans and horses are fundamentally similar.[38]

The worldview of the new religions is one of harmony and interconnection. Individual actions incrementally affect the body, society, nature, and the universe. While all levels of this worldview are important, the self is paramount because it is most inclined to cultivation and the development of virtue. As one who subscribes to the worldview of the new religions improves, expected benefits and results can be reflected in all other elements of his or her worldview: with the body through physical health and aesthetics, with society through positive and constructive relationships, with the state through peace and prosperity, and with the cosmos through a satisfying understanding of premortal, mortal, and postmortal existence for oneself and others. This worldview turns both other people and situations that the self encounters into mirrors that reflect and even magnify religious cultivation and individual virtues. The worldview of the new religions provides the self with much more control and requires the individual to internalize religious conceptions and specific contexts. The promises of the new religions' worldview are great, but so are the responsibilities.[39]

The question then becomes whether this new religion worldview adequately describes a prevalent worldview in the LDS Church. Without falling into the trap of dividing or reducing this worldview into discrete characteristics or traits, several general questions should be asked. Does the LDS Church teach an interconnection between the self, the body, society, nature, and the cosmos? Does it teach an interconnection between cultivation of the self or the development of virtue and the realization of health, beauty, love, prosperity, immortality, and eternal life? Hardacre argues, "If the self is awakened and resolutely so, sincerely striving for virtue and the conquest of egotism, then nothing is impossible."[40] It could be argued that this is similar to several verses found in the scriptures of the LDS canon. The thirteenth article of faith lists the virtues sought by the LDS faithful as a process of individual moral cultivation, societal renewal, and a pathway to divine promises. In Moses 7:18–21, the qualities of Enoch's ideal society are described. The establishment of the kingdom of God on earth (Zion) is a goal of the LDS Church, and this millennial

Tokyo Japan Temple. (Photo by Greg Wilkinson.)

society should emulate the spirituality and harmony experienced by the city of Enoch as both an individual and communal promise.

The Traditions and Cultures of New Religions

Even if the LDS Church appears to be a Japanese new religion through an analysis of chronology, characteristics, and even worldview, the question must be asked whether a foreign or Christian religion could be accepted and defined as a Japanese new religion. Most Japanese new religion research focuses solely on religions that are founded in Japan within a specific Japanese cultural and social context. While many Japanese new religions have successfully internationalized and expanded their organizations beyond Japan through evangelical efforts,[41] their headquarters, top organizational leadership, and bureaucracy, as well as a vast majority of members, remain in Japan. This certainly could not be said of the LDS Church. Looking for other organizations that are either foreign-based or Christian, or even both, and yet are still deemed Japanese new religions will help in determining whether the LDS Church is too foreign or too Christian to be included in the category.

Several foreign-based religions are commonly called new religions in Japan within academic or journalistic publications and other sources of media.[42] Most notable among these foreign new religions are the Jehovah's Witnesses (United States), The Unification Church (Korea), and Falun Gong (China). These are certainly not the only foreign religious organizations in Japan that would comply with general characteristics or definitions of new religions, but these groups have been numerically successful and are aggressively evangelical, making academic and media coverage more common.

As for Christian movements (foreign or indigenous) being deemed new religions, much has been published, most notably by Mark Mullins.[43] Mullins claims that while not all Christian churches in Japan should be labeled new religions, many that are explicitly sectarian and make unique claims of authority and legitimacy that separate them from traditional Christian denominations could and should be included with other new religions in Japan that are based on Buddhism, Shinto, or a syncretism of several elements.[44] Shimazono Susumu concurs and has stated that the new religions in modern Japan include "Christian imports."[45]

Advantages and Disadvantages of New Religion Categorization

If the above analysis is correct and the LDS Church is a Japanese new religion and is perceived as such by Japanese who come in contact with the Church, is there anything the LDS Church could do to change perceptions and thus categorization?[46] If Shimazono Susumu is correct, changing perceptions or categorizations would probably require lessening evangelic fervor and even abandoning certain proselyting tactics.[47] If Mark Mullins is correct and new religious categorization derives from a sectarian rather than denominational stance in regard to other Christian organizations, then changing categories would require doctrinal concessions to a pluralistic definition of legitimacy.[48] However, before prescriptions to change the Church's image are considered, the question must be asked whether the LDS Church should try to distance itself from its new religion categorization or characteristics. While perhaps not readily apparent, there may be some persuasive advantages to the LDS Church accepting and even embracing a new religion categorization and the ties with other new religions that could result. While most Latter-day Saints might prefer ecumenical cooperation with groups other than Jehovah's Witnesses or the Unification Church, issued-oriented collaboration with other new religions could result in significant benefits.

Japan's new religions face many challenges, including changes in the law or the enforcement of laws, an increasingly skeptical media and public, and the occasional unethical or illegal acts by individuals or organizations within the new religion category. Responding to these challenges may be more effective through issue-based ecumenical cooperation among the new religions. The oil shocks of the late 1970s and the terrorist acts of Aum Shinrikyō in 1995 have resulted in paradigm shifts in Japan.[49] Previously, religions were seen to be constitutionally protected from intrusion, or even supervision, because religion could provide necessary societal benefits. Now, constitutional protection, rights of incorporation, and tax benefits are increasingly seen as privileges religions must earn rather than rights they inherently enjoy.[50] New laws such as the Personal Information Protection Law[51] and door-to-door sales laws[52] have the potential to seriously alter the organizational and evangelical activities of the LDS Church along with most new religions. However, some of the larger new religions in Japan, most notably Sōka Gakkai, hold strategic political influence and have successfully lobbied for religious exclusions from such laws.[53] Cooperation with large new religions, like Sōka Gakkai, to prevent consumer protection or personal information laws from becoming an undue burden on religious activities is probably a worthwhile goal. However, because the LDS Church is so small in Japan in comparison to groups like Sōka Gakkai, Kōfuku no Kagaku, or Risshō Kōsei-kai, it does run the risk of being primarily known by many Japanese for their cooperation with these organizations. Issue-based ecumenism can quickly become far-reaching entanglement.

Another opportunity for ecumenical cooperation comes from times of crisis or natural disaster like the Kobe earthquake in 1995 or the Tohoku tsunami in 2011. Certainly the resources and logistical support of large new religions would improve the LDS Church's ability to meet certain objectives, and perhaps cooperation could work towards the common good. However, navigating opportunities, even the most promising, must be approached carefully and prudently. LDS leaders and members should understand how their Church is associated with Japanese new religions and common perceptions, and even the stereotypes the categorization may engender. Often, the LDS Church does not easily fit into common religious categories. As Janine Sawada has argued, this can result in serious consequences in times of turmoil or religious persecution because religions without categorization do not enjoy ecumenical support and are often singled out and more severely persecuted.[54] The LDS Church and its members should carefully consider the significant advantages and disadvantages of being perceived as new religion and if embracing that categorization may be preferable to the lack of categorization altogether.

Notes

1. See Trevor Astley, "New Religions," in *Nanzan Guide to Japanese Religions*, ed. Paul Swanson and Clark Chilson (Honolulu: University of Hawaii, 2006), 91–114.
2. This terminology is borrowed from J. B. Haws. See J. B. Haws, *The Mormon Image in the American Mind: Fifty Years of Public Perception* (New York City: Oxford University Press, 2013).
3. Sydney Ahlstrom, *A Religious History of the American People* (New Haven, CT: Yale University Press, 1972), 508.

4. See Ian Reader, *Religious Violence in Contemporary Japan: The Case of Aum Shinrikyō* (Honolulu: University of Hawaii Press, 2000).
5. See Asami Sadao, *Naze Karuto Shūkyō wa Umareru no ka* (なぜカルト宗教は生まれるのか) (Tokyo: Nihon Kirisuto Kyōdan Shuppankyoku, 1997), 15–28.
6. See J. Gordon Melton, foreword to *New Religions: A Guide*, ed. Christopher Partridge (New York City: Oxford University Press, 2004), 10–13.
7. For example, several new religions have formed the *Shinshūren* (新宗連), or the Federation of New Religious Organizations, and publish the New Religions Newspaper (*Shinshūkyō Shinbun* or 新宗教新聞). See Shin-Nihon Shūkyō Dantai Rengōkai, "Shinshūren," http://www.shinshuren.or.jp/.
8. Quoted in Shinji Takagi, "Mormons in the Press: Reactions to the 1901 Opening of the Japan Mission," *BYU Studies* 40, no. 1 (2001): 160. The translation of the Osaka editorial was taken directly from Takagi's article.
9. See Janine Tasca Sawada, *Practical Pursuits: Religion, Politics, and Personal Cultivation in Nineteenth-Century Japan* (Honolulu: University of Hawaii Press, 2004), 236–61, for analysis of the controversies and criticism surrounding Tenrikyō and Renmonkyō in the late nineteenth century as precursor to the opinions expressed by groups in the Osaka Mainichi editorial. Sawada argues that criticism and persecution of Renmonkyō resulted from its status and characteristics that were extraneous to traditional religious categories and even ecumenical associations among the new religions, which left Renmonkyō vulnerable to political or societal definitions of religious orthodoxy. A similar argument could be made about the LDS Church in Japan because its characteristics could place it extraneous to categorization as a Protestant Christian denomination or new religious movement/*shinshūkyō*.
10. See Mark R. Mullins, "Christianity as a New Religion," in *Religion and Society in Modern Japan*, ed. Mark R. Mullins, Shimazono Susumu, and Paul L. Swanson (Berkeley, CA: Asian Humanities Press, 1993), 259.
11. Susumu Shimazono, *From Salvation to Spirituality: Popular Religious Movements in Modern Japan* (Melbourne: Trans Pacific Press, 2004).
12. Shimazono, *From Salvation to Spirituality*, 3.
13. Shimazono, *From Salvation to Spirituality*, 18, 28.

14. Shimazono, *From Salvation to Spirituality*, 18, 28, 230, 259.
15. Ian Reader, *Religion in Contemporary Japan* (Honolulu: University of Hawaii Press, 1991), 13, 198, 200, 249. Reader cites Numata Kenya, *Gendai Nihon no Shinshūkyō* (Osaka: Sōgensha, 1988), as evidence for Mormonism's inclusion within the new religion category by Japanese academics.
16. See, for example, Winston Davis, *Japanese Religion and Society: Paradigms of Structure and Change* (Albany, NY: SUNY Press, 1992), or Shigeyoshi Murakami, *Japanese Religion in the Modern Century* (Tokyo: University of Tokyo Press, 1980).
17. Examples of case studies include Winston Davis, *Dojo: Magic and Exorcism in Modern Japan* (Stanford, CA: Stanford University Press, 1980); Brian McVeigh, *Spirits, Selves, and Subjectivity in a Japanese New Religion: The Cultural Psychology of Belief in Sūkyō Mahikari* (Lewiston, NY: Edwin Mellen Press, 1997); H. Byron Earhart, *Gedatsukai and Religion in Contemporary Japan* (Bloomington, IN: Indiana University Press, 1989); and Ian Reader, *Religious Violence in Contemporary Japan*.
18. Shinshūkyō Kenkyū-kai, ed., *21-seiki no Nihon o rīdo suru shin shūkyō 100* (21世紀の日本をリードする新宗教) (Tokyo: KK Besuto Bukku, 2000), 212. The cover page of this book states that it is the perfect introduction for anyone interested in the new religions or seeking to join a new religion.
19. An oral history of Kitamura was recorded by Richard Turley in 2001 and is cataloged in the LDS Church History Library as OH 2900, but is unfortunately closed to research. At the time of publication, the director for temporal affairs and the Church representative in Japan was Wada Takashi.
20. In Japanese this description is *Katei o taisetsu ni shite iru Kirisuto-kyō* / 家庭を大切にしているキリスト教.
21. Shinshūkyō Kenkyū-kai, ed., *Zukai Shinshūkyō Gaido* (図解新宗教ガイド) (Tokyo: Kyūtensha, 2006), 255.
22. While awkward, "another" is the translation given for *shokyōkei* in the original Japanese text.
23. The Spirit of Jesus Church or *Iesu no Mitama Kyōkai Kyōdan*/イエス之御霊教会教団 was founded by Murai Jun in 1941. *The Illustrated New Religions Guide* records current membership as just over 40,000, but reports of membership

over ten times that number have been claimed by the group. Similar to the LDS Church, Spirit of Jesus performs baptisms for the dead as a form of ancestor veneration, and some have speculated that this could explain the group's claims of over 400,000 members, which is nearly half of the total number of Christians in Japan. See Mullins, "Christianity as a New Religion," 269.

24. Don Rich is listed as ダニエル ゴードン リッチ.
25. Hiromi Shimada, *Yoku Wakaru! Nihon no Shinshūkyō* (よくわかる！ 日本の新宗教)(Tokyo: Kasakura Shuppansha, 2009).
26. This membership number is taken from Bunkachō, ed., *Shūkyō Nenkan* (Japan's yearbook of religion) (Tokyo: Kyosei, 2009), 84–85.
27. *21-seiki no Nihon o rīdo suru shin shūkyō 100* and *Zukai Shinshūkyō Gaido* include profiles of 100 and 90 groups, respectively.
28. See H. Neill McFarland, *The Rush Hour of the Gods* (New York City: Harper Colophon Books, 1967), 54–67; Susumu Shimazono, *Gendai Kyūsai Shūkyō-ron* (Tokyo: Seikyūsha, 1997); and Helen Hardacre, *Kurozumikyō and the New Religions of Japan* (Princeton, NJ: Princeton University Press, 1986).
29. For a chronological list of new religions by date of founding, see Susumu Shimazono, "Introduction to Part 4: New Religious Movements," in *Religion and Society in Modern Japan*, 221–30.
30. See Karel Dobbelaere, *Sōka Gakkai: From Lay Movement to Religion* (Salt Lake City: CESNUR, 2001), for an analysis of Soka Gakkai's early development and split with Nichiren Shōshū.
31. See Sheldon Garon, *Molding Japanese Minds* (Princeton, NJ: Princeton University Press, 1997), 60–87, for an example of Ōmoto's early history, especially instances of state persecution from 1930 to 1945.
32. See McFarland, *The Rush Hour of the Gods*, 71–96; and Harry Thomsen, *The New Religions of Japan* (Rutland, VT: Charles E. Tuttle, 1963), 20–31.
33. See Davis, *Dojo*; Earhart, *Gedatsukai and Religion in Contemporary Japan*; and Hardacre, *Kurozumikyō and the New Religions of Japan*.
34. See Grant Underwood, *The Millenarian World of Early Mormonism* (Urbana, IL: University of Illinois Press, 1993).
35. Hardacre, *Kurozumikyō and the New Religions of Japan*.

36. Hardacre, *Kurozumikyō and the New Religions of Japan*, 6.
37. Hardacre, *Kurozumikyō and the New Religions of Japan*, 7.
38. Gordon B. Hinckley made this same analogy to argue that despite similar characteristics, The Book of Mormon and Solomon Spaulding's or Ethan Smith's works are fundamentally dissimilar. See Gordon B. Hinckley, "My Testimony," *Ensign*, November 1993, 51–52.
39. Hardacre, *Kurozumikyō and the New Religions of Japan*, 8–21.
40. Hardacre, *Kurozumikyō and the New Religions of Japan*, 12.
41. See Peter B. Clarke, ed., *Japanese New Religions in Global Perspective* (Richmond, Surrey: Curzon, 2000).
42. See Kenya Numata, *Gendai Nihon no Shinshūkyō*, 1988.
43. See Mullins, "Christianity as a New Religion," 257–72.
44. See Mullins, "Christianity as a New Religion," 258–59.
45. Shimazono, *From Salvation to Spirituality*, 18, 28.
46. Tomoko Aizawa, "The LDS Church as a New Religious Movement in Japan" (master's thesis, Brigham Young University, 1995). Aizawa argues that new religion categorization has severely limited LDS Church growth and development. A new religion label does not need to be an obstacle to growth; several new religions have experienced significant growth. However, I do not contend with Aizawa's conclusions. In 1995, shortly after the subway terrorist attacks of Aum Shinrikyō, new religion categorization had several disadvantages, which severely limited evangelical activity and organizational development.
47. Shimazono, *From Salvation to Spirituality*, 28.
48. Mark Mullins, "Christianity as a New Religion," 269. LDS sociologist John Hoffmann concurs with Mullins and states that "Christianity in Japan—whether of a Western or Japanese form—continues to suffer from chronic denominationalism. . . . Syncretism is more consistent with Japanese history and tradition." See John P. Hoffmann, *Japanese Saints: Mormons in the Land of the Rising Sun* (Lanham, MD: Lexington Books, 2007), 43–44.
49. See Ian Reader, "Consensus Shattered: Japanese Paradigm Shifts and Moral Panic in the Post-Aum Era," *Nova Religio: The Journal of Alternative and Emergent Religions* 4, no. 2 (April 2001): 225–34.

50. See Richard Kisala and Mark R. Mullins, *Religion and Social Crisis in Japan: Understanding Japanese Society through the Aum Affair* (New York City: Palgrave Macmillan, 2001).
51. The Personal Information Protection Act (*Kojin Jōhō Hogo Hō*/個人情報保護法) was passed in 2003. Religious issues with the law included the dissemination of membership information (even internally), the kind of membership information religions could permanently maintain, and the rights individual members had about the information religions could keep, especially when members want to sever ties with their religion.
52. Door-to-door sales regulations have been included in several laws on commercial transactions and consumer protection. Many of these regulations could have severely limited door-to-door canvassing which is common by many of Japan's new religions (Soka Gakkai, Mahikari, Jehovah's Witnesses, Mormons, and so forth). However, members of the Diet from the Kōmeitō or New Kōmeitō Party (NKP) have consistently been able to add exceptions for religious organizations into laws that regulate door-to-door sales.
53. In 1954 Sōka Gakkai organized the Kōmeitō political party. Kōmeitō has elected members to several local, prefectural, and national offices. At the time of writing, Kōmeitō was a part of the majority coalition with the Liberal Democratic Party (LDP) in the National Diet with twenty party members in the House of Councillors or upper house (*Sangi-in*/参議院) and thirty-five members in the House of Representatives or lower house (*Shūgiin*/衆議院). See Kōmeitō, https://www.komei.or.jp/en/.
54. Sawada, *Practical Pursuits*, 236–61.

Eurasia

Ezra Taft Benson, fifteenth secretary of agriculture, January 21, 1953–January 20, 1961.

8

A Light in the Darkness

Apostle Ezra Taft Benson's 1959 Sermon at Moscow's Central Baptist Church

Reid L. Neilson

While visiting members and missionaries of The Church of Jesus Christ of Latter-day Saints in Eastern Europe in the summer of 2009, President Dieter F. Uchtdorf and Elder Neil L. Andersen toured Moscow's Central Baptist Church. The two LDS officials toured the historic structure on June 2 with Baptist leaders Vitaly Vlasenko and Sergey Zolotarevsky. What prompted twenty-first-century Mormon leaders to seek out this historic Baptist church in Russia of all places?

Five decades earlier, this two-hundred-year-old Protestant chapel, located near the Russian Kremlin and Red Square, was the site of a remarkable Christian sermon by one of President Uchtdorf and Elder Andersen's apostolic predecessors. On October 1, 1959, Elder Ezra Taft Benson,[1] then U.S. secretary of agriculture under President Dwight D. Eisenhower, visited the Moscow church during

Reid L. Neilson is an Assistant Church Historian and Recorder as well as the managing director of the Church History Department of The Church of Jesus Christ of Latter-day Saints.

his two-week diplomatic tour of Eastern Europe and there offered an impromptu Christian sermon during the height of the Cold War.

"Fifty years go fast, and lots of things have changed. But the desires of the heart have not changed," President Uchtdorf remarked to Zolotarevsky. "And we appreciate very much that Apostle Benson could come here and talk about Christ as you still do here, and as we try to do." The Mormon leaders reflected on the warm welcome they received from Moscow's Baptist officials. "Our friends from the Baptist church were very kind, very friendly. They invited us to come. We met with them in this historic place and stood at the pulpit with them and could feel how the message of Jesus Christ—even with different doctrinal feelings and different beliefs—unites us [as] people as we try to follow Him, our Savior," President Uchtdorf commented.[2]

Pastor Sergey N. Zolotarevsky, Vitaliy K. Vlasenkov, President Dieter F. Uchtdorf, and Elder Neil L. Andersen stand at the pulpit Elder Ezra Taft Benson spoke from in 1959, at the Central Baptist Church, Moscow, Russia, June 2, 2009. (© Intellectual Reserve, Inc.)

Although the Prophet Joseph Smith called two missionaries to preach in Russia in 1843 (they never made it), and a few scattered members were baptized in the 1890s, it was not until the fall of communism and the end of the Cold War that Latter-day Saints truly made a proselyting push into Russia, despite dedicating the land for the preaching of the gosepl in 1903. In fact, Mormon missionaries first arrived in St. Petersburg in 1990, and Russian lawmakers officially recognized the Church in May 1991.[3] Since Benson's visit in 1959, Moscow's Central Baptist Church has been a favorite place for local Latter-day Saints and visiting Church authorities to tour. General Authorities and other Church guests are regularly brought to the location and photographed outside its walls.

Secretary Ezra Taft Benson Confronts Communism

Ezra Taft Benson was born in August 1899 in the small farming community of Whitney, Idaho. After serving in the military during World War I, he served as a missionary to England and thereafter graduated from Brigham Young University with honors. He then attended Iowa State College for graduate training in agricultural science. Upon graduation, he worked as a farm agent for his hometown community, served as a specialist for the University of Idaho, and promoted farm cooperatives. Eventually he was named the executive secretary of the National Council of Farmer Cooperatives, one of America's largest agricultural organizations, and served on President Franklin D. Roosevelt's National Agricultural Advisory Committee during the dark years of World War II. He also served as a stake president in Boise, Idaho, and later in Washington, DC.[4]

Church leaders called Benson to the Quorum of the Twelve Apostles in October 1943. Following the devastation of World War II, he presided over the European Mission and oversaw the humanitarian efforts of the Church in those war-torn nations, beginning in 1946. This leadership experience abroad had a major influence on his worldview. "Confronting the horrors of National Socialism and Stalinist Communism, he developed a deep, abiding hatred of fascism, socialism, and especially Communism," one historian noted. "For Benson, individual liberty lay at the heart of God's plan for his children."[5] He was particularly troubled by the rise of nonbelief and the demise of civil liberties in the Soviet Bloc. To Benson, Communism and atheism "were an affront to his role as an Apostle of Jesus Christ and a denial of everything he held sacred. There could be no compromise with such a system. He was willing to debate the political and the economic issues involved in the conflicts between capitalism and Communism, but his mind was closed irrevocably against any concession to atheism," one of his biographers explained. "This accounts for his unyielding, implacable opposition to Communism and Communistic governments."[6] Benson returned from the European Mission an ardent opponent of these noncapitalistic and anti-Christian systems.

In 1953, ten years after Benson's apostolic ordination, President Dwight D. Eisenhower invited him to serve in his cabinet as secretary of agriculture, a post he would hold until 1961.[7] Never before had a Latter-day Saint held such a high position in the government of the United States. He quickly became known for his conservative political views and innovative agricultural initiatives. In the fall of 1959, Soviet premier Nikita S. Khrushchev announced an official state visit to Washington, DC, preliminary to a reciprocal diplomatic visit to Moscow by Eisenhower planned for the following year. The political frost of the Cold War seemed to be thawing, and leaders of both superpowers, along with the rest of humanity, hoped to ease tensions and promote world peace. Khrushchev desired to see America and its supposedly flawed capitalist system firsthand.

That September, the U.S. State Department asked Benson to escort Khrushchev's envoy to one of the Department of Agriculture's

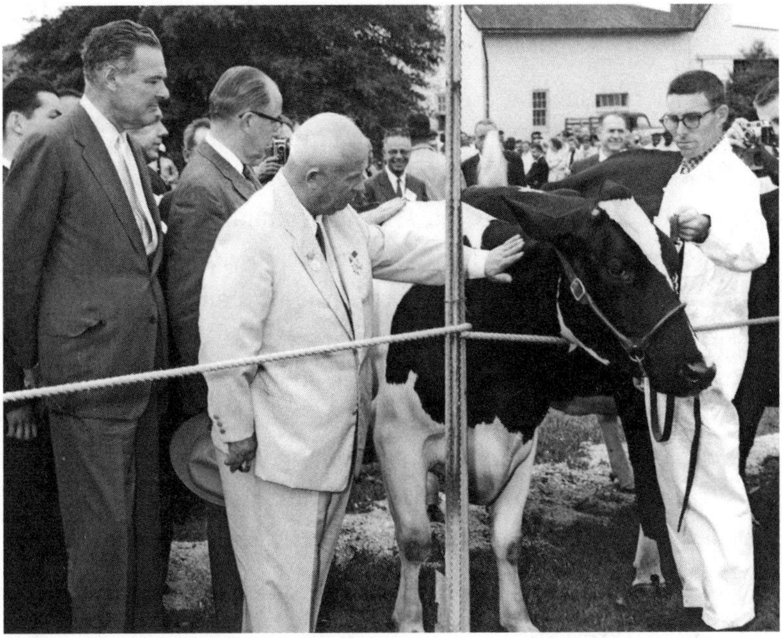

Premier Nikita S. Khrushchev with Agriculture Secretary Ezra Taft Benson and U.S. ambassador to the United Nations Henry Cabot Lodge during his visit on September 16, 1959, to the Agricultural Research Service Center. Left to right: U.S. ambassador to the United Nations Henry Cabot Lodge, Secretary Ezra Taft Benson, Premier Nikita S. Khrushchev, and high milk producer Impgodo Alice. (Courtesy of National Archives and Records Administration.)

experimental agricultural stations. "I, of course, agreed, but I must say my enthusiasm for the project could have been put in a small thimble," he wrote. "By my lights, Khrushchev was, and is, an evil man. He has about as much conception of moral right and wrong as a jungle animal. I just couldn't picture President Eisenhower sitting down with him and accomplishing anything worthwhile."[8] Notwithstanding his personal reservations, Benson accompanied the Soviet leader to the USDA's Research Center, located in nearby Beltsville, Maryland, on the morning of September 16. Khrushchev recalled in his memoir, "It was suggested I go there, and I accepted the invitation. There I was shown chickens, geese, ducks, and above all turkeys. Turkey meat is especially valued in the United States. On holidays every American considers it obligatory to have a roast turkey on the table. I inspected their poultry farming installations with interest."[9]

Khrushchev had more than a passing curiosity in American fowl and farming. During the Cold War, agricultural output, along with every other productivity metric, was used by Russian and American leaders alike to "keep score" in the battle between communism and capitalism in the public square. Not surprisingly, Khrushchev and Benson postured accordingly during their strained encounter on the animal farm. There is no question that the two men were advocating radically different economic and political systems, and neither was shy about expressing his divergent hopes for the future. Although fairly cordial that day in Maryland, each man would go away convinced that the other was misguided at best and dangerous to political aspirations for the world at large. Benson despised Khrushchev in the years to come.[10]

Secretary Benson's 1959 Tour of Eastern Europe

The Soviet premier remained in America until September 27, touring a number of cities and sites. A week after meeting with Khrushchev in Maryland and Washington, DC, Benson departed the United States on a diplomatic tour of the Soviet Union. Joined by his wife, Flora, and daughters Beverly and Bonnie, Benson and four USDA staffers flew out of the nation's capital on a chartered military plane. Ten American journalists assigned to cover Benson's European travels accompanied the group. Between September 23 and October 9, the Bensons and their entourage toured Yugoslavia, West Germany, Poland, Russia, Ukraine, Finland, Sweden, and Norway. During his trip, the Mormon Apostle often reflected on how much had changed since the dark days of World War II, but also on the contemporary problems he encountered. Given his previous humanitarian experiences in Europe in 1946 and his resulting disdain for all things communistic, he did not relish the opportunity to be back in Soviet territory.

The American diplomatic envoy visited Belgrade, Yugoslavia, its first stop on the European tour, and Benson was granted an audience with President Tito. "Tito is head of a totalitarian, Communist government and I never lost sight of that fact, yet he did impress me as being sincerely desirous of peace between east and west and of improving economic conditions in his country. If only he could be made to see the dynamic quality of freedom!" Next they traveled to Germany, which was then divided between west and east. "In Germany we continued the pattern, visiting government officials, holding press conferences, and visiting farms." The juxtaposition of Allied versus Soviet Berlin left a confirming imprint on Benson's worldview.

Benson and his party next toured Warsaw, Poland, and the surrounding environs. He noted that the Polish farmers seemed bent against communal ownership of agricultural lands, preferring to own and farm their own properties. Not surprisingly, Benson focused his attention on the produce, dairy, and meat production capabilities of the Communist system, just as Khrushchev had viewed American farms with a close eye earlier that year. Although Benson's guides kept him from some less-developed agricultural centers, even what he was permitted to see was underwhelming.[11]

As both a seasoned political official and an ordained Apostle of Jesus Christ, Benson was even more concerned about the religious hunger in communist Poland. Thirteen years earlier he had visited Warsaw during his post–World War II humanitarian mission and witnessed firsthand the physical and spiritual devastation there. As Benson and his American entourage passed through the Jewish ghetto, he became heartsick as memories of his previous visit combined with his present reality. Thirteen years had passed, but not much had improved for the Polish people in Benson's mind.

Secretary Benson's private plane next flew from Poland to Russia, arriving in Moscow on Tuesday, September 29. "The Soviet Union insisted on putting a Russian crew aboard to assist our U.S. crew," he groused. Benson and his associates were curious and unsure what to expect as they landed in the heart of the Soviet Union. "Flying into Moscow, perhaps because we had been so heavily briefed, we were looking forward to new experiences. We carried much disconnected knowledge of Russia with us, but we knew the Russians would only let us see the picture they wanted us to see," he recalled.[12] Benson later described in detail the choreographed and deceptive nature of his Russian hosts. He would leave the Soviet Union feeling even more disillusioned and pessimistic about the future of communism than he did upon his arrival. This would be Benson's first and last trip to Russia as a member of Eisenhower's cabinet and of the Quorum of the Twelve Apostles.

Soviet minister of agriculture Vladimir V. Matskevich, Benson's governmental counterpart, greeted the Americans at the Moscow airport with the Russian news media in tow. That evening the Americans planned to attend a Christian service at the Central Baptist Church, at Benson's request, but due to their delayed flight, they missed their chance to worship Christ in the Soviet Union that night. The following day they visited the Russian Ministry of Agriculture, toured the Exhibition of Economic Achievements of the USSR, and walked through the All Union Academy of Agricultural Sciences. That evening they attended the world-renowned Bolshoi Theater and were dazzled by the Soviet performance. In fact, this cultural event provided one of the few positive moments of the trip for Benson.[13]

On their final day in Russia, October 1, Benson and his team were shown additional Soviet state farms and agriculture displays in the morning. That afternoon their Russian hosts took them to see downtown Moscow. They first toured Red Square, including the Christian St. Basil's Cathedral (which Benson complained was closed) and the open tombs of Communist leaders, which were a major tourist draw. Even the world-class Kremlin Museum and treasures of the czars failed to impress the Apostle. The tour of Red Square ended at the famous GUM department store. Everywhere he looked in the Soviet Empire, Benson saw the deleterious effects of Communism and the deception of a ruling class bent on their own aggrandizement and power, the antithesis of his idealized America. He described, "The Russian leaders are very conscious of their limitations and they try to compensate by putting up a big front."[14] Virtually nothing about Russia was particularly impressive, noteworthy, or worthy of emulation, in Benson's mind, not even the czar's tourist traps along the Muscovy River.

Ezra Taft Benson on Red Square in front of St. Basil's Cathedral and Lenin's Tomb, Moscow, Russia, October 1, 1959. Left to right: Ezra Taft Benson, Flora Benson, and daughters Beverly (Parker) and Bonnie (Madsen). (Courtesy of Church History Library.)

Moscow's Central Baptist Church

After touring the historic heart and Communist center of Russia, Benson and his party were scheduled to travel on to Kiev, Ukraine. "The most remarkable incident of the entire trip occurred our last evening in Moscow," Benson reminisced.[15] Up to this point he had been experiencing his trip as secretary of agriculture for the United States, and the vast majority of his comments were offered from that perspective. But on that October 1959 night, he was an Apostle of Jesus Christ. (Years earlier he had been "set apart" as a U.S. cabinet member by Church leaders and told to share his testimony.) He noted in his memoir that for the past four decades the leadership of the Soviet Union encouraged atheism and discouraged religion. Lenin, Marx, and Stalin had all embraced Communism and rejected Christianity. Benson did note, however, that a few churches were open for worship in Moscow but were viewed as "merely to create a pretense of freedom." According to his sources, in a city of over five million inhabitants, there were only twenty-eight churches in Moscow holding services, twenty-three of them being Russian Orthodox, with two Baptist churches, two Jewish synagogues, and one Muslim mosque. He continued, "The Communists say those who go to church do so out of curiosity, not devotion or belief. The young people don't go, we were told, only the old."[16]

Recall that two days earlier Benson and the American delegation had arrived in Moscow too late at night to worship in Russia. Now, as they headed to their airport to depart, it seemed that he would never have the chance to celebrate Jesus Christ on Soviet soil. For several days, the Mormon Apostle had requested to visit one of the capital city's Christian churches, and his host, Matskevich, promised to deliver the desired opportunity. But Benson's Russian guides had done nothing to make this a reality and actually seemed bent on thwarting his request. Finally he took matters into his own hands and learned the location of the historic Christian congregation not far from Red Square. Having run out of excuses about the same moment the Americans were almost out of time, the Russians at last gave in to his request. "I mentioned again to one of our guides my disappointment that we had had no opportunity to visit a church in Russia," recalled Benson. "He said a few words to the chauffeur, the car swung around in the middle of the avenue and we eventually pulled up before an old stucco building on a dark, narrow, cobblestone side street not far from Red Square. This was the Central Baptist Church."[17] Benson's wish was finally granted—he would be able to worship with other Christians in the center of Communism.

The American reporters accompanying Benson and his family did not initially share the Mormon leader's enthusiasm for church services in Moscow. For example, Grant Salisbury and Warren K. Leffler, the writer-photographer team for *U.S. News and World Report*, remembered that they and their fellow journalists laughed about this possibility in atheist Russia—the previous Sunday all members of the press corps had declined Benson's invitation to join him and his family at a West Berlin chapel. "In Moscow, we had no choice because the cars picked us up at the hotel and stopped at the church on the way to the airport. It was around 7:30 o'clock on the chill, rainy evening of October 1. As the cavalcade of cars arrived at the Central Baptist Church, on a narrow side street not far from Red Square, somebody wisecracked, 'Well, boys, you're going to get to church whether you like it or not,'" the two reporters noted.[18] The American leader and Mormon Apostle took the American press group to church, giving them a memory they would never forget.

The Americans were not sure what to expect when they disembarked from their Russian limousines at the historic Baptist building that night. Certainly, they did not anticipate many Russian Christians to be in attendance. Benson explained, "Our guides had told us that the churches were empty, that no one attended church any more, that religion was the opiate of the people, and that the people had risen above religion." So he and the others expected few worshippers to be in the chapel. "It was a rainy, disagreeable October night with a distinct chill in the air. But when we entered the church, we found it filled; people were standing in the hall, in the entry, even in the street. Every Sunday, Tuesday, and Thursday, we learned, similar crowds turnout," Benson described. "I looked at the faces of the people. Many were middle-aged and older but a surprising number were young. About four out of every five were women, most of them with scarves about their heads. We were ushered into a place beside the pulpit."[19]

The scene likewise took the American journalists by surprise. Tom Anderson, editor and publisher of *Farm and Ranch* magazine, wrote with emotion, "Every face in the old sanctuary gaped incredulously as our obviously-American group was led down the aisle. They grabbed for our hands as we proceeded to our pews, which were gladly vacated for our unexpected visit. Their wrinkled, old faces looked at us pleadingly. They reached out to touch us almost as one would reach out for the last final caress of one's most-beloved just before the casket is lowered. They were in misery and yet a light shone through the misery. They gripped our hands like frightened children."[20] Others likewise described the surprisingly cramped quarters: "The small church was packed, with people standing wherever they could find room."[21] Over a thousand Christians filled the small chapel that evening. None of the Americans in attendance anticipated such a meeting in atheistic Russia.

While Benson had sought to worship with a Christian congregation in the Soviet Union, he did not plan on speaking that October evening. After being ushered into the Baptist building, the Bensons and the American journalists were seated on the rostrum, overlooking the congregants. Benson was moved by what happened next: "The minister spoke a few words, and then the organ struck a chord or two and began a hymn in which the entire congregation joined as one. Hearing a thousand to 1,500 voices raised there became one of the most affecting experiences of my entire life. In our common faith as Christians, they reached out to us with a message of welcome that bridged all differences of language, of government, of history." Following the opening hymn, the Baptist minister invited the still emotionally reeling Mormon Apostle, through an interpreter, to share a Christian sermon. "It took me a moment of hard struggle to master my feelings sufficiently to agree," Benson noted.[22] He would not miss this opportunity to share his feelings on the Savior with the beleaguered Baptists and other Christians in attendance.

Benson had not come prepared to speak, but he shared his testimony of the Christian gospel and a loving Heavenly Father who esteemed all of his earthly children, whether Russian or American. His spontaneous remarks were translated from English into Russian for the assembled crowd and captured on paper by journalists. "It was very kind of your minister to ask me to extend greetings to you," Benson began his impromptu sermon. He continued:

> I bring you greetings from the millions and millions of church people in America and around the world.
>
> Our Heavenly Father is not far away. He can be very close to us. I know that God lives. He is our Father. Jesus Christ, the Redeemer of the World, watches over this earth. He will direct all things. Be unafraid, keep His commandments, love one another, pray for peace and all will be well.
>
> This life is only a part of eternity. We lived before we came here as spiritual children of God. We will live again after we leave this life. Christ broke the bonds of death and was resurrected. We will all be resurrected.
>
> [I believe very firmly in prayer. I know it is possible to reach out and tap that unseen power which gives us strength and such an anchor in time of need.]
>
> I leave you my witness as a church servant for many years that the truth will endure. Time is always on our side. God bless you and keep you all the days of your life. I pray in the name of Jesus Christ.[23]

The Mormon Apostle reminisced that his words seemed to naturally flow and that his ideas seemingly reached the hearts of his listeners. As the Russian translator shared each of his short sentences, women waved their handkerchiefs, men nodded their heads, and many shed tears. When he lifted his eyes over the congregation, Benson noticed that even the second-story gallery was filled to capacity. An older woman caught his eye, and he directed his remarks to her: "With each sentence I uttered, the old head nodded assent. And old, feeble, wrinkled as she was, that woman was beautiful in her devotion."[24] Two reporters described, "Watching the Russian congregation, you could see tears welling up in the eyes of people as the Secretary's words were relayed to them through a translator." Salisbury and Leffler continued, "At the mention of the promise of life hereafter, muffled sobs could be heard in the small church. These people, after all, were sacrificing their chances of participating in the gains of the Communist society of Russia. Though worshipping God no longer is forbidden in the Soviet Union, those who do so usually find themselves cut off from advancement."[25]

Benson's talk was not a long one, even with the Russian interpreter's translation, but it was heartfelt and full of love. He shared, "I don't remember all that I said, but I recall feeling lifted up, inspired by the rapt faces of these men and women who were so steadfastly proving their faith in the God they served and loved."[26] The Mormon Apostle concluded his remarks when he was overcome by emotion and could no longer address the audience. Journalists Salisbury and Leffler described the final scene: "As the Secretary returned to his seat, the congregation broke into the familiar hymn, 'God Be With You Till We Meet Again.' They were still singing and waving their handkerchiefs as we followed Mr. Benson out of the church. All the way along the crowded aisle, hands were outstretched to shake our hands." The duo further recalled that on the way to the Moscow airport, one of the female Soviet interpreters confessed that she felt like crying as she listened to Benson's message that October evening.[27]

A Night Never to Be Forgotten

Secretary Benson and his press entourage arrived back in the United States in early October 1959, after about a week in Eastern Europe. Not surprisingly, Benson returned to America more pessimistic about the agricultural production, political oppression, and spiritual starvation in the Soviet empire. Their goodwill mission had deepened his suspicions and confirmed his worst fears about Communism. "Compared with typical American country life, Soviet rural standards are almost primitive," he later described. "Few Soviet farms have electricity compared with 97 per cent of ours and with electricity in the United States have come running water, radios, televisions, refrigerators, deep freezers, vacuum cleaners, and a whole multitude of conveniences that make the typical farm home as modern as those in the cities. Many families on Soviet farms live in wooden cabins, even mud huts. They get to town about as often as farmers in this country used to sixty or seventy-five years ago." Benson further noted how advanced America was in comparison to Russia in terms of transportation and telecommunication infrastructure: "Our farm families drive modern cars on hard-surface highways. The Soviet farm family rides in horse-drawn carts over roads to match. We have more telephones on farms in this country than can be found in all of Russia, city and farm combined."[28] Russia had little to offer the free markets and political system of the United States, except for a case study in the futility of Communism, according to Benson.

Benson's firsthand observations during that autumn colored his perception of the Soviet Union for the rest of his political career and Church service. In November 1959, one month after Benson's return from Eastern Europe, President Eisenhower met with Benson and his other advisors, including Christian A. Herter, secretary of state; Henry Cabot Lodge Jr., U.S. ambassador to the United Nations; and John A. McCone, chairman of the U.S. Atomic Energy Commission. Two months had passed since Khrushchev's visit to the United States, and Eisenhower wanted to hear his inner circle's impressions of the Soviet premier and his nation. When several cabinet members suggested that the Communists were making notable progress, Benson strongly countered their sentiments with his recent experiences in Eastern Europe. One attendee remembered, "A somewhat discordant note was produced by Benson, who had found nothing good in the USSR on his visit to see agriculture. He ended his speech on a very emotional note, describing his visit to a crowded church in Moscow and said this was the only favorable point in his visit to Russia."[29] In hindsight, the fall of 1959 was one of the few positive moments in U.S.-Soviet relations after World War II. The Cold War continued to thaw until May 1960, when the Soviets shot down an American plane spying over Russia and a deep freeze returned.

When Richard Nixon, Eisenhower's vice president and the Republican nominee, lost to Democrat John F. Kennedy in the November 1960 presidential election, Benson also vacated his cabinet appointment. After eight years of living in the nation's capital, he and his family were ready to return to Utah. In early 1961 Benson resumed his full-time apostolic responsibilities at Church headquarters in Salt Lake City. While he had left the politics and government affairs of Washington, DC, behind him, he "continued to express himself on political matters—frequently in a blunt, outspoken manner," according to historians Newell G. Bringhurst and Craig L. Foster. "Above all, Benson increasingly clamored to alert the nation to the dangers of Communism, which, he believed posed a grave, imminent threat to American civilization.... In the period from 1961 to 1963, Benson promoted his increasingly strident anti-Communist views in various forums both inside and outside of his official capacity as a Mormon apostle." He also associated closely with and advocated for the John Birch Society, a right-wing activist group bent on the defeat of Communism at home and abroad.[30]

Benson's remarkable career and Church service would continue to crescendo in the coming decades. He succeeded Spencer W. Kimball as President of the Quorum of the Twelve Apostles in 1973 and as President of the Church in 1985. Benson passed away in late May 1994 at the age of ninety-four, the only Latter-day Saint to have served in the highest government and ecclesiastical circles. Given everything that he experienced and accomplished during his lifetime, it is remarkable to think that his spur-of-the-moment speaking opportunity in a Moscow Baptist church during the height of the Cold War remained one of his most meaningful experiences. The significance of that 1959 night in Russia stayed with Benson throughout his life, and he referred to it often in his apostolic ministry. "It has been my privilege to speak before many church bodies in all parts of the world, but the impact of that experience is almost indescribable. I shall never forget that evening as long as I live," Benson reminisced. "Seldom, if ever, have I felt the oneness of mankind and the unquenchable yearning of the human heart for freedom so keenly as at that moment."[31]

Significantly, Benson was not the only one present who felt the Spirit of Christ in the Central Baptist Church that rainy October night. To him, the power of that evening was that others heard his apostolic witness and felt a confirming testimony of God's love for all of his children. It was a communal, not individual, experience. One American reporter described, "The Communist plan is that when these 'last believers' die off, religion will die with them. What the atheists don't know is that God can't be stamped out either by legislated atheism or firing squad. This Methodist back-slider who occasionally grumbles about having to go to church, stood crying unashamedly, throat lumped, and chills running from spine to toes. It was the most heart-rending and most inspiring scene I've ever witnessed."[32] His testimonial was supported by other reporters present that evening. "It turned out to be one of the most moving experiences in the lifetime of many of us. One newsman, a former marine, ranked it with the sight of the American flag rising over the old American compound in Tientsin, China, at the end of World War II," Salisbury and Leffler wrote for their national magazine.[33]

As an Apostle of Jesus Christ, Benson was a light in the darkness that night in Moscow, and his words "time is always on our side" proved to be prophetic. In June 1991, the Mormon Tabernacle Choir toured Central and Eastern Europe and performed in Moscow on June 24. After the concert, at a dinner hosted by Church officials, newly elected Russian vice president Alexander Rutskoi announced that as of May 28, 1991, the Russian Republic of the Soviet Union had legally recognized the Church and welcomed the Latter-day Saints' efforts to "assist in the spiritual regeneration of Russia."[34] A few days after this historic event, Elders Russell M. Nelson and Dallin H. Oaks reported this to President Ezra Taft Benson, recalling his visit to Moscow in 1959. The light of the gospel had prevailed, and time proved to be on President Benson's side.

Notes

1. Biographies of Ezra Taft Benson include Sheri L. Dew, *Ezra Taft Benson: A Biography* (Salt Lake City: Deseret Book, 1987); and Francis M. Gibbons, *Ezra Taft Benson: Statesman, Patriot, Prophet of God* (Salt Lake City: Deseret Book, 1996).
2. "Apostles Recall Historic Sermon by Ezra Taft Benson at a Moscow Baptist Church," *Mormon Newsroom*, June 5, 2009.
3. See Gary L. Browning, *Russia and the Restored Gospel* (Salt Lake City: Deseret Book, 1997); and Kahlile B. Mehr, *Mormon Missionaries Enter Eastern Europe* (Provo, UT: Brigham Young University Press; Salt Lake City: Deseret Book, 2002).
4. Reed A. Benson, "Ezra Taft Benson," in *Encyclopedia of Latter-day Saint History*, ed. Arnold K. Garr, Donald Q. Cannon, and Richard O. Cowan (Salt Lake City: Deseret Book, 2000), 93–94.
5. Gary James Bergera, "Ezra Taft Benson's 1946 Mission to Europe," *Journal of Mormon History* 34, no. 2 (Spring 2008): 112. See also Ezra Taft Benson, *A Labor of Love: The 1946 European Mission of Ezra Taft Benson* (Salt Lake City: Deseret Book, 1989).
6. Gibbons, *Ezra Taft Benson*, 227.
7. Reed A. Benson, "Ezra Taft Benson: The Eisenhower Years," in *Out of Obscurity: The LDS Church in the Twentieth Century* (Salt Lake City: Deseret Book, 2000), 53–62. See also Gary James Bergera, "'Rising above Principle': Ezra Taft Benson as U.S. Secretary of Agriculture, 1953–61, Part 1," *Dialogue: A Journal of Mormon Thought* 41, no. 3 (Fall 2008): 81–122; Gary James Bergera, "'Weak-Kneed Republicans and Socialist Democrats': Ezra Taft Benson as U.S. Secretary of Agriculture, 1953–61, Part 2," *Dialogue* 41, no. 4 (Winter 2008): 55–95; and Edward L. Schapsmeier and Frederick H. Schapsmeier, *Ezra Taft Benson and the Politics of Agriculture: The Eisenhower Years, 1953–1961* (Danville, IL: Interstate Printers and Publishers, 1975).

8. Ezra Taft Benson, *Cross Fire: The Eight Years with Eisenhower* (Garden City, NY: Doubleday, 1962), 467.
9. Sergei Khrushchev, ed., *Memoirs of Nikita Khrushchev*, vol. 3: *Statesman, 1953–1964* (University Park, PA: Penn State Press, 2007), 158; see 187n1 for clarifying details.
10. During his October 25, 1966, address to Brigham Young University's student body, Benson shared details surrounding Khrushchev's visit to the United States seven years earlier: "I have personally witnessed the heart-rending results of the loss of freedom. I have talked face-to-face with the godless Communist leaders. It may surprise you to learn that I was host to Mr. Khrushchev for a half-day when he visited the United States. Not that I'm proud of it. I opposed his coming then, and I still feel it was a mistake to welcome this atheistic murderer as a state visitor." Ezra Taft Benson, "Our Immediate Responsibility," *BYU Speeches of the Year, 1966–67* (Provo, UT: Brigham Young University Press, 1966), [page].

    In his political memoir, Benson described the Russian premier thus: "Khrushchev himself was the personification of Kipling's bear who walks like a man—a short, stocky, powerful body, a round head, a full rather coarse-featured face, a great reservoir of animal energy. Khrushchev is undeniably a shrewd and single-purposed mind, cunning and alert. The more I studied him, the more I saw the bear. Like those denizens of my native West, he could be playful and jovial one moment and dangerously aggressive the next. What lay behind those appraising eyes, the loud laugh and bluff mannerisms?" Benson, *Cross Fire*, 468.

    Benson would continue to reflect on and recall his 1959 interaction with Khrushchev in later speeches and publications. See Gary James Bergera, "Ezra Taft Benson Meets Nikita Khrushchev, 1959: The Embellishment of Memory," unpublished paper, copy in author's possession.
11. Benson, *Cross Fire*, 475–76.
12. Benson, *Cross Fire*, 477; emphasis in original.
13. Benson, *Cross Fire*, 477–79.
14. Benson, *Cross Fire*, 480–81.
15. Benson, *Cross Fire*, 485.
16. Benson, *Cross Fire*, 485.

17. Benson, *Cross Fire*, 485–86.
18. Grant Salisbury and Warren K. Leffler, "A Church Service in Soviet Russia," *U.S. News and World Report*, October 26, 1959, 76.
19. Ezra Taft Benson, *This Nation Shall Endure* (Salt Lake City: Deseret Book, 1977), 83.
20. Tom Anderson, "Straight Talk," *Farm and Ranch*, December 1959, 8.
21. Salisbury and Leffler, "Church Service in Soviet Russia," 76.
22. Benson, *Cross Fire*, 486.
23. Salisbury and Leffler, "Church Service in Soviet Russia," 76. Benson's bracketed fifth paragraph on the efficacy of prayer did not appear in contemporary accounts of his 1959 speech. It first appeared in his 1962 political service memoir, *Cross Fire*, 487.
24. Benson, *Cross Fire*, 487.
25. Salisbury and Leffler, "Church Service in Soviet Russia," 76.
26. Benson, *Cross Fire*, 487.
27. Salisbury and Leffler, "Church Service in Soviet Russia," 76.
28. Benson, *Cross Fire*, 482.
29. George Bogdan Kistiakowsky, *A Scientist at the White House: The Private Diary of President Eisenhower's Special Assistant for Science and Technology* (Cambridge, MA: Harvard University Press, 1976), 145.
30. Newell G. Bringhurst and Craig L. Foster, *The Mormon Quest for the Presidency* (Independence, MO: John Whitmer Books, 2008), 141–43. See also Gregory A. Prince, "The Red Peril, the Candy Maker, and the Apostle: David O. McKay's Confrontation with Communism," *Dialogue* 37, no. 2 (Summer 2004): 37–94.
31. Benson, *Cross Fire*, 487.
32. Anderson, "Straight Talk," 8.
33. Salisbury and Leffler, "Church Service in Soviet Russia," 76.
34. Browning, *Russia and the Restored Gospel*, 156–57.

9

The Non-Mormon *Mormony*

Authority, Religious Tolerance, and Sectarian Identification in Late Imperial Russia

Andrew C. Reed

In early 1913, a clipping of a previously published article in the Russian newspaper *Kolokol* (the Bell) was sent to government officials in Samara province (located in the southern part of Russia). The article was filled with rumors that originated in the village of Nikolaevskii, also in Samara province. It identified a religious sect that conducted a series of religious rites of passage that involved sexual acts with young girls. The article, titled "Po svobode sovesti" (On Freedom of Conscience), argued that a group of *Mormony* (Mormons), as they were locally known, carried out mysterious religious practices within their large homes in the village.[1]

The author suggested that the *Mormony* were a sect of religious fanatics who lived communally in the village, and included in their number were wealthy farmers, elderly women, children, and some peasants. Further, this group of *Mormony* was subjected

Andrew C. Reed is an assistant professor of Church history and doctrine at Brigham Young University.

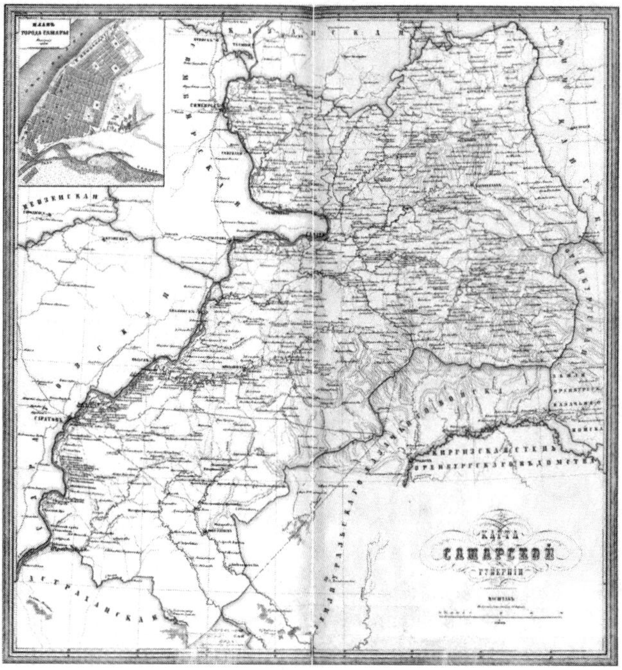

A. Il'ina, Podrobnyi Atlas Rossiiskoi Imperii c planami glavnykh gorodov *(St. Petersburg: Izdanie kartograficheskago zavedeniia, 1871).*

with some regularity to the scoffing and laughing of the local peasants who perpetuated a broad range of rumors about the community's members. Locals saw this religious group as troublesome and enigmatic; therefore, they argued its members ought to be investigated by government officials to determine whether they were heretics and criminals or merely a divergent branch of the Orthodox Church. Since they were known by the appellation "Mormons," the Russian government decided that the most appropriate beginning point for such an investigation was to identify parallels between the practices and rituals of the Russian *Mormony* those of the American religion associated with Joseph Smith, the Book of Mormon, and Salt Lake City. A search of available records in Russian central state archives suggests that late nineteenth-century and early twentieth-century Russian emphasis on the *Mormony* was only a passing interest, and fears of connection to the American Mormon movement were quickly dispelled. This fact is supported by the paucity of Church records and available knowledge about early Latter-day Saint attempts to proselyte in the Russian Empire during the late tsarist period.[2]

The subject of Russian *Mormony* is not altogether new. When Latter-day Saint missionaries began proselyting in Russia in the late 1980s and early 1990s, those located in the southern Volga region occasionally encountered individuals or groups referred to as *Mormony*. Researchers Gary Browning and Eric Eliason spent several weeks traveling through the region in 2000 in hopes of finding the roots of the group they referred to, rather confusingly, as "pre-perestroika Saints."[3] Aleksandr Klibanov, a Russian expert on sectarian movements, argued that the name *Mormony* was given to a group of Molokans (named for their drinking of milk, or *moloko*, during Lent and other fast days which was prohibited by Russian Orthodoxy) by Orthodox believers because they suspected that the former practiced polygamy.[4] When such efforts proved fruitless, Browning and Eliason settled on four hypotheses about the potential roots of this group to account for a missing historical record.[5] The two researchers concluded that the most probable explanation for the origins of the group were not to be found in searching for theological parallels. Rather, the use of the term "Mormon" served as a descriptor of public religious practice that diverged from normative Russian Orthodoxy. While some of these aberrant practices were similar to Latter-day Saint practices, they were not related theologically. In order to fill in the gaps, Browning and Eliason worked through oral interviews with Russian members of The Church of Jesus Christ of Latter-day Saints, with President Sheridan T. Gashler (1998–2001) of the Samara Mission, and with at least one "Old Molokan" man who lived in the region.[6] Their work, while foundational in many respects to the study of Russian *Mormony*, failed to account for the work of the Russian Orthodox Church and the Russian government nearly eighty years earlier to solve this very question about the origins of this group.

The primary aim of this chapter is to highlight the available sources in the Russian State Historical Archive (RGIA) that remained unexamined even during the heyday of *Mormony* studies in the early 2000s. These early sources show quite clearly that as early as 1913 *Mormony* were determined by Russian officialdom to have no connection to The Church of Jesus Christ of Latter-day Saints. It was not until Latter-day Saint missionaries began proselyting in Russia after the collapse of the Soviet Union that the question became interesting once again for members of the Church seeking lost members of the Church. Thus one of the secondary contributions of this paper is to provide a case study where scholars interested in international Church history would be well served to consult not only archives located in Salt Lake City but also the relevant archival sources in the countries of interest.

In this short article I analyze two previously unstudied sets of documents that comprise reports submitted to the Russian Imperial Department of Spiritual Affairs (*Departament Dukhovnykh Del*), the ministerial organ of the Russian government responsible for regulating religious life within the Russian Empire. The investigations described in these two reports examine the beliefs, practices, and culture of the *Mormony* by juxtaposing the Russian group with the American religion between 1912 and 1915. In doing so, they also show the major characteristics, most often through stereotypes, attributed to American Mormonism within early twentieth-century Russia. Locals criticized Russian *Mormony* because of their rituals and practices that presumably crossed certain moral and cultural boundaries. The local population, as evidenced in these reports and letters, was most disturbed by the sectarians' polygamous lifestyle, their general treatment of women, and the secretive nature of their religious meetings.

Thus this examination of American Mormonism and Russian *Mormony* shows the interplay between these possible threats to Russian Orthodoxy. In the process of weeding out heretical movements, Russian church and state authorities practiced politics by categorization, defined by those elements that were dogmatically acceptable and those viewed by the Orthodox Church as heretical. The government reports highlighted the interplay between center and periphery in the Russian Empire while also testing, as it were, nineteenth-century Russian knowledge of American Mormonism. The Russian government needed a definition of "Mormonism," which it garnered from a broad range of material to define a native sectarian movement. In doing so, Mormonism as practiced in late nineteenth-century America became the standard by which these investigators measured the origins and beliefs of the Russian *Mormony*. While the official reports and investigative documents proved that no identifiable connection existed between the *Mormony* and the Mormons, in the process they also provided insights into the extent of their knowledge of Mormonism in a land that had very little, if any, previous Latter-day Saint missionary activity in it. Unsurprisingly, the conclusions they reached about American Mormonism emphasized Latter-day Saint uniqueness (or rather bizarreness) when compared to Russian religious sensibilities.

Conversion and Religious Identity in a Confessional Empire

In order to understand why government officials fixated on finding a definition of Mormonism in 1913, it must be kept in mind that during the imperial period, Russia was "a confessional state."[7] During the nineteenth century, the tsarist government maintained a fair degree of stability through the regulation of confessions, or religious identification. Although the government fully endorsed and privileged Russian Orthodoxy above all other religions, officials also routinely co-opted local schismatic Christian and non-Christian groups to assure stability and loyalty. As part of this process, tsarist officials sought to classify aberrant Christian practices and communities—hence the interest in identifying the roots of the *Mormony*. The empire contained a broad range of sectarian groups that fell under the umbrella term "*dukhovnye khristiane*" (Spiritual Christians).[8] Spiritual Christians were consistently on the mind of the Russian imperial authorities because they mirrored Russian Orthodoxy at times while also threatening the very core of Orthodox doctrine and tradition.[9] Lumped within this broad category of Spiritual Christians were the *Mormony*, and because of this association they were therefore suspect in the eyes of the Russian government and Orthodox Church. Spiritual Christians tended toward pacifism, drew upon apocalyptic renderings of scripture, and generally refused the sacraments, church ecclesiastical authority, and rejected icons as necessary for worship.[10] Some of them chose to drink milk during *Velikii Post* (Lent) and other fast days, a forbidden practice within Russian Orthodoxy; others valued self-castration (*Skoptsy*), and others chose to reject external authority in favor of personal revelation (*Dukhobors*). After 1870, the term *Mormony* was used by opponents to Spiritual Christian groups interchangeably with Molokans, Skoptsy, and Dukhobors, and often in connection with claims of a deviant sexual culture that promoted immorality and hostility toward church authority and de-emphasized the centrality of the Bible.

One modern definition of these groups suggested that the designation "Spiritual Christians" ought to be used "when generally referring to . . . non-Orthodox, non-Jewish, non-Muslim, and similar faiths and/or groups in Old Russia whose ancestry may be a mixture of Armenian, Chuvash, Finn, German, Russian, Tatar, Ukrainian, Mordvin, etc."[11] Indeed, a definition such as this is so inclusive that it might negate any usefulness. In order to sort out the various differences between these many groups, Russian bureaucrats and clergy needed to identify and classify their various beliefs and practices. It was the process of classification of religious faith and practice that led government officials to take on this question of the Russian *Mormony*. The Russian government had a long-held tradition of protecting Orthodoxy from potential threats—a task that was assigned to various government ministries and offices that functioned in spiritual and secular spaces simultaneously.[12] In this effort, the government was driven by a sense of controlling the boundaries of Orthodoxy and limiting the spread of seemingly heretical movements within the empire.

The imperial government tightly controlled all religious affairs, including conversion and liturgical developments, and it identified its population by religious affiliation. Earlier rulers sought to bring the Church under the auspices of the imperial government and used the clergy to help encourage allegiance to the tsars and their policies. Thus the symbiotic relationship of church and state in imperial Russia served an important function of creating boundaries of belief and religious practice. Conversion in a confessional empire such as Russia was a tightly regulated process because it involved the transformation for potential converts from minority positions into majority, mainstream religious identity and thereby allowed the newly converted individual to access the rights and privileges associated with Russian Orthodoxy identity. In many cases, conversion was not a matter of personal preference or spiritual promptings in the Russian Empire, but might be more easily understood as a religious *and* political act. This is not to suggest that converts understood conversion only as a means to attain greater rights, though some certainly saw it in this way, but to highlight potential incentives of conversion.

Fears of a gradual wearing away of the buttresses of official Russian identity—Orthodoxy, autocracy, and nationality—led government officials to further protect evangelized Russians from potential threats by adherents of aberrant religious sects.[13] Thus, religious conversion must be viewed as a potential wellspring of religious and political dissent in a society that was ideologically built upon solid state-church foundations. In her broad study of conversion and its meaning, Gauri Viswanathan argued:

> In its most transparent meaning as a change of religion, conversion is arguably one of the most unsettling political events in the life of a society. This is irrespective of whether conversion involves a single individual or an entire community, whether it is forced or voluntary, or whether it is the result of proselytization or inner spiritual illumination. Not only does conversion alter the demographic equation within a society and produce numerical imbalances, but it also challenges an established community's assent to religious doctrines and practices.[14]

Given the confessional nature of the Russian Empire, government officials aggressively attempted to control the process by which sectarian groups actively sought new proselytes because individual adoptions of non-Orthodox faith potentially undermined the legitimacy of the imperial claim to religious and cultural unity. In order to convert to Russian Orthodoxy (it was illegal to convert to a non-Christian religion until 1905), one needed to submit a series of letters of intent, as well as testimonials from reliable sources, to local church officials, state bureaucrats, in some cases even the Ministry of Internal Affairs (which oversaw the police force), and—in exceptional cases—the tsar himself.[15]

When the *Kolokol* article was brought to the attention of government officials, they did just as they had for other potentially "heretical" or subversive religious movements. Official investigations into the sect initiated at the local level and later moved to the state level. In the case of the *Mormony*, the local population had already begun this process of inquiry and inquisition into the religious practices and beliefs of the group. It was the local population that applied the term

Mormony to this sect and did so because of a preexisting (albeit vague) knowledge of The Church of Jesus Christ of Latter-day Saints in the United States and Europe.[16] Although the Russian investigation highlighted the differences between the two movements, it also showed how some degree of minor heresy was preferred over full adoption of a foreign religion that, according to the investigation's perspective, emphasized the gradual overthrow of world governments, encouraged polygamous relations, and sought to add to the Bible.

Early Church Efforts to Evangelize Russia

The history of Russian interaction with missionaries of The Church of Jesus Christ of Latter-day Saints is yet to be written. Missionaries from the Church never fully engaged in proselytizing in Russia during the nineteenth century. However, Joseph Smith identified Russia as a site of important missionary activity in the early years of the Church. Russia was on the mind of Joseph Smith in 1843 when he called upon Elders Orson Hyde and George Adams to fulfill missions to Russia. Orson Hyde's communication to the Saints in Nauvoo, Illinois, and Liverpool, England, during his journey through Palestine and Europe in 1841 and 1842 suggests that he possessed an interest in Russia as a critical location for the future proclamation of the gospel.[17] From his earliest days in the Church, Orson Hyde was picked out as one who was "called by his ordination to proclaim the everlasting gospel, by the Spirit of the living God, from people to people, and from land to land, in the congregations of the wicked, in their synagogues, reasoning and expounding scriptures with them."[18] Joseph Smith indicated in an article in the *Times and Seasons* that Hyde and Adams had received a call to go to Russia and begin spreading the gospel in that land.[19] Although the missions were never fulfilled, evidence suggests that Joseph Smith understood Russia as a critical link to the expansion of the Church across the globe. The *Times and Seasons* pronouncement noted, "Our worthy brother, Elder George J. Adams, has been appointed by the First Presidency of the Church of Jesus Christ of Latter-day Saints at Nauvoo to present to them the importance, as well as things connected with his mission to Russia, to introduce the fullness of the Gospel to the people of that vast empire, and also to which is attached some of the most important things concerning the advancement and building up of the kingdom of God in the last days, which cannot be explained at this time."[20] Hyde and Adams never made the trip to Russia.

Despite the failed efforts of Orson Hyde and Joseph Smith to evangelize the empire, Russians gradually became aware of the Mormon movement through a variety of sources and possible connections. The first real evidence of Mormon missionaries who actively taught potential converts in Russia is contained in a short article printed in the *Millennial Star* in 1895.[21] Elder A. J. Höglund traveled from Gothenburg, Sweden, to St. Petersburg, Russia, to meet with a family that had earlier communicated their interest in the Church to the president of the Scandinavian Mission, Peter Sundwall.[22] Höglund met with the Lindelof family in St. Petersburg beginning Sunday, June 9, and then baptized the family on June 11, 1895.[23] Before leaving St. Petersburg, Höglund ordained Brother Lindelof an elder and taught him about his responsibilities.[24] The energetic Lindelof family appears to have been the only group of Mormon converts in St. Petersburg at the time. They were exiled out during the Soviet period, and no further missionary efforts were made within Russia.

The Official Government Report on the *Mormony*

The persecutory tone in the *Kolokol* article attempted to build a case against the religious sect based on unacceptable sexual practices, suspicious (i.e., un-Orthodox) religious rites, and a seemingly offensive "communal" lifestyle. A local Samara court authority, Evgenii Menkin, wrote to the governor of Samara province and included seven "clippings" of the *Kolokol* article, along with a plea that "your Excellency not deny the facts listed in the report."[25] Menkin's request remained either unanswered or not taken seriously until late September 1913 when another bureaucratic arm of the Russian government, the Ministry of Internal Affairs (*Ministerstva Vnutrennykh Del*), got involved. The ministry apparently had heard further reports (not included in the file contained in RGIA) that the *Mormony* were again causing havoc in Nikolaevskii. The letters continued to petition the government for assistance in dealing with this aberrant sect of religious fanatics and, by mid-1914, the local population began calling for the local *Mormony* to be removed from the village. According to this letter, the *Mormony* in nearby villages were rather troublesome and difficult for the local populations to deal with on a daily basis. One report (dated June 23, 1914) indicated that parishioners in the village of Blagodarovki had earlier held a town hall meeting (March 24, 1913) and determined to ask for assistance in "petitioning for the removal of followers of the *Mormony* religious sect and the complete removal of them from society."[26] These reports followed a formulaic nature for the most part and included accusations of poor treatment of women, polygamy, and portrayals of poor health and filth among some of the members. Before the *Mormony* could legally be exiled from the community, an investigation needed to define the offense and determine if such suspicions were indeed verifiable.

Within this report there is evidence of some maneuvering around the question of "Are these American Mormons?" More importantly, however, was the initial interest in possible cases of sexual abuse and polygamy. The frame of reference for the investigation remained the American Mormons, but the investigators seemed more concerned about the welfare of the women in the community. Russians were aware of the challenges that the American church members faced

Tsar Nicholas II, 1896 *by Il'ia Efimovich Repin (1844–1930).*

leading up to 1913, including the efforts to distance themselves from polygamy. Polygamy was seen as a foreign idea and thus a clear marker of a non-Orthodox movement. Thus it served as the key category of difference for these investigations. In the final years of Nicholas II's reign, a last-ditch effort to reassert Russian national sentiment based on a claim to Orthodoxy led to a broad range of official and unofficial searches into the mysterious world of the Russian "Spiritual Christian" world.

Another report from Baku (current day Azerbaijan), near Armenia, is even more instructive in this investigation into prerevolutionary *Mormony*.[27] From 1912 until 1915, local leaders began to investigate the arrests of *Mormony* in Baku (fifteen individuals were arrested) and tried to figure out where they came from and what they believed. With Baku's central location on the Caspian Sea, it was not out of the realm of possibility that in fact some small group of individuals might have met early Mormon missionaries in the Near East.[28] In the Baku report about the arrests of *Mormony*, the questions that officials sought to answer involved those associated with the specific differences between the *Skoptsy*, Molokans, and Mormons. Beyond trying to differentiate between American religious groups and the *Mormony*, the government went further to show how they (the *Mormony*) matched up with similar Spiritual Christian groups. On the Russian frontier, where these groups were found, the term

Spiritual Christian was used broadly to define any and all sectarian movements, with the distinctions between them often confused or used interchangeably.

In doing so, what developed on the pages of the 1913 Department of Spiritual Affairs in St. Petersburg's report about religious practices in Baku are fairly detailed discussions of sacraments, religious meetings (nature of hymns and prayers) and the role of religious authority within each sect. The report indicated that there were two groups (*dve gruppy*) of *Mormony* in the city.[29] The government looked specifically at the case of one Pavel Evdokimov Riashentsev, who is labeled a "Mormon leader" in the report and who "decided upon the desire to attach himself (via conversion) to the sect of Spiritual Christians (Molokans)."[30] While the Russian government could hardly closely govern the movement of Spiritual Christians back and forth amongst the competing sectarian groups, it did become concerned when the issue of women was involved. Riashentsev was married to Ksenia Grigor'evna, and although the report focused heavily on Riashenstev, it later turned to Ksenia, a potentially plural wife. The threat of polygamy in the Russian Empire raised flags among Russian authorities because of the long history of these Spiritual Christians mutilating their bodies (as in the case of the self-castrating *Skoptsy*) and deviant sexual practices.

The investigator became preoccupied with the pattern of worship and the practices within the prayer house. Spiritual Christians in the Samara and Saratov regions often met secretly in homes and even went so far as to place "watchmen" to scout for danger lurking in the streets. "It is observed," the report noted, "that for prayer the sectarians meet often in their homes, sing psalms and other spiritual songs. However, no statute or regulation that precisely defined the essence of the teachings of the local Mormons is available. We have not observed any instance of polygamy and know only that their chief goal is to "*dostizheniia Cv. Dukha*" (obtain the Holy Ghost).[31] In this regard, the *Mormony* were not altogether different than the broader categories of Spiritual Christians, as they all sought spiritual experience and knowledge through mystical communion with the Holy Spirit. In cases where polygamy and sexual abuse factors could not be proven, the investigators seemed willing to turn the individual jurisdiction over to the local priest to make decisions regarding religious praxis and orthodoxy. This reflected the empire's privileging Russian Orthodoxy over other Christian groups—the priest could legally intervene in the affairs of sectarian religious life when it was seen as a merely religious affair that was not particularly dangerous to Russian society generally.

Ultimately, Leonid Pospelov (the local priest in Baku) declared that Riashenstev's Mormonism "bears no resemblance to the American Mormon sect" and even went so far as to argue that there were two distinct communities, the "American Mormons" (who did not exist in Russia) and the "Russian Mormons." The report shunned American Mormonism in the end because ultimately, it concluded, "Baku region and Samara region *mormony* don't have anything in common with American Mormons, because among Russian Mormons there is no polygamy or theocracy (*teokratia*) that exists among American Mormons."[32]

It is interesting that the two definitive "American" Mormon traits that emerged out of a lengthy investigation into a heretical group were polygamy (which was no longer practiced by 1913) and the claim of theocracy. Noticeably absent from the discussion was any discussion of Joseph Smith, the Book of Mormon, or even the possibility of prophetic figures who could talk with God. Theocracy was not a foreign idea to the Russian rulers nor to the Russian Orthodox Church; indeed, a significant group of Russian Silver Age (late nineteenth century through the early twentieth century) writers including Vladimir Solov'ev (who wrote about Mormons), Sergei Bulgakov, and Pavel Florenskii wrote extensively about the idea and longed for a future date when the rule of God would unite the world.[33] In this way, American Mormonism embodied a model for some disillusioned Russians who longed for a greater religiosity (often through mystical means) than they experienced. In the United States, contemporary anti-Mormons discovered an emphasis on an imminent rule of Joseph Smith, the Nauvoo Council of Fifty, and ideally, the ushering in of the Kingdom of God on earth in the modern world.[34] Thus, when the Russian theological journals and writers picked up on the ideas, they did so out of a familiarity with early anti-Mormon themes but also out of an awareness of some of the most prescient religious ideas gaining currency in late tsarist intellectual circles. At the same time, they tended to mirror the early complaints while ignoring some of the contemporary developments within Latter-day Saint history that moved the American church away from the substance of these earlier attacks.[35]

Available Knowledge about Mormonism

How do we account for the broad yet flawed knowledge of The Church of Jesus Christ of Latter-day Saints among Russian clergy and intellectuals from the 1860s onwards? There were many avenues for them to gain knowledge about Mormonism—namely, the theological journals and popular literary works. Some individuals corresponded with members in Europe and even a few in the United States. I provide two examples here to show the breadth and source of available knowledge.

One such example might well be the famed writer Leo Tolstoy (1828–1910). Between January 11 and January 13, 1889, Tolstoy recorded the following in his journal: "I've had dinner and want to write up the days I missed. Made a few rough entries. Read *The Mormons' Bible* and *The Life of Smith* (George Q. Cannon's 1888 *Life of Joseph Smith The Prophet*) and was horrified. Yes, religion, actually religion, is a work of deceit. Lies for a good purpose."[36] Two days later, Tolstoy continued:

> Read about the Mormons, and understood the whole story. Yes, here is a glaringly obvious example of that deliberate deceit which is a part of every religion. I even wondered whether this element of conscious fabrication—not cold blooded fabrication, but a poetic, enthusiastic half-belief in itself—isn't an exclusive sign of what is called religion. There is fabrication in Mohammad and Paul. There isn't with Christ. It has been falsely imputed to Him. He would not have been turned into a religion had it not been for the fabrication of the resurrection, and the chief fabricator was Paul.[37]

Around the same time that Tolstoy reflected on Joseph Smith and modern religion, he wrote a letter to Nikolai Vasilievich Mikhailov, a university student from Kharkov, about the potential benefits of reading the "great books." In his letter, the Russian writer suggested that of all the books in the world, those of greatest importance were the sacred texts of the world's major religions. One ought to know, he argued, that the "ideas of people which are the basis of beliefs and the guiding principles of life of millions and millions of people are the most necessary and the most important ideas."[38] In another letter to Gavril Andreievich Rusanov, Tolstoy suggested that the books "I always carry with me, and which I would like to have always, are the unwritten books: The Prophets, the Gospels, Beal's Buddha, Confucius, Mencius, Lao-Tzu," and others.[39] For someone of Tolstoy's stature to

Lev Tolstoy, 1887, *by Il'ia Efimovich Repin.*

comment on the American Mormons should not surprise us, given the abundance of material available to the reading public. And yet, it is interesting that it is his curiosity about Mormonism that provoked his ranting about the nature of all religions in this case. Great thinkers who were Tolstoy's contemporaries in other countries considered the "Mormon Question" and critically analyzed Mormon theology, and more importantly, Mormon "civilization in the west."[40] Tolstoy's fascination with Mormonism—as evidenced by the edition of the Book of Mormon (a gift from Brigham Young's daughter, Susa Young Gates) located on his bookshelf in the museum dedicated to him—has often received popular attention among members of the Church today.[41]

Another avenue for knowledge about Mormons and Mormonism for nineteenth-century Russians was the expansive *Tserkovnyi Vestnik* (Church Bulletin). *Tserkovnyi Vestnik* was the journal of the St. Petersburg Orthodox Theological Academy. In September 1877, the journal, which was read widely by many seminarians, priests, professors, and government bureaucrats, published an obituary of the prophet Brigham Young.[42] Brigham Young figured prominently only one year earlier in a detailed "history" of the American religion in the same journal, simply titled "*Mormony*."[43] This article is important because it shows the degree to which the writers (and by extension, many of the readers) were familiar with The Church of Jesus Christ of Latter-day Saints and the migration to Salt Lake City (an object of fascination for many of them). Within the obituary of Brigham Young, his many wives figured more prominently than he did at times—particularly Ann Eliza, who "*bezhala*" (ran) to New York—polygamy again reigning supreme in terms of interesting subjects. In 1879, *Tserkovnyi Vestnik* also carried a brief article titled "Religious Sects in America" that supplied statistical data on the Church and reflected the growing international composition of the Church.[44] Thus it is clear that many years before the 1912–15 investigations of the *Mormony*, there existed a broad knowledge about The Church of Jesus Christ of

Latter-day Saints, albeit more fanciful and stereotyped than members of the Church might hope.

Conclusion

In the end, both of these reports concluded that these groups known as *Mormony* were nothing more than odd mixtures of Old Belief, sectarian offshoots, and Spiritual Christians that through some unknown path gained the appellation that associated them with The Church of Jesus Christ of Latter-day Saints. By examining the reports submitted to government officials during a particularly contentious period in Russian history (1911–15) when matters of religion and the reassertion of the primacy of Russian Orthodoxy were at the forefront of Nicholas II's policies, we learn a great deal about how Russian intellectuals, priests, and everyday folks thought about the term "Mormons." The attempts to delineate between religious groups were critical for supplanting heresies that threatened to shatter the Orthodox world by promoting new religions. We learn something of the way that people used "foreign" faiths to describe those that were unusual or deemed harmful within Orthodoxy and gain greater insight into the ways that confessional empires operate by projecting otherness onto foreign beliefs to distance heretical groups from their own tradition. Finally, by examining their categories of belief, we also learn more about how they understood and characterized American Mormonism. Indeed, we find that the global reach of Mormonism transcended borders and reached into places where there were *Mormony* but not Mormons.

Notes

1. "Po svobode sovesti," *Kolokol*, no. 2075. A copy of the article is available in microfilm form as part of the Department of Spiritual Affairs report located

in *Rossiiskii gosudarstvennyi istoricheskii arkhiv* (Russian State Historical Archive, St. Petersburg). The collection reference is RGIA, collection (fond) 821, section (opis) 133, document (delo) 230 (4 April 1913–5 December 1913). The term "*Mormony*" is used here as it was in the documents found in the Russian State Historical Archive.

2. The one exception was the Finnish Duchy, where as many as two hundred converts joined the Church between 1875 and 1895. See Zachary R. Jones, "Conversion amid Conflict: Mormon Proselytizing in Russian Finland, 1867–1914," *Journal of Mormon History* 35, no. 3 (Summer 2009): 1–41.

3. Eric A. Eliason and Gary L. Browning, "Russia's Other 'Mormons': Their Origins and Relationship to the Church of Jesus Christ of Latter-day Saints," *BYU Studies* 40, no. 1 (2001): 7–34. The use of "pre-perestroika Saints" is confusing as the authors' concluded that there is no connection between the *Mormony* and The Church of Jesus Christ of Latter-day Saints. Further, there is no archival source that employs "Saints" as an appellation for these groups in Russia. It should also be noted that about one year after the researchers' trip to the Samara region, one of Browning's undergraduate students, James W. Scott, traveled to the area to conduct similar research on the *Mormony* groups in the region. Scott subsequently posted his conclusions on his personal webpage, "Russian Mormonism: History of a Native Russian Sect," scottcorner.org /russianmormons.

4. Aleksandr Klibanov, *Narodnaia sotsial'naia utopia v Rossii: XIX vek* (Moscow: Izd. Nauka, 1978). Klibanov discussed this issue and clearly articulated the idea that there was no connection between the Molokans and Mormons. See also Klibanov, *History of Religious Sectarianism in Russia, 1860–1917* (Oxford: Pergamon Press, 1982), 152–53. To avoid confusion, *Mormony* is used in this paper to describe the Russian group known by the term.

5. Browning and Eliason suggested that the most probable explanation for the origins of the group was not to be found in searching for theological parallels, but rather in recognizing the use of the term "Mormon" in Russia as a potential descriptor of a religious practices that, although similar to Latter-day Saint practice historically, are maintained publically by individuals within normative Russian Orthodoxy.

6. The audiocassettes with the recorded conversations between Eliason, Browning, and Gashler are located in Eric A. Eliason papers, Vault MSS 7914, box 1, folder 11, L. Tom Perry Special Collections, Harold B. Lee Library, Brigham Young University, Provo, UT. It is clear that Browning and Eliason were rightly skeptical of an actual relationship between the groups, despite Gashler's passionate claims that the Russian *Mormony* were in fact lost Mormons with real connections to American Mormons.
7. Robert Crews, "Empire and the Confessional State: Islam and Religious Politics in Nineteenth-Century Russia," *American Historical Review* 108, no. 1 (2003): 50–83.
8. The *dukhovnye khristiane* movement splintered by the beginning of the nineteenth century when the two major factions, the Dukhobors (dukhobortsy) and the Molokans, disagreed over the place of authority. Dukhobors emphasized individual spiritual experience while Molokans believed in the primacy of authority located in the biblical text.
9. Laura Engelstein, *Castration and the Heavenly Kingdom: A Russian Folktale* (Ithaca, NY: Cornell University Press, 2003), 56–59. Engelstein shows how the *Skoptsy* (self-castrators) were the object of a similar investigation in 1844 when the well-respected lexicographer Vladimir Dal headed an investigation within the Ministry of Internal Affairs to classify and illuminate *Skoptsy* religious practice and belief.
10. J. Eugene Clay, "The Woman Clothed in the Sun: Pacifism and Apocalyptic Discourse among Russian Spiritual Christian Molokan-Jumpers," *Church History* 80, no. 1 (March 2011): 109–38.
11. Andrei Conovaloff, "Taxonomy of 3 Spiritual Christian Groups: *Molokane, Pryguny* and *Dukhizhizniki*—Books, Fellowship, Holidays, Prophets, and Songs," www.molokane.org/taxonomy/.
12. Gregory L. Freeze, *The Parish Clergy in Nineteenth-Century Russia: Crisis, Reform, Counter-Reform* (Princeton: Princeton University Press, 1983), xxxi.
13. The Minister of Education, Sergei Semenovich Uvarov (1786–1855) during the reign of Nicholas I (1825–55) articulated the threefold definition of Russian identity.
14. Gauri Viswanathan, *Outside the Fold: Conversion, Modernity, and Belief* (Princeton: Princeton University Press, 1998), xi.

15. For one example of the documentary evidence of potential converts and the due diligence associated with the conversion process, see the file associated with the conversion of Vasilli Abram Levison (1814–1869), a Jewish convert from the German territories who came to Russia during his conversion to Russian Orthodoxy. The files are located in RGIA collection 797, section 9, document 25232, pages 16–17. Delo Kantseliarii Ober-Prokurora Sviateishago Pravitel'stvuiushchago Sinoda, "O zhelanii evreev Levisona primet' pravoslavnuiu veru."
16. Tania Rands Lyon, "The Discovery of Native 'Mormon' Communities in Russia," *Dialogue: A Journal of Mormon Thought* 33, no. 1 (Spring 2000): 1–24.
17. Hyde's interest in Russia as a possible site of future missionary work was connected to his primary interest in the "return" of Jews in Europe to Palestine. See Hyde's letter to Parley P. Pratt, Letter IV in Orson Hyde, *A Voice from Jerusalem or a Sketch of the Travels and Ministry of Elder Orson Hyde, Missionary of the Church of Jesus Christ of Latter Day Saints to Germany, Constantinople, and Jerusalem* (Liverpool: P. P. Pratt, 1842), 34.
18. Doctrine and Covenants 68:1. When Orson Hyde was baptized a member of The Church of Jesus Christ of Latter-day Saints in October 1831 by his former pastor Sidney Rigdon, he, along with others, asked Joseph Smith for a revelation about what he ought to do for the kingdom of God. Joseph Smith received a revelation on Hyde's behalf the following day, November 1, 1831.
19. Joseph Smith, "Recommendatory," *Times and Seasons*, June 1, 1843, 218. In the June 28, 1843, edition, the *Nauvoo Neighbor* mentioned that Hyde had addressed a large crowd during the Fourth of July celebrations and that he was a newly appointed missionary to St. Petersburg, Russia. See "The 4th of July," *Nauvoo Neighbor*, June 28, 1843, 38.
20. Smith, "Recommendatory," 218. On Adams, see Andrew H. Hedges, Alex D. Smith, and Richard Lloyd Anderson, eds., *Journals, Volume 2: December 1841–April 1843*, vol. 2 of the Journals series of the *The Joseph Smith Papers*, ed. Dean C. Jessee, Ronald K. Esplin, and Richard Lyman Bushman (Salt Lake City: Church Historian's Press, 2011), 440.
21. Anthon H. Lund, "Introduction of the Gospel into Russia," *Millennial Star*, vol. 57, no. 26 (27 June 1895): 413–15. This is a report originally written by Höglund

and then published in the *Millennial Star* by President Anthon H. Lund in Liverpool, England. See also the report contained in Andrew Jenson, *History of the Scandinavian Mission* (Salt Lake City: Deseret News, 1927), 343–44.

22. For a biographical statement on Sundwall, see Andrew Jenson, "Sundwall, Peter," in *Latter-day Saint Biographical Encyclopedia* (Salt Lake City: Deseret News, 1941), 3:724.
23. Jenson, *Biographical Encyclopedia*, 414.
24. Jenson, *History of the Scandinavian Mission*, 343.
25. RGIA, collection 821, section 133, document 230, page 10.
26. RGIA, collection 821, section 133, document 230, page 14.
27. RGIA, collection 821, section 133, document 230, page 8.
28. Richard O. Cowan mentions that Jacob Spori and Mischa Markow met while on a steamship from Alexandria to Constantinople in about 1887. See "Mischa Markow: Mormon Missionary to the Balkans," *BYU Studies* 11, no. 1 (Autumn 1970): 92–98.
29. RGIA, collection 821, section 133, document 230, page 4.
30. RGIA, collection 821, section 133, document 230, page 5.
31. RGIA, collection 821, section 133, document 230, page 4.
32. RGIA, collection 821, section 133, document 230, page 7.
33. See Vladimir Solov'ev, "Mormonstvo," in *Entisklopedicheskii slovar,* ed. F. A. Brokhaus (St. Petersburg: Brokgauz i Efron, 1896), 19:863–66.
34. For one argument along these lines, see Alex Beam, *American Crucifixion: The Murder of Joseph Smith and the Fate of Mormonism* (New York: Public Affairs, 2014), 31–33.
35. There existed a broad range of possible sources that reflected a more updated view of Mormonism available in Russian to them, though these collections tended to be more damaging than the earlier American anti-Mormon tracts. See, for example, Eduard Romanovich Tsimmerman, *Puteshestvie po Amerike v 1869–1870* (Moscow: K. T. Soldatnekova, 1872), 296–305. For a good summary of this work, see Zachary R. Jones, "Conversion amid Conflict," 6–7.
36. R. F. Christian, ed. and trans., *Tolstoy's Diaries*, vol. 1, *1847–1894* (New York: Scribner Press, 1985), 236.

37. Christian, *Tolstoy's Diaries*, 1:236.
38. "Letter to N. V. Mikhailov, 16 February 1889," in *Tolstoy's Letters*, vol. 2, *1880–1910*, ed. and trans. R. F. Christian (London: University of London, Athlone Press, 1978), 439.
39. "Letter to G. A. Rusanov, 12 March 1889," in *Tolstoy's Letters*, 2:442. Rusanov was a landowner from Voronezh who attributed to Tolstoy his decision to become a Christian.
40. See, for example, Paul E. Kerry, "Thomas Carlyle's Draft Essay on the Mormons," in *Literature and Belief* 25, nos. 1 and 2 (2005): 261–88.
41. See Thomas J. Yates, "Count Tolstoi and the American Religion," *Improvement Era*, February 1939, 94. See also Leland A. Fetzer, "Tolstoy and Mormonism," *Dialogue: A Journal of Mormon Thought* 6 (Spring 1971): 27; and Harold Bloom, *The American Religion: The Emergence of the Post-Christian Nation* (New York: Simon and Schuster, 1992), 21–22, 97.
42. *Tserkovnyi Vestnik* 2, no. 35 (September 13, 1877): 13.
43. "*Mormony*," *Tserkovnyi vestnik* 1, no. 46 (November 20, 1876): 11–13; Chast' Neofitsial'naia (Unofficial Section).
44. "Religioznya sekti v Amerike," *Tserkovnyi vestnik* 3, nos. 51–52 (December 22–29, 1879): 7–8; Chast' Neofitsial'naia (Unofficial Section).

Freedom Monument in Riga, Latvia.

10

To Every Tongue

The Church and Language in the Former Soviet Union

James A. Miller

About a month after their arrival in Latvia in 1992, the first Latter-day Saint missionaries from the Russia St. Petersburg Mission assigned to Riga set up a street display about the Church in an attempt to find potential converts. Once they put up the display, however, and began talking to Latvians passing by, a mild uproar ensued among those they contacted. The missionaries' chosen location was the Freedom Monument, a memorial honoring Latvian independence. But the missionaries' display and materials were in Russian, a language many Latvians considered the tongue of their country's former occupiers. Boris Schiel, an ethnic Latvian Latter-day Saint who had returned to his native land as a senior missionary, came to the rescue and defused the situation somewhat by explaining that the young missionaries had studied Russian in America.[1] However, even if the four young

James A. Miller is a Church History specialist at the Church History Department, The Church of Jesus Christ of Latter-day Saints.

Russian-speaking missionaries had understood the national sensitivities beforehand, they still would only have been able to communicate in Russian. Although their leaders had sent them to Latvia, the Church had neither literature available in Latvian nor an established language-training program in Latvian for missionaries.

This and other episodes from early Latter-day Saint history in the former Soviet Union illustrate the role that language plays in the Church's efforts to fulfill its divinely appointed mission of preaching the gospel "to every nation, and kindred, and tongue, and people" (D&C 133:37). Indeed, since the Church's nineteenth-century founding in America, reaching this intended global audience has required overcoming linguistic divisions that define the world in which we live. International Church history is replete with examples of the Church establishing a presence in previously unreached nations, initially having limited literature available in the local language and lacking personnel with needed language skills. In some regions, though, the Church has relied on the initial use of a second language commonly understood by some in the new area. Following its establishment in the area, it seeks to make its message available in other languages, meeting the needs of converts and extending its reach. Examining the Church's beginnings in the former Soviet Union in the 1990s offers an opportunity to explore how this approach affects the Church's outreach and how it influences the spiritual lives of those who adopt the faith.

Reliance on a widespread regional language, Russian, enabled the Church to establish footholds in several nations in the former Soviet Union relatively quickly, showing the effectiveness of an approach relying on a second language. However, it also shows that the transition to using other local languages can require more time than initially anticipated. In the interim, the Church's members and missionaries face limitations in learning and sharing the gospel message. The national and ethnic tensions of Eastern Europe made the situation in this region additionally complex. Thus Latter-day Saint history in the former Soviet Union reveals the inherent advantages and limitations of the Church's language procedures.

Language in the Former Soviet Union

While linguistic diversity presents challenges to Church growth in many parts of the world, language in Eastern Europe—and particularly the former Soviet Union—presents unique concerns. The imperial and communist powers that ruled the region in the past often used language policy as a tool of the state to attack or subvert the identities of ethnic groups and nationalities on the periphery of their lands. The Russian Empire, for example, employed assimilation policies in its borderlands in the nineteenth century to "Russify" local elites and society. Later, under Stalin, the Soviet Union renewed and intensified Russification in some of the same areas. Fearful of perceived, foreign-backed conspiracies and nationalist movements in their borderlands, Soviet authorities also targeted various nationalities through terror, murder, and mass deportations. Ethnic Russians, by far the largest ethnic group in the Soviet Union, were also relocated to these areas to supply needed labor or to influence local political leadership.[2] When the Soviet Union ended its existence in 1991, large groups of ethnic Russians suddenly found themselves minorities in newly independent states.

Discriminatory policies and attitudes in state-party institutions throughout the Soviet period made Russian the language of opportunity of the USSR. This trend of Russification was perhaps most successful in the urban and industrialized regions of Ukraine and Belarus, where similarities between Russian and its sister Slavic languages made it easier for the local population to adopt.[3] Nonetheless, many in the non-Slavic regions still learned Russian to gain additional education, advance their careers, or even simply to interact with ethnic Russians living in their areas who did not understand the local language. The prevalence of Russian, though, led many non-Russians to resent the language as a symbol of oppression or repression of their national culture.[4]

Following the fall of the Soviet Union, many of the former Soviet republics took active steps to decrease the role of the Russian language in society, causing backlash in areas with large ethnic Russian or Russian-speaking populations. In Estonia and Latvia, for example, government language policies promoting the use of Estonian and Latvian angered their ethnic Russian minorities (about 30 percent of the population of Estonia and 34 percent of Latvia),[5] many of whom had not learned the national language. Coupled with additional decisions to deny most ethnic Russians citizenship, these policies marginalized Russians and fanned ethnic tensions.

The expansion of the Church in the former Soviet sphere in the early 1990s, though, depended largely on the Church's ability to communicate and provide materials in the Russian language. While problems did arise, using Russian enabled the Church to establish footholds or foundations in several countries. Russian-speaking missionaries were assigned to Ukraine beginning in October 1990, even before the fall of the Soviet Union.[6] Missionaries serving in the Russia St. Petersburg Mission opened the capital cities of Latvia and Lithuania in 1992 and found converts among ethnic Russians in Estonia.[7] Additionally, missionaries from the Ukraine Kyiv Mission proselytized for a time in Minsk, Belarus, in 1993 and 1994.[8]

In each case, the widespread understanding of Russian as a first or second language benefited the Church's initial establishment across the region. With a few exceptions, most missionaries taught in Russian, most early converts read the Book of Mormon in Russian, and most early Church services were conducted in Russian. As membership grew and the Church sought to expand into other areas, the lack of materials in other languages began to limit the Church's ability to edify the faithful and spread the gospel. Adopting the use of other languages, however, required time and additional resources, including qualified and trained translators. A basic understanding of the Church's translation procedures will help better examine how the Church and its members adapted and worked to overcome these challenges.

Church Translation

Translation is at the core of the Church's efforts to share the gospel globally. Without literature—especially the scriptures—in a language accessible to members and potential converts, the Church would neither grow nor help individuals internalize the gospel message. In the nineteenth and early twentieth centuries, area leaders organized local translation projects for needed language materials. Church leaders in Salt Lake City provided some direction for translation projects, especially the Book of Mormon and other scriptures, but the Church

Building with Church offices in downtown Kyiv where the Book of Mormon was first translated into Ukrainian. (Courtesy of James A. Miller.)

lacked an organized program that could implement and coordinate translation efforts; consequentially, "considerable autonomy existed within the various language areas of the Church for the important function of translation."[9] While translation policy covers a wide range of issues—from Sunday School manuals to Church websites—focusing principally on scripture translation in this discussion provides sufficient examples to examine.

Translations of Latter-day Saint scripture were often produced by individuals called by senior Church leaders serving abroad or volunteers who then donated their work to the Church. Such was the case with early Russian translations that enabled the Church's initial growth in the former Soviet Union. While the Church eventually arranged reviews of the texts and provided some guidance, the translation process largely depended on the initiative of the translator without close oversight from Church headquarters.

The first-known Russian translator in the Church was Joseph C. Littke, whose efforts produced the first Mormon missionary tract in Russian. Littke, a Russian German who joined the Church after leaving his homeland, translated the pamphlet *The Prophet Joseph Smith Tells His Own Story*, and it was published through a Russian printing company in San Francisco in 1936.[10] He also began work on a Russian translation of the Book of Mormon. According to his personal account, Joseph Fielding Smith—then serving as Church Historian—called him to begin the translation in February 1932.[11] He labored on the project over the next several years and submitted the manuscript of the translation to the Church in 1940. His work, however, was never published.

During the same period, Andre Anastasion, a native-Russian speaker in England, began his own translation of the Book of Mormon after receiving an assignment from European Mission President James E. Talmage in the 1920s.[12] Over the course of the next several decades, and with the assistance of other Russian immigrants in the United States, he revised and corrected his translation before submitting it to the Church. After undergoing additional revisions, including reviews initiated by the Translation Department, Anastasion's translation was published in 1980 and became available the next year.[13]

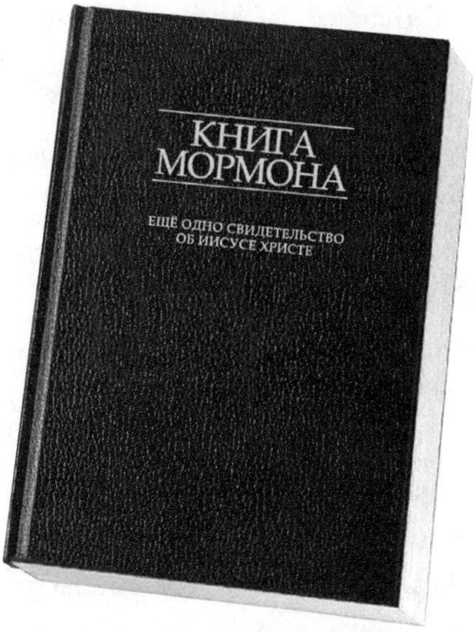

Russian Book of Mormon, © IRI.

By the end of the twentieth century, however, Church translation had evolved into a more centrally controlled and organized program, moving away from decentralized and uncoordinated origins. Beginning with the creation of the Translation Services Department—later the Translation Department and today the Translation Division—in 1965, professional staff at Church headquarters began developing numerous translation resources and aids to improve the quality of translations.[14] Church leaders and Translation Division staff established and refined policies governing the philosophy of scripture translation, standards for the translation process, and procedures for obtaining approval for translation projects.

According to current policies, area leaders must submit official requests to Church headquarters for the Translation Division to begin translating into a needed language. They must explain the need for a new language, whether that need is current or anticipated and how materials in other languages do not sufficiently meet the needs of Church members in the area. Ecclesiastical leaders at headquarters then review their requests with input from the Translation Division.[15]

The text of approved scripture projects must go through a stringent review process. Under the leadership of the Scriptures Committee, which oversees the publication of LDS scripture, the Translation Division organizes translation teams and ensures that they follow policy set forth by the First Presidency and Quorum of the Twelve that "requires translations of the standard works to be literal translations, insofar as possible."[16] The teams—preferably composed of in-country, native-speaking Latter-day Saints—generally include translators who produce the text, content reviewers who check for meaning, and language reviewers who correct grammatical or other technical mistakes. The translation is then proofread and "undergoes an ecclesiastic review by a committee of native-speaking local leaders who provide a certification that the translation is doctrinally accurate as well as acceptable to the intended audience." The certifications of the ecclesiastical reviewers are then submitted to the "presiding councils" in Salt Lake City who approve publication.[17]

Translation in Eastern Europe

Not all of the current procedures described above were established as the Church began facilitating translation into the languages of the former Soviet Union. Nonetheless, the translation projects that the Church undertook in the region followed the general approval and review processes and even contributed to their further development. The task of organizing and running these projects, however, proved challenging as the Church rapidly expanded across the region and new converts representing different languages adopted the faith.

Finding and training translation team members presented one of the main challenges to organizing and running the projects. In late 1991 and early 1992, missionary couple Steven and Jean Struk were assigned to establish a program to translate Church literature, including scripture, into the Ukrainian language. The Struks helped identify and select translation staff, including the Book of Mormon translation team.[18] The initial translation work for the Book of Mormon took about nineteen months and was followed by additional years of reviews and proofreading. The first edition was published in 1997.

In some situations, though, concerns about translation quality or challenges with establishing effective project teams can require additional time to resolve, extending the already lengthy translation process. The translation of the Estonian Book of Mormon, for example, required additional years of reviews and revisions before it was approved for publication. In 1953, Aimo Teemant, an Estonian woman who fled her native land with her husband in 1944 and joined the Church in 1952, began translating the book of scripture after receiving an impression in a dream. Over the next few decades, she continued translating as circumstances allowed, completing her work in December 1988, shortly before the Church was able to enter the Soviet Union.[19] Later, the Estonian Latter-day Saints selected to review her work raised concerns about the quality of the translation, leading to nearly a nearly decade-long reworking of the text, which was finally published in 2000.[20]

In other cases, problems can lead to the temporary suspension of scripture translation projects, resulting in similar delays. In 1992 and 1993, the Church organized teams to begin translation work on the Book of Mormon in Latvian and Armenian, respectively. Disagreements between members of the translation teams, in addition to worries about translation quality, soon led the Church to cancel the projects for a time.[21] In 1998, Translation Services staff organized a new translation team, which included some members of the original teams.[22] Both translations were published in 2000 and distributed to Church members in early 2001.[23]

Publication Year of LDS Scripture Translations

Language	Book of Mormon	Revised Book of Mormon	D&C and Pearl of Great Price
Armenian East	2000	2006	2006
Armenian West	1937	1983 (Selections)	1941
Belarusian	None	None	None
Estonian	2000	2011	2011
Latvian	2000	2006	2006
Lithuanian	2000	2006	2006
Russian	1981	2012	1996
Ukranian	1997	2005	2005

Challenges to Church Growth

Of course, as the scripture translation process unfolded, translators and Church staff gradually produced other gospel literature in the new languages, and local leaders and members sometimes took their own initiative to meet language needs. In Estonia, for example, one individual translated the missionary discussions into Estonian before the Church released an official publication, and copies of the translation even found their way to the Provo Missionary Training Center where they circulated among missionaries assigned to the country.[24] In 1993, the Latvia Riga Mission took the initiative to train selected Russian-speaking missionaries in the field to teach the gospel in Latvian and Lithuanian for the first time.[25] Nonetheless, the delayed availability of the scriptures and other materials became a limiting factor to the Church's development.

Reliance on a secondary language in which the Church already has materials translated does not eliminate all language barriers. Even as missionaries began to teach in the national languages of the Baltics, their use of the Russian translation of the Book of Mormon made it difficult for those that did not know Russian well to receive or understand the gospel message. Many Latvian members and potential converts, for example, found it difficult to read Church literature even if they could communicate with the missionaries in Latvian. One former missionary explained, "The hardest thing was when I sat in a discussion, and I asked [Latvians] to read a passage from the Book of Mormon, and they started to read it, and I could see that they couldn't read. They could not read Russian. They could read the letters, but they didn't understand what they were reading at all."[26]

The Church's language approach in the region also complicated its outreach to even those with whom there was no language barrier. The unwillingness of many to use Russian with missionaries, even if they understood it, complicated proselytizing. In addition to individuals refusing to respond or becoming angry with missionaries when addressed in Russian (such as at the Freedom Monument incident in July 1992), some missionaries themselves limited their own public interactions due to language concerns. Those who knew only one mission language sometimes avoided reaching out or teaching speakers of the other tongue.[27]

In Armenia, however, the lack of Eastern Armenian scriptures and other literature presented obstacles similar to those the Church faces in nations where it cannot initially rely on a second language. Although some Church literature was available in Western Armenian, which was spoken by Armenian Latter-day Saint converts from Turkey and Syria in the early twentieth century, few recent converts in Armenia itself, where Eastern Armenian is used, could understand it.[28] Moreover, the lesser extent of Russification in Armenia meant that knowledge of Russian varied by age and locality. One of the Church's translators explained, "If the Church is going to spread all over Armenia in villages and in other regions, you can't find a lot of people who speak good Russian and understand everything in Russian."[29] Some of these people, especially among the older generations, had not attended schools where Russian was taught.[30]

In other situations, Church leaders imposed such growth limits themselves, as was the case in Ukraine. While mission leaders in the Baltic trained missionaries to teach in the national language and expanded into non-Russian speaking areas before literature was available, the Church leaders in Ukraine focused primarily on Russian-speaking regions in the country's east and south until the mid-late 1990s.[31] Western Ukraine, where Ukrainian was dominant, saw very little Church activity until the second half of the decade when Ukrainian-speaking missionaries were called and assigned to the region shortly before the release of the Ukrainian Book of Mormon.[32]

In the face of these challenges to Church growth and access to the gospel, members and missionaries still found ways to strengthen their faith and adapt to the circumstances. Some missionaries, though they could not always offer literature in an investigator's preferred language, learned to use one of the national languages as well as Russian to communicate with as many people as possible.[33] Latter-day Saints in Estonia turned to Church materials in Finnish, a close relative of their native language, instead of using Russian.[34] As a result of such efforts, the Church was able to continue its growth despite the obstacles.

Eventually, the release of the Book of Mormon and other materials in national languages of these other republics eventually helped the Church overcome some of its challenges and enter a new chapter of development. In the Baltics, members and investigators no longer needed to rely on the Russian Book of Mormon. Also, when the Book of Mormon was released in Eastern Armenian, a missionary commented, "It has opened so many doors that weren't open before we received the Book of Mormon in Armenian. It has strengthened people's testimonies in the Church and has helped new converts become a lot stronger."[35]

One Faith, Different Languages

The Church's efforts to make the gospel message available and publish scriptures in the national languages of the former Soviet republics, however, did not represent a complete transition away from the use of Russian. The Church could not ignore the language needs and preferences of its ethnic Russian and Russian-speaking members even as it worked to meet the needs and preferences of other groups. This challenge, though, not only affected translation and public outreach, but also the spiritual health and unity of the Church's members.

In Ukraine, Ukrainians' bilingualism generally rendered the language question a non-issue, and the Church now uses both Ukrainian and Russian without much incident. Latter-day Saints in Ukraine tend to use the most dominant language of the region in their Church meetings, whether it be Ukrainian or Russian. In the center of the country, where both languages are regularly used, leaders usually conduct in Ukrainian and Church members use whichever language they prefer in sermons, prayers, and lessons.[36]

Language differences among members in the Baltics, however, led the Church to adopt a different approach. Most early Church meetings were held in Russian to accommodate ethnic Russian converts, some of whom did not understand the national language well and felt marginalized by their governments' language policies. As the other converts began to use their native languages in Church meetings, however, some Russian members became discontent because they could not understand what was being said.[37]

Church leaders attempted to resolve the issue by creating separate branches for speakers of the different languages. Instead of attending weekly worship services based on geographic location, members could attend branch meetings in the language of their preference. The practice of creating branches and wards for speakers of a given language can be traced back to efforts to proselytize and engage speakers of minority languages in North America in the mid-twentieth century.[38] Church leaders did not intentionally aim to divide Latter-day Saints along ethnic lines, rather they wished to accommodate Latter-day Saints with differing language needs and backgrounds.[39]

While perhaps solving the logistical issues surrounding multilingual Church meetings and engaging members and investigators in their preferred language, this approach did not resolve all tensions between Latter-day Saints. In some instances, it may have reinforced previously present divisions between some Church members. Language already presented a barrier between members and offered an excuse for some not to interact with the other groups.[40] When they began meeting separately, though, their interaction with each other decreased further. In Riga, some did not want to participate in activities held jointly by the Latvian and Russian branches due to language concerns.[41] The divisions between ethnic groups, though, extended beyond language barriers. On one occasion, animosity erupted between the Estonian and Russian branches in Tallinn over disagreements about the distribution of humanitarian aid between the two groups of members.[42] Although the Church's approach to the language differences between members did not directly cause such disunity, it may have made it simpler for the ethnic tensions present in society to manifest themselves in a similar fashion among Latter-day Saints.

Still, language was not a point of contention for all Latter-day Saints in the Baltics. In the early Vilnius Branch in Lithuania, missionaries and local members prized relations between speakers of different languages. A former sister missionary explained, "In Lithuania we had one combined branch, but they had a rule in the branch to speak their own language."[43] A local woman shared her own concern regarding the division of the branch: "We all were very worried when they divided us by nationality because one of the most important aspects in the Church is that it is not a national Church."[44]

Addressing Future Language Issues

To a certain degree, the experiences of Latter-day Saints in the former Soviet Union are unique; but in other ways, they are typical of what thousands of other Latter-day Saints have experienced across the world. As in other regions, the Church in the former Soviet Union could not fully meet the needs of many faithful members and grow to reach more souls without adopting the other languages. Eventually, Church literature—especially the scriptures—became available, improving the spiritual lives of members and enabling greater outreach. If the Church could somehow make its literature available quicker in new languages, or better anticipate emerging needs, it could mitigate some of the challenges it faces in the interim.

With limited resources, of course, it is not feasible to address every language need as quickly or efficiently as some might hope. The history of the Church's translation program shows how it has already greatly improved since its beginnings, and modern technology has enhanced the process. Opening up the translation process of at least nonscripture publications for wider, volunteer-based participation with oversight from professional staff could further improve the Church's translation capacity. In recent years, crowdsourcing translation has enabled many organizations and websites to make products available in many languages. More volunteer translation work could allow the Church to reallocate some resources to priority projects, produce translations quicker, and translate into a wider range of languages, including some that may not be immediate priorities. The Church in the early 2010s experimented with crowdsourcing translation on its website *The Vineyard*. However, as of August 2015, the translation section of the site had been removed, leaving the future of crowdsourcing translation in the Church unclear.[45]

The challenge of preserving unity among a multilingual membership in a divided society also remains. In later years, Church leaders repeatedly combined, divided, and again recombined language branches in Tallinn, Riga, and Vilnius, but it is unclear from currently available records how this affected relations between Church members. The history of these branches' creation in the early 1990s, though, suggests that Church leaders should not expect to resolve ethnic or national prejudices by organizing separate groups to address language differences.

Within the larger context of Mormonism's global expansion, the history of how the Church approached these linguistic challenges offers relevant insight into role of language in the Church's development. While in some nations, the Church begins with almost nothing in the primary local language, elsewhere it can rely upon another language to take advantage of growth opportunities. Still, the limited availability of the gospel message in the nation's primary language holds the Church back for a time. In some situations, language can present additional obstacles to unity among the Church membership. Overcoming some of these challenges is a matter of time and resources, but by drawing upon these and similar experiences from international Church history, Latter-day Saints and their leaders will better understand both the positive and the negative aspects of the Church's efforts to share the gospel message with them.

Notes

1. Boris Schiel, Latvia Church History, ca. 2002, 5, MS 18634, Church History Library, Salt Lake City. Boris and Liselotte Schiel interview, March–April 1996, interviewed by Matthew K. Heiss, Orem, Utah, typescript, 17, James Moyle Oral History Program, Church History Library.

2. For an overview of Soviet class and ethnic policies in the western regions of the USSR, see Timothy Snyder, *Bloodlands: Europe between Hitler and Stalin* (New York: Basic Books, 2010), 21–154.
3. The language situation in Belarus provides one of the most dramatic examples of Russification. By 1999, only 36.7 percent of Belarusians used Belarusian in their homes. 1999 Belarus Census data, National Statistics Committee of the Republic of Belarus, 2014, http://belstat.gov.by/perepis-naseleniya/perepis-naseleniya-1999-goda/tablichnye-dannye/raspredelenie-naseleniya-respubliki-belarus-po-natsionalnostyam-i-yazykam-v-1999-godu/. The translation of the title of the table is "Distribution of the population of the Republic of Belarus on nationality and language in 1999."
4. As evidenced by the response elicited by the Russian-speaking missionaries' street display in Riga, Latvia, in July 1992. See Schiel, Latvia Church history, 5.
5. "1989 All-Union Census: National Composition of Population of USSR by Republic," *Demoskop Weekly*, online application (in Russian) by Institute of Demography, Higher School of Economics, http://demoscope.ru/weekly/ssp/sng_nac_89.php?reg=15.
6. Howard L. Biddulph, *The Morning Breaks: Stories of Conversion and Faith in the Former Soviet Union* (Salt Lake City: Deseret Book, 1996), 38.
7. Kahlile B. Mehr, *Mormon Missionaries Enter Eastern Europe* (Provo, UT: Brigham Young University, 2002), 231–35.
8. Mehr, *Mormon Missionaries Enter Eastern Europe*, 228.
9. John E. Carr, *"For in That Day—": A History of Translation and Distribution, 1965–1980*," 1985, 41, MS 258 C311f, Church History Library.
10. See *The Prophet Joseph Smith Tells His Own Story* (San Francisco: Russian News Life Publishing, 1936), trans. Andre K. Anastasion, MS270.2 S653pRUS, Church History Library.
11. Joseph C. Littke, *History of the Translation of the Book of Mormon into the Russian Languague* [*sic*], 1933, 2, MS 4353, Church History Library.
12. Andre K. Anastasion to Missionary Executive Committee, December 22, 1965, in Andrew K. Anastasion articles, circa 1965–1970, MS 4646 2, Church History Library.

13. Gary Browning, *Russia and the Restored Gospel* (Salt Lake City: Deseret Book, 1997), 13–14.
14. Justus Ernst describes some of the early translation aids that the department developed in "Every Man . . . in His Own Language," *Ensign*, July 1974, 23–27. See also Joseph G. Stringham, "The Church and Translation," *BYU Studies* 21, no. 1 (Winter 1981): 69–90.
15. Tod R. Harris (manager of scriptures translation) interview, January 13, 2014, interview by the author, Salt Lake City. Recording in author's possession.
16. Tod R. Harris, "Translation in The Church of Jesus Christ of Latter-day Saints," *BYU Studies* 50, no. 4 (2011): 55–56. This two-page article was written in response to Van C. Gessel, "Coming to Terms: Creating Christian Vocabulary in a Non-Christian Land," *BYU Studies* 50, no. 4 (2011): 33–59.
17. Harris, "Translation in The Church," 55–56. Harris's response to Gessel's article was published with Gessel's article. See the citation above.
18. Biddulph, *The Morning Breaks*, 77.
19. Paul V. Johnson, "Out of the Dust," *Religious Educator* 6, no. 3 (2005): 25–26.
20. David Stewart, "Book of Mormon Assists Work in Estonia," *Church News*, November 4, 2000, 4.
21. Hasvira V. Minasaryan interview, September 22, 1997, interviewed by Matthew K. Heiss, Yerevan, Armenia, typescript, 29, OH 1708, James Moyle Oral History Program, Church History Library; and Viesturs Y. Tivums interview, April 26, 1996, interviewed by Matthew K. Heiss, Salt Lake City, typescript, 8–9, James Moyle Oral History Program, OH 1440, Church History Library.
22. The translation of the Book of Mormon into Latvian began anew in 1998 and concluded in 2000. See Schiel, Latvia Church history, 49, 55–56.
23. Johnson, "Out of the Dust," 26; and "Open Houses Introduce Eastern Armenian Book of Mormon," *Ensign*, October 2001, 77.
24. Missionary discussion in Estonian, circa 1993, MS 15024, Church History Library. See also Steven S. Potter interview, June 1, 1996, interviewed by Matthew K. Heiss, Tallinn, Estonia, typescript, 3, James Moyle Oral History Program, OH 1502, Church History Library.

25. See Marvin and Ruth Folsom interview, March 12, 1996, interviewed by Matthew K. Heiss, Provo, Utah, typescript, 13–14, James Moyle Oral History Program, OH 1431, Church History Library.
26. Amy M. Searle in Amy M. Searle and Jennifer Rebecca Turner interview, March 23, 1995, interview by Matthew K. Heiss, Provo, UT, typescript, 13, James Moyle Oral History Program, OH 1422, Church History Library.
27. Potter interview, 10.
28. Minasaryan interview, 30.
29. Minasaryan interview, 29.
30. Narine Sarkissian in Sergey Hamayaki, Susanna Sergeyi, and Narine Sergeyi Srkissian, interview, March 23, 1995, interviewed by Matthew K. Heiss, Provo Utah, typescript, 25, James Moyle Oral History Program, OH 2163, Church History Library.
31. Biddulph, *The Morning Breaks*, 62–65.
32. John Moroz Smith, "He Has Witnessed the Fulfillment of Prophecy in Ukraine," *Church News*, October 2, 2010, 6, 13.
33. Alexander O. Bazarski interview, May 30, 1996, interviewed by Matthew K. Heiss, Vilnius, Lithuania, typescript, 19–20, James Moyle Oral History Program, OH 1515, Church History Library.
34. Erki Koiv interview, June 2, 1996, interviewed by Matthew K. Heiss, Tallinn, Estonia, typescript, 9, James Moyle Oral History Program, OH 1504, Church History Library.
35. "News of the Church: Open Houses Introduce Eastern Armenian Book of Mormon," in *Ensign*, October 2001, 77.
36. Based on the personal experiences of the author in Ukraine (2008–14).
37. Searle and Turner, interview, 8.
38. For a review of the development of Spanish-speaking LDS congregations in the United States, see Jessie L. Embry, in *"In His Own Language": Mormon Spanish Speaking Congregations in the United States* (Provo, UT: The Charles Redd Center for Western Studies, Brigham Young University, 1997), 13–34.
39. For an overview of the Church leaders' position towards "ethnic congregations," see Jessie L. Embry, *Asian American Mormons: Bridging Cultures* (Provo, UT:

Charles Redd Center for Western Studies, Brigham Young University, 1999), 66–68.

40. Koiv interview, 8–9; and Katherine Michele Secrist and Nicole Curtis interview, May 24, 2001, interview by Matthew K. Heiss, Riga, Latvia, typescript, 9, James Moyle Oral History Program, OH 1509, Church History Library.
41. Searle and Turner interview, 7–8.
42. Koiv interview, 8–9.
43. Amy Searle in Searle and Turner interview, 8.
44. Tatyana A. Grishkovskaya interview, May 30, 1996, interview by Matthew K. Heiss, Vilnius, Lithuania, typescript, 6, James Moyle Oral History Program, OH 1488, Church History Library. Translation from Russian by the author.
45. See "LDS Community Translation," *The Vineyard*, vineyard.lds.org.

EUROPE

President Wallace F. Toronto, Brno, Czechoslovakia, 1947.

11

Moses of Czechoslovakia

Wallace F. Toronto, the Thirty-Two-Year Mission President

Mary Jane Woodger

Wallace F. Toronto could be called a modern-day Moses, for his path and that of the ancient prophet were similar. Both were called to a land of bondage to spread the gospel. Both trained local converts to lead in their absence. Both spent almost forty years establishing the church of God, and both were prevented from joining their followers in a land of promise once freedom was obtained. For Moses, the promised land was Canaan. For Toronto, it was twentieth-century Czechoslovakia (present-day Czech Republic and Slovak Republic).

To introduce The Church of Jesus Christ of Latter-day Saints in Czechoslovakia, a modern Moses was needed who could withstand the pharaohs of Nazism and Communism while raising up a people prepared to cling to the gospel despite horrendous hardships. Wallace F. Toronto was that man. Toronto became the leader

Mary Jane Woodger is a professor of Church history and doctrine at Brigham Young University.

and exemplar for the people of Czechoslovakia. Demonstrating superior leadership and great spiritual strength through the most difficult of circumstances, he served as the president of the Czechoslovak Mission for thirty-two years—a record in LDS Church history.

First Mission

In October 1928, at the age of twenty-one, Wallace Toronto was called on a mission to Germany. After serving a year, he was assigned with five other German missionaries to open the Czechoslovak Mission.[1] In Czechoslovakia, Toronto met a people that differed in many ways from Germans. He immersed himself in the life of Czechs and Slovaks in order to learn the traits, characteristics, and attitudes of them. "Among the many things he discovered, he found that they were great lovers of individual freedom."[2]

Toronto spent most of his time in the Czech part of then-Czechoslovakia. He picked up the Czech language quickly, becoming one of the first missionaries to learn it.[3] His daughter, Marion Toronto Miller, felt that one of the reasons her father was later chosen to become the mission president was because "he learned the language in a snap, and he could converse with these people."[4]

After Toronto returned from his three-and-a-half-year mission, he met and married Martha Sharp on September 15, 1933.[5] Martha later became vital to his future service in Czechoslovakia.

President Toronto and the Mission Princess

A little over two years after Toronto's marriage, on March 4, 1936, President David O. McKay of the First Presidency called Toronto and asked him if he would be willing to preside over the Czechoslovak Mission. Toronto was surprised, but not as much as Martha was. She came from a privileged background, and "nothing

Wallace, Martha, and Marion Toronto, 1938.

but a testimony of the gospel" would have had her accept such a call.[6] Because many of the missionaries were older than she was, twenty-four-year-old Martha became known as the "mission princess" rather than the mission mother.[7]

Wallace remembered, "I felt grave misgivings about successfully carrying on the work which [Mission President] Gaeth, a man of great ability, foresight and humility, had so ably begun and conducted. I voiced my fears and apprehensions to him. His reply sunk deep into my heart. 'Just remember, Wally, that one and the Lord are always a majority.'"[8] With that counsel, Wallace felt that the Lord would bless him and that he would also bless Martha "to the end that [they] too may accomplish great good among these people."[9]

Leader and Exemplar

The trait that contributed most to Toronto's success was his ability to make himself at home in a new culture. He said in 1940, "By seeking, at least in spirit, to become one of them . . . [I] learned to love, honor and admire this people. . . . [My] intimate experience in Bohemian [Bohemia is a central and western part of present-day Czech Republic] life and culture, gave [me] a profitable insight into their nature and manner of living."[10] Toronto was known by the local Czech Saints as "Bear" because "he was always optimistic and full of smiles."[11]

Former Czechoslovak missionary Ed Morrell remembered that Toronto's great love for people was evident.[12] "He had a love of people, . . . strong faith, knowledge of the doctrine and scriptures, an acceptance of inspiration, joyfulness, kindness and empathy for all, [along with] intelligence, courage and incredible optimism with a constant smile. He was not weary of any work or labor. He was respectful to people—regardless of their position in life."[13] Local historian Johann Wondra concurred that Toronto "understood that each person is different and that . . . his approach must be different and this is what his missionaries learned."[14]

Dale Tingey, also a former missionary in Czechoslovakia, remembered that Toronto was "very, very protective and also a very brave risk-taking person." A captivating speaker, Toronto would have meetings where a thousand people would come, even at the risk of irritating the Communists. Czech and Slovak Latter-day Saints remember he was committed to help people and felt that the gospel could help them more than anything in troubled times.[15] Wondra explains, "It's hard for Americans to understand Europeans, and for the west Europeans to understand east Europeans. . . . [Yet Toronto] was different from many other people from America. He had a feeling for the people."[16] Toronto was the force that held the Czechoslovak Mission together through the very difficult times of two totalitarian regimes. Son Bob Toronto declares, "For that period of time he was the Czech Mission."[17] "Not only was Toronto a likeable leader, he was also an inspired one, foreseeing the trouble that the new Saints would have long before it came."[18]

Settling into the Mission amidst Rumors of War

As time went on in Toronto's mission presidency, he became comfortable in his role, even making requests that today appear demanding. For instance, he decided to use music and sports to spread the gospel. Toronto wrote the First Presidency, asking for missionaries with certain abilities to be sent to the Czechoslovak Mission. President David O. McKay of the First Presidency obliged Toronto, writing that he would send missionaries before May 1, 1939, and that they would try, according to Toronto's request, to include a pianist and a first tenor.[19]

Such concerns may have seemed trivial in the impending threat of war, but Toronto's priority was always spreading the gospel. Following the *Anschluss* (essentially an annexation) of Austria by Nazi Germany in March 1938, the conquest of Czechoslovakia became Hitler's next ambition. The incorporation of the Sudetenland (the German name for the northern, southwest, and western areas of Czechoslovakia, which were inhabited primarily by German speakers) into Nazi Germany left the rest of Czechoslovakia weak and powerless to resist subsequent occupation. Slovakia separated from the country on March 14, 1939, becoming the Slovak State, which was a Nazi client state. On March 16, 1939, the German Wehrmacht, or the unified armed forces of Nazi Germany, moved into the remainder of Czechoslovakia. As war seemed imminent, Toronto used his great talent of working with government officials to the Church's advantage. In April, he met with the police commissioner to see if it would be possible to still conduct meetings under Nazi rule. Although he had prayed hard the night before, he was still surprised when permission was given. This eased Toronto's mind considerably, but there were still moments of great apprehension.[20]

Other tenuous situations occurred in the mission under the new regime. During Sunday services in May 1939, a tall Nazi officer entered. The congregation froze in their seats. A German officer did not bring good news. Toronto got up and walked towards the Nazi soldier, speaking to him in German. The young man and Toronto shook hands and conversed for a minute. At last, Toronto announced that the officer had something to say. The officer explained, "'I am Brother Schrul from Kiel. . . . I am an elder of the Church. . . . I would like to be accepted and worship with you, if you will allow me that privilege. . . .' By [then] all the women were in tears and the men were nodding in approval."[21]

In July, the most stressful situation of Toronto's entire mission presidency occurred when four young missionaries were arrested by the Gestapo for illegally exchanging money with an individual rather than at a bank. The individual turned out to be a Gestapo agent, who arrested the four, all of whom ended up in Pankrac Prison. Conditions in the prison were terrible, and the prisoners barely subsisted on bread and water.[22]

When Toronto found out about the arrest, he met with one Gestapo official after another. In order to have the missionaries released, he was told he would have to provide a bail of ten thousand dollars. When he went to another Gestapo office and offered to pay the amount, to his great disappointment, he learned they could not be released, even on bond, until a decision came down from the currently uninterested protectorate.[23] In August, Toronto recorded the following:

> I was thinking over this whole affair, and found that although it has been a great worry and very disagreeable, yet it has brought me into contact with official personalities, whom I would otherwise have never met. And it has given us the opportunity to tell them something of the Gospel plan. Thus it is certain that blessings have flown from it. Such contacts may be very helpful to us in our future work and activities.[24]

War seemed imminent. On August 24, 1939, a cablegram from Church headquarters directed all European missionaries to evacuate. Martha Toronto and the children immediately went to Denmark while President Toronto stayed behind.[25] In Denmark, Elder Joseph Fielding Smith of the Quorum of the Twelve assured her that the war would not start until her husband and all the missionaries had escaped.[26]

The four missionaries were released from prison just one day before Toronto received word to leave the country. President Toronto obtained passage on the last train to leave Czechoslovakia before war engulfed Europe on August 31. Upon Toronto's arrival in Denmark, Elder Smith told Toronto that he and his family would now return home.[27]

Between Nazism and Communism

The Torontos had five children when they returned to Salt Lake City, where life regained a sense of normalcy. Months after World War II officially ended, the Torontos were again called into the office of the First Presidency and asked to reopen the Czechoslovak Mission. Never having been released as mission president during the war, Toronto had kept in touch as much as possible with the Czechoslovakian Saints. There was no doubt in Wallace's mind that he and Martha would accept the call to serve again. President McKay informed the couple that Wallace would have to go ahead of Martha and the family. At the time, it was impossible to take a family of five children to a European country so recently ravaged by war, with no place to stay and no mission home.

On June 28, 1946, President Toronto, along with two other missionaries—Victor Bell and Heber Jacob—reentered Czechoslovakia.[28] The membership of the Church had waited seven long years for any contact from Church headquarters.[29] The year Toronto spent without his family was one of hard work, challenging both physically and mentally. He spent many hours trying to find Church members, some of whom had become lost, moved to other countries, or been imprisoned.[30]

One member Toronto was able to find was a Jewish Latter-day Saint, Elfrieda (Frieda) Glasnerová Vaněčková, who had been put in a concentration camp along with her small sons. When the Germans finally released her in 1945, her feet were so frozen she could not walk. Toronto found her recovering in the hospital. She broke into tears when she saw him, thinking she was looking at a vision. She then handed him a little bag with her tithing that she had saved.[31]

Church members had survived every hardship imaginable. With the help of the two elders, Toronto distributed foodstuffs and clothing from a train-car load of welfare supplies from Church headquarters. Several Saints reported that this had practically saved their lives.[32]

It took more than a year for Wallace to secure a mission home and send for his family. Martha and the five children arrived in June 1947.[33] The Torontos found that "opposition engendered a greater commitment among members." Attendance at Church meetings increased to levels never known before, a majority of members reported a full tithing, and Toronto began to hold lectures that drew large crowds anywhere from seventy to nine hundred people.[34]

A Mission under Communist Rule

Czechoslovakian Mission Home, 1947.

Free Czechoslovakia survived for just three years. In February 1948, just a year and a half after Toronto returned, a Communist coup began to control businesses, industries, churches, and schools. Historian Kahlile B. Mehr explains:

> Mormon missionaries came under secret police surveillance. The police ordered publication of the mission magazine, *Nový Hlas* (New Voice), to cease, ending its influence over three thousand readers, mostly members of other faiths. Church sermons and lessons had to be submitted to the authorities six weeks before being delivered. When the materials returned censored, they had to be rewritten. Agents attended meetings to ensure everything was said as written. Police threatened members who came to meetings and ordered some to spy. If they refused, they could lose their jobs or have their rations reduced.[35]

During the year and a half Toronto had worked under free Czechoslovakia before the Communists took over, his great talent of making good friends and becoming well known was vital in the government. Those friends would later help him cancel the expulsion notices missionaries received.[36] During this time of political uncertainty, Toronto was constantly trying to keep missionaries out of prison and prevent them from being expelled from the country.[37] Fortunately, he knew the proper things to say to government authorities so that missionaries were allowed to stay as long as possible. As missionary Don Whipperman observed, under Toronto's direction the missionaries learned how to deal with the Communists: "We worked under them—around them—as best we could."[38]

Under Communist rule, the mission came into peril. Food was rationed.[39] Missionaries were falsely accused of espionage and threatened with expulsion. Many, including the Toronto children, were followed by the secret police. The government was waiting for the mission to slip up, and the missionaries had good cause to be nervous. People would disappear from the streets and never be heard from again. Everyone walked in fear, and even family members could not trust each other.[40]

Czech Saint Gad Vojkuvka explained that the Communist party was an atheist organization that repressed all forms of religion. By 1949, all churches had to request official permission to operate from the Department of State. The Church of Jesus Christ of Latter-day Saints was never given that permission.[41] The Communist government then ceased to grant or renew resident permits for missionaries, making them illegal aliens. In May 1949, three missionaries were expelled because of the claim that they were a danger to the Czechoslovakian nation's safety and security. By October 1949, the number of missionaries had been reduced by 50 percent.[42] As Martha Toronto remembers, "The missionary work really suffered. We had nothing but problems, the biggest of which was trying to keep our missionaries in the country. Eventually the accusations of espionage became intolerable. Little by little the missionaries [in Czechoslovakia] would receive a notice of expulsion, or an invitation to leave the country within a certain time."[43]

In January 1950, two elders disappeared in a remote area. Toronto later found out that they had been arrested for entering a restricted border zone when they were trying to visit a member's home. Because they had some written directions, the authorities accused them of spying. They were in prison for twenty-seven days without a bath or change of clothing, were constantly interrogated, and subsisted on a diet of Postum, a little black bread, and soup. Eventually the government told Toronto that the elders would be released if he could find passage for them within two hours. Toronto was able to get to the airport and find tickets for them that same day.[44] This was nothing short of miraculous, considering all of the red tape that was usually involved in leaving the Communist country.

The Communists threatened LDS members because of their meeting attendance, and many were blackmailed by the secret police into spying on the Torontos and the missionaries at the risk of losing their jobs or being given reduced rations. The conflicted members came to Toronto in tears to ask him what they should do, and every time he advised them to go along with it. He explained that they need not endanger themselves or their families in an effort to try to protect the privacy of the mission, especially when the authorities usually found out what they wanted to one way or another.[45]

A summary of Czech archive documents recorded by Ed Morrell in the 1940s and in 1950 shows that the Communists considered as espionage such innocent actions as asking for city map signs. This record also shows a January 1950 request for the expiration dates of missionaries' permits and reports on the interrogations of various elders and President Toronto.[46] When missionary Mel Maybe was summoned for an interview, he asked Toronto, "Shall I answer the questions?" Toronto answered, "Be honest in everything you say, answer every question." Elder Maybe was interrogated for four hours and then given a twenty-four-hour notice to get out of the country. The notice was dated from the previous day, so the twenty-four hours were already gone. Toronto asked Maybe if he would take the mission history with him and give it to the First Presidency. Just before leaving, Toronto changed his mind and told Maybe to let his companion carry the mission history instead. When the missionaries got to the customs officials, they searched Maybe but did not even look at his companion. The papers got through safely.[47]

The evacuation of the Czechoslovak Mission gained national attention in the United States "because of [Toronto's] successful efforts to win the release of several missionaries who had been imprisoned by the Communists."[48] Finally, the time came for the Torontos to be expelled. They were given forty-eight hours. While the Torontos were packing, the secret police came and requested that Toronto come with them. Handing the tickets and money to Martha, Toronto instructed, "If I don't come back, go without me." He was interrogated for seven long, tense hours. The next morning, much to their relief, he was allowed to drop his family off at the train station.[49]

Toronto was given seven extra days to make plans for the mission and for the local priesthood to carry on the Church without him. On April 6, 1950, Toronto drove out of Czechoslovakia to Basel, Switzerland, where he stayed for a month, keeping in constant contact, either by phone or telegram, with the Prague priesthood leaders. Finding he could do the work just as well from Salt Lake City as from Basel, he returned home.[50]

President Toronto and the Prague Mission, 1937.

Mission President De Facto

The Torontos' escape from Communism took its toll upon the family. Martha, in particular, suffered a mental collapse and did not recover for over a year. Fifteen-year-old Marion Toronto took care of the family until Martha recovered.[51]

Wallace was not released as mission president when he returned to Utah. The First Presidency asked him to continue to act as liaison, so the Torontos did what they could to help those they had left behind. At Christmastime, the Toronto children would stuff envelopes with innocuous Christmas messages for the Czechoslovakian Saints. There were no messages of Christ, religion, or Christmas—just a wish that they would have a happy holiday.[52]

Czech members, forbidden to observe their religion openly or even interact with the Church outside the country, guarded their belief in secret for nearly fourteen years. Toronto did all he could to help from where he was, taking every chance to correspond with the members and send financial aid, clothing, medicine, and Church publications. He never gave up trying to return, and in the course of fifteen years he applied nine times for a [Czech] visa and was denied each time.[53]

The Torontos Return

It was a visit of a Czechoslovakian sister to the Torontos that opened the way for them to at least briefly return. In 1963, Marie Vesela, who had served as Toronto's personal secretary in Prague, came to Salt Lake.[54] Vesela's stay included a visit with President McKay, who asked the Torontos, "How is it that this woman can get out of the country and visit here for three months?" Toronto explained that Czechoslovakia was on the brink of economic ruin and would do anything to get foreign money, especially American dollars. Because

Vesela's entire trip was paid in dollars to the travel bureau in Prague, they decided to let her come to the United States. President McKay turned and exclaimed, "Brother Toronto! If this is the case, why would they refuse you a visa into that country?" Toronto answered, "I am still considered a threat to the peace and security of that nation, and money or not, I don't think they would let me in, not with my record. In their eyes I am still the leader of a spy ring and they are not about to let me do it again." President McKay replied, "Our members need you at this time. They have been carrying on underground long enough. They need the authority of their mission president. I advise you and Sister Toronto go home, make application again, and if it's the Lord's will, He will open the way." So the Torontos went through the routine of applying once again. Much to their surprise, after just one week, they were granted a visa for fifteen days in Czechoslovakia.[55]

Before leaving, President McKay gave the Torontos a blessing, wherein they were promised that they would "have the inspiration of the Lord in doing what was needed for the good of the mission and necessary for the morale of our members who were by this time feeling the oppression and discouragement of a downtrodden people." They were also promised that they "would go safely into the country and come back out without bodily harm or be unduly detained."[56]

In late December 1964, the Torontos drove through Austria to the Czechoslovakian border, where they encountered a barbed-wire barrier and vicious dogs on guard. After Martha said a prayer, they parked the car and went into a border station, where they declared all their valuables, including a large amount of dollars given to them by the First Presidency—not only so they could impress the guards, but that they might be able to help people in the mission. President McKay had said, "If dollars will get you in, and it is obvious that is what they want, we will give you plenty to show them." The border guards took their passports into an inner office as the Torontos held hands and prayed inwardly that they would not open the "black book" and see Wallace Toronto's name at the top of the "undesirable characters" list. Even in 1964, he was still considered the leader of a spy ring. Martha thought that if the border guards had looked at the "black book," perhaps the guards had passed over it, or the Lord had blinded them, or all the money had been too much to refuse, because the Torontos were allowed to enter Czechoslovakia.[57]

Members thought it was miraculous that the Torontos had returned. In the first town they came to, a Latter-day Saint woman came out on the sidewalk. When she saw the Torontos approaching she said, "It must be the eternities. I never expected to see you again."[58] So was the reaction of many Saints when they saw the Torontos once again.

The law stated that no more than five people could meet in the same place at one time, but the members "learned to be very clever in skirting the law if they wanted something bad enough." Much to the Torontos' surprise, when they entered one home, ten Church members were present, including counselors in the branch presidency. Martha remembered that "at the sight of us, the return of their beloved mission president, tears came freely. They stood looking at us, crying with joy. . . . We extended our arms to them and they all came at once to kiss and embrace us."[59]

Martha recorded that they felt the Lord had a particular reason for their being there in 1964.[60] Toronto finally realized the Lord's purpose for bringing them back to the mission: the most important thing they could do in their short stay there was to try to see each member if possible. "Morale was very low after fifteen years of servitude and oppression, and a visit [from the Torontos] was like a shot in the arm for them." Despite the great joy the Torontos felt during those fifteen days, they also felt great sorrow for a country that was in deep despair as they returned to Utah.[61]

Unintended National Exposure

Every five years, all nations were invited by the government to attend a sport event in Czechoslovakia named "Spatakiad." In July 1965, when Latter-day Saint Gad Vojkuvka turned on the TV to watch the event, much to his surprise, he saw Wallace Toronto on the screen.[62]

Early in 1965, Toronto had gone to President McKay and asked his advice on taking another trip to Czechoslovakia. The purpose of this trip was not to visit members but rather the authorities in the ministry of religion and education. His purpose was to get permission for public meetings again as a way to reopen the door. President McKay agreed and said that he would send Toronoto in an official capacity this time, but McKay advised him to go alone. Amazingly, as Toronto sat in a crowd of 25,000 people at the Spatakiad in Prague, a cameraman singled him out and asked him to tell the nation why he was there.[63] Toronto replied in perfect Czech that he loved the people and their land.[64] In a blessing given long before to Toronto, he had been told he would testify to the nation. In that moment that prophecy began to be fulfilled.[65]

He visited the offices of various ministries and many recognized him as the man they had seen on TV. Many Latter-day Saints came to Prague to visit him, but that was exactly what he wished to avoid. He did not want to jeopardize his mission with the officials of the government.[66]

On July 8, 1965, Toronto was talking with Latter-day Saint Brother Kubiska when four secret police in a big black car drove up and arrested him, demanding he go to the Ministry of Interior for interrogation. He started to tremble with fear as never before. Toronto felt he had the same feeling that Joseph Smith must have had in Carthage. He wondered what was going to happen to him. During the interrogation, he was accused of "such subversive activities as stirring up people and inciting them against the regime, trying to establish the Church illegally again in Czechoslovakia and bringing in missionaries."[67]

During the severe interrogation, Toronto began to question the interrogators: "Why are you afraid of 500 Mormons? Why did you pick me up?" They replied, "We want you out of the country tonight." Toronto had reservations to fly out of the country in the morning, but they wanted him out that night. One of the interrogators said to him, "When the hammer and sickle are emblazoned across all of America, then you will know that the Communist way is the right way."[68]

President McKay had blessed Toronto that he would have the opportunity to bear his testimony in high places. When he was brought back to the ministry to stand before very high officials as they accused him, he had that opportunity. The very man Toronto had hoped to have an appointment with, the man in charge of all the religious affairs of the country, was called in. Toronto felt that appearing on TV at the sports festival was orchestrated by the Lord. Otherwise, he never would have been permitted to see the top-ranking officials and make his request for the Church to be recognized.[69] After many hours, the same big thugs that had picked him up drove him to the border and made him walk across to Germany.[70]

On Toronto's last trip in 1965, "some of the members looked at him with tears in their eyes and said, 'Why are we going through this? Why are we suffering like this?'" Toronto replied, "It's because you're going to be witnesses. . . . So keep your faith and keep strong."[71]

Moses of Czechoslovakia

Toronto had always planned to go back to Czechoslovakia at a later day to complete what he was unable to do. His life was devoted to the Czechoslovak Mission and people, and he would do anything to get the Church above ground again.[72] But in August 1967, as Toronto went in for a kidney stone operation, he discovered he had cancer. He passed away in January 1968, never having been released as president of the Czechoslovak Mission.[73] At Toronto's death, President McKay asked Martha to continue as the de facto mission president of Czechoslovakia until another could be called.[74]

The Czech Saints were devastated when Toronto died. A letter written to President McKay by local leader Jiří Šnedefler reveals how they felt:

> Prague, July 10, 1968.
>
> Dear President McKay,
>
> We are sincerely concerned about the future of our Mission in Czechoslovakia. Since the untimely death of our dear Pres. Toronto we do not have any contact to receive direction and encouragement from the First Presidency and Church leaders. . . .
>
> We realize you are so busy you personally cannot be concerned about us, but would it be possible to designate someone who understands us, who would correspond with us, who could help us enjoy the blessings we so much want and need.[75]

During the "Prague Spring" of 1968, the same year that Toronto died, "Alexander Dubcek became leader of the Czechoslovak Communist Party and instituted a series of liberal reforms, including more freedom of the press and increased contact with non-Communist countries. Encouraged by these actions, Čeněk Vrba, Jiří Šnedefler, and Miroslav Děkanovský—three stalwarts of the Church—petitioned for religious recognition. However, hopes were dashed when Warsaw Pact troops and tanks, under Soviet orders, crushed the progressive regime and quelled any hope of reviving the Church."[76]

Latter-day Saint Gad Vojkuvka remembers President Toronto and his visits, the joy of the members, their testimonies, and the advice and support given to them. Many members asked why they had to go through what they went through and why religious freedom was never granted again during Toronto's lifetime. Vojkuvka compared the modern Czech Saints with the Israelites. "Just like Israelites had to wander for 40 years in the desert and not even Moses could enter the promised land, even so we had to suffer being illegal/prohibited for 40 years and President Toronto died before the Church became again legal here."[77] Like Moses, Toronto helped in preparing Czechoslovakia for the freedom that would come after his death.

Farewell program for Elder Wallace Toronto and family.

Wallace Toronto's ministry opened the gospel door to the Slavic people. As Mehr explains, "For sixty years before the demise of Communism in 1989, the Czechoslovak Mission was the backbone of the Church in Slavic Europe, which also includes Poland, Bulgaria, Yugoslavia, and the states of the former Soviet Union." Though during his thirty-two years as mission president "missionaries had open access for only fourteen years, 1929–39 and 1946–50, [and] baptized [only] 277 new members. . . . The small group of Saints that had been converted were isolated but enduring, deprived of a public voice but silently believing." The practices instituted by Toronto prepared a people to endure forty years of Communism and can still be used today in similar situations.[78]

Brigham Young University professor of Church history and doctrine Richard O. Cowan says, "When the police banned door-to-door tracting, missionaries were forced to develop a more efficient 'friend-to-friend' referral system."[79] This referral system was the beginning of a different missionary approach that has endured into the twenty-first century. When Toronto served as a mission president, few had heard about the Church, and those that had often only knew about the Church's connection with polygamy. Toronto developed "a simpler way of breaking down the barriers and presenting a picture of wholesome recreation by attractive, skilled, and good-natured young Americans." As Jessie L. Embry, historian of Western studies, observes, Toronto "capitalized on the talents of their missionaries. When they had good basketball players, they formed a basketball team. When they had musicians, they formed a choir." These activities were effective in meeting people in a friendlier, less direct way. Such approaches evolved into the subtler and less intrusive methods used today, such as teaching English classes or providing community service.[80]

Cowan reiterates that Toronto "helped to build goodwill for Mormons in areas where they had generally been unknown or misunderstood."[81] Toronto's ability to make government contacts, draw large crowds at public meetings, and use the press effectively resulted in a flood of publicity, which made the people more "Mormon conscious" than ever before.[82] Such tactics are still applicable in other less-receptive countries. BYU emeritus professor of history Thomas G. Alexander concurs that Toronto provides a pattern to be emulated as the Church moves forward in "publiciz[ing] Mormonism widely through sports, public displays, concerts, and lectures." Under Toronto's leadership "the nation was much better informed about Mormonism, [and though the Czechs were] not disposed to accept it in significant numbers . . . those who chose this new and demanding religion found richer meaning in life."[83]

Toronto's ability to convert and train local leaders was also an impetus for survival of the Church in these regions and greatly contributed to the current growth the Church is experiencing. As David F. Boone, BYU associate professor of Church history and doctrine, observes, "Much of the recent growth in Europe, as reflected in the number of members, local missionaries, stakes, and temples, can be traced to the leadership developed during an era when, because of the evacuation of the American missionaries, local individuals had to stand up and be counted."[84] This is especially seen in Czechoslovakia today (2015), where membership has grown to 2,396 members in 13 branches.[85]

Toronto was one of the most successful mission presidents of his era. Mehr explains that "the Saints in Czechoslovakia had the same amount of time to prepare themselves for resistance" to the Communist and Nazi regimes as those in other countries. Yet they fared much better. As the Church continued to grow during the twentieth century, nowhere were the challenges greater than in Czechoslovakia. Wallace Toronto experienced missionary work in the most diverse of circumstances that cause feelings of uneasiness and concern among members. As seen in this narrative, Toronto shows future missionaries and Church leaders how to function under similar conditions and still hold fast to the LDS tenets of obeying the laws of the land and respecting separation of Church and state.[86] Toronto observed that his converts' "testimonies of the truthfulness of the gospel have not wavered even in the worst moments of this great conflict."[87] Despite these great challenges, including "few missionaries, internal disputes, social opposition, and limited facilities and funds, the small band of Saints established a foothold so firm that they endured war and almost sixty years of repression as stubborn believers."[88] Toronto's methods, teachings, and practices were largely responsible for this success and provide an example for others to follow as the Church moves forward to encounter similar challenges and conflicts in other parts of the world.

Notes

1. Martha Toronto Anderson, *A Cherry Tree Behind the Iron Curtain: The Autobiography of Martha Toronto Anderson* (Salt Lake City: Martha Toronto Anderson, 1977), 11.
2. Wallace F. Toronto, "Some Socio-psychological Aspects of the Czecho-Slovakian Crisis of 1938–39" (master's thesis, University of Utah, 1940), 7.
3. Carma Toronto interview, February 26, 2004, interviewed by Daniel Toronto, Salt Lake City, Utah, 2, transcript in author's possession.
4. Marion Toronto Miller and Judith Toronto Richards interview, May 3, 2013, interviewed by Mary Jane Woodger, Salt Lake City, 13, transcript in author's possession; Bob and David Toronto interview, August 20, 2013, interviewed by Mary Jane Woodger, Sandy, Utah, 5, transcript in author's possession.
5. Anderson, *A Cherry Tree*, 12.
6. Carma Toronto interview, 7.
7. Bob and David Toronto interview, 5.
8. Wallace F. Toronto, "Lord's Help Indispensable," *Hvězdička* [*The Star*, Czechoslovakian Mission newsletter], July 1938, found in Jiri Snederfler papers, Europe Church History Center, Bad Homburg, Germany, copy in author's possession.
9. Wallace Toronto, journal, July 19–25, 1936, 15, copy in author's possession.
10. Toronto, "Socio-psychological Aspects," 8.
11. Gad Vojkuvka, "Memories of President Wallace Felt Toronto," email to Mary Jane Woodger, November 9, 2013, 5, in author's possession.
12. Ed and Norma Morrell interview, May 8, 2013, interviewed by Mary Jane Woodger, Provo, Utah, 7, transcript in author's possession.
13. Vojkuvka, "Memories," 7.
14. Johann Wondra interview, May 30, 2013, interviewed by Mary Jane Woodger, Vienna, Austria, 4, transcript in author's possession.
15. Dale Tingey interview, October 2, 2013, interviewed by Kalli Searle, Provo, Utah, 2, transcript in author's possession.
16. Johann Wondra interview, 2, 4.

17. Bob and David Toronto interview, 16.
18. Dale Tingey interview.
19. Wallace Toronto journal, March 5–11, 1939, 339.
20. Wallace Toronto journal, April 2–8, 1939, 348–49; and June 25–July 1, 1939, 377.
21. Anderson, *A Cherry Tree*, 19–20.
22. Anderson, *A Cherry Tree*, 23, 26; Kahlile Mehr, "Czech Saints: A Brighter Day," *Ensign*, August 1994, 49.
23. Wallace Toronto journal, July 9–15, 1939, 380–82.
24. Wallace Toronto journal, August 20–26, 1939, 399.
25. Mehr, "A Brighter Day," 49–50.
26. Anderson, *A Cherry Tree*, 32. For information on mission evacuation in Europe see David F. Boone, "The Evacuation of the Czechoslovak and German Missions at the Outbreak of World War II," *BYU Studies* 40, no. 3 (2001): 123–54; Kahlile Mehr, *Mormon Missionaries Enter Eastern Europe* (Salt Lake City: Deseret Book, 2002), 72–73.
27. Wallace Toronto journal, August 27–September 2, 1939, 405.
28. After World War II, the Slovak Republic ceased to exist and was reabsorbed into Czechoslovakia.
29. Mehr, "Czech Saints: A Brighter Day," 50.
30. Anderson, *A Cherry Tree*, 38.
31. Marion Toronto Miller and Judith Toronto Richards interview, 14; Mehr, "A Brighter Day," 50.
32. Anderson, *A Cherry Tree*, 39.
33. Mehr, *Mormon Missionaries Enter Eastern Europe*, 83.
34. Mehr, *Mormon Missionaries Enter Eastern Europe*, 84.
35. Mehr, *Mormon Missionaries Enter Eastern Europe*, 83.
36. Don Whipperman interview, October 9, 2013, interviewed by Mary Jane Woodger, 1, transcript in author's possession.
37. Marion Toronto Miller, "My Story: The Dream (The Early Years)" (presentation, December 1998), 14.
38. Whipperman interview, 1, 4 .

39. Mel Maybe interview, August 13, 2013, interviewed by Mary Jane Woodger, Alpine, Utah, 8, transcript in author's possession.
40. Marion Toronto Miller, "My Story," 14.
41. Vojkuvka, "Memories," 2.
42. Mehr, *Mormon Missionaries Enter Eastern Europe*, 84.
43. Anderson, *A Cherry Tree*, 56.
44. Mehr, *Mormon Missionaries Enter Eastern Europe*, 85.
45. Anderson, *A Cherry Tree*, 50.
46. Ed Morell, "Summary of Czechoslovak Archive Documents, dated in the 1940s and 1950, turned over to the Torontos in 2007," 1–2, in author's possession.
47. Mel Maybe interview, 3,6; Marion Toronto Miller and Judith Toronto Richards interview, 12.
48. "Cancer Crusader W. F. Toronto Dies," *Deseret News*, January 10, 1968, B1, B5.
49. Marion Toronto Miller and Judith Toronto Richards interview, 11; Mehr, *Mormon Missionaries Enter Eastern Europe*, 85.
50. Anderson, *A Cherry Tree*, 65–66; Vojkuvka, "Memories," 4; Mehr, *Mormon Missionaries Enter Eastern Europe*, 86.
51. Marion Toronto Miller, "My Story," 17.
52. David Toronto interview, 2010, interviewed by Daniel Toronto, 1, copy in possession of the author; Bob and David Toronto interview, 28.
53. Mehr, "A Brighter Day," 51.
54. Anderson, *A Cherry Tree*, 75; Mehr, *Mormon Missionaries Enter Eastern Europe*, 90.
55. Anderson, *A Cherry Tree*, 76–77.
56. Anderson, *A Cherry Tree*, 79.
57. Anderson, *A Cherry Tree*, 83–84.
58. Ed and Norma Morrell interview, May 8, 2013, interviewed by Mary Jane Woodger, May 8, 2013, Provo, Utah, transcript in author's possession, 5.
59. Anderson, *A Cherry Tree*, 86–87.
60. Anderson, *A Cherry Tree*, 88.

61. Anderson, *A Cherry Tree*, 91 and 93.
62. Vojkuvka, "Memories," 5.
63. Anderson, *A Cherry Tree*, 100–102.
64. Mehr, *Mormon Missionaries Enter Eastern Europe*, 90–92.
65. Anderson, *A Cherry Tree*, 102.
66. Anderson, *A Cherry Tree*, 102.
67. Anderson, *A Cherry Tree*, 102–3; see also Ed and Norma Morrell interview, 15–16.
68. Bob and David Toronto interview, 27.
69. Anderson, *A Cherry Tree*, 103.
70. Bob and David Toronto interview, 27.
71. Marion Toronto Miller and Judith Toronto Richards interview, 15–16.
72. Anderson, *A Cherry Tree*, 106.
73. "Cancer Crusader W. F. Toronto Dies," B1.
74. Bob and David Toronto interview, 29.
75. Jiri Snedefler to President David O. McKay, July 10, 1968, Jiri Snederfler Papers, Europe Church History Center, Bad Homburg, Germany, copy in author's possession.
76. Mehr, *Mormon Missionaries Enter Eastern Europe*, 92–93.
77. Vojkuvka, "Memories."
78. Kahlile Mehr, "Enduring Believers: Czechoslovakia and the LDS Church 1884–1990," *Journal of Mormon History* 18, no. 2 (1992): 111–12.
79. Richard O. Cowan, *The Latter-day Saint Century* (Salt Lake City: Bookcraft, 1999), 111.
80. Jessie L. Embry and John H. Brambaugh, "Preaching through Playing: Using Sports and Recreation in Missionary Work, 1911–64," *Journal of Mormon History* 35, no. 4 (Fall 2009): 58.
81. Cowan, *The Latter-day Saint Century*, 112.
82. "Czechoslovakia Welcomes President Grant," *Church News*, August 14, 1937, 2, 6, 8.

83. Mehr, "Enduring Believers," 137.
84. David F. Boone, "The Evacuation of the Czechoslovak and German Missions at the Outbreak of World War II," *BYU Studies* 40, no. 3 (2001): 149.
85. "Facts and Statistics: Czech Republic," The Church of Jesus Christ of Latter-day Saints Newsroom, www.mormonnewsroom.org/facts-and-statistics/country/czech-republic.
86. Mehr, "Enduring Believers," 125.
87. "First Report Comes from Czechoslovakia," *Church News*, July 21, 1945, 9.
88. Mehr, "Enduring Believers," 125.

12

From Conflict to Collaboration

Mormons and Waldensians in Italy

Mauro Properzi and James A. Toronto

A historic event for the LDS Church in Italy took place in Rome on July 30, 2012. Giorgio Napolitano, president of the Italian Republic, signed legislation that recognized The Church of Jesus Christ of Latter-day Saints, along with two other religious organizations, as full legal partners of the state. This *Intesa,* or "agreement," has both legal and practical significance in that it gives the Church every right and benefit available to other similarly recognized religious institutions. Among other things, "the Intesa gave Church leaders unhindered access in their pastoral support for members in the military, in hospitals, and in prisons, and guaranteed confidentiality in their communications with members; permitted church members a modest tax deduction for charitable donations; provided authorization for LDS seminaries and institutes, with the possibility that courses might even

Mauro Properzi is an assistant professor of Church history and doctrine at Brigham Young University. James A. Toronto is an associate professor of Arabic and Islamic studies at Brigham Young University.

be eligible for public school credit; allowed teaching of LDS religion courses in public school, if the Church decided to do so; stabilized the visa situation for missionaries and mission presidents and the granting of residency permits; and denied police and military the right to enter and search LDS Church buildings without authorization."[1] As one of only eleven non-Catholic churches to have signed an Intesa with the Italian government, the Church achieved a status that symbolically and psychologically represents "a badge of authenticity and legitimacy—a public affirmation that the religious community has come of age and attained an equal standing in Italy's public square."[2] It was undoubtedly a historical milestone for Mormonism in Italy, which will be rivaled in significance only by the completion of the Rome Italy Temple, presently expected in 2016.

While the Intesa process took over fifteen years from the day of the application's submission to the day in which the law took full effect, the whole history of Mormonism in Italy functions as the necessary background and foundation for this important achievement. It is a history with a large one-century gap within a 162-year timeframe extending from the day in which the first Mormon missionary set foot on Italian soil to Napolitano's signing of the Intesa. Two phases are clearly recognizable: the first covering a limited fifteen-year period between 1850 and 1865, and the second ranging from 1965 to the present.[3] A comparison of these stages highlights significant differences in context, focus, approach, and objectives to such an extent that any continuity between the nineteenth-century LDS presence in Italy and later twentieth- and early twenty-first-century Italian Mormonism is not immediately apparent. Yet our exploration of the recent path to the Intesa has revealed a somewhat surprising bridge between the two historical phases of Mormonism in Italy: the interactions, tensions, and interfaith relations between Mormons and Waldensians, which range from conflict to friendship and from competition to cooperation. Our analysis aims to shed light on this intriguing and partially neglected dimension of the history of Mormonism in Italy and to examine some implications that these developments might have for the LDS Church's efforts to establish a stable presence in other emerging areas of international growth.

The historical origins of the Waldensians can be traced to Lyon (southern France) in the twelfth century when a man named Valdès (or Waldesius) and his followers distinguished themselves by preaching a form of Christianity that was based, among other things, on strict adherence to the Bible and on voluntary poverty.[4] It did not take long for the group to be declared heretical by Catholic authorities and for Waldo and his "Waldensians" to have to relocate to the Piedmont valleys of present-day northwest Italy.[5] Although persecution occurred in subsequent centuries, including an order of extermination issued against them in 1487, the movement managed to survive due in part to the isolation provided by their alpine surroundings.[6] Following the Protestant Reformation in the sixteenth century, Waldensian leaders joined the Swiss Reformed tradition of John Calvin and became, for all intents and purposes, a Protestant denomination. In 1848, Charles Albert, the ruler of the Kingdom of Piedmont-Sardinia, extended civil rights to the Waldensians, who, for the first time in their history, were assured liberty of conscience.[7] Only two years later, in 1850, the first Mormon missionaries arrived in Piedmont to begin their evangelization of a land that would officially become the Kingdom of Italy in 1861.

Lorenzo Snow, a member of the Quorum of the Twelve and one of the first Mormon missionaries to Italy, explained the decision to begin proselytizing among the Waldensians to be only partially due to the favorable legal setting brought about by Charles Albert.[8] Snow was fascinated by the history of the Waldensians and in fact thought of them as "the rose in the wilderness or the bow in the cloud." When he visited a public library in Liverpool to obtain more information on this people, he read that they were a remnant of the primitive Christian

Church and that they "had been the means of preserving the doctrines of the gospel in their primitive simplicity."[9] He and other Church leaders such as Sidney Rigdon, Brigham Young, and John Taylor saw striking parallels between the persecutions that both Mormons and Waldensians had had to endure. They undoubtedly felt that the doctrinal parallels between the two faiths—including a focus on Christian primitivism, a belief in the Apostasy, and the affirmation of spiritual gifts—would mean that the Waldensians would be receptive to the Mormon message.[10] Consequently, the first phase of missionary work in Italy, which extended from 1850 to 1865, was almost exclusively concentrated in the Waldensian valleys of Piedmont.

Notwithstanding numerous obstacles—including language barriers, political and social hurdles, difficulties of travel on challenging alpine terrain, isolation, discouragement, and conflicts internal to the Church—the missionaries obtained a degree of success in nearly two decades of early Mormon proselytism in Italy.[11] Three branches would be established in the valleys and about 180 Waldensians would convert to Mormonism during the mission's existence, although most joined in the first five years of missionary activities. About a third of all converts would emigrate to Utah, where they would contribute to the establishment of the Church in the West; the remaining converts were either excommunicated, returned to the Waldensian Church, or are unaccounted for.[12] While a harvest of less than two hundred souls, with about eighty representing permanent conversions, may appear meager, it must be remembered that the Waldensian population in the valleys only amounted to about twenty thousand individuals, a number that kept decreasing because of emigration. In other words, Mormon missionary activity was certainly noticed and, unsurprisingly, it encountered stiff opposition.

In 1851 in particular, following the conversion of some prominent families, Waldensian ministers began to actively counter LDS missionary activities through anti-Mormon literature, public debates, and denunciations from the pulpit. Rumors and printed material stated that "the missionaries were agents sent to Italy to find polygamous wives for Mormon Church leaders in Utah;" Mormon meetings were occasionally disturbed and verbal threats exchanged.[13] Pastors used both preaching and practical means to protect their flocks from the Mormon message. They reminded their parishioners about their ancestors' sacrifices for the Waldensian faith in order to dissuade them from accepting a different baptism,[14] and when crop failures and economic crises led many inhabitants to turn to the ministers for assistance, the clergy made help conditional on the person's renunciation of Mormonism.[15] Moreover, since a few hundred Waldensians were already emigrating every year in search of better opportunities, leaders in the valley were particularly wary of the Mormon focus on emigration to America.[16] In the summer of 1854, this concern even reached the Piedmont House of Deputies, where Joseph Malan, himself a Waldensian, wondered whether the Mormons should be driven out "immediately."[17]

While the 1850s conflict between the Mormon missionaries and the Waldensian pastors is undeniable, it rarely reached proportions where the elders or local members came to fear for their lives. Furthermore, when one looks at the history and size of this persecuted religious minority, Waldensian defensiveness in response to Mormon proselytizing efforts is certainly understandable. Yet defensiveness did not translate into refusal to extend basic religious freedoms to a competing religious group. LDS missionaries would not have been able to organize three branches and convert almost two hundred individuals had there not been a degree of religious freedom within mostly isolated valleys that were practically monolithic in terms of religious affiliation. In other words, when faced with the opportunity to show whether their protracted advocacy for religious freedom was purely self-interested or rather based on a deep commitment to a foundational human value, the Waldensians responded by and large in favor of the latter. In fact, this was one of the main reasons missionary work began in the valleys of Piedmont; this kind of freedom of religion in nineteenth-century Italy was more of an anomaly than a standard. This same thought was expressed by those early missionaries who attempted to expand the work beyond the Waldensian valleys into Catholic Italy.[18]

Following the departure of the last Mormon missionary from the valleys of Piedmont in 1865, the LDS Church would not officially return to the land of Italy for a full century. The reasons for this absence are complex and can be traced both to factors within the LDS Church and to outside historical events that affected Italy's openness to Mormon proselytism.[19] Among the latter, the Second Vatican Council, which took place between 1962 and 1965, is worth a brief mention. This ecumenical council represented an *aggiornamento*, or updating, of the Catholic Church's approach to the modern world, which had been mostly negative up to that point in time. Vatican II would bring about significant changes in the direction of greater openness. For example, in the declaration *Dignitatis Humanae*, the council affirmed unequivocally that every human being has a foundational right to religious liberty.[20] Interestingly, the Italian zone of the LDS Swiss Mission had been opened only a few months earlier, with missionaries being sent to seven Italian cities where LDS American servicemen or a handful of Italian members were already residing.

This second phase of missionary work in Italy began with great enthusiasm. In August 1966, following the Italian zone's considerable success, a separate Italian mission was organized.[21] The country was rededicated by Elder Ezra Taft Benson during a small, private service in Torre Pellice, the Waldensian town in Piedmont that had been the residence of the earliest Mormon missionaries; the 1966 flood of the Arno River had prevented the ceremony from taking place in Florence, the originally selected location.[22] Missionary work in Italy continued in its steady advance, notwithstanding difficulties in public

Elder and Sister Benson and President and Sister Duns at the mission conference held in Florence on August 2, 1966, to formally reestablish the Italian Mission.

relations, challenges in training native leadership, and other obstacles typical of an emergent-church setting. In 1971 a second Italian mission was created, and statistics indicate the presence of almost fifteen hundred members organized into twenty-five Italian branches and four servicemen's groups.[23] Two additional missions were created in the later '70s, bringing the total number to four (later consolidated

A photo of Torre Pellice in 1889, probably similar to what it would have looked like in the 1850s and '60s when the early Mormon missionaries labored there. Clearly seen dominating the skyline in the background are Monte Vandalino and the prominent rock protrusion called Monte Castelluzzo on its left slope, which was the location for the dedication of the country of Italy to missionary work by Elder Lorenzo Snow in 1850. (Carlo Papini, ed., Come Vivevano: Val Pellice, Valli D'Angrogna e di Luserna fin de siècle (1870–1910) *[Torino: Claudiana, 1980, 1998], image 54.)*

back to two), and visits by two Church prophets, Harold B. Lee and Spencer W. Kimball, galvanized the Italian Saints and brought added media exposure to the Church. Overall, the 1970s and early '80s were characterized by accelerated rates of conversion to Mormonism as demonstrated by the formation of the first two Italian stakes in Milan (1981) and Venice (1985).[24]

This "golden" period of missionary work was followed by three decades of slower growth but increasing maturity, stability within the Church, and greater acceptance and integration into Italian public life. Presently, ten Church stakes dot the Italian map, and evidence of the maturation of the local leadership can "be found in the calling of many Italians to senior positions in the church hierarchy: seven mission presidents . . . a Swiss Temple president . . . and numerous regional representatives, area seventies, and stake presidents."[25] Landmark events also played a role in this slow but steady trajectory of growth and public visibility. A highlight of the 1990s was the Mormon Tabernacle Choir's European tour, which included a visit to Italy in 1998. President Monson's 2008 announcement of the Church's plans to construct a temple in Rome certainly marked a historic moment. More history was made in 2012 with the achievement of the previously mentioned Intesa and the signing of a contract between the Italian National Archives and FamilySearch, allowing for the complete digitization of the archives' historical records.[26] The next milestone will be the temple's dedication, which is anticipated to take place in 2016.

Although cursory and highly simplified, this sketch of Mormonism's progress in Italy highlights a few significant differences between its early and later phases. The nineteenth-century Italian mission had less than a two-decade lifespan, whereas the later mission organization, begun about half a century ago, was to be permanent in nature. Similarly, the early organization of three branches within the Waldensian valleys was not as much a step in the establishment of a permanent Mormon presence in Italy as it was the response to a need to provide temporary spiritual shelter for members preparing to emigrate to Zion. Limited resources and the strongly millenarian view of the nineteenth-century Church gave such an urgency to the "gathering of the elect" that the Church did not set roots into Italian soil then like it would begin to do in the twentieth century.

Another big difference between the earlier and the later Mormon phases of evangelization was their area of focus. Nineteenth-century efforts were almost exclusively centered around a small Protestant minority in a very limited geographical location, whereas the "new"

"The fountain of Carlo Alberto (1845), a rare example of a monument erected by a king in tribute to his people 'who welcomed him with great affection.' Having come to Torre Pellice the previous year for the inauguration of a Catholic church, he received such a warm and spontaneous reception from the Waldensian population that he was deeply moved. When the king learned, a little later, that the community council of Torre Pellice had decided to erect a monumental fountain in memory of his visit, he insisted on covering all the expenses and provided the wording for the inscription." The fountain has since been relocated to the middle of the piazza among the trees. (Carlo Papini, ed., Come Vivevano: Val Pellice, Valli D'Angrogna e di Luserna fin de siècle (1870–1910) *[Torino: Claudiana, 1980, 1998], image 53.)*

Italian missions expanded to reach all corners of the country, without concern for people's religious backgrounds or beliefs. In short, there appears to be a significant discontinuity between the two phases of the Mormon presence in Italy.

Yet one also finds points of contact between the first and the second Italian missions. One significant line of continuity emerges in the Mormon-Waldensian interactions that began in the nineteenth century and have continued into the twenty-first. To be sure, at the general membership level, such contact was and remains limited. Both Italian Mormons and Italian Waldensians are few in number, and the LDS Church does not presently have congregations in the Piedmont valleys where Waldensians are in highest concentration. Although a handful of Waldensians have joined the LDS Church in Italy and LDS missionaries have, as recently as the year 2000, spent some time in the proselyting areas of the "first" mission, the interaction between the Mormons and Waldensians has not primarily emerged through missionary activities. Instead, Church leaders and public relations representatives have made an effort to maintain and strengthen relationships with prominent Waldensians, even as present-day Mormonism has moved to bigger and greener "Catholic" pastures in its proselytizing endeavors. In short, Mormons and Waldensians have come to interact and to know each other not primarily as potential converts but as friends and partners in the defense of religious freedom and of other shared values.

For example, "many LDS members have benefited from receiving access to the Waldensian archives in order to get ancestral information for their own genealogical research, and the FamilySearch department has established very good relations with Italian Waldensians."[27] The sincerity of Waldensian friendship has also been demonstrated throughout the process that led to the Intesa between the Italian government and the LDS Church. Indeed, the support and mediation that prominent Waldensians offered spontaneously to Latter-day Saints was a significant contributor to the success of the endeavor. This agreement was not finalized without having to surpass some hurdles, which took about fifteen years to be resolved. These difficulties varied in nature and were mostly unrelated to any specific doctrinal or practical concerns associated with the LDS Church. Anna Nardini, the Italian government representative who helped oversee the whole process, indicated that some politicians were not as concerned about the Mormons as they were about the possibility that granting full legal recognition to any religious group might eventually mean having to recognize all of them. In the months following the events of 9/11, this prospect was worrisome to some. Other politicians simply needed to become better educated about the LDS Church, and in this context, as Nardini highlighted, they greatly benefited from the exposure that Mitt Romney's 2012 candidacy for president of the United States gave to the Church and its teachings.[28] Yet explicit support and sustained advocacy from non-Mormons would still be needed to overcome the impasse of the Italian bureaucratic machinery.

Waldensians have been consistent advocates for the extension of religious equality to an increasing number of religious minorities. For example, before the June 1946 national assembly elections immediately following World War II, as Italy transitioned from a monarchy to a republic, the Waldensians (as well as other Protestants) issued a statement that was printed on posters and displayed in cities throughout the country. The statement asserted, among other things, that "authentic civil and political freedom cannot flourish unless there be the foundation of freedom of religion equal for all," and it called for the elimination of "every vestige of the old confessional state." It set forth three principles to achieve this goal: (1) "The full and complete freedom of conscience and of religion for all, so that anyone . . . can worship God and witness to God's truth as conscience directs"; (2) "The full independence of all the churches from the state"; and (3) "Impartiality and neutrality in matters of religion on the part of a non-confessional state."[29]

Later, in 1984, being the first non-Catholic religious group to have reached an Intesa with the Italian government (following their merger with Italian Methodists in the '70s), the Waldensians did not see this achievement as a reason to retreat from direct involvement in other religions' efforts to reach the same objective. In fact, in 2008 the Waldensian-Methodist Church supported and participated in a Coalition for Religious Agreements that had been formed by the five religions that were seeking the Intesa, the LDS Church being one of the five.[30] Moreover, prominent Waldensians have repeatedly proposed and sponsored legislation aimed at extending and guaranteeing religious freedom for all. In 2007, Waldensian member of Parliament Valdo Spini sponsored a proposed law on religious freedom and in that context gave LDS Church representatives the chance to make their case publicly when they were invited, alongside members of other Italian religious minorities, to a parliamentary inquiry into the recommended legislation. At present, Waldensian professor Paolo Naso, from the La Sapienza University in Rome, is spearheading efforts for a new law on religious freedom in Italy in cooperation with representatives of different religions, including the Latter-day Saints.

In the specific context of the parliamentary process leading to the Intesa, Spini counseled and assisted LDS Church representatives at the early stages of the proposal.[31] Another Waldensian member of Parliament, Senator Lucio Malan, was a key contributor to the success of the legislation in the months leading up to its signing. In fact, in 2011 Malan cosponsored the draft of the proposed agreements between the state and the five religions of the Coalition. He then proceeded to advocate for these proposals as they were being debated in the Italian Senate. Following the approval of three of these proposed agreements, the LDS Church being the recipient of one of them, Malan stated that the new legislation represented "three important steps for religious liberty in Italy." He also added, "I am especially pleased to have worked for these measures since my religious community, the Waldensian Church, was the first to attain an Intesa in 1984 and from that time until now we have fought hard to guarantee the same right for others."[32] Indeed, although the Waldensians mentioned so far span the whole range of the political spectrum, they all share a solid commitment to religious freedom, which seems to be deeply ingrained in their Waldensian DNA. Thus, when asked about the meaning of being a Waldensian in the twenty-first century, Malan responded: "It means being a Christian with a responsibility not to stain the memory of our poor and humble ancestors. For many centuries they experienced persecution, discrimination, and poverty to be faithful to the gospel message. It is then our human responsibility today to prevent other religious groups from being similarly persecuted."[33]

Love for religious freedom has then been at the root of Waldensian involvement in the LDS cause, but the sincere friendship that has developed in the process between these Waldensian personalities and LDS officials should not be underestimated. Paolo Naso, Domenico Maselli, and Lucio Malan are considered "friends" by Giuseppe Pasta, a public affairs representative for the LDS Church in Italy, a feeling which is fully reciprocated. Malan highlights that he "would have done what he did for the Mormons no matter what, but the fact that they are so likable, courteous, devoted to their faith, and trustworthy citizens made it easier to advocate for them without any reservations."[34] Parenthetically, Malan's interaction with Mormonism is also strongly associated with the faith's sacred buildings. When asked about his first contact with the LDS Church, he recalled attending the open house of the newly built Las Vegas Nevada Temple at a time when he was living in the United States. Malan also attended the groundbreaking ceremony of the Rome temple in October of 2010, presided over by President Monson himself. In that setting, the Waldensian senator hailed the groundbreaking as "a positive day for

Some representatives of the coalition and their political partners gather to discuss plans and strategy. Left to right: Giuseppe Pasta, The Church of Jesus Christ of Latter-day Saints; Ms. Maria Fala', vice-president of the Buddhist Union; Ms. Dora Bognandi, pastor of the Seventh-day Adventist Church; Mr. Franco Di Maria, president of the Italy Hindu Union; Senator Vannino Chiti, vice-president of the Italian Senate; Archimandrite Symeone Catsinas, Orthodox Church; Senator Stefano Ceccanti, PD Party; Mr. Claudio Tanca, APCO; Senator Lucio Malan, PDL Party. (Courtesy of Giuseppe Pasta, LDS public affairs, Italy.)

Italy because those who profess to obey the laws of the state and the laws of God make the country in which they live a better place."[35] Certainly, relationships of trust of this kind emerge only through encounter, dialogue, and sincere desire to know and understand the religious "other."

Many years have passed since the days in which Lorenzo Snow and his companions walked the Waldensian valleys of Piedmont. Few are familiar with the story beyond LDS Church historians, some Italian members, and the descendants of those early converts to

Mission histories record that thirty-five missionaries witnessed the rededication of Italy by Elder Benson near Torre Pellice, November 10, 1966. (Church History Library.)

Mormonism who emigrated to Utah. Malan, who grew up in that area, recalls hearing in his youth that the Mormons had renamed their local Monte Vandalino "Mount Brigham," but beyond that the rest of the story was mostly unknown. The Mormons had come, converted some, had conflicts with the local pastors, and finally left. Yet, at the end of the twentieth and at the beginning of the twenty-first century, the two groups would meet again, this time mostly outside of Piedmont and in collaboration and friendship rather than in conflict. These meetings culminated in one of the most significant achievements of the LDS Church in Italy: the signing of the Intesa with the Italian government. Certainly, those early Mormon missionaries could not have anticipated that descendants of the Waldensians among whom they had served would contribute to make the Church a full partner of the Italian state more than 150 years later.

To be sure, the significance of the Waldensian support for the achievement of the Intesa should not be singled out as the one determining cause of its success. Catholics and individuals of different persuasions also courageously backed the legislation and gave their valued contribution to its success, and, although friendship and interfaith cooperation brought momentum to the proposal, the effective work of the LDS public relations team and extensive community and humanitarian service by Italian LDS members were no less significant. Indeed, interviews with government officials, legal scholars, and Church leaders and attorneys in Italy shed further light on how the LDS Church achieved the significant milestones of the Intesa with the state and the construction of a temple.[36]

Several factors were key to the LDS Church's successful Intesa campaign. First, a focused, team-oriented, and patient strategy prevented the Mormons from becoming discouraged during the long process of pursuing the Intesa and allowed them to cross the finish line. Second, friends of many faiths (particularly Waldensians and Catholics)—individuals who were brave enough to take a public stand on behalf of the LDS Church—helped open doors and assisted in the advancement of the Intesa. Third, the Mormon campaign had important stakeholders in state government offices, the Senate, and the Chamber of Deputies who offered strong support. Allies outside of government—including noted scholars such as Silvio Ferrari, Massimo Introvigne, and Stefano Ceccanti—were also very supportive of the Church's effort.

Finally, the Parliament was generally willing (although there was some dispute on this point) to recognize Mormonism as a "Christian" faith—globally recognized and well-respected—which enhanced the Church's ability to advance with the other two Christian faiths in the Coalition, although not at the same pace. There was respect for Mormonism's reputation as a well-known, influential religious organization in the United States and for its support of principles of sound government and loyal citizenship. Moreover, as a member of the Coalition, the LDS Church was the driving force behind the strategy, execution, government relations outreach, and communication plan that earned the admiration of other Coalition members and Italian politicians.

Conversely, political factors such as instability in the government and lack of political priority on the issue prevented some religious groups from attaining Intesa status. In general, these groups were not supported, and in some cases were explicitly opposed by certain political parties like the Northern League. Some churches did not succeed in their Intesa petitions because they lacked a champion willing to advocate their cause and because the state and political parties did not consider them strategically important. Because of Italy's prominently Catholic status, it is understandable that there were strong biases against non-Christian faiths (e.g., Buddhists, Hindus, and Muslims) as well as against faiths considered to be opponents of the state (Jehovah's Witnesses).[37] Significant efforts were made by three groups who had previously achieved Intesa status (the Evangelical Federation, the Seventh-Day Adventists, and the Waldensian-Methodist Church) and by the three successful Intesa applicants (the Orthodox Church, the Apostolic Church, and the LDS Church) to bring the Buddhist Union and the Hindu Union along with them in the Senate. However, these two groups were handicapped because they did not have the resources to invest sufficient time, finances, and strategic positioning to follow up with key stakeholders regarding their faith-specific issues; hence, their agreements with the government required several additional months in order to be finalized.[38]

The Mormon experience in Italy shows that religious equality in any country is not freely granted, and this is a lesson that may have implications for the Church's efforts to establish an enduring presence in other international areas. Religious liberty is a closely guarded commodity that the state distributes selectively and incrementally; political acumen and lobbying muscle, not a transparent legal process, determine the recipients. In other words, religious, ethnic, and other social minorities attain their constitutionally guaranteed rights and freedoms not by merely requesting them but by proactively and tenaciously pursuing them, most effectively in league with individuals and groups who share a common cause. The kind of faith that produces miracles, such as signing an Intesa or building a temple, remains dead unless accompanied by civic activism, community service, interfaith outreach, and other works. Thus one of the lessons to be drawn from the Italian case, which could transfer to other emerging areas of Church growth, is that common political, legal, and social interests can be achieved by granting local leaders and members a more visible and substantive role in building coalitions at the community and national levels. In Italy, this approach proved to be crucial as it fostered mutual respect, achieved legal recognition, helped dispel stereotypes, and hastened social integration.

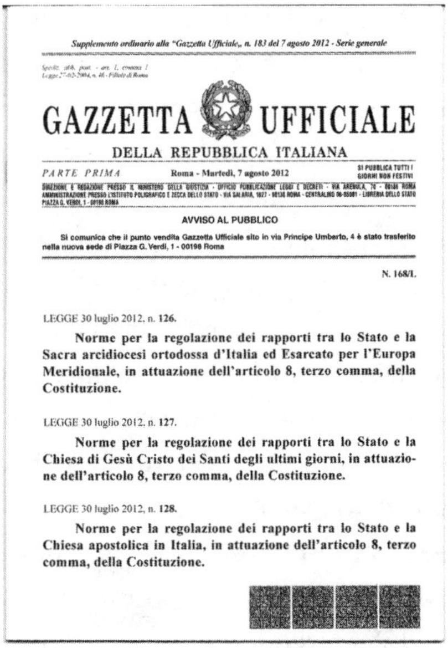
Supplemento ordinario alla "Gazzetta Ufficiale" n. 183 del 7 agosto 2012 - Serie generale

Spediz. abb. post. - art. 1, comma 1
Legge 27-02-2004, n. 46 - Filiale di Roma

GAZZETTA UFFICIALE
DELLA REPUBBLICA ITALIANA

PARTE PRIMA Roma - Martedì, 7 agosto 2012 SI PUBBLICA TUTTI I GIORNI NON FESTIVI

DIREZIONE E REDAZIONE PRESSO IL MINISTERO DELLA GIUSTIZIA - UFFICIO PUBBLICAZIONE LEGGI E DECRETI - VIA ARENULA, 70 - 00186 ROMA
AMMINISTRAZIONE PRESSO L'ISTITUTO POLIGRAFICO E ZECCA DELLO STATO - VIA SALARIA, 1027 - 00138 ROMA - CENTRALINO 06-85081 - LIBRERIA DELLO STATO PIAZZA G. VERDI, 1 - 00198 ROMA

AVVISO AL PUBBLICO

Si comunica che il punto vendita Gazzetta Ufficiale sito in via Principe Umberto, 4 è stato trasferito nella nuova sede di Piazza G. Verdi, 1 - 00198 Roma

N. 168/L

LEGGE 30 luglio 2012, n. **126.**

Norme per la regolazione dei rapporti tra lo Stato e la Sacra arcidiocesi ortodossa d'Italia ed Esarcato per l'Europa Meridionale, in attuazione dell'articolo 8, terzo comma, della Costituzione.

LEGGE 30 luglio 2012, n. **127.**

Norme per la regolazione dei rapporti tra lo Stato e la Chiesa di Gesù Cristo dei Santi degli ultimi giorni, in attuazione dell'articolo 8, terzo comma, della Costituzione.

LEGGE 30 luglio 2012, n. **128.**

Norme per la regolazione dei rapporti tra lo Stato e la Chiesa apostolica in Italia, in attuazione dell'articolo 8, terzo comma, della Costituzione.

A copy of the Gazzetta Ufficiale *(the official journal that promulgates acts of the Italian Parliament) containing the announcement of the LDS Church's Intesa with the Italian State, August 2012. (Courtesy of Giuseppe Pasta, national director of public affairs in Italy.)*

In conclusion, given the unique background of nineteenth-century Mormon-Waldensian interactions, it is both interesting and inspiring to recognize a line of continuity between the past and the present through these historical developments from which the Italian LDS Church has greatly benefited. The nature of these interactions certainly leads us to reflect upon the value of mutually respectful interfaith relations and upon the importance of going beyond self-serving motivations in order to fully embrace religious freedom. Indeed, such a context of understanding and cooperation can give proselytization a less-competitive flavor as various faith communities recognize that alternative religious messages can coexist and contribute positively to society.

Latter-day Saints have been counseled "to join with people of all faiths who feel accountable to God in defending religious freedom so it can be a beacon for morality."[39] In Italy, the Waldensians continue to be leaders in these kinds of endeavors as well as being one of Mormonism's strongest allies. When one recognizes that these Reformed Protestants were willing to respect the newly extended principle of religious liberty when the Mormon missionaries arrived in 1850, even at the cost of losing several of their own to the new religion and to the New World, this partnership acquires added significance. It functions as an instructive example of the widespread benefits that emerge from joining hands in advocating for religious freedom, and it provides an inspiring illustration of the need to go beyond conflicts or divisions in order to successfully meet the challenges of modern society.

Notes

1. James A. Toronto, Eric R. Dursteler, and Michael W. Homer, *Mormons in the Piazza: The History of the Latter-day Saints in Italy* (Provo, UT: Religious Studies Center, forthcoming), 516.
2. Toronto, Dursteler, and Homer, *Mormons in the Piazza*, 497.
3. These dates focus on the time frame of organized missionary presence as opposed to official time length of administrative units. In fact, the "first" Italian mission would not be closed until 1867, but missionaries had ceased to operate in Italy by 1865. The "second" Italian mission would open in 1966, but an

Italian zone of the Swiss Mission had been organized eighteen months earlier in 1965.

4. The preferred phonetic spelling of the founder's name is Valdès, although he has also been referred to as Vaudès, Waldo, and even Peter Waldo. See Gabriel Audisio, *Preachers by Night: The Waldensian Barbes (15th–16th Centuries)* (Leiden, Netherlands: Brill, 2011); also Giorgio Tourn, Giorgio Bouchard, Roger Geymonat, and Giorgio Spini, *You Are My Witnesses: The Waldensians across 800 Years* (Torino, Italy: Claudiana, 1989), 309. Other excellent general sources on the origins of the Waldensians and their establishment in northern Italy are Giorgio Tourn, *I Valdesi: La Singolare Vicenda di un Popolo-Chiesa* (Torino, Italy: Claudiana, 1977); Giorgio Spini, *Risorgimento e Protestanti* (Torino, Italy: Claudiana, 1998); and Augusto Armand Hugon, *Torre Pellice: Dieci Secoli di Storia e di Vicende* (Torre Pellice: Società di Studi Valdesi, 1980).
5. In English, both "Waldensians" and "Waldenses" are used, but the former term is preferred today. The Waldensians are called *Valdesi* in Italian and *Vaudois* in French. On the question of English terminology, see Tourn et al., *You Are My Witnesses*, 309.
6. See Euan Cameron, *The Reformation of the Heretics: The Waldensians of the Alps, 1480–1580* (Oxford: Clarendon Press, 1984); and Gabriel Audisio, *The Waldensian Dissent, Persecution and Survival, c. 1170–c. 1570* (Cambridge: Cambridge University Press, 1999).
7. "History," American Waldensian Society, http://www.waldensian.org/3-history/. See also Michael W. Homer, "The Waldensian Valleys: Seeking 'Primitive Christianity' in Italy," *Journal of Mormon History* 31, no. 2 (Summer 2005): 134–87.
8. For Snow's account of his activities, see Lorenzo Snow, *The Italian Mission* (London: W. Aubrey, 1851); and Eliza R. Snow Smith, *Biography and Family Record of Lorenzo Snow* (Salt Lake City: Deseret News, 1884). Concerning the Italian Mission, see Michael W. Homer, "'Like the Rose in the Wilderness': The Mormon Mission in the Kingdom of Sardinia," *Mormon Historical Studies* 1, no. 2 (Fall 2000): 25–62; Homer, "The Italian Mission, 1850–1867," *Sunstone* 7 (May/June 1982): 16–21; James A. Toronto, "'A Continual War, Not of

Arguments, but of Bread and Cheese': Opening the First LDS Mission in Italy, 1849–1867," *Journal of Mormon History* 31, no. 2 (Summer 2005): 188–232; Diane Stokoe, "The Mormon Waldensians" (master's thesis, Brigham Young University, 1985); and Flora Ferrero, "L'emigrazione valdese nello Utah nella seconda metà dell'800" (master's thesis, University of Torino, 1999).

9. Snow, *The Italian Mission*, 10–11. Numerous Protestant publications in the nineteenth century promulgated this ancient origins thesis regarding the Waldensians. See, for example, Alexis Muston, *Histoire des Vaudois des vallées du Piémont, et de leurs colonies depuis leur origine jusqu'a nos jours* (Paris: F. G. Levrault, 1834); Mrs. William Fison, *The Evangelists of Italy: Or the Mission of the Apostolic Waldensian Church* (London: Werthein & Macintosh, 1855); and J. A. Wylie, *The History of Protestantism*, 3 vols. (London: Cassell & Company). Other writers, many of whom were Catholic, sought to prove this thesis false. See, for example, André Charvaz, *Recherches Historiques sur la véritable origine dei Valdesi* (Torino: G. Bocca, 1838). For details of this historical controversy, see Homer, "The Waldensian Valleys: Seeking 'Primitive Christianity' in Italy."
10. "Faith of the Church of Christ in These Last Days, No. IV," *The Evening and the Morning Star*, June 1834, 162; *Journal of Discourses* (Liverpool: F. D. Richards, 1855–86), 5:342 (October 18, 1857); and *Journal of Discourses*, 24:352 (December 9, 1883).
11. Homer, "Like the Rose in the Wilderness"; and Toronto, "A Continual War."
12. Toronto, Dursteler, and Homer, *Mormons in the Piazza*, 99. See "Record of the Italian Mission," in Daniel B. Richards, *The Scriptural Allegory in Three Parts* (Salt Lake City: Magazine Printing Company, 1931), 301; also Italian Mission Manuscript History and Historical Reports (1849–1854), LR 4140 2, Church History Library, Salt Lake City.
13. Marie Madaline Cardon Guild, Autobiography, Family History Library, Salt Lake City, Utah, 5–7.
14. G. D. Keaton, "The Italian Mission," *Millennial Star* 16, no. 13 (April 1, 1854), 204–6.
15. Samuel Francis, "Foreign Correspondence," *Millennial Star* 17, no. 29 (July 21, 1855), 454–55.

16. "Comunicazioni con l'estero, 1836–1899," folder 1562, Archivio Storico del Comune, Torre Pellice, Italy.
17. Toronto, Dursteler, and Homer, *Mormons in the Piazza,* 152.
18. Toronto, Dursteler, and Homer, *Mormons in the Piazza,* 111; Samuel Francis journals, December 11, 1856, MS 8832, Church History Library.
19. Eric R. Dursteler, "One Hundred Years of Solitude: Mormonism in Italy, 1867–1964," *International Journal of Mormon Studies* 4 (2011): 119–48.
20. Second Vatican Council, "*Dignitatis Humanae,*" Declaration on Religious Freedom, December 7, 1965, http://www.vatican.va/archive/hist_councils/ii_vatican_council/documents/vat-ii_decl_19651207_dignitatis-humanae_en.html.
21. Regarding the early years of the second mission in Italy, see James A. Toronto, "The 'Wild West' of Missionary Work: Reopening the Italian Mission, 1965–71," *Journal of Mormon History* 40, no. 4 (Fall 2014): 1–72.
22. James A. Toronto and Richard Neitzel Holzapfel, "The LDS Church in Italy: the 1966 Rededication by Elder Ezra Taft Benson," *BYU Studies Quarterly* 51, no. 3 (2012): 83–100.
23. Leavitt Christensen, "Leavitt Christensen papers, 1960–1989," MS 13473, Church History Library. Christensen served as a counselor in the Italian Mission presidency and later as the president of the Italian Mission.
24. Toronto, Dursteler, and Homer, *Mormons in the Piazza,* 350–73.
25. Toronto, Dursteler, and Homer, *Mormons in the Piazza,* 389.
26. "Italian Ancestors," FamilySearch, https://familysearch.org/italian-ancestors/.
27. Giuseppe Pasta (director of institutional relations for the LDS Church in Italy), email to Mauro Properzi, June 26, 2014. For many years, Mormon historians have been given access to the resources of the Waldensian library and archives at the headquarters of the Waldensian Church in Torre Pellice. For the account of how LDS officials received authorization in 1947 from Virgilio Sommani—the moderator of the *Tavola Valdese* (governing committee)—to microfilm the baptismal, marriage, and death registers of Waldensian parishes in the valleys, see Archibald F. Bennett, "The Vaudois Revisited," *Improvement Era*, January 1948, 12–14, 56–58.

28. Cons. Anna Nardini (coordinator of the Office of Institutional Relations, Presidency of the Council of Ministers) interview, May 27, 2014, interviewed by Mauro Properzi and James A. Toronto.
29. Tourn et al., *You Are My Witnesses*, 305.
30. Coalizione per le Intese Religiose, "Brief History," http://www.coalizioneintese religiose.it/jsps/portal/coalizione/la_coalizione.jsp. Pasta highlights the role of Professor Domenico Maselli, Waldensian pastor and former member of the Italian Parliament, as "giving a great contribution in helping" the religious coalition reach its goals. Pasta, email, June 26, 2014.
31. Meeting report, Hon. Valdo Spini, July 25, 2007, Rome. Document in possession of the authors.
32. Dora Bognandi, "Libertà religiosa. Ora le Intese non sono più sei ma nove," Unione Italiana delle Chiese Cristiane Avventiste del Settimo Giorno (July 27, 2012), http://www.avventistimilano.org/2012/07/liberta-religiosa-ora-le-intese -non-sono-piu-sei-ma-nove/.
33. Senator Lucio Malan interview, May 28, 2014, interviewed by Mauro Properzi.
34. Malan, interview, May 28, 2014.
35. "President Monson Breaks Ground for Rome Italy Temple," October 23, 2010, http://www.mormonnewsroom.org/article/president-monson-breaks-ground -for-rome-italy-temple.
36. The analysis in this section is drawn primarily from information and observations provided by David Colton, the Church's legal counsel in Frankfurt, and Giuseppe Pasta, former national director of public affairs in Italy. Email interviews, July 27, 2012, copies in author's possession.
37. Nardini, interview, May 27, 2014.
38. The Hindu and Buddhist Intese were finally approved in February 2013. See Fabrizio Caccia, "Baggio, Guzzanti, e gli altri che hanno scelto il buddismo,'" *Corriere della Sera,* January 31, 2013, http://www.corriere.it/cronache/13_gen naio_30/baggio-guzzanti-convertiti_11c525a4-6aa7-11e2-9446-e5967f79d7 ac.shtml; "Religioni: Zaccaria (Pd), Approvate Intese con Induisti e Buddhisti, Risultato Storico," *Agenparl* (Rome, Italy), December 11, 2012, copy in author's possession. See also Massimo Introvigne, "Italy Enters into Concordates with

Buddhists and Hinduists, Who Follow Mormons, Apostolic Pentecostals, and an Orthodox Church," Center for Studies on New Religions, http://www.cesnur.org/2012/mi1807.htm; and http://www.ashramgita.com/en/.

39. Elder Quentin L. Cook, "The Restoration of Morality and Religious Freedom," Brigham Young University–Idaho commencement address, December 16, 2011, http://www.mormonnewsroom.org/article/the-restoration-of-morality-and-religious-freedom.

Fleet Street, London 1886, home of the British news and print industries.

13

Mormonism and the British Press, 1880–90

Penrose, Roberts, and Sloan Fight for Fair Treatment

Susan W. Howard

The rise in literacy rates in Britain's middle and working classes in the nineteenth century created a tremendous demand for inexpensive publications that could inform, entertain, and educate readers. Technological improvements in the printing press and the manufacture of cheap paper, along with the final repeal of the Stamp Act in 1855, "the tax on knowledge,"[1] resulted in an explosion of newspapers, periodicals, tracts, and pamphlets. The successful completion of the transatlantic cable in 1866 cut the time news took to travel from New York to London from around ten days, depending on the weather, to less than one. In order to meet the demand from new readers, London became the center of "the manufacture of words," and Fleet Street, "the street of ink,"[2] became the heart of the rapidly growing newspaper industry. The spread of the printed word and the

Susan W. Howard is an independent researcher and retired attorney in San Jose, California.

introduction of Mormonism into Europe also created a demand for information about this new religion from the United States.

The British press prided itself on being a fair and ethical institution, yet on occasion newspapers had published "willfully dishonest and grossly untrue fabrications."[3] When false or misleading information about Mormonism did appear in print, the task of writing and submitting corrections often fell on the missionaries who wrote and edited the *Millennial Star*. The subject of this paper is the work of three Salt Lake City journalists, all talented writers and orators, who lobbied for "fair play and justice" from the British press while serving missions during the latter half of the 1880s. They were Charles W. Penrose, editor in chief of the *Deseret News*; Robert W. Sloan, prize-winning essayist and editor with the *Salt Lake Herald*; and Brigham H. Roberts, an associate editor of the *Salt Lake Herald*.

Shortly after arriving in London in March 1885, Charles Penrose wrote to the *Deseret News*, "The storm that has been raging in Utah has had no effect in this part of the world. . . . It is difficult to explain the situation in Utah to an Englishman, . . . for he could not comprehend how or why people would put up with such infamous outrages."[4] By "infamous outrages" Penrose meant the actions of the U.S. marshal and his deputies, together with the conduct of federal judges, court officials, and grand juries under the Edmunds Anti-Polygamy Act of 1882. Under the new law, federal officials in Utah Territory in October 1884 successfully tried and convicted Rudger Clawson of polygamy, signaling that noncompliance with Edmunds would be punished.

In early February 1885, a Salt Lake City grand jury indicted Penrose for unlawful cohabitation after subpoenaing members of his family, including his eight-year-old son, to appear for questioning. At the time, Penrose was in Washington, DC, on a mission to promote statehood so that the citizens of Utah, rather than federal officials, would administer the laws. Rather than have him return home,

President John Taylor sent Penrose to the British Mission, where he had begun his journalism career on the staff of the *Millennial Star* during two earlier missions, (from 1851 to 1861 and 1865 to 1868). From 1870 to 1877 he was the editor of the *Ogden Junction*. He then joined the staff of the *Deseret News*, where he became editor in chief in September 1880. As editor, he exchanged critical and at times rancorous editorials with C. C. Goodwin of the *Salt Lake Tribune*, whose editorial policy was aimed at eliminating polygamy and undermining the power of the "Mormon Theocracy." Now at age fifty-three, well seasoned in journalism and politics, Penrose began his third mission in his native land.

European Mission president Daniel H. Wells appointed Penrose to be president of the London Conference. The assignment suited him: Penrose had been born and raised in London, where he converted and where his mother and three sisters still lived. He remained there for seven months before being released to return to Utah in late October.

Penrose's mission overlapped with that of the second missionary, Robert Wallace Sloan. Born in Cavan, Ireland, Sloan was a young boy when his family joined the Church. After settling in Salt Lake, his father, Edward L. Sloan, cofounded an independent newspaper, the *Salt Lake Herald*, in 1870. Rob, as Penrose called Sloan, was recognized as a brilliant young writer. He was twenty-eight and unmarried when called to his first missionary assignment, which was to assist Penrose and Utah lobbyists in New York and Washington, DC, for three months before sailing for Great Britain. He arrived in April and was assigned to the Irish Mission until his release in August 1886.

The third missionary, Brigham H. Roberts, was called to the British Mission shortly after he was arrested for unlawful cohabitation in December 1886. During a hasty meeting in the offices of the *Salt Lake Herald*, the two Apostles present made the decision to send him to Liverpool, where President Wells could use his talents with the *Millennial Star*.[5] Although he was only thirty, Roberts, a native of Warrington, Lancashire, had served two missions in the southern states and had presided over the Tennessee Conference, where he saw first-hand the tragic consequences of an irresponsible anti-Mormon press.[6] In August 1884, Roberts disguised himself as a tramp and risked his life to recover the bodies of two missionaries killed during a violent attack on a local branch in what became known as the Cane Creek Massacre.

Mormonism in Print

Within a year of the arrival of the first Mormon missionaries at Liverpool in 1837, anti-Mormon tracts appeared in areas where the elders had been preaching. Craig L. Foster's *Penny Tracts and Polemics*[7] traced the first anti-Mormon pamphlet to a Methodist minister who found his material in newspapers while living in Massachusetts. Foster analyzed the content of thousands of these documents that appeared in response to the presence of American missionaries in Great Britain in the years from 1837 to 1860.

Many British readers' first encounter with Mormonism may have been in fiction rather than newspapers or tracts. The first novel about Mormonism appeared in 1843 when British author Frederick Marryat published *Travels and Adventures of Monsieur Violet*. A new subgenre, the antipolygamy novel, appeared in the mid-1850s. Almost one hundred novels (which featured stereotypical Mormon characters and melodramatic plots), along with countless exposés[8] and magazine and newspaper stories, were published before the end of the century.[9] By the time Arthur Conan Doyle's first Sherlock Holmes detective story, *A Study in Scarlet* (which painted Mormon characters as kidnappers and murderers), arrived in London book-stores in 1887, readers had encountered the stock characters in books by British travel writers, such as Emily Faithful,[10] as well as in the theater. In the 1880s they could see a comedy, "The Exiles from Erin: or St. Abe and His Seven Wives,"[11] later performed as "The Mormons" or "The Danites," a hit so in demand that simultaneous performances took place in different London theaters in the mid-1880s.[12]

In historian Jan Shipps's analysis of the Mormon image in the American press, Shipps found that negative attitudes peaked in the nineteenth century during the years between 1881 and 1885.[13] Shipps excluded British magazines and books, and while no comparable study has been done for Great Britain, it seems likely that the trends there would echo the results of Shipps's study. J. Spencer Fluhman also excluded British materials from his history of nineteenth-century anti-Mormonism,[14] but as Craig Foster's research found, the sources for the earliest British anti-Mormon tracts came from old American newspapers. Patrick Q. Mason explored how nineteenth-century journalism was a part of a broader anti-Mormonism that contributed to a "culture of violence" against Mormons in the American South.[15] Rebecca Bartholomew's *Audacious Women: Early British Mormon Immigrants* examined how the fictional stereotypes differed from the actual lives of the British women who did convert and move to Utah.[16]

Two British authors did write honest travel accounts of Mormon life. The Honorable James W. Barclay, a British member of Parliament, described his visit to Utah in 1883 in a positive article for the *Nineteenth Century*, an important British periodical.[17] In the same year Phil Robinson, a war correspondent and reporter for the *London Telegraph*, traveled through Utah Territory and the western territories on behalf of the *New York World*. Although Robinson did not approve of polygamy, the Saints regarded his articles and his book on his experiences, *Sinners and Saints*,[18] to be fair as well as complimentary in their portrayal of Mormon Utah.[19]

Robinson complained, however, that the Mormons were "most foolishly negligent of the power of the press, and of the immense value in forming public opinion of a free use of type."[20] He also noted that they did not understand that with a "public contradiction of a public calumny," or "that by anticipating malicious versions of events,"[21] they could as often as not get an accurate statement before the public.

Yet, as one *Millennial Star* editorial put it, Mormonism was unpopular in Great Britain, and editors were "afraid to be impartial towards such an unpopular cause."[22] The critics of Mormonism often claimed that it was not so much the religion itself, but rather the practice of polygamy, that they opposed. Many regarded the practice as barbaric and "Asiatic,"[23] an institution "never meant to flourish on American soil,"[24] and in a modern age that was increasingly cognizant of the rights of women, a step backward. The missionaries defended polygamy as a commandment of God supported by biblical precedent and a pragmatic solution to certain modern ills.

Baptismal statistics show that in the fourth year after the missionaries arrived in Britain, more than two thousand converts joined the Church. During the peak years of 1849, 1850, and 1851, more than eight thousand British men and women joined the Church annually. In January 1853, after the *Millennial Star* announced the doctrine of plural marriage, the number of convert baptisms dropped dramatically, and by the 1880s the numbers were less than 10 percent of what they had been in peak years.[25] While other factors contributed to the decline, the popularity of books and news articles about polygamy and predatory Mormon missionaries sold more newspapers than did portrayals of the Saints as honest people who were victims of unjust persecution. The press had become more commercialized, and advertisers looked at circulation numbers in deciding where to place their ads.[26]

The British Press, 1885

Ongoing digitization of British newspapers has made an enormous supply of materials available to researchers.[27] In my survey of Mormon topics in the decades from 1870 to 1890, I found that many of the straight news articles on Mormons were one or two paragraphs long, usually in the back pages. Frequent news topics were notices of the departure of a Mormon emigration company, local district conference reports, and occasionally a letter to the editor from a missionary or member. During the 1870s, British readers could read about controversial topics such as Brigham Young, the "Mormon Murders," and the trials of John D. Lee. Depending on the newspaper, the reports were generally straightforward and accurate, and if they needed correction, follow-ups appeared—although these articles were not always timely.[28] Occasionally a reporter visited a Mormon branch meeting and followed up with a review, which was usually unflattering.[29] After the Supreme Court decision in *Reynolds v. United States* in 1879, however, overall reporting on Mormonism took a darker turn.

The British papers contained more reprints from the press in the eastern United States, where the antipolygamy movement—disappointed by the failure to pressure the Saints into giving up polygamy—pushed for passage of the Edmunds-Tucker Act of 1887. Once the stricter law took effect, headlines such as "The Last Struggle of Mormonism" predicted not only the end of polygamy, but also the possible demise of the Church.[30] While these articles were not written with the caustic tone that often appeared in the *New York Times*, for example, it is understandable that mission leaders believed the press was aligned against Mormonism.

Press reports of the mobbing of British missionaries marked a disturbing trend that began as early as 1881.[31] In 1883 the *Star* alerted its readers that William Jarman, former resident of Utah who called himself an "Ex-Mormon Priest," had founded the British Anti-Mormon Association with the goal of driving the Mormon missionaries out of the British Isles. Based in Exeter, Devon County, Jarman had published an exposé of Mormonism, *U.S.A.: Uncle Sam's Abscess, or Hell upon*

One version of the cover to William Jarman's 1884 exposé of Mormonism.

Earth.[32] Jarman attracted large crowds to his lectures, which often took place wherever a Mormon district conference had been announced. He drew upon the stereotypes of Mormons found in fiction and travel reports, embellishing exaggerated stories about life in Utah, including easily disproved claims that the Mormons had murdered over five hundred thousand people, including Jarman's own son. He never tired of proclaiming that the missionaries enticed British women into polygamy and lives of misery and slavery in Utah.

Sloan and Penrose both wrote for the *Millennial Star*, but during their missions they continued to write for home newspapers as well. Penrose signed his letters to the *Deseret News* with the alias "Exile." He wrote about life and politics in Great Britain and defended the Utah Saints. Sloan wrote columns on his travels and politics for the *Herald* as "Wanderer," or, according to the *Salt Lake Tribune*, "Wandering Bobbie."[33]

For the April 1885 general conference the First Presidency had prepared a letter to be read to the Saints, claiming that the federal government had violated basic rights of the Latter-day Saints (for example, the right to a fair jury trial and the right of an accused to be deemed innocent until proven guilty). Penrose initially approached the London press in May to submit copies of the letter to the major

Circulation

Utah		Great Britain	
Utah population (1884)	145,000	Great Britain Population	35,000,000
Salt Lake Population	45,000	London Population	4,500,000
Combined Editions		Weeklies	
Deseret News	9,500	Lloyd's	750,000
Salt Lake Herald	13,000	Times	200,000
Salt Lake Tribune	19,340	Reynolds' (1870)	200,000
British Mission		Dailies	
Millennial Star (1850)	18,000	London Star	200,000
		London Times	100,000
		Manchester Guardian	38,000

Comparison of population and newspaper circulation in the 1880s in Utah and Great Britain.

London dailies. On May 20 he sent copies to more than six of the leading dailies: "Times, Telegraph, Standard, Chronicle, Globe, Echo, etc."[34] The next day he sent copies to at least four weeklies—namely, "Lloyds, Reynolds', Dispatch, News of the World etc." On Friday, May 22, he sent the letter to the *Nineteenth Century*. The letter was long, taking up nearly one full page in the *Deseret News*, so in each case Penrose offered to condense it and turn it into an article. Within days he received rejections from every single paper, although the summary was eventually printed in the *Western Mail* in Wales.[35] The length of the letter alone could have been reason enough for editors to reject it.

Two weeks later Penrose again sent copies of an official protest by the Saints addressed to Congress and President Cleveland to leading London papers, again with no acceptances, although at least two articles appeared, one in a Scots newspaper and the other in Wales.[36] Missionaries did have success with letters to the editor in areas

Charles W. Penrose, editor at the Deseret News, *London Conference, October 1885. (Used by permission of the Utah State Historical Society.)*

outside metropolitan London. Penrose's first acceptance was a letter to the editor of the *Belfast Evening Telegraph* (Ireland) after an unruly crowd prevented him from speaking on the Custom House steps.[37]

In Penrose's opinion, the British press was dull. In his June letter to the *Desesret News* he wrote:

> What a dreary and leaden thing is ordinary
>
> ENGLISH JOURNALISM
>
> It lacks the spice, piquancy, snap and enterprise of American newspaperdom. Much fault is found with the Associated Press at home, but something of the kind here would put new life into the sleepy columns of the London dailies. . . . There is more "meat" in the Deseret News in a week, than in an English paper for six months.[38]

In July, London's *Pall Mall Gazette* remedied the lack of "spice" in a demonstration of "the New Journalism" in Britain.[39] Beginning July 6, the *Gazette* published a series titled "The Maiden Tribute of Modern Babylon,"[40] based on several months of investigative research into practices that resulted in the sexual exploitation of innocent girls and young women. Before publishing the articles, *Gazette* editor William T. Stead assembled a secret commission to assist Stead's reporters in finding solid evidence to prove the newspaper's allegations. He was motivated by the failure of Parliament to pass a law changing the age of consent for women from thirteen to fifteen after the bill had passed the House of Lords three times.[41] The series sparked controversies in the press that continued for months in Britain and in the United States. Inevitably, comparisons between corrupt Englishmen and Mormon elders were made.[42]

Nevertheless, the "Maiden Tribute" series may have opened the door for Penrose to gain access to the London press in a roundabout way. In mid-August, after a crowd stirred up by Jarman confronted Wells, Penrose, and other leaders at a district conference in Sheffield, it became necessary for the police to escort them to safety through what Penrose described as a "howling crowd."[43] Although as recorded

MORMONS MOBBED

Elders in London are Attacked by Infuriated Rioters.

A RICH MAN'S MURDER.

Sullivan Preparing for Another Pugilistic Encounter—General News.

By Western Ass'd Press to the Herald.

Cholera Record.

Toulon, Aug. 27.—Seventeen persons died here yesterday from cholera.

Marseilles, Aug. 27.—Eleven deaths from cholera were reported here yesterday

ANTI-MORMON RIOT.

Missionaries Slandered and Terribly Abused by a Mob.

New York, Aug. 26.—*Sun's* London: For some time past several Mormon missionaries have been laboring with great energy in the East End of London, and have succeeded in making many converts and proselytes, in spite of persistant opposition. There have recently been reports that these missionaries have been systematically kidnapping young women and shipping them to Utah to be "sealed" to rich Mormons. All sorts of stories have been told about the harems kept by wealthy Mormons, and the indignities inflicted upon girls who were entrapped into becoming their concubines. These reports have greatly exasperated the East Enders and to night an infuriated mob invaded and took possession of the hall in which the missionaries were speaking. The invaders stormed the platform, smashed most of the furniture in the hall, and made a wreck of everything on the platform. Seven elders who had been conducting the services fled for their lives. The rioters chased them through the streets, pelting them with mud and every missile that could be picked up. Several of the elders were captured and terribly abused by the mob. Their clothing was torn to shreds, and they were beaten until they were unconscious and almost lifeless. The rioters, evidently believing them dead, fled and left the Mormons lying naked and bleeding on the pavement, where they were afterward found by the police.

This page one article appeared in papers throughout Great Britain and the United States. The story was not true.

in Penrose's diary the incident did have comical aspects, the threat of violence was genuine.

Ten days later a news item headlined "A Mormon Riot at the East End of London" appeared in several London newspapers on August 26 and again the following day. The story was reprinted in the weeklies, in local presses, and in newspapers in the United States and in Utah, but not the *Deseret News*.[44] According to the report, on Tuesday evening, August 25, a mob attacked and beat Mormon missionaries after becoming enraged by reports that the elders were "systematically kidnapping young women and shipping them to Utah to be 'sealed' to rich Mormons,"[45] thus evoking the July series in the *Pall Mall Gazette*. On August 29 the *Salt Lake Tribune* noted that Jarman had sent a letter to the editor indicating that he "mean[t] business and that the mobbing may have been due to his work."[46] The letter was dated August 16, the day of the Sheffield disturbance. Following an investigation, the *Millennial Star* denied the attack story. The *London Evening Standard* rejected a letter from Penrose, who then published it in the *Millennial Star*. Penrose asserted, "I am in a position to state, positively, that no attack whatever has been made upon the 'Mormon' missionaries in London during the present year."[47] He himself had been in London that evening in the area near Mile End Road where the incident supposedly took place.[48]

Penrose objected to two items in the London *Daily Chronicle*: a September 1 editorial followed by a September 3 letter to the editor, both stating that while there were Irish people in Utah, none of them had ever joined the Mormon Church. The *Chronicle* agreed to publish Penrose's rebuttal, "Irish in Salt Lake City," signed "A Londoner from Utah."[49] Penrose complimented the *Chronicle*, noting that it "gave place to the 'other side'" and that "it is so seldom that the 'Mormon' side of any question relating to Utah is permitted to occupy the columns of English newspapers, in spite of their boasts about freedom of speech and British fairness."[50] The *Evening*

Standard, however, ignored Penrose's offer of a response to an untruthful article.[51]

Although the *Pall Mall Gazette* had published the report of the East End attack, W. T. Stead decided to send a reporter to interview Penrose on September 9.[52] With unintentional irony, the *Gazette*'s account of the interview began, "So little is known about Mormonism, and so much curiosity has recently been shown respecting that sect, that we decided to take advantage of the conference which the Latter Day Saints are at present holding in London in order to gather a few actual facts from one of themselves."[53] Penrose's opinion of the interview which was published September 15, was that it was "garbled but not hostile."[54] He must have been pleased with the reporter's description as "an Interview with Mr. C. W. Penrose, the intelligent and talented president of the conference."[55] This was Penrose's last opportunity to influence the British press. Penrose was called back to Utah in October.

Overall, rejections had outnumbered acceptances. Penrose summarized his nearly seven months of struggle with the London press in his September 28 editorial: "The metropolitan press fights shy of anything that would indicate the slightest favor to the Latter-day Saints, and communications containing facts or rectifying errors about Utah or 'The Mormons' are usually drowned in the cold depths of utter silence."[56]

"The Battle Cry," 1886

Robert Sloan was released from his mission the following year, in August 1886. President Wells asked him to remain a few weeks longer to organize a series of meetings in London intended to bring to the attention of the metropolitan press the Mormons' claims that the U.S. government was unjustly persecuting them. Sloan approached Phil Robinson, who agreed to host and act as chair for the program. Robinson scheduled St. George's Hall for the first event, held Tuesday evening, October 12. According to the *Salt Lake Herald*, St. George's, a theater located on Langham Place, Regent Street, in London's West End, was "one of the finest and most aristocratic halls in London."[57] Ten thousand handbills were printed and distributed, and larger bills were "placed on boards and carried through Fleet Street, Strand, Regent Street and many of the principal thoroughfares by twenty men, all in a row, commonly knows as 'Sandwichmen,' and of which the streets are never free." The bills were titled "A Bitter Cry from the Persecuted Mormons of Utah" and "For Fair Play and Justice." The organizers chose the location, three-quarters of a mile from Fleet Street, in order to attract newspapermen and a class of nearby residents who otherwise would have little contact with the missionaries.

Nineteenth-century sandwichmen strolled the Strand to advertise events and products.

On Tuesday evening attendance was sparse, in part perhaps due to the rain. A reporter for the *Salt Lake Tribune* counted sixty-three in the audience, while the correspondent for the *Herald* estimated one hundred in a hall that held more than five hundred. In introducing the speakers, Robinson proclaimed his objectivity and monogamous status as well as his admiration for the Mormons.[58] The crowd was antagonistic, and heckling grew more intense when Rob Sloan began to speak in defense of polygamy, yet his wit and sincerity won over several of the reporters.

Robert W. Sloan, compiler of Utah Gazetteer, *1884. (Used by permission of the Utah State Historical Society.)*

Sloan later wrote that the evening was a financial failure and that Robinson, who had backed it, was out twenty pounds.[59] According to his survey, the meeting was noticed in five of the morning dailies and an equal number of evening papers—and only one of them was "extremely fair." With this exception, the reviews of the evening were almost universally negative. The *Salt Lake Tribune* printed a letter from its correspondent in London, Mr. E. Hamilton, who said that Elder Sloan was the "only really sincere Mormon he had ever seen. He is a smart young fellow and pleased the audience hugely."[60] A second *Tribune* article printed negative reviews quoted from several London papers: the *Globe*, *Standard*, and *Telegraph*,[61] where the reporter pointed out that the elders "left practically untouched the question of persecution."[62] The *Herald* story submitted by "Varah" quoted the *Echo*, the *London Daily Times*, the *Telegraph*, and the *Daily Chronicle*.[63] Varah wrote that until the meeting it had been nearly impossible for the Mormons to preach to the wealth and the aristocracy of London, but now, despite contempt, the newspapers provided the means for readers to conclude that the Mormons had been wronged.

According to George Osmond, an assistant editor of the *Star* who was tireless in denouncing misleading press reports, the account in the *Chronicle* was "tolerably fair,"[64] and the uniformity of the newspaper reports seemed to indicate "an almost common origin." Osmond noted that the *London Daily Telegraph*, "one of the greatest newspapers in the world," deemed Mormonism sufficiently important to publish three articles on it. Yet, when asked for space in the paper to deny the most reckless charges, the *Telegraph* invariably denied requests.[65]

No further meetings were held. Sloan returned to Utah in October 1886, but within weeks he was sent back to the East to lobby on behalf of the Church.[66]

The Debate Challenges, 1887–1888

B. H. Roberts arrived in Liverpool in March 1887. Throughout 1886 and 1887, Jarman and his anti-Mormon colleagues con tinued to confront the missionaries. Jarman issued repeated challenges to meet in a public debate on the doctrines and practices of the Utah church.[67] At the request of local missionaries, Roberts accepted the challenge, but he insisted on a neutral chairman to preside and a set of rules to be followed.[68] The debates, which drew crowds in the thousands, took place in Yorkshire, London, and Sussex, with a final confrontation in

Brigham H. Roberts, editor at the Salt Lake Herald. *(Used by permission of the Utah State Historical Society.)*

Swansea, Wales, in July 1888. At the final debate, three thousand noisy, antagonistic listeners made it difficult for Roberts to be heard. The crowd voted that Jarman had proven his charges against the Church. Although Roberts lost the vote, his performance resulted in his letters appearing in the *Barnsley Independent* and the *Cambrian Daily Leader*.[69] The *Herald* of Wales sent a reporter to interview him, allowing Roberts to counteract and offer proof against Jarman's falsehoods.[70] Brief articles on the debates appeared in newspapers as far away as Manchester.[71] Moreover, several witnesses to the lectures by Jarman and his society members expressed their disgust with his behavior in letters to the local papers.[72]

Jarman's campaigns against the Mormons brought negative attention to his activities and turned public opinion against him. Readers had a chance to see another side of the anti-Mormon in news reports of a criminal case brought against him in the Swansea Police Court on a charge of inciting violence against a Mormon, and later a lawsuit by two of his deputies who claimed he had defrauded them.[73] The *Deseret News* later reported that after years of "apathetic indifference," there had been a remarkable revival of interest in Mormonism in Wales.[74] A number of newspapers opened their columns to favorable reports on the subject of Mormonism. The *Pall Mall Gazette* published a brief piece commending the Swansea court for not tolerating interference with liberty of speech.[75]

While carrying out his editorial duties at the *Millennial Star*, Roberts began the work of research and writing that would occupy much of his later career. The materials for his debate preparations became the basis for pamphlets published for the use of missionaries. The mission office printed and sold thousands of copies to be distributed in advance of Jarman's lectures. With the encouragement of the mission president, he researched and published his first book, *The Gospel: Man's Relationship to Deity* (1888).[76] Shortly after he returned home, Roberts was called to the First Council of the Seventy. During the antipolygamy prosecution, he decided to surrender to the federal prosecutor and plead guilty, then served a four-month prison sentence for unlawful cohabitation.

The three missionaries returned home at a time of crucial importance for the Church and Utah. Penrose and Sloan soon became involved in lobbying efforts in Washington and New York against the Edmunds-Tucker Bill as well as the 1887 attempt to win statehood for Utah. Penrose also took on the challenge of trying to place more positive articles about the Church into the eastern press.[77] With one hiatus in the 1890s when the *Deseret News* was privately owned, Penrose served as editor in chief until 1906 when he became president of the European Mission, returning to his native land as a member of the Quorum of Twelve. Roberts continued writing and speaking and served as assistant Church historian, army chaplain, and mission president. In 1889 Robert Sloan bought an interest in the *Logan Journal* and became its editor. The People's Party, which was organized in Utah Territory 1870 to counter non-Mormon influence, was disbanded in 1891, leaving members free to join either national party. Penrose, Sloan, and Roberts joined the Democratic Party and became active in party politics and political controversies.

In the decades following the Manifesto, anti-Mormonism did not disappear from the press. Another era of violent anti-Mormonism arose in Britain in the early twentieth century.[78] The threatening figure of the predatory Mormon missionary continued to haunt the pages of newspapers, fiction, and eventually, silent movies. Mormonism, however, had gained a powerful defender. When stories about elders luring English girls into polygamy surfaced once again prior to World War I, editor W. T. Stead of the *Pall Mall Gazette* took the press to task. He wrote to the London *Daily Press* demanding that unscrupulous journalists provide proof of salacious stories about Mormonism before publishing such in the British newspapers. He publicly urged opponents of Mormonism to remember "the principle of religious toleration."[79]

Conclusion

Charles W. Penrose, Robert W. Sloan, and Brigham H. Roberts did not succeed overall in achieving a change in the public image of Mormonism in Great Britain during the 1880s. It is important to remember that their primary duties lay in missionary work and assisting the members. They were among the better-known Mormon journalists who took on Phil Robinson's challenge to answer the calumnies against their adopted religion, yet there were many others—not professional journalists—who took up the challenge as well, and whose experiences remain to be told. Most histories of Mormonism during this critical decade understandably have focused on the struggle between church and state on the North American continent. Systematic studies of Mormonism and local presses throughout the world will be a great resource for future Mormon studies.

Notes

1. Mark Hampton, *Visions of the Press in Britain, 1850–1950* (Urbana: University of Illinois Press, 2004), 31–33.
2. Jerry White, *London in the Nineteenth Century: A Human Awful Wonder of God* (London: Vintage Books, 2007), 226, 230.
3. Richard L. Evans, *A Century of "Mormonism" in Great Britain* (Salt Lake City: Publisher's Press, 1984), 202.
4. Exile, "A Voice from Abroad," *Deseret News*, May 1, 1885.
5. Gary James Bergera, ed., *The Autobiography of B. H. Roberts* (Salt Lake City: Signature Books, 1990), 163–64.
6. Patrick Q. Mason, *The Mormon Menace: Violence and Anti-Mormonism in the Postbellum South* (New York: Oxford University Press, 2011), 40–41, 52–53. See also J. Spencer Fluhman, *"A Peculiar People": Anti-Mormonism and the Making of Religion in Nineteenth-Century America* (Chapel Hill: University of North Carolina Press, 2012).

7. Craig L. Foster, *Penny Tracts and Polemics: A Critical Analysis of Anti-Mormon Pamphleteering in Great Britain, 1837–1860* (Salt Lake City: Greg Kofford Books, 2002), 51–52.
8. A reviewer for a British illustrated weekly called Fanny Stenhouse's 1880 book, *An Englishwoman in Utah*, "more sensational than the wildest novel." "The Reader," the *Graphic* (London), April 24, 1880. Permission for quotations from British newspapers has been granted by the source, the British Newspaper Archive, http://www.britishnewspaperarchive.co.uk/
9. Leonard J. Arrington and Jon Haupt, "Intolerable Zion: The Image of Mormonism in Nineteenth Century Literature," *Western Humanities Review* 22, no. 3 (Summer 1968): 243–60; Leonard J. Arrington and Rebecca Foster Cornwall, "Perpetuation of a Myth: Mormon Danites in Five Western Novels, 1840–90," *BYU Studies* 23, no. 2 (Spring 1983): 149. Terryl L. Givens updated and deepened the understanding of how these stereotypes affected American readers' perceptions of Mormonism. See Terryl L. Givens, *The Viper on the Hearth: Mormons, Myths, and the Construction of Heresy* (New York: Oxford University Press, 1997, 2013).
10. Karen M. Morin and Jeanne K. Guelke, "Strategies of Representation, Relationship, and Resistance, British Women Travelers and Mormon Plural Wives, ca. 1879–1890," *Annals of the Association of American Geographers* 88, no. 3 (September 1998): 436–62, 449.
11. Described as "illustrations of the social inconveniences of polygamy," "The London Theaters," the *Era* (London), May 14, 1881; a page one review, "Last Night's Theatricals," *Lloyd's Weekly*, May 1, 1881.
12. Leonard J. Arrington, "Mormonism: Views from Without and Within," *BYU Studies* 14, no. 2 (Winter 1974): 144.
13. Jan Shipps, "From Satyr to Saint: American Perception of the Mormons, 1860–1960," in *Sojourner in the Promised Land: Forty Years among the Mormons* (Urbana: University of Illinois Press, 2000), 58, 64.
14. Fluhman, *"A Peculiar People,"* 19.
15. Mason, *Mormon Menace*, 29–32, 164–65.

16. Rebecca Bartholomew, *Audacious Women: Early British Mormon Immigrants* (Salt Lake City: Signature Books, 1995), 1–24.
17. James W. Barclay, "A New View of Mormonism," *Nineteenth Century* 15, no. 83, (January 1884): 167–84.
18. Phil Robinson, *Sinners and Saints: A Tour Across the States, and Round Them; with Three Months among the Mormons* (1883; repr., Ulan Press, 2013).
19. "A Distinguished Journalist," *Salt Lake Tribune*, February 28, 1883. The *Tribune* accused Robinson of being in the pay of the Mormons, but he had in fact written the articles for the *World*.
20. Robinson, *Sinners and Saints*, 245.
21. Robinson, *Sinners and Saints*, 246; Arrington, "Mormonism: Views from Without and Within," 140–41. Leonard Arrington later confirmed Robinson's observations. He wrote that after they settled in Utah, "the Saints were not aggressive and resourceful in their own image creations" until the 1930s.
22. G. O., "The London Meeting," *Millennial Star*, October 25, 1886, 680–83. See also "Popular Governments and Unpopular Religions," *Pall Mall Gazette*, May 15, 1880.
23. "Asiatic" and "Oriental" were derogatory terms sometimes used along with "harem" to describe Mormon plural marriage.
24. Christine Talbot, *A Foreign Kingdom: Mormons and Polygamy in American Political Culture, 1852–1890* (Urbana: University of Illinois Press, 2013), 133.
25. Evans, *Century of "Mormonism,"* 244. See also Richard L. Jensen and Malcolm R. Thorp, eds., *Mormons in Early Victorian Britain* (Salt Lake City: University of Utah Press, 1989), 25–26.
26. Hampton, *Visions of the Press in Britain*, 164–65.
27. British Newspaper Archive, Findmypast Newspaper Archive Limited, http://www.britishnewspaperarchive.co.uk/
28. The first correction to the erroneous report appeared in the *Millennial Star* days, if not weeks, in advance of general press reports: S. S. Jones, "President Young's Resignation," *Millennial Star*, April 22, 1873, 248–49, supplement to the *Nottinghamshire Guardian*, May 2, 1873 (reprint of Brigham Young's letter

to *New York Herald*); "Resignation of Brigham Young," *Royal Cornwall Gazette*, May 10, 1882.

29. "The Mormons in London," the *Standard* (London), January 27, 1872 (reporter attended a Sunday meeting at Barnsbury Road); "A Sunday with the Mormons," *Pall Mall Gazette*, March 7, 1882 (reporter attended meeting at Pentonville Branch, London).
30. "The Last Struggle of Mormonism," *York Herald*, April 3, 1886; "Decay of Mormonism," *Birmingham Daily Post*, August 4, 1887; "Disestablishment in Deseret," *Shields Daily Gazette* (Tyne and Wear, Northeast England), August 22, 1887.
31. "The Mormons in London," *Portsmouth Evening News*, December 31, 1881; "Mormons in London," *Morning Post*, January 28, 1882.
32. William Jarman, *U.S.A.: Uncle Sam's Abscess, or Hell upon Earth for U. S. Uncle Sam* (Exeter, England: H. Leduc's Steam Printing Works, 1884).
33. "Wandering Bobbie," *Salt Lake Tribune*, September 2, 1885, 4.
34. Charles W. Penrose, diary, May 20, 1885, Utah State Historical Society, Salt Lake City; transcript in possession of the author.
35. Penrose, diary, May 27, 1885. See also "Mormonism on Its Trial: A Remarkable Presidential Address," *Western Mail* (Cardiff, Wales), June 2, 1885.
36. "The Latter-day Saints and Their Grievances," *Glasgow Herald*, June 8, 1885; "Mormons and the United States Government: Declaration of Grievances and Protest," *Western Mail*, June 16, 1885. See also Charles W. Penrose, "How to Roll On the Work," *Millennial Star*, June 15, 1885, 376–78.
37. Charles W. Penrose, "Mormonism in Belfast," *Millennial Star*, August 10, 1885, 497–98; reprinted from *Belfast Evening Telegraph*, July 21, 1885. Penrose was prevented from preaching as had been advertised. Robert W. Sloan's account of the meeting is found in "On the Ould Sod," *Salt Lake Herald*, August 16, 1885.
38. Exile, "Exile's Letter: Affairs Political, Religious, and Otherwise, in Europe, and Reflections on Doings in Utah," *Deseret News*, July 8, 1885, 398. Robert Sloan agreed: "There is more news, a greater variety of style, better taste, and infinitely more profitable reading in an average, or even ordinary American daily in a city the size of Salt Lake than there is in two-thirds the English, or British papers

combined." Wanderer, "Home News: Dublin Items. The Prince of Wales Blown to Atoms," *Salt Lake Herald,* May 3, 1885, 6.

39. Hampton, *Visions of the Press in Britain*, 36–39, 76.
40. W. T. Stead, "The Maiden Tribute of Modern Babylon," *Pall Mall Gazette* (London), July 6–10, 1885. See full series at http://www.attackingthedevil.co.uk/pmg/tribute/mt1.php
41. The Criminal Law Amendment Act passed August 14, 1885. The act raised the age of consent to sixteen and criminalized additional acts of sexual exploitation reported by the *Gazette.*
42. "The Mormon Threat," *Salt Lake Tribune,* July 29, 1885, 4, quoting *New York Commercial Advertiser.*
43. Penrose, diary, August 16, 1885. Penrose wrote that no one was hurt.
44. "Special Telegrams: Seven Mormon Elders Whipped in London: Anti Mormon Riots in London," *Salt Lake Tribune*, August 27, 1885, 1. Versions also were published in the following: *Pall Mall Gazette*, August 26; *Daily London*, August 26; *London Sun*, August 26; *Birmingham Daily Post*, August 27; *Liverpool Mercury*, August 27; *Belfast News-Letter*, August 29; *Lloyd's Weekly* (London), August 30; *Reynolds's* (London), August 30.
45. "Special Telegrams," *Salt Lake Tribune*, 1.
46. "Elder Jarman: He is Showing Up the Monkey Game in England," *Salt Lake Tribune*, August 29, 1885, 4.
47. Charles Penrose, "'Mormonism' and the Press," *Millennial Star*, September 28, 1885.
48. Penrose, diary, August 25, 1885; Penrose, "'Mormonism' and the Press," 616; "Explanation," *Millennial Star*, September 7, 1885, 570. The news reports placed the attack at the location of the Whitechapel Branch meetings, Orson's Hall (Orson's Academy).
49. Penrose, diary, September 5, 1887.
50. Penrose, "'Mormonism' and the Press," 616.
51. Penrose, diary, September 11, 1885; "'Mormonism' and the Press," 616.
52. Penrose, diary, September 9, 1885.
53. "Among the Mormons," *Pall Mall Gazette*, September 15, 1885.

54. Penrose, diary, September 17, 1885.
55. The *New York Times* published a negative comment on Penrose in "The Defiant Polygamists," *New York Times*, September 28, 1885.
56. Penrose, "'Mormonism' and the Press," 616.
57. Varah, "Mormonism in Style," *Salt Lake Herald*, October 31, 1886, 12. (He was probably British missionary John Varah Long.)
58. Earlier that day, the *Pall Mall Gazette* published an article by Phil Robinson, "The Mormons in Trouble." "Phil Robinson and the 'Mormons,'" *Millennial Star*, December 13, 1886.
59. Constance L. Lieber and John Sillito, eds., *Letters from Exile: The Correspondence of Martha Hughes Cannon and Angus M. Cannon, 1886–1888* (Salt Lake City: Signature Books, 1989), 67–70, http://signaturebookslibrary.org/?p=7017. Sloan asked Dr. Martha Hughes Cannon, a plural wife of Angus M. Cannon, to speak at the meeting. Despite his persuasive plea, she refused for fear that news of her presence in London would jeopardize her husband's freedom. Twenty pounds in 1886 was equivalent to ninety-seven dollars then, approximately worth $2,450 purchasing power in today's dollars.
60. "Mormons in London," *Salt Lake Tribune*, October 31, 1886, 6.
61. "The St. George's Hall Meeting," *Salt Lake Tribune*, November 2, 1886, 2.
62. Varah, "Mormonism in Style," 12.
63. Varah, "Mormonism in Style," 12.
64. George Osmond, "The London Meeting," *Millennial Star*, October 25, 1886, 680.
65. George Osmond, "The London Telegraph on 'Mormonism,'" *Millennial Star*, November 1, 1886, 698–70.
66. "Jottings," *Salt Lake Tribune*, December 7, 1886, 3.
67. "Mormonism on the Stump in Swansea," *Millennial Star*, September 19, 1887, 604–7.
68. Bergera, *Autobiography of B.H. Roberts*, 165–73.
69. "Correspondence," *Millennial Star*, November 21, 1887, 748–50; "The Mormon Controversy: Jarman Challenged," *Millennial Star*, November 21, 1887, 750;

B. H. Roberts, "A Lover of Fair Play," *Millennial Star*, November 28, 1887, 760–63; "The Notorious Jarman," *Deseret News*, December 21, 1887, 768; "Discussion on Mormonism at Swansea," *Millennial Star*, July 16, 1888, 461; B. H. Roberts, "Elder Roberts' Letter to the *Leader*," *Millennial Star*, July 23, 1888, 475–76; John Hays, "Old Country Correspondence," *Deseret News*, August 15, 1888, 493.

70. "Interviewing Elder Roberts, The Mormon," *Millennial Star*, July 30, 1888, 484–87, published July 14 in *Herald of Wales*.
71. "The Mormons in Wales: An Extraordinary Scene," *Manchester Courier and Lancashire General Advertiser*, September 24, 1887.
72. Exile, "Anti-Mormonism in Bristol," *Deseret News*, November 11, 1885, 686. An Englishman, John H. White, citing "British Fair Play" met Jarman's debate challenge armed with police and reports on Jarman's divorces from his two wives in Utah. Jarman turned the meeting against him. Swayne's Eye, "Mr. Jarman and the Mormons," *Millennial Star*, October 15, 1888, 660.
73. *Western Mail* (Cardiff, Wales), September 18, 1888, quoted in "Jarman's Trial," *Deseret News*, October 24, 1888, 645.
74. "In Wales: A Remarkable Revival of Interest in 'Mormonism,'" *Deseret News*, December 12, 1888, 756. See also D. M. McAllister, "The Anti-'Mormon' Show," *Deseret News*, September 14, 1889, reprint from *Eccles Advertiser* (Manchester), July 27.
75. "Occasional Notes," *Pall Mall Gazette*, September 18, 1888. "In the good time coming even policemen will not be allowed to break the heads of the preachers of unpopular doctrines, and even now that is a luxury which no constables are allowed outside London."
76. Truman G. Madsen, *Defender of the Faith: The B. H. Roberts Story* (Salt Lake City: Deseret Book, 1980), 441. Roberts wrote over thirty books, three hundred articles, and over a thousand sermons and discourses.
77. Edward Leo Lyman, *Political Deliverance: The Mormon Quest for Utah Statehood* (Urbana: University of Illinois Press, 1986), 43–48, 76.
78. Malcolm R. Thorp, "'The Mormon Peril': The Crusade Against the Saints in Britain, 1910–1914," *Journal of Mormon History* 2 (1975); Malcolm R. Thorp,

"Winifred Graham and the Mormon Image in England," *Journal of Mormon History* 6 (1979).

79. Peter J. Vousden, "The English Editor and the 'Mormon Scare' of 1911," *BYU Studies* 41, no. 1 (2002): 70.

14

The Church's Cultural Challenges in Europe

Gerald Hansen Jr., Hans Noot, and Medlir Mema

From its small beginnings in the early nineteenth century, The Church of Jesus Christ of Latter-day Saints has been a proselyting church, aiming to expand worldwide. Indeed, the Church has developed into a generally accepted organization in the United States and in other countries as well. This rapid growth has given us cause to stop and reflect on the challenges that the Church faces or is likely to face in the future. In this chapter, we will focus on the interaction between the doctrines and practices of the LDS Church and Europeans and attempt to explore some of the challenges the Church runs into as it tries to fulfill its mission in an increasingly secular Western Europe as well as in parts of Eastern Europe where countries are still coming to terms with their communist past.

Gerald Hansen Jr. is a faculty member in the Political Science Department at Brigham Young University–Idaho. Hans Noot is assistant associate area director for the Church Educational System in Eastern Europe, the Balkans, and Italy. Medlir Mema (PhD, George Washington University) is director of research at the Institute of Leadership in Tirana, Albania.

Working Out Our Salvation

One of the perennial debates in Mormonism, and indeed in Christianity, has been that of *praxis* vs. *doxis*, or practice versus doctrine. Although our understanding of doctrinal truth and access to it varies, its essential nature is unchanging. But working out how those truths are reflected in our everyday life takes time and often turns into a trial-and-error process. Sometimes error can be the result of incomplete understanding. However, more often than not, errors can be attributed to the environment in which these doctrinal truths are disseminated or from where they become disseminated. Cultural backgrounds, linguistic differences, and socioeconomic differences can then become important aspects of the acting out of one's doctrinal teachings and beliefs.[1] Swidler argues that "culture influences action not by providing the ultimate values toward which action is oriented, but by shaping a repertoire or 'tool kit' of habits, skills, and styles from which people construct 'strategies of actions.'"[2] Related to the impact that one's culture has on that person's understanding and practice of received knowledge is what Federici refers to as one's own "intertextual literary, linguistic and cultural 'baggage' due to [one's] 'location' and identity politics."[3] Meanwhile, the interaction between one's socioeconomic status and religious practices has been demonstrated through numerous studies, most of them following the publication of Weber's *The Protestant Ethic and the Spirit of Capitalism* in 1905.

Distinguishing between Doctrines, Practices, and Local Customs and Culture

For the purposes of this paper, when we use the term "gospel," we mean the doctrines and commandments, as taught by the prophets and the scriptures. When we speak of LDS practices, we mean a set of procedures that the Church and the Saints have accrued throughout their history and that have been accepted generally by the Church at large, as they are taught by Church leaders. Examples of such practices include dress and grooming standards, prayer observances such as folding our arms and closing our eyes, the nonuse of crucifixes, the absence of facial hair for men serving in senior leadership positions, a lack of visible tattoos for missionaries, and the wearing of a white shirt and a tie when passing the sacrament.[4] By local customs and cultures, we mean those accretions which have little to do with the gospel and yet, at times, are as pervasive and risk becoming as distinctively "Mormon" as the previous two categories.[5] Of particular importance and consequence here is the association with and the attempt to justify and propagate one's ideological, cultural,[6] political, or socioeconomic views and preferences in the context of doctrinal truths. If we are to truly become an international church while keeping the doctrine pure from local practices and cultures, it is important that we distinguish between doctrinal truth or the gospel, Church practices, and local customs and cultures. It is with this distinction and understanding in mind that we offer the following observations.

The Early New Testament Church and the Modern Challenge

The challenge of disentangling the gospel teachings and inspired practices from local practices, cultures, and traditions is not new. Instructively, the Apostle Paul's fight against the Judaizers illustrates this well. After Christ's death, as the first-century Christian Church attempted to leave the law of Moses behind and expand past its Jewish culture into the Gentile world, it struggled to escape its more recent past. Even after a powerful revelation to Peter, the chief Apostle (see Acts 10), and an official declaration by the Church (see Acts 15) stating that new members did not have to first accept the Mosaic law before becoming Christians, these Judaizers continued to push their

Jewish culture onto the Church, making it more difficult to fulfill its missionary assignment to the non-Jewish world.[7]

In addition, the government of the Roman Empire, while offering the advantages of security and order to Christian missionaries, nonetheless adjudicated disputes involving the young Church in seriously disadvantageous ways, including the execution of its founder and many of its leaders, partly because the empire conflated the Christian Church with its Jewish roots and questioned the New Testament Church's political loyalty.[8] The modern Church still faces the same double-edged dilemma: it must take a pure gospel to the rest of the world—untainted by the cultural accoutrements which always collect around organizations—and it must also adhere to its own doctrines and practices without appearing disloyal and subversive to the world's governments and their citizens.

The Church's greatest modern challenge in this regard occurred towards the end of the nineteenth century and the beginning of the twentieth century as it dealt with unrelenting pressure from the American government and society to conform to the dominant moral and cultural standards which existed in the United States at the time.[9] How the Church reacted to this challenge provides a good example of how the earthly Church of God, not yet part of the millennial kingdom of God, must accommodate itself to the various governments within which it must coexist, as well as explaining why the Church currently grapples with its American roots.

A Roman denarius, with the image of Tiberius Caesar on the front. He was the Roman emperor during the period of the Savior's ministry. It was his image that would likely have appeared on the coin that Jesus showed to the Herodians and said, "Render therefore to Caesar the things that are Caesar's, and to God the things that are God's" (Matthew 22:21).

After being chased out of Illinois in 1847, the

Latter-day Saints settled in what was then part of Mexico, though within a year's time the United States had defeated Mexico in war and acquired the territory where the Church had settled. Mostly isolated from the greater United States, the Church over the next two decades developed a culture atypical of the American norm—one that was economically cooperative, politically oriented to God's kingdom, and socially unacceptable to most Americans because it accepted the validity of both monogamist and polygamist marriages.[10] After the American Civil War ended, as the nation's attention turned to other issues, the construction of the cross-continent railroad helped end Utah's isolation. The American government then began to insist that the Latter-day Saints adopt "American" values, meaning specifically that they become steadfast capitalists, patriotic and loyal members of the American republic, and strict monogamists.[11]

Map of Mexico in 1847 showing that the Utah Territory was not in the United States at the time that the Latter-day Saints first arrived there.

President Wilford Woodruff, 1894.

This insistence by the U.S. government moved the Church's leadership to petition the Lord for guidance. Their choice was, as President Wilford Woodruff put it, to choose between keeping the original commandment regarding plural marriage and thus maintaining the political, economic, and social culture that it had developed over its first few decades (and by so doing suffer persistent legal harassment and possible dissolution at the hands of the U.S. government), or adapt the kingdom of God to the traditions and laws of the American republic so that the Church could fulfill its primary mission of preaching to and administering the ordinances to the living and the dead.[12] Faced with this terrible choice, those who held the keys of the priesthood, the First Presidency and Quorum of the Twelve Apostles, wisely chose to seek new revelation which resulted in a change to the commandment as well as the cultural practices surrounding it.

Over time, the Latter-day Saints, following suit, adopted American patriotism, capitalism, and monogamy with great enthusiasm.[13] Reflecting on the difficulties of this transformation of the Mormon economic and social life following this turbulent period and the length of time it took to do so, one commentator questions Bloom's[14] assessment of Mormonism as a quintessentially American religion, at least initially, since Mormonism did not acquire many of its practices identifiable with the larger American culture until the twentieth century, once "the economic and political behavior of Mormons ha[d] mirrored that of 'middle America,'" leading to diminished tensions and partial assimilation.[15] Reflecting the indomitable spirit of the Church members and the indispensability of divine guidance, this adoption served the Church well, allowing it to emerge out of obscurity and to obtain a level of respectability that helped it use its base in the United States to take the gospel to the nations of the world.

An American Church in a European Court?

The Church is sometimes referred to as an American world religion,[16] and not just because it was founded in the United States and because its headquarters are in Salt Lake City. While the principle in this quote by J. Reuben Clark Jr.—"This is not an American church. This is the Church of Jesus Christ of Latter-day Saints and its destiny as well as its mission is to fill the earth"[17]—is a basic premise, unavoidably, understandably, and often beneficially, much Americanism exists within this global institution. Unfortunately, the necessary cultural transformation of the Church, while contributing positively to the kingdom of God, may risk, at times, becoming a liability. As the Church continues to move into other countries and has to deal with other types of republics and monarchies, as well as economic, social, and cultural loyalties, a sometimes excessive allegiance by the Church's membership and some of its leaders to American culture, tradition, and politics often generates counterproductive reactions—ranging from bemusement to frustration and even to spiritual confusion—in the souls of some Latter-day Saints. This does not mean that non-American members do not appreciate the role the United States played and continues to play in the restored Church, only that they sometimes find it hard to deal with the parochialism and ethnocentrism that at times accompanies the acknowledgement of that role.

Europeans can and generally do politely listen to the occasional sacrament talk by U.S. missionary couples promoting good government—complete with extensive quotes from Thomas Jefferson and James Madison. But the use of American political, economic, and cultural perspectives in preaching, teaching, and decision making creates an inappropriate expectation for some members of the Church. An Australian member, Marjorie Newton, explains it as follows: "No Latter-day Saint would argue with the premise that America is a choice land, a promised land. Problems arise when American Latter-day Saints assume that America is the only choice land; that because the gospel was restored in America, American culture is also better than any other; and that, therefore, the Church has a mission not only to spread the gospel of Jesus Christ but to spread the gospel of Americanism."[18]

To spread this "gospel of Americanism" would imply that American capitalism and its vision for the role of government is superior, which in the European context often can become an impediment to the spread of the gospel. Typically, as John McCormick explains, "in terms of how they conceive political rights, Europeans stand in particular distinction to Americans; while the latter emphasize individual rights and place an emphasis on self-reliance, Europeans are more communitarian in their approach: they support more of a balance between individual and community interests. On the economic front, Europeans are committed capitalists and supporters of the free market, but they place a premium on the redistribution of wealth and opportunity, and on the responsibility of government to maintain a level playing field."[19]

It could be argued that this European willingness to lean toward community good and government and the social responsibility of faith communities on the ideological spectrum is an equally valid viewpoint. Conflicts and misunderstandings can arise from an insufficient self-awareness of these socioeconomic patterns and understandings. Another potential conflict exists between many American and European Latter-day Saints with regards to religious pronouncements on politics, war, and other important events. Many Europeans have a suspicion of religions in general and have learned through past experience that mixing church and state can lead to diminished freedom and rights by those who are not supported by a state religion. As a result, many Europeans are sensitive to the need for a strong separation between church and state.[20]

As the Church continues to expand its missionary efforts globally in places which face diverse, complex, and often unique political problems, any assumptions by Church members that America's political system is the only way to organize a democratic government, or that a particular American political ideology or party is the correct one, would accentuate the perception of parochialism, belying its claim to be a worldwide church. Moreover, at a time when most of the Church membership lives outside of the United States, official Church statements on American political matters carry greater risk than in the past because of the increased potential for adverse reaction outside the United States or because they would run against the grain of what the Church is actually trying to accomplish.[21]

These concerns have been evident for some time, even as early as the 1980s. For instance, although the Church gave very reasonable arguments against the U.S. government's plan to place MX missiles in Utah in 1981,[22] the statement still seemed incongruent to many Europeans,[23] especially because the Church did not similarly protest the placement of nuclear warheads in Europe during the same period, when demonstrations in Europe played an important role in the ending of the Cold War between East and West. The Church's MX missile statement may have been the correct response to the proposed policy, but the somewhat negative reaction to it in Europe emphasizes the Church's growing challenge to communicate its own policies and administrative decisions to an increasingly culturally and politically diverse membership in such a way as to avoid giving unnecessary offense[24] or promoting unintended viewpoints and consequences.

Other Cultural Challenges

Conflation with American culture is not the only challenge to sharing the gospel worldwide. Another dimension is communication between various cultures. What one thinks to have said and what others actually hear often depends on their traditions. Language invariably involves interpretation and carries its own historical and cultural meaning. It comes preloaded with cultural and historical baggage, eliciting culturally specific memories and understandings, which endow certain words and ideas with different meanings depending on the context. Short of adopting a universal language for all its membership, we would be wise to keep these features in mind. At stake in this discussion is our ability to accurately teach and relay essential gospel principles, such as the "gospel plan," "baptism," or "repentance."

For example, some members of the Church in Belgium and the Netherlands debate how to understand the gospel term "plan of salvation." In the southern and predominantly Catholic-influenced part of the Netherlands and Flanders, members of the Church prefer Catholic terminology, *het plan van zaligheid*, meaning "plan of joy" or "plan of bliss." On the other hand, to members in the Protestant-influenced northern part of the Netherlands the term *heilsplan* is preferred, meaning "plan of saving/healing/making whole." The two different interpretations are culturally and historically significant and arguably transmit different facets of one doctrinal truth. Furthermore, the term *heilsplan* carries additional baggage in that it can evoke memories of World War II and the German salute, "*sieg Heil.*" Some older Dutch people, therefore, take offense when they hear the term *heilsplan*.

In a similar dispute, some German Latter-day Saints argue that the Catholic phrase *buße tun*, meaning "penitence" or "paying the price", best connotes a true understanding of the gospel principle of repentance; others argue that the more typical Protestant term *umkehr*, meaning "turning around," more aptly interprets its true sense.[25] In this debate, the preference for which translation best fits an LDS understanding of the principle of repentance once again may hinge on one's Catholic or Protestant cultural heritage. Both examples demonstrate the influence that one's cultural and historical background, and even regional origin, can have on one's understanding or conceptualization of what are considered basic gospel principles. As such, it behooves members and missionaries alike to pay attention to the impact of our own use of language and the potential effect it may have on how even basic gospel principles are taught and understood.

Another implication of the aforementioned examples is that as missionaries selflessly leave the comfort of their homes in the United States, they need to be extra sensitive to these cultural and historical differences. This is especially true in former communist countries where the term "loyalty," for example, carries heavy baggage because for decades the Communist government demanded total loyalty to the party, the proletariat, and the Communist regime. In language similar to the admonitions given to Mormons to be faithful, true, and consecrated to the kingdom of God, Communist leaders called on the party members to develop certain qualities that make for a good and loyal communist.

For example, outlining the characteristics a party member should possess, Mao Zedong said, "At no time and in no circumstance should a communist place one's own personal interests first. . . . Hence, selfishness, slacking, corruption, seeking the limelight are most contemptible, while selflessness, working with all one's energy, wholehearted devotion to one's [. . .] duty, and quiet hard work will command respect."[26] Likewise, Liu Shaoqi noted a true communist "possesses high communist morality; acts with [. . .] courage; seeks the truth from fact and distinguishes what is true from what is false; most sincere, most candid, and happiest of men; should possess the finest and highest human virtues; and consider it a matter of course to die for the sake of the cause, to lay down their lives for justice, when that is necessary."[27] The point of this comparison is not to suggest that one is the source of inspiration for the other or that they are interchangeable ideologies. Far from it; rather, it demonstrates the challenge the Church can face in making sure that it is not misunderstood in its teachings and pronouncements, as well as the necessity for increased sensitivity to local cultures. Propagandized by this type of communist dogma, a member from former communist countries may react to talks on obedience, sacrifice, and consecration much differently than would a member from America or Western Europe.

Other examples of this challenge exist. In Albania, as well as in many countries in Eastern Europe, fears of government infiltration and spying on the Church and its programs are often the subject of gossip and discussion among the members. Some have suggested at times that the home and visiting teaching program suffers due to the members' suspicions about the true motives of the visit. Events like general sustaining votes, Church conferences either at the local level or beyond, and even visits from Church dignitaries enter the minds of some of these members through a very different filter than in Northern Europe or the United States. While these attitudes are not overly pervasive or long-lasting (and most Church members perform their responsibilities and attend their meetings with the same degree of devotion, safety, and comfort as any congregation in any other areas of the world), they do exist, especially among a very specific demographic.

Should the Church cease using such terms, language, or practices in any of its meetinghouses in former communist countries? Or should it do away with home and visiting teaching? The answer is clearly no. But as the Church expands the need to be sensitive to cultural backgrounds when teaching gospel truths or instituting Church procedures, members must understand that the local populations are not a *tabula rasa* and that such practices are not implemented in a vacuum. This phenomenon and therefore the need to increase our awareness as the Church increases its global reach is relevant in the case of Western Europe as well, where instead of the communist legacy, it is the religiously informed traditions and customs that influence a baptismal candidate's or a recent convert's thinking.

It should not be surprising, then, that even the basic idea of what it means to "go to church" can elicit different responses from individuals investigating the Church depending on their background. For some European Catholics, for example, going to church typically means going through the ritual of the mass and other Catholic sacraments in order to obtain God's grace and approval.[28] Priests are men who have studied extensively for their office, have dedicated their lives to the ministry, and are recognized by their black liturgical and clerical clothing, not sixteen-year-old boys who wear white shirts.[29] For some, being a Catholic is often just as much about being part of a long history of familial, national, and religious tradition as it is about learning and practicing one's belief system. As a consequence, for some former Catholics, part of the conversion process to the LDS Church means learning to see Church activity as a way to build the kingdom of God and develop personal spiritual inclinations and to learn about God in ways that were not part of the older tradition.

Some European Protestants, on the other hand, while typically interpreting religiosity as a way to learn about God and his expectations for good behavior, would not favorably view joining a church led by a dominant priesthood hierarchy. Protestants typically do not have a hierarchical priesthood (though Anglicans are an exception). For most Protestant congregations, ministers do not have or need any more priesthood than anyone else in the church, other than a personal call from God. Ministers are not authorized leaders, but paid servants to serve among the flock. Thus for a Protestant, the conversion process to the Church includes learning to sustain those who hold priesthood keys and discovering the reasons for receiving priesthood ordinances and keeping one's covenants.

Similarly, a candidate for baptism would approach an invitation to become baptized very differently depending on his or her religious background. Catholics often think of baptism as sanctification of a child. Protestants often think of it as accepting Jesus into their hearts. For Mormons, it means committing oneself to follow Christ and enduring to the end. Awareness of the meaning of gospel terminology in the investigator's mental context can help a missionary or member explain the Mormon meaning more precisely.

The Church's close association and identification with the United States as a quintessentially American religion has additional drawbacks. Even in countries such as Poland and Albania, in which people generally love most things American, the identification of the Church as the "American Church" has been a mixed blessing. In Albania, for example, in the short run, the identification has proven helpful to the missionary and outreach efforts because it provides the Church with immediate prestige with the population and the government officials. However, a potentially long-term detrimental aspect of the association of the Church with the American culture and its body politic is the opposition that investigators encounter from their local communities who accuse them of selling out their heritage and national identity.

This sentiment has been especially pronounced in areas where national identity and religious identity have become interchangeable and where taking up the latter also implies, in the minds of many, the surrender of the former. Under such conditions, any religious affiliation other than the inherited national religion is seen as betrayal of one's heritage.[30] Recent events in Kosovo and the Former Yugoslav Republic of Macedonia (FYROM) have raised concerns about the possible targeting of the LDS membership and especially of the missionaries in some areas by extremist elements associated with Islamic fundamentalism. In this regard, the more the Church can be seen as a universal church, rather than an American one, the safer it is.[31]

Anticipating Zion

Because the theocratic millennial kingdom of God does not yet exist, its precursor, The Church of Jesus Christ of Latter-day Saints, must by necessity navigate the legal and social constraints of the countries that it finds itself part of. The twelfth article of faith prescribes that we be "subject to" local governments in "obeying, honoring, and sustaining the law." In Europe, history has shown that as we give heed to this exhortation, the potential for accrued good to the Church increases in marvelous, if not miraculous, ways. The permission to build an LDS temple in Freiberg, Germany (dedicated in 1985), by the Communist German Democratic Republic government provides a supreme, well-known example for this argument,[32] as does this follow-up story that occurred three years after the temple dedication.

In the month of October 1988, Erich Honecker, who as the general secretary of the Socialist Unity Party led the East German government from 1971 to 1989, invited the three main LDS leaders in East Germany, Manfred Schütze and Frank Apel (both stake presidents) and Henry Burkhardt (the temple president) to his office. They were told by Honecker that the government was considering presenting a gift to the LDS Church and that they were to come up with an appropriate proposal on what this gift should be. Not wanting to abuse the government's offer and making sure that the Church presented itself properly, the Church leadership offered three options and suggested that German Democratic Government could choose whichever one it deemed best.

The first option was to allow East German boys to attend a Church-sponsored, Europe-wide, Boy Scout jamboree to be held in Brexbachtal, West Germany. The second was to allow young men from East Germany to go to the West and serve full-time missions. The third was to allow foreign missionaries to enter East Germany in order to proselyte. In spite of the fact that all three options were extremely sensitive issues at the time, Mr. Honecker, as head of the East German government, granted the Church all three in gratitude for the contributions and good behavior of the Church members who lived in his country. He said that he was impressed with the way the

The Freiberg Temple, 2006.

Church organized the open house for the temple in East Germany a few years earlier and the way the Church supported the family. In fact, on this last issue, Honecker said that if all East Germans were Mormons, the country would be much stronger, since the basis for strong society is the family.[33]

The Savior's admonition to "render . . . unto Caesar the things which are Caesar's" (Matthew 22:21) is more than a clever way for Jesus to fend off the Pharisees. It acknowledges the reality, which all institutions incorporated into a larger political entity must do, that God's Church must and will abide by the government rules and regulations of its resident political entity. Recognizing the political complexities that exist in a globalized world is important, remembering that on more than one occasion—notably Missouri in the 1830s, Illinois in the 1840s, and Utah through most of the later part of the nineteenth century—the perception of the Church's over-involvement in politics unleashed serious backlash against it.

Erich Honecker, general secretary and chairman of the GDR's Council of State. May 1976.

The Church has, over the last few decades, attempted to maintain strict neutrality in partisan politics,[34] and it has advised its members that as a worldwide institution, it adopts no political party or ideology as its own. In fact, in its marvelous statement on political civility, the Church unambiguously declares: "As the Church operates in countries around the world, it embraces the richness of pluralism. Thus, the political diversity of Latter-day Saints spans the ideological spectrum. Individual members are free to choose their own political philosophy and affiliation. Moreover, the Church itself is not aligned with any particular political ideology or movement. It defies category. Its moral values may be expressed in a number of parties and ideologies."[35]

Minus an official Church political ideology, Latter-day Saints need not fall into the psychological trap of believing that the politics and culture of their particular country are the same as God's. Indeed, in making his case for government by God, John Taylor suggested that all governments are deficient when compared to God's: "Happiness and Peace are the gifts of God, and come from him. Every kind of government has its good and evil properties. . . . Our systems, our policy, our legislation, our education, and philosophy, are all wrong . . . and our present position is a manifest proof of our incompetency to govern; and our past failures make it evident, that any future effort, with the same means, would be as useless."[36]

As the Church continues its push toward becoming a global institution, it will likewise continue to move past its American cultural underpinnings and, by so doing, flourish. Without having to change the doctrine or even its core essential practices, much can be done to find a way to get the message across in a diversity of cultures. Recognizing which elements of the Church need to stay centralized and which elements could be left up to the leadership of local cultures will be a crucial element of this navigation. Those who hold the keys of the priesthood have helped the Church traverse rough political and cultural waters in the past during difficult transitional periods. They will continue to do so through this globalizing period. In fact, in ways perhaps unnoticed by many members, many leaders have, over the last few decades, given talks meant to broaden the Church's cultural and political vision preparatory to greater international growth, none being any better than this statement by President Gordon B. Hinckley: "Let us be good citizens of the nations in which we live. Let us be good neighbors in our communities. Let us acknowledge the diversity of our society, recognizing the good in all people. We need not make any surrender of our theology. But we can set aside any element of suspicion, of provincialism, of parochialism."[37]

Notes

1. Max Weber, *Economy and Society: An Outline of Interpretive Sociology*, vol. 1 (Berkeley: University of California Press, 1978); Max Weber, *The Protestant Ethic and the Spirit of Capitalism: and Other Writings* (New York: Penguin, 2002); Ann Swidler, "Culture in Action: Symbols and Strategies," *American Sociological Review* 50, no. 2 (April 1986): 273–86; Eleonora Federici, "The Translator's Intertextual Baggage," *Forum for Modern Language Studies* 43, no. 2 (April 2007): 147–60.

2. Swidler, "Culture in Action," 273.
3. Federici, "The Translator's Intertextual Baggage," 147.
4. For an excellent overview of different ways to look at "Mormon Culture," we refer the reader to Wilfried Decoo, "In Search of Mormon Identity: Mormon Culture, Gospel Culture, and an American Worldwide Church," *International Journal of Mormon Studies* 6 (December 2013); and Armand L. Mauss, "Feelings, Faith, and Folkways: A Personal Essay on Mormon Popular Culture," in *Proving Contraries: A Collection of Writings in Honor of Eugene England*, ed. Robert A. Rees (Salt Lake City: Signature Books, 2004), 23–38.
5. J. M. Penning, "Americans' Views of Muslims and Mormons: A Social Identity Theory Approach," *Politics and Religion* 2, no. 2 (August 2009): 277–302.
6. For examples, see Decoo, "In Search of Mormon Identity," 32.
7. Armand L. Mauss, *All Abraham's Children* (Urbana: University of Illinois Press, 2003), 4.
8. Robert L. Wilken, *The Christians as the Romans Saw Them* (New Haven, CT: Yale University Press, 1984).
9. K. D. Driggs, "Mormon Church-State Confrontation in Nineteenth-Century America," *Journal of Church and State* 30, no. 2 (1988): 273–89. See also Leonard J. Arrington, *Great Basin Kingdom: An Economic History of the Latter-day Saints, 1830–1900* (Cambridge, MA: Harvard University Press, 1958).
10. Leonard J. Arrington and Davis Bitton, *The Mormon Experience: A History of the Latter-day Saints* (New York: Vintage Books, 1980); Gustive O. Larson, *The "Americanization" of Utah for Statehood* (San Marino, CA: The Huntington Library, 1971); Gustive O. Larson, *Outline History of Utah and the Mormons* (Salt Lake City: Deseret News, 1958).
11. Thomas Alexander, *Mormonism in Transition: A History of the Latter-day Saints* (Urbana: University of Illinois Press, 1986); Sarah Barringer Gordon, *The Mormon Question: Polygamy and Constitutional Conflict in Nineteenth-Century America* (Chapel Hill, NC: The University of North Carolina Press, 2002); Ethan R. Yorgason, *Transformation of the Mormon Culture Region* (Urbana: University of Illinois Press, 2003); Lawrence Young, "Confronting Turbulent Environments: Issues in the Organizational Growth and Globalization of

Mormonism," in *Contemporary Mormonism: Social Science Perspectives*, ed. Marie Cornwall, Tim B. Heaton, and Lawrence Alfred Young (Urbana: University of Illinois Press, 2001)

12. Wilford Woodruff, "Excerpts from Three Addresses by President Wilford Woodruff Regarding the Manifesto," April 1893, www.lds.org/scriptures /dc-testament/od/1?lang=eng.
13. Arrington, *Great Basin Kingdom.*
14. Harold Bloom, *The American Religion: The Emergence of the Post-Christian Nation* (New York: Simon and Schuster, 1992).
15. Young, "Confronting Turbulent Environments," 46.
16. Eric A. Eliason, *Mormons and Mormonism: An Introduction to an American World Religion* (Urbana: University of Illinois Press, 2001).
17. J. Reuben Clark Jr., in Conference Report, October 1937, 107.
18. Marjorie Newton, "'Almost Like Us': The American Socialization of Australian Converts," *Dialogue: A Journal of Mormon Thought* 24, no. 3 (Fall 1991): 9–20. www.dialoguejournal.com/wp-content/uploads/sbi/articles/Dialogue_V24N 03_11.pdf.
19. John McCormick, *Understanding the European Union*, (New York: Palgrave Macmillan, 2014), 41–42.
20. S. V. Monsma and J. C. Soper, *The Challenge of Pluralism: Church and State in Five Democracies* (Lanham, MD: Rowman & Littlefield, 2008).
21. Tad Walch, "LDS Conference Talks May Be Given in Native Languages," *Deseret News*, September 8, 2014, www.deseretnews.com/article/865610540/LDS -conference-talks-may-be-given-in-native-languages.html?pg=all.
22. Joann Jolley, "First Presidency Statement on Basing MX Missile," www.lds.org /ensign/1981/06/news-of-the-church?lang=eng.
23. Personal conversations between European members of the Church and Hans Noot.
24. The Savior strongly suggests that we cannot simply tell the "little ones"—probably new members or those still weak in the faith—"Don't be offended." Instead, he warns the Apostles that they must not give offense (see Matthew 18:6). Paul taught the same principle when he advised those who could make

the distinction between the actual worship of idols and simply eating sacrificed meat, to refrain from such a meal if it would spiritually injure those who could not make the distinction (see 1 Corinthians 8:8). By so doing, he placed the burden of cultural assimilation into the church on the spiritually strong members rather than the weak.

25. ReversoContext, "Repent," http://context.reverso.net/%C3%BCbersetzung/englisch-deutsch/repent+1.
26. Mao Tse-Tung, "The Role of the Chinese Communist Party in the National War," *Selected Works of Mao Tse-Tung*, vol. 2 (Beijing: Foreign Languages Press, 1965), 198, cited in Liu Shaoqi, "How to Be a Good Communist," 1939, available at http://www.marxists.org/reference/archive/liu-shaoqi/1939/how-to-be/ch01.htm. Shaoqi was chairman of the Chinese National People's Congress Standing Committee (NPC) from 1954 to 1959.
27. Liu Shaoqi, "How to Be a Good Communist."
28. For more examples on Catholicism and Mormonism, see Wilfried Decoo, "'As Our Two Faiths Have Worked Together'—Catholicism and Mormonism on Human Life Ethics and Same-Sex Marriage," *Dialogue: A Journal of Mormon Thought* 46, no. 3 (Fall 2013): 1–44.
29. The idea of white shirts as a formality started in the Highland Park Ward in Salt Lake City in 1928–1940. Instead of neckties, bowties were used, because they "do more to build morale and pride in organization-membership, than a 10,000 word lecture." See Justin R. Bray, "Excessive Formalities in the Mormon Sacrament, 1928–1940," *Intermountain West Journal of Religious Studies* 4, no. 1 (2013). http://digitalcommons.usu.edu/cgi/viewcontent.cgi?article=1021&context=imwjournal.
30. Albanian cultural loyalties strongly exemplify the complexities and challenges faced by the Church on this issue. For many Albanians in Kosovo and the Former Republic of Macedonia (FYROM), even though the United States is seen as sympathetic to Albanian interests in the region, conversion to the Church would signify the submerging of their national identity to that of the (Christian) Slavic populations around them.
31. See Milos Teodorovic and Ron Synovitz, "Balkan Militants Join Syria's Rebel Cause," *Radio Free Europe*, January 29, 2014, http://www.rferl.org/content

/syria-balkan-militants-join-rebel-cause/25011213.html. According to a *Salt Lake Tribune* report in November of last year, two sister missionaries were attacked by two ethnic Albanians who were also "suspected of planning an attack on an unidentified target with four other suspects, allegedly inspired by extreme Islamist ideology. . . . The six men were arrested Nov. 5, two days after the missionaries were attacked in Pristina." See Erin Alberty, "Two Mormon Sister Missionaries Beaten in Kosovo," *Salt Lake Tribune*, November 13, 2013, http://www.sltrib.com/sltrib/news/57125799-78/police-kosovo-suspects-official.html.csp.

32. David F. Boone and Richard O. Cowan, "The Freiberg Temple: A Latter-Day Miracle," in *Regional Studies in Latter-day Church History: Europe*, ed. Donald Q. Cannon and Brent L. Top (Provo, UT: Religious Studies Center, 2003), 147–67, http://rsc.byu.edu/archived/regional-studies-latter-day-saint-church-history-europe/8-freiberg-germany-temple-latter-day.
33. Manfred Schütze, then stake president of Dresden Germany Stake, to Hans Noot, email, June 14, 2014.
34. The Church of Jesus Christ of Latter-day Saints, "Political Neutrality," http://www.mormonnewsroom.org/official-statement/political-neutrality.
35. The Church of Jesus Christ of Latter-day Saints, "The Mormon Ethic of Civility," October 16, 2009, http://www.mormonnewsroom.org/ldsnewsroom/eng/commentary/the-mormon-ethic-of-civility.
36. John Taylor, *The Government of God* (Liverpool: S.W. Richards, 1852), 24–26, https://archive.org/details/governmentofgodb03tayl.
37. Gordon B. Hinckley, in Conference Report, April 1997, 116.

South and Central America

15

Latin America and the Globalization of the LDS Church

From an American to an Americas Church

Mark L. Grover

The title of the Church-produced graphic on the Public Relations Department website had a distinct message: "A Global Christ-Centered Faith." The LDS Church was no longer a U.S. Church but a worldwide religion. The statistics presented were impressive, clearly demonstrating the internationalization of the Church. The Book of Mormon was translated into 109 languages, general conference was broadcast in over 90 languages, and a high percentage of the membership spoke a language other than English. Though this graphic suggested a Church with a broad and extensive geographic presence, upon examining the numbers it was clear that the strength of the international Church was in the Americas. In the international Church, 70 percent of the Church population was located in Latin America, with 30 percent in the rest of the world. English continued

---

Mark L. Grover is a retired Latin American and African studies librarian, Brigham Young University.

to be the primary language spoken by members, but Spanish and Portuguese combined represented a very close second.[1]

The LDS Church in Latin America has an interesting and diverse story. Mormonism came late to Latin America in comparison to other parts of the world. Though the first mission was established in Mexico in 1879, it was only with the change in focus that came with President David O. McKay in the 1950s that an environment and impetus was created for significant Church growth in Latin America. Due to changes instituted by President McKay, the Church was in a position to take advantage of momentous social fluctuations that were occurring in Latin America. The outcome was unprecedented growth in Latin America on the scale of the mid-nineteenth-century missionary success in Great Britain. The declining growth of the Church in Europe at the end of the twentieth century, and the steady expansion of the Church in the United States combined with an unprecedented growth of the Church throughout Latin America, resulted in a Mormonism that was not just American. The LDS Church of the twenty-first century has become an Americas church.

This growth in Latin America has not been an anomaly, but part of a changing global religious pattern of Christianity in general. Philip Jenkins, religious historian from Pennsylvania State University, suggested in his 2002 examination of global Christianity that the Christianity of the future would be very different from its historical past due to the growth of conservative and evangelical religions among the poor in the third world. Jenkins suggested that not only has Christianity changed, but the center of Christianity has shifted south. "By 2050, only about one-fifth of the world's 3 billion Christians will be non-Hispanic Whites. . . . The era of Western Christianity has passed within our lifetimes, and the day of Southern Christianity is dawning." Thus the growth of Mormonism in Latin America is not unique, but part of a global pattern of worldwide religious transformation.[2]

David O. McKay and Globalization: The Preparation of Latin America

At the end of World War II, the world moved from a traumatic global struggle into a period of relative peace and economic growth. For the LDS Church, it ended an era of looking inward—focusing on the Church in the western United States—and introduced and era of anticipating an expansive and growing international Church. Just as the United States emerged from this period with a new view of its role as a world political and economic leader, the LDS Church during this time significantly revised the view of who and what it was. The most noteworthy change was that Church leaders began to see the possibility of Mormonism becoming a global religion. The direction of the Church was fully embraced and advocated by President David O. McKay, who became the prophet in April of 1951. This new Mormonism exemplified who he was and his long-held vision for a worldwide church.[3]

It took time for Latin America to become a central part of the expansion of the Church worldwide. Latin America, through the mid-twentieth century, was seen by Church members and leaders primarily for its link to the Book of Mormon. Since its publication in 1830, there has been speculation concerning where the events described in the Book of Mormon actually occurred. In the early 1840s, Joseph Smith and other Church leaders became aware of significant pre-Columbian ruins in Mexico and Central America that fueled their belief that Latin America might be the place. Most Latter-day Saints since then have believed that the Book of Mormon identifies the descendants of these civilizations, all the indigenous populations of the Americas, as part of Israel and thus a chosen people. The Prophet Joseph Smith also identified all of the Americas as Zion, further focusing interest on the region. These ideas are important because they established in the minds of leaders and members that the primary purpose for expansion into Latin America would be to work with the indigenous and mestizo populations, not the Europeans or Africans.[4]

That interest, however, did not result in significant Church expansion into Latin America for over a hundred years. The primary focus of missionary work of the Church was the United States, the United Kingdom, and northern Europe. New converts were encouraged to immigrate to the Great Basin. Attempts to establish the Church in other regions had minimal success. A failed mission by Parley P. Pratt to Chile in 1851–52 was only followed up when missionaries went to Mexico in 1879. Forty-five years later, in 1925, missionaries were finally sent to South America, first to Argentina and then Brazil and Uruguay. None of these countries had a noticeable indigenous population, and missionary work focused almost exclusively on the European immigrant population. The number of missionaries in Latin America remained small, and expansion to all of Latin America did not occur until the 1960s, with a smaller final expansion in the Caribbean after 1978.[5]

The expansion of the Church in Latin America during the presidency of President McKay was not a priority but a byproduct of his focus on the international Church. Early in McKay's presidency, he took a worldwide tour similar to one he took between 1920 and 1921 when he was a young Apostle. In January of 1954, he visited Latin America and was pleasantly surprised with what he found. He stated, "I came to South America with the feeling that there would be plenty of opposition to the Church. I go away feeling that all the people need is a better understanding of the Church and its teachings. These are great countries."[6] He suggested administrative changes indicating that the Church was finally willing to make a permanent investment in Latin America. Noting the condition of meetinghouses—mostly renovated homes—he approved the purchase of land for the construction of chapels. He encouraged strengthening and refocusing missionary work. He pushed for the development of native leadership by suggesting the replacement of missionaries as unit leaders with local members.

President McKay's positive attitude toward South America can be seen in an increased interest paid to the region by General Authorities. For example, during the first twenty-five years of the original Brazil mission, it was visited by one General Authority. Between 1954 and 1960, eight General Authorities—mostly Apostles—made extensive tours of the Brazilian missions, visiting most of the congregations and holding numerous missionary conferences. They were pleasantly surprised with what they found. These visits enabled leaders from Salt Lake City to become familiar with the country and realize that there was a possibility for growth and development.[7]

One important change was to assign a General Authority to live in South America as a regional administrator. In 1961, Elder A. Theodore Tuttle, a young member of the First Quorum of the Seventy, moved to Montevideo, Uruguay, to direct the missions of South America. He reinforced missionary work by making sure all missions had similar goals and a similar focus. He insisted that missionaries be totally involved in the work, not branch and district administration. He instituted numerous changes to strengthen the local units for the purpose of bringing them to the level found in other parts of the world. Elder Tuttle's plan for local leadership development had as its ultimate goal the organization of stakes in all Latin American countries. He lobbied Church leaders in Salt Lake City on behalf of Latin America and emphasized the potential for growth. Part of Elder Tuttle's plan was to expand the Church throughout all of South America, and he focused on the northern and western areas of the continent that had large indigenous populations. By 1966, missionaries were in all of Latin America, with the exception of the small Afro-Latin countries of South America and the Caribbean. The first stake was organized in 1961 in Mexico, a second in Brazil in 1966, and in subsequent years stakes were organized in all the countries of Latin

Elder A. Theodore Tuttle arriving in Brazil, 1962.

America. New missions were established, and the number of missionaries increased significantly. The first Latin American temple was dedicated in Brazil in 1978.[8]

Latin America benefited significantly from the introduction of a Churchwide program called Priesthood Correlation because of the equalizing effect it had on the Church outside of the United States.[9] One of the goals of Correlation was the creation of Church programs and structures throughout the world. The Church was expected to be similar all over the world under the supervision and direction of the priesthood. There was a centralization of most decisions to the priesthood and Church bureaucracy in Salt Lake City. In order for Church correlation to be effective in Latin America, there had to be centralized translation and publishing programs under the direction of Church leadership. No longer were manuals translated, written, and produced in the local mission homes as had happened earlier.[10] Guidelines were established for unit creation, chapel construction, and regional administrative development. When the requisite conditions were met, no matter where in the world, a unit would be organized or a chapel would be constructed. Under the direction of the Twelve Apostles, all regions of the world began to evolve with relative similarities.[11]

The administrative changes that occurred in the Church in the '50s and '60s were important in the evolution of the Church into a global religion. However, for this to occur there had to be growth and expansion in convert baptisms outside of the United States. Though this had begun to occur during the presidency of David O. McKay, it was the expansion of the Church in the last two decades of the twentieth century that provided the statistical proof of a global Church. These numbers, in large part, were provided by the expansion of the Church in Latin America.

Unprecedented Growth and Expansion in Latin America

What happened in Latin America from the 1980s through the end of the century was remarkable. The growth in this region had an effect on the Church similar to that of baptisms in the British missions in the nineteenth century. The simplest method to demonstrate what happened is to look at growth statistics. Statistics only are not completely satisfactory in describing what occurred, but they are a quick method to analyze trends in global Mormonism.

In 1978, there were about 4.2 million members of the Church worldwide, with half a million in Latin America. By 2005, the total number of Church members in Latin America had risen to 4.7 million. In twenty-five years, the Church in Latin America grew as much as it took the entire Church to grow in 148 years. In 1978, the Church in Latin America was 12 percent of the entire Church. By 2014, it was almost 40 percent of the Church. In total numbers of Church members,

President David O. McKay speaking in Rosario, Argentina. His son Robert is translating.

fourteen of the top twenty countries in the world are from Latin America.[12]

Providing an explanation for this growth using secular analysis requires an understanding of Latin America in general during this time. The expansion of the Church in Latin America is the result of a combination of external factors as well as internal changes within the Church. This combination placed the Church in Latin America in a position to benefit from momentous social and economic changes that were occurring in all of Latin America. Those changes were the consequence of political and economic events, both positive and negative, that culminated in a series of interacting social and psychological changes in Latin American society. After World War II, economic modernization and industrialization increased migration in Latin America from rural areas to the cities. This demographic shift was accompanied by shifting power from traditional patrimonial elites to democratic states, thus weakening a social system based on local and regional control.[13]

One of the consequences was a weakening of the Catholic Church's dominance throughout the region. The Catholic Church experienced an erosion in its influence, resulting in an unprecedented separation of religion from culture and issues of national identity. That change began first with the rural migrants but expanded to the rest of the population. The result was that a larger pool of Latin Americans became susceptible to religious conversion in a society that earlier had discouraged or even criminalized religious change.[14] When a Latin American developed spiritual needs, regardless of his or her social class, the pressure to seek answers only from the traditional sources diminished because the relationship between traditional religion and society was weakened.[15] By 2010, only 70 percent of Latin Americans considered themselves Catholic as compared to 90 percent in 1990. This 20 percent decrease in a twenty-year span is a remarkable indication of a major psychological shift in the religious foundation of the region. A change in religion not only became more acceptable but was often considered to be a positive and favorable action.[16]

Though economic, social, and psychological changes are compelling factors that help explain the changing religious environment in Latin America, it is important not to place too much emphasis on secular factors. For the most part, people make decisions about religion not for social or economic needs but for reasons of the Spirit. The struggles of life, both secular and spiritual, create a need for contact and help from a divine source. It is that desire that encourages the search for spiritual assistance. Social disruptions create a larger pool in the population who are susceptible to religious change, but that does not mean religious change will necessarily occur. All people, rich or poor, go through times in their lives in which there is a need for spiritual assistance. If they do not find that help in the institutions and relationships that are already part of their lives, it is likely that they will seek spiritual assistance from other sources.[17]

The religious atmosphere of competition that existed in Latin America can be compared to the religious environment that existed in nineteenth-century New York when Joseph Smith also found himself in a pool of potential converts to a large variety of religions. As there was in New York, there is significant competition for converts among numerous religions in Latin America, primarily evangelical churches. These religious groups are varied and diverse. The fastest-growing alternative religion manifests a greater perception of connection with Deity than does the Catholic Church. There are small churches in the new growing poor neighborhoods, as well as large religions who hold revival meetings in soccer stadiums with more than 100,000 participants. The Catholic Church Charismatics are also part of the competition. Though the LDS Church is a partaker in the religious change that is occurring, it is not close to being the largest or fastest growing.[18]

Those who have studied the growth of Latin American evangelical religions point to growth factors that are not significantly part of the Mormon experience. One important study by Andrew Chesnut looked at the movements in terms of religious economy, suggesting three groups were the most successful: evangelical Protestants, African diaspora religions, and Catholic Charismatics. The fastest-growing evangelical groups use the media to attract investigators. They hold large group activities, often involving thousands of participants, to effectively influence potential converts. Chesnut suggested that the three most important factors in the growth of these movements were that most converts were female, the growth was coming from the lowest economic and social strata of society, and these religions had prominent pneumatic or spiritual experiences—often public faith healings—in their religious services. Dr. Chesnut suggested that Mormonism has not grown at the same level because the Mormon Church is not particularly strong in any of these areas.[19]

The internal changes in the LDS Church during this time were also important. Two events are central in the expansion of Mormonism in Latin America. The first was the priesthood revelation in 1978 that changed a longtime delimiting policy that restricted blacks of African descent from fully participating in the Church. The elimination of these restrictions allowed for the opening of new areas of the world in Africa and the Caribbean to missionary work but also resulted in the expansion of the Church into already established regions of Brazil, as well as parts of Colombia, Venezuela, Ecuador, and Peru.

A second internal event in 1984 was the organization of regional Area Presidencies. The significance of Area Presidencies was that they were constituted primarily of members of the First and Second

Quorums of the Seventy who lived in the assigned regions and had Church local administrative support in the area. There were originally thirteen areas, with three in Latin America. By 2014, there were sixteen areas outside of North America, with six in Latin America and the Caribbean. The most important consequence of this organizational adjustment was the decentralization of decisions from Salt Lake City to the areas, which accelerated development in all aspects of the Church. A second factor was the increasing influence of local native leaders. These leaders encourage a broader missionary focus that included going into economically depressed areas that had been avoided in earlier years.[20]

The statistical growth in numbers alone is remarkable. From 1980 to 1999, Latin America experienced an annual growth rate of 10.4 percent, compared to the annual general Church growth rate of 4.6 percent. The rate after 2000 slowed considerably due to concerns over retention but was still above Church average. Between

Elder Hélio da Rocha Camargo, first Brazilian General Authority.

2000 and 2013, the Latin American average growth was 3.2 percent as compared to a Church growth rate of 2.4 percent. The growth in Brazil and Mexico was especially significant, with over a million members in both countries. Growth in Chile and Uruguay was substantial enough that both countries registered over 3 percent of their national population as Mormons; Chile had 3.4 percent and Uruguay 3.1 percent.

A hypothetical statistical examination further suggests the importance of Latin America in Church growth. In January of 2013, the total membership of the Church was 14,782,473. Without including Latin America, it was only 8,951,004. I decided to look at the size of the Church in 1980 and hypothesized that if the Church in Latin America had grown at the same rate as the rest of the Church between 1980 and 2013, without the high growth figures from Latin America, the size of the Church in 2013 would only have been 9,913,382—almost 4 million less than it was. With this decreased growth, Latin America would have only 1 million members. These hypothetical statistics show the importance of the growth of the Church in Latin America at the end of the twentieth century to the evolution of the Church as a worldwide Church.

With this growth, there has been a significant shift in how the Church views Latin America. It is no longer seen as an outpost or far-flung missionary destination, but as the area of the Church where growth is significant and institutional development noteworthy. It is the region that gives vibrancy and global significance to the Church in the world. Scholars who are members as well as nonmembers point to the growth in Latin America as evidence of the emergence of Mormonism as a world religion.[21]

Issues

Unfortunately, statistics do not always adequately demonstrate what is happening. Throughout the history of missionary work in the entire Church, baptisms have not turned into an equal number of actual converts to the Church. Consequently, even though Latin America has experienced growth and development, it also highlights the challenges and occasional unexpected effects of a rapidly expanding Church. Thus Latin America can be seen as both the hero and scapegoat in an understanding of the evolution of the modern international Church. Questions of retention and poverty of the converts are issues that are regularly part of the discussion on the evolution of the Church in Latin America.

With the growth of the Church in Latin America, the question of retention became a concern that brought into question the legitimacy of growth claims in the LDS Church. Difficulty with retention and keeping new converts active is not a recent phenomenon but has historically been a challenge for the Church throughout the world.[22] David Knowlton, an anthropologist and professor of behavioral science at Utah Valley University, has shown the challenges in two different studies. Since the Church does not publish activity or attendance statistics, other methods have to be used to indicate retention. Knowlton compared published Church statistics with the number of people who identified themselves as Mormon in two national censuses and found significant differences between the Church statistics and the census results.[23] In addition, he made a comparison of the total numbers found in stakes in Latin America compared to the United States, finding much larger stakes in Latin America, which again suggests high levels of inactivity. His conclusions were that the numbers in Latin America who regularly attend meetings, pay tithing, and claim membership are significantly lower than the official statistics of the Church.[24]

The differences between statistical numbers and actual activity are seldom advertised outside the Church, but they have been mentioned several times to members and leaders at general conference. Retention was a weighty concern of President Gordon B. Hinckley, who discussed these challenges in several of his conference talks. In an emotional talk given to priesthood holders in October of 1997, President Hinckley expressed both frustration and ire. "This is serious business. There is no point in doing missionary work unless we hold on to the fruits of that effort. The two must be inseparable. . . . Brethren, this loss must stop. It is unnecessary. I am satisfied the Lord is not pleased with us."[25]

This was not an easy challenge to overcome. Growth is important for the Church but has to be combined with a focus on retention. During a visit to Chile in April of 1999, President Hinckley delivered a message to the missionaries:

> The days are past—the days are gone—the days are no longer here when we will baptize hundreds of thousands of people in Chile and then they will drift away from the Church. . . . When you begin to count those who are not active, you are almost driven to tears over the terrible losses we have suffered in this nation. . . . Now, I am sure you have understood my message. I have stated it as plainly as I know how.[26]

There were several institutional changes made whose purpose was to slow down the growth of the Church while at the same time increasing retention rates. In a rare action in 2002, Apostle Jeffrey R. Holland was sent to preside over and live in Chile for two years. He instituted numerous modifications to have missionaries spend more time visiting less-active members and encouraging their return to the Church. Missionaries were required to continue visits to converts after they were baptized. Programs of integration and teaching of new members in the branches and wards were strengthened. Wards and stakes were consolidated so that the resulting units had larger congregations and stronger leadership. The number of stakes went from 112 to 87.[27] Chile consequently experienced a significant drop in convert baptisms, transitioning from a 10.27 percent yearly growth in 2002 to .52 percent in 2003. In 2012, the growth rate was 1.21 percent, the lowest in all of South America. Some form of retrenchment was introduced throughout all of Latin America, and the percentage of growth for the entire area dropped to between 2 and 3 percent—close to the general Church average.

The challenges of retention encouraged the Church to look at issues of poverty and education. President Spencer W. Kimball during his presidency (1973–85) expanded missionary efforts by significantly increasing the number of non-Americans serving missions. This effort was successful, and the numbers of Latin Americans who became missionaries increased from a small percentage to close to 50 percent of the missionary force in Latin America. Financial support for many of these young missionaries came from a special missionary fund supported by Church membership, generally in the United States.[28]

The missionary program highlighted the economic challenges facing many Church members in Latin America. The lower economic status of converts joining the Church was evident in the young men and women called on missions. Coming from challenging home environments, many had not been able to obtain enough education to prepare them to get adequate jobs when they returned from their missions. These economic challenges were significant, and many remained unemployed or seriously underemployed for long periods following their missions. Education and technological training were necessary, but many of these missionaries did not have the economic means to attend school. Church leaders realized that a significant percentage of the returned missionaries who struggled economically also struggled to maintain activity in the Church. By the end of the twentieth century, a small Church loan program administered by Seminaries and Institutes had been established in some of the countries, but the funds were limited. A few private foundations were also established by former American missionaries to provide scholarships and loans to young returning missionaries. Millions of dollars were donated to fund scholarships, particularly in Brazil and Chile.

Unfortunately, the available funding was still limited in comparison to what was needed.[29]

In the spring of 2001, after studying the problem, the Church established a program meant to help young members of the Church with their educational challenges. President Gordon B. Hinckley announced a program called the Perpetual Educational Fund (PEF), a Church-administered educational fund supported by donations to provide loans to young members (mostly returned missionaries) to attend school and obtain enough technical training that would make them competitive in the job market. The expectation was that with financial assistance, not only would these young members obtain better employment, but there would be higher retention in the Church.

The program was similar to the Perpetual Emigration Fund, an important Church effort of the nineteenth century. New converts from Europe were encouraged to immigrate to the United States but often lacked the financial means to make the expensive journey. In 1849, the Church established a fund called the Perpetual Emigration Fund (PEF), designed to help new converts finance the journey. The similarities between the nineteenth-century program and the educational program of the twenty-first century are significant because although they respond to different situations, they suggest a similar philosophy as the Church confronts twenty-first-century challenges resulting from growth and expansion in the Third World.[30]

Conclusion

The history of the Church in Latin America provides a valuable case study of the globalization of the Church. The presidency of David O. McKay was momentous, but the subsequent evolution under later Presidents was just as significant. Later presidents expanded on many of the ideas of President McKay. President Kimball repeated often his vision of the importance of Latin America by comparing the Church to an eagle. "Zion was all of North and South America, like the wide, spreading wings of a great eagle, the one being North and the other South America."[31]

The influence of Latin America in the Church is significant. Latin America has been a focus of financial and administrative expansion seen symbolically by the 42 temples constructed and announced in Latin America by 2015. Three Latin Americans—Elders Claudio R. M. Costa and Ulisses Soares from Brazil, and Elder Walter F. González from Uruguay—have served in the Presidency of the Seventy. Probably the most important symbolic evidence of recognition would come with the call of a Latin American to the Quorum of the Twelve Apostles, which would put him in line for the presidency of the Church.

I am positive about what is happening in the Church in Latin America. Yes, there continue to be problems of retention, poverty, and leadership development; however, there has been a remarkable maturation of the Church organization. There is a vibrancy among the membership in general and strong leaders who are equal to any in the Church. There are active members in Latin America who are owners and CEOs of companies, professors in universities, and politicians. There are numerous examples of young members who have faced social and economic challenges and have impressive success stories that rival any in the Church. There is respect from outside the Church for its members and organization. There is an impressive commitment and faithfulness among many. Part of their vibrancy comes from the fact that they live in a Church environment that is growing and reaching out to their fellow Latin Americans.[32]

I also find solace in what is happening in Latin America in general. Regardless of the stories found in the press about Latin America that focus on the violent, the silly, and the profane, there is a new sense of confidence in most countries. It is led by Brazil and Chile, with their impressive economic growth and political maturation.

Latin Americans are confident in their lives and look positively towards the future. This growing self-confidence is resulting in a lessening of dependence on and control from the outside, particularly from the United States. The political systems are functioning and maturing, and economic challenges are being addressed. This is felt by the members in Latin America as they see themselves as equal to their North American brothers and sisters. That confidence will affect the Church as Latin America continues to grow, expand, and become even more important in the Church in general.[33]

Notes

1. See Larry Richman, "LDS Infographic: A Global, Christ-Centered Faith," LDS Media Talk, November 4, 2013. There were 6,872,074 English speakers and a combined 6,204,941 Spanish and Portuguese speakers. The distinct fourth language was Tagalog, with 219,054.
2. Philip Jenkins, *The Next Christendom: The Coming of Global Christianity* (New York: Oxford University Press, 2002), 3.
3. See Gregory A. Prince and William Robert Wright, *David O. McKay and the Rise of Modern Mormonism* (Salt Lake City: University of Utah Press, 2005), 1. Much of the history of the Church internationally has been focused on converts immigrating to the United States. That idea continued during the first half of the twentieth century even though leaders talked about members remaining in their countries of origin. The Church did not allocate significant resources outside the United States. The focus by President McKay was on creating a continuing Mormon presence throughout the world by constructing buildings, developing organizations, and expanding activities.
4. This idea permeates most discussions about Latin America, though in reality Church expansion occurred initially among the urban European immigrant population, and later among descendants from African slaves. Church success has occurred in countries with a large mestizo population, but only limited success has occurred with the indigenous. See Richard O. Cowan, "The Lamanites:

A More Accurate Image," in *The Book of Mormon: Helaman through 3 Nephi 8, according to Thy Word*, ed. Monte S. Nyman and Charles D. Tate Jr. (Provo, UT: Religious Studies Center, 1992), 251–64.

5. A few missionaries did go to Paraguay in 1949, which does have a large indigenous population, but missionaries focused on the European population for many years. Important insight into missionary work during this period is found in Armand L. Mauss, *All Abraham's Children: Changing Mormon Conceptions of Race and Lineage* (Champaign: University of Illinois Press, 2003).
6. As quoted in Francis M. Gibbons, *David O. McKay: Apostle to the World, Prophet of God* (Salt Lake City: Deseret Book, 1986), 338.
7. For a description of the changes, see Mark L. Grover, *A Land of Promise and Prophecy: Elder A. Theodore Tuttle in South America, 1960–1965* (Provo, UT: Religious Studies Center, 2008).
8. For a history of this period, see Grover, *Land of Promise and Prophecy.*
9. See Daniel H. Ludlow, "Correlation," in *Encyclopedia of Latter-day Saint History*, ed. Arnold K. Garr et. al (Salt Lake City: Deseret Book, 2000), 250–51; Jerry Rose, "The Correlation Program of The Church of Jesus Christ of Latter-day Saints During the Twentieth Century" (master's thesis, Brigham Young University, 1973); and Prince and Wright, "Correlation and Church Administration," in *Rise of Modern Mormonism*, 139–58.
10. In 1965, translation, publication, and distribution of Spanish-language materials were centralized under direction of the Presiding Bishopric and administered by J. Thomas Fyans, recently returned mission president from Uruguay. See Justus Ernst, "'Every Man . . . in His Own Language,'" *Ensign*, July 1974, 23.
11. Reaction to the importance and effect of correlation has varied. One author characterized it as a revolution. Others have been critical because it centralized the Church and advanced and established American culture by insisting that all of the Church be the same worldwide. See Peter Wiley, "The Lee Revolution and the Rise of Correlation," *Sunstone* 10 (January 1985): 18–22; and J. Michael Cleverley, "Mormonism on the Big Mac Standard," *Dialogue: A Journal of Mormon Thought* 29, no. 2 (Summer 1996): 69–75.

12. The statistics up through 2013 come from the annual publication *Deseret News Almanac of the Church of Jesus Christ of Latter-day Saints* (Salt Lake City). The publication has since been discontinued.
13. For a discussion of these occurrences in Brazil, see Ignacy Sachs, Jorge Wilheim, and Paulo Sérgio Pinheiro, eds., *Brazil: A Century of Change* (Chapel Hill, NC: University of North Carolina Press, 2009).
14. See Sidney M. Greenfield and André Droogers, eds., *Reinventing Religions: Syncretism and Transformation in Africa and the Americas* (Lanham, MD: Rowman & Littlefield, 2001).
15. A number of explanations for religious change in Latin America in general have been suggested by scholars. See Christian Lalive d'Epinay, *El Refugio de las Masas: Estudio Sociológico del Protestantismo Chileno* (Santiago, Chile: Editorial del Pacifico, 1968); David Martin, *Tongues of Fire: The Explosion of Protestantism in Latin America* (Oxford: B. Blackwell, 1990); David Stoll, *Is Latin America Turning Protestant?: The Politics of Evangelical Growth* (Berkeley, CA: University of California Press, 1991); and Brian H. Smith, *Religious Politics in Latin America, Pentecostal vs. Catholic* (Notre Dame, IN: University of Notre Dame Press, 1998). For a more extensive discussion of this change as it relates to the Church, see Mark L. Grover, "The Maturing of the Oak: The Dynamics of Latter-day Saint Growth in Latin America," *Dialogue* 38, no. 2 (Summer 2005): 79–104.
16. See "Latin America's Catholics in the Spotlight as Pope Francis is Installed," Pew Research: Religion and Public Life Project, March 18, 2013. See also Phillip Berryman, *Religion in the Megacity: Catholic and Protestant Portraits from Latin America* (Maryknoll, NY: Orbis Books, 1996), 2–3.
17. See Edward L. Cleary, introduction to *Power, Politics, and Pentecostals in Latin America*, ed. Edward L. Cleary and Hannah Stewart-Gambino (Boulder, CO: Westview Press, 1996), 4–5. See also David Lehmann, *Struggle for the Spirit: Religious Transformation and Popular Culture in Brazil and Latin America* (Cambridge, MA: Polity Press, 1996); and Cecília Loreto Mariz, *Coping with Poverty: Pentecostals and Christian Base Communities in Brazil* (Philadelphia: Temple University Press, 1994).
18. See Grover, "Maturing of the Oak."

19. Dr. Chesnut made the comment on the LDS Church in a private conversation with the author at a conference in Austin, Texas, in 2010. See Andrew Chesnut, *Competitive Spirits: Latin America's New Religious Economy* (New York: Oxford University Press, 2003), 3–15. For a recent report that suggests the same factor, see "Religion in Latin America: Widespread Change in a Historically Catholic Region," Pew Research Center, November 13, 2014.
20. See Kahlile Mehr, "Area Supervision: Administration of the Worldwide Church, 1960–2002," *Journal of Mormon History* 27, no. 1 (Spring 2001): 192–214. Missionaries seldom went into slums prior to the 1980s. The baptism of teenagers without their families had been discouraged but became a regular part of missionary work.
21. See Rodney Stark, *The Rise of Mormonism*, ed. Reid L. Neilson (New York: Columbia University Press, 2005), 103–8.
22. The worldwide challenge of retention is examined in this important study of missionary work: David Stewart, *The Law of the Harvest: Practical Principles of Effective Missionary Work* (Henderson, NV: Cumorah Foundation, 2007).
23. For all who study the Church in Latin America, it is obvious that the retention rates are very low. The challenge is finding the statistical data to adequately demonstrate the challenges. See David Knowlton, "How Many Members Are There Really? Two Censuses and the Meaning of LDS Membership in Chile and Mexico," *Dialogue* 38, no. 2 (Summer 2005): 53–78.
24. See David Knowlton, "Mormonism in Latin America: Towards the Twenty-First Century," *Dialogue* 29, no. 1 (Spring 1996): 159–76.
25. Gordon B. Hinckley, "Some Thoughts on Temples, Retention of Converts, and Missionary Service," *Ensign*, November 1997, 49. See also Gordon B. Hinckley, "May We Be Faithful and True," *Ensign*, May 1997, 6.
26. "Special Mission Conference—April 25, 1999 (excerpts from President Hinckley's Address)"; copy in possession of the author.
27. At the same time, Elder Dallin H. Oaks of the Quorum of the Twelve was assigned to the Philippines, another area with high growth and low retention.
28. See Edward L. Kimball, *Lengthen Your Stride: The Presidency of Spencer W. Kimball* (Salt Lake City: Deseret Book, 2005), 113–28.

29. For a discussion of the two earlier programs, see the interviews conducted by Mark L. Grover of Pedro Brassanini, May 20, 2004, Provo, UT; A. Duke Cowley, February 25, 2011, Provo, UT; and Wilford Allen Cardin, July 30, 2006, São Paulo, Brazil. All interviews in possession of the author.
30. See John K. Carmack, *A Bright Ray of Hope: The Perpetual Education Fund* (Salt Lake City: Deseret Book, 2004).
31. Spencer W. Kimball, in Conference Report, April 1975, 4.
32. One interesting challenge is over the renewed focus on the role and position of the United States in the world. The issue of immigration in the United States in particular has created a hostility not only towards Latin Americans but all the world. The evangelical conservative right has renewed its call for protection of American culture from the believed degenerative nature of non-American influences. Those ideas have found resonance in the conservative right in the Church, which calls for a preservation of American culture and protection of what many call the "sacred role" afforded to the United States and its European immigrant population. Just how many of those ideas have permeated the Church in general is not known, but the ideas are manifesting themselves in the conflict over immigration.
33. That feeling is supported by a Gallup study that suggests Latin Americans are the most positive in the world. See Jon Clifton, "People Worldwide Are Reporting a Lot of Positive Emotions," *Gallup Daily*, May 21, 2014.

16

A Century of LDS Church Schools in Mexico Influenced by Lamanite Identity

Barbara E. Morgan

Since its inception, The Church of Jesus Christ of Latter-day Saints has been interested in proclaiming the gospel through missionary work and through educating its members. As early as 1831, Joseph Smith established schools for children of members living in Ohio.[1] The School of the Prophets was established two years later.[2] In 1837, the Kirtland High School met with an enrollment of 145.[3] Parley P. Pratt taught a school of elders in Missouri until the Mormons were driven to Nauvoo, and there they established schools in each ward and the University of the City of Nauvoo. Following the death of the Prophet Joseph Smith, the Saints moved west to the Great Basin, building schools in all their settlements.[4] By the 1870s, the Church requested that every stake fund an academy. Between 1875 and 1911, thirty-four academies were organized; one of these, the Juárez Academy, was officially dedicated in Mexico in 1897.[5]

Barbara E. Morgan is an assistant professor of Church history and doctrine at Brigham Young University.

Although it was built primarily to educate the Mormon American colonizers, it was a forerunner to the creation of a massive Church Educational System throughout Mexico.

Since the Church's beginning, the Lord's focus on education was at the heart of the gospel. In July 1828, two years before the Restoration of the Church, the Lord revealed that one reason for the plates' preservation was in part "that the Lamanites might come to knowledge of their fathers, and that they might know of the promises of the Lord."[6] While we don't know the complete ancestral pedigree of the indigenous inhabitants of the Americas, we do affirm that the peoples of the Book of Mormon are among their ancestors. Hence, they have often been called "Lamanites," and we affirm that they are heirs to the great promises made in that sacred volume.[7] Thus, it not only became incumbent upon Church members to find and baptize those considered to be "Lamanites" at the time, but also to teach them who they were and prepare them to receive the promises of the Lord. Because the Saints felt the urge to fulfill this mandate, one of the first official Latter-day Saint missions commenced in 1830 with a call for Parley P. Pratt and Ziba Peterson to join Oliver Cowdery and Peter Whitmer Jr. in the preaching of the gospel to the "Lamanites."[8] In 1845, the Church issued a proclamation that stated in part that "the sons and daughters of Zion will soon be required to devote a portion of their time in instructing the children of the forest (Indians) . . . and glorify them as the sons and daughters of the royal house of Israel and of Joseph."[9]

For the next century, the LDS emphasis on converting and educating the perceived Lamanites would wax and wane. During the presidencies of David O. McKay and Spencer W. Kimball, however, the emphasis increased dramatically, causing not only an increase in baptisms among this people, but ultimately the creation of an immense educational system. In addition to placing American Indian students with Latter-day Saint families so they could go to school and creating Lamanite seminary programs in areas highly populated with Latter-day

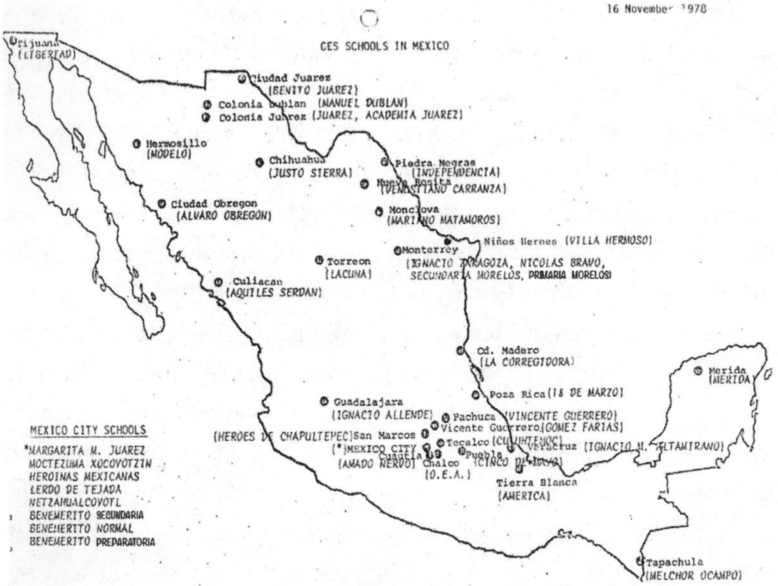

Map of Church schools in Mexico as of November 16, 1978, by Ephraim Villalobos Vasquez.

Saints, the Church also instituted a large-scale international educational system for those then considered to be Lamanite children and youth throughout the Pacific Islands, New Zealand, Central and South America, and Mexico. By examining the historical, political, social, and religious underpinnings of more than a century of LDS Church existence in Mexico, this paper will attempt to show how the Church's emphasis on educating and converting those whom its leaders considered to be "Lamanites" influenced its educational endeavors in Mexico.

Mexico as a Mormon Refuge and Mission Field

When the Mormons escaped the violent and bitter persecution in Nauvoo and began their trek west to the Rocky Mountains, they were leaving not only a state, but a country. The Treaty of Guadalupe Hidalgo between Mexico and the United States was not signed until after the Mormons had lived in the Salt Lake Valley for over half a year. Less than fifty years later, some Latter-day Saints would again seek refuge and colonization in Mexico as a result of religious persecution aimed at those practicing plural marriage. Not only was Mexico a place of refuge which led to future colonization, but it provided a fertile ground for missionary work, especially among those that the early Latter-day Saints considered Lamanites. Indeed, from the earliest days of the history of the Church, it was widely accepted that the inhabitants of Mexico were Lamanites.

In 1874, Brigham Young announced that the time was near to take the gospel to millions of Lehi's Mexican descendants.[10] After the many years of political and religious turmoil in Mexico known as La Reforma, that time finally came in 1876. La Reforma opened the doors to many Christian religions, including Mormonism. Although early proselyting efforts were difficult for the missionaries, the prophet earnestly granted his approval of their mission. However, he felt that their efforts were best spent focusing on one group in particular. "I feel that it would be wise for you to visit the old original blood as much as possible,"[11] Young advised.

Brigham Young's announcement came at a critical time in Mexican history, because Benito Juárez's Reforma had fostered a renewed pride in Mexicans' Indian heritage. As a result, many contacts were made and sustained among the liberal Mexicans who were sympathetic to the indigenous citizens, and they appreciated the teachings contained in the Book of Mormon and its possible connection to their own people. Taking advantage of this newfound Indian pride, early Mormon missionaries sent over five hundred copies of important Book of Mormon selections, all containing the same scriptures, to nearly one hundred of Mexico's major cities and to its most prominent men.

Impressed with their report upon arriving home, Brigham Young immediately continued the missionary work and land scouting by sending new missionaries. In 1876, the first five members of the

Church from Mexico were taught and baptized, and by 1879, the first Mormon congregation in Mexico was organized. On April 6, 1881, Apostle Moses Thatcher, with several missionaries and a handful of Saints, dedicated the land for the preaching of the gospel.

By 1885, Mormon leaders had secured land in northern Mexico, and immediately some of the Church's most able families began colonizing there, because the twenty-five-year attempt to defend the Church's stance on plural marriage had failed in the United States. Appreciative of the Mexican refuge but wary of outside influences, these early colonists isolated themselves from their immediate surroundings. Because education was foundational to Mormon theology and culture, schools became a top priority for these early colonists. In 1886, Ana Maria Woodbury Romney began educating the children in her own home, and by 1897 the Juárez Stake Academy had officially commenced.[12] Little did these early colonists know that as they were forming these small schools for their own children, they were laying the foundation for empowering thousands of Mexican students and thus partially fulfilling their call to teach those then considered Lamanites. These students would eventually be taught, mentored, and graduated from nearly fifty LDS Church schools nationwide. These schools would not come immediately, however, and the Mexican Saints, both natives and immigrants, would be put through a refiner's fire before receiving the blessings of their sacrifices.

For example, shortly after a failed attempt by President Helaman Pratt of the Mexico Mission to unify the native Mexican members with the mature Latter-day Saint American colonists, the Mexican mission was closed in June 1899, primarily due to cultural differences between the two parties. Hundreds of recent converts were left as orphans to fend for themselves until the mission was reopened in 1901.[13] With the reopening of the mission, great care was taken by the now-fluent Spanish-speaking missionaries—well versed in Mexican law and culture and educated primarily in the colonies—in order to find the earlier converts and continue the work of conversion. During the next decade, these missionaries would not only baptize over a thousand Mexican natives but also use the educational training they received prior to their missions from their families, church, and the Juárez Academy to train the converts as leaders and assist them in building a strong foundation for the newly formed branches. The results of their efforts would prove critical to the Church's existence and growth when political and social unrest in the country would require the Church to depend on its own native members to survive the impending Mexican revolution and its long-lasting effects.

From 1876 to 1910, Porfirio Díaz ruled Mexico. He was a popular leader when he first took office, but his increasing support for international growth, favoritism towards the elite, and antagonism toward the native Indians resulted in major national discord. This eventually led to the expulsion of all Americans, including the four thousand Mormon colonists in northern Mexico and all American missionaries. With only sporadic visits from the missionaries and their mission president, opportunities for leadership responsibility increased among the local Mexican members. As a result, native members quickly became self-reliant and independent. Although progress and expansion were slow, the members pressed forward. Two prominent Mexican members baptized during this time were Rafael Monroy, who became the first branch president in San Marcos, Hidalgo, and the first Church martyr in Mexico, and Bernabe Parra, who opened the first Mormon school outside of the colonies.

Native Mexican Growing Pains

In many ways, the maturity of the Church in Mexico paralleled the journey of childhood to adulthood. With increased independence and responsibility came growing pains, experience, and consequences. Several events resulted in a great wedge between many native Mexican

August 7, 1945. A group of students from the San Marcos Hidalgo primary school accompanied by their teachers Leonor Lozano and Luis Gutierrez. Photo from record book kept by staff of San Marcos Hidalgo Primary. (Courtesy of author.)

Mormons, who now considered themselves Lamanites, and their North American "Gentile" leaders. First came their newfound ecclesiastical independence, then the tragic death of their beloved mission president, President Rey L. Pratt, in 1931. The pains continued when there seemed to be no adequate replacement—Mexican national pride enhanced the desire to be led by one of their own and increased deep antagonistic feelings toward the Americans, whom they blamed for unfairly taking over half of their country in the Mexican-American War. Mexican Saints desired their own native Mexican mission president to represent their people and prove their capability, thus further fulfilling the perceived role of the Lamanites. American Mormon leaders perceived the Mexican members' desire for a native mission president as a form of apostasy and rebellion against general priesthood authority.[14]

This divide led to nearly ten years of internal conflict from about 1935 to 1945 as Mexican nationalism and perceptions of Lamanite growth and responsibility clashed with loyalty to American Church authority and personal testimony. "If the Church does not give us the means as well as open the way for complete development, we will never be able to carry forth this important work for ourselves and our people," one member declared. "It will be impossible for us to make the necessary progress without this leadership opportunity."[15] Members feared that without adequate experience they could never "blossom as the rose."[16] As these and similar sentiments continued to build, some influential native Mexican leaders took more drastic steps, forming a separate organization with local native leadership, which led to a ten-year separation and excommunication (later changed to disfellowship) of nearly one-third of the native Mexican members.[17] Even though this group did not sustain the mission leadership sent from Church headquarters in Utah, they regarded themselves as faithful Church members.[18]

Recognizing the need for new leadership, presiding ecclesiastical authorities in Salt Lake City called Arwell L. Pierce to preside over the Mexican mission with a special charge by J. Reuben Clark Jr., an Apostle and former U.S. ambassador to Mexico, to reunify the Church there. The Church was once again unified thanks to Pierce's incredible leadership and great love for the Mexican people; the efforts of many local leaders, including Isasias Juárez, Julio Garcia, Bernabe Parra; general Church leadership; and the newly sustained prophet, George Albert Smith (who successfully spoke at a Mexican Area Conference to reunite the members in 1946). Focus now could be turned to strengthening the Saints and preparing the rising generation "to blossom as the rose," primarily through education, as was the pattern in the early Church history.

In 1944, recognizing the need to educate his own children as well as many of the other illiterate members, Bernabe Parra, a well-off native Mexican convert and branch president, founded his own private school at San Marcos Tula, Hidalgo, about thirty miles northwest of Mexico City.[19] By 1946, over seventy-nine children were enrolled in this elementary school.[20] Unlike the reports of their sister schools in the colonies, who in 1942 reportedly failed to give the child much more of Mexico than his cousin receives from his Spanish class in Salt Lake City,[21] this school was Mexican through and through. They celebrated Mexican Independence Day, taught Mexican history, spoke Spanish, and involved the community in all types of Mexican festivities. One year later, President Arwell Pierce joined Parra and others in requesting assistance from the Church for the school.

The timing of Parra's request for help from Church leaders could not have been better. David O. McKay, then serving as one of the senior Apostles, not only had a professional background in teaching, but was the first member of the Quorum of the Twelve to have taken an international tour around the world. For a year, he had taken notice of the needs of members of the Church, resulting in, among other things, a desire to educate the underprivileged Saints. In addition, Elder Spencer W. Kimball, who was called to the Quorum of the Twelve in 1943, was admonished in his patriarchal blessing to "preach the gospel to many people, but more especially the Lamanites." Then, in May of 1945, President George Albert Smith assigned Elder Kimball to "look after the indians—they are neglected. Take charge and watch after the Indians in all the world." [22] Needless to say, Parra's request was heard. Later that year at a general conference, Elder Spencer W. Kimball announced, "We are looking forward to a new day in schooling where our Lamanites may receive many of the advantages that our own children have."[23]

During the next two decades, the Church ran a Lamanite Seminary program, commenced the Indian Placement Program (primarily in the western United States), initiated the Lamanite Generation at BYU, founded the Church College of Hawaii, and started an international Church Educational System that reached students from elementary to high school throughout the Pacific Islands, New Zealand, Central and South America, and Mexico. A writer for the Church's official magazine, the *Ensign* (whose entire issue for the month was devoted to the progress of those then considered Lamanites), wrote of these educational endeavors, "Possibly the most important thing that could be said about the Lamanite programs of the Church is that they are developing leadership and strength among the Lamanites. The gospel of Jesus Christ," he continues, "brings men and women to a greater measure of their potential, and nowhere is this more evident than among the Lamanite members of the Church."[24]

The Church's international growth was accelerating, and member conversion in Mexico was extraordinary. Between the years 1946 and 1961, Mexican membership grew from approximately 5,000 members to nearly 25,000.[25] With this increase in membership, especially among the underprivileged class, came a glaring realization of the lack of education and resources among them. Although the Church supported and approved of Bernabe Parra's school, the need for more resources became apparent. Many native members looked to the well-established and successful Mormon Colonies in the northern Mexico state of Chihuahua for further secular and religious education and leadership training of their children. Some wondered why these same resources given to the American colonists were not available for the natives. No longer could the need for good education be ignored. Desiring to help these new converts and their children, Mexico mission president Claudio Bowman encouraged a study to be done to assess the needs of education in Mexico.

Mexico's Educational Needs

In 1957, President David O. McKay formed a committee to investigate the possibility of establishing Church schools in Mexico. He named Elder Marion G. Romney of the Quorum of the Twelve, who was responsible for the overall direction for Church programs of special interest to the Lamanites, as director of the committee, with Joseph T. Bentley and Claudius Bowman, both mission presidents serving in Mexico, as members of the committee.[26] These capable leaders ascertained the number of students, the buildings necessary, the legality of the Church operating educational facilities in Mexico, the political leanings of the government, and the available state educational system in each area. The results of this study led to the development of the Sociedad Educativa y Cultural, S. C. (Educational and Cultural Society), which would be the catalyst to building and organizing over forty elementary schools, two additional secondary schools, one preparatory school, and one normal school during the next decade.[27]

From 1957 to 1960, constant correspondence occurred among local LDS ecclesiastical and educational leaders in Mexico and the General Authorities. Major concerns addressed through the correspondence were the politics of the Mexican educational system (which had strong Communist and atheistic influence),[28] the buying and owning of land, and official recognition of the Church by the Mexican government.[29] Partially in reaction to the religious domination of the Catholic Church, the Mexican constitution placed strict limits on all churches, including prohibiting churches to purchase land, separating religion and education, and requiring native teachers to avoid proselyting to their children.[30]

After a thorough investigation of educational resources and needs, Elder Romney and Joseph Bentley recommended the development of a large private educational system supported by the Church to be completed by the fall of 1960. They also recommended that a high school be built which "could well form the nucleus of a center not only for Mexico, but for all the Latin American missions where priesthood manuals and materials for church auxiliaries could be prepared."[31] With the expansion of the Church in mind and with the necessity to build strong ties with the Mexican people and government, they wrote, "We have a great work yet to do in these lands, . . . developing our programs around the native cultures. Stories and illustrations for Mexico should be taken from Mexican history and from the lives of Mexican heroes such as Benito Juárez and Hidalgo."[32] On January 21, 1960, the First Presidency approved the recommendations and assigned Elder Romney and Ernest Wilkinson to take charge.[33]

During the October general conference of the same year, in his talk "The Day of the Lamanites," Elder Spencer W. Kimball reported, "[The Lamanites in general] are facing an open door to education, culture, refinement, progress, and the gospel of Jesus Christ. The Church has spent its millions in Hawaii and New Zealand, and other islands to provide schools for the young Lehites. Surely, no descendants need go now without an education, and schools in Mexico will be followed by schools in other nations. Surely the number of deprived ones is being reduced, and opportunity is knocking at their door." He continued, "A new world is open to them, and they are grasping the opportunities. God bless the Lamanites and hasten the day of their total emancipation from the thralldom of yesteryear."[34]

Commencement of Church Education throughout Mexico

Under the new LDS educational advisory board in Mexico and superintendent Daniel Taylor from the Mormon colonies (who had extensive experience in Mexican education, law, and culture and who was trusted by leaders of the Church), the society built schools, trained and hired teachers, and enrolled students by the thousands. In fact, by the end of 1969, thirty-nine schools were created throughout Mexico, named after "outstanding Mexican civil servants independent of religious influence." When asked nearly half a century later about the connection between the school building and the empowerment of the Lamanites, Dan Taylor responded, "The two had everything in common. We were helping the Lamanites 'blossom as a rose.'"[35]

Due to the high rate of graduation from the LDS primary schools and inadequate secondary schools provided by the government, Church educational leaders in Mexico turned next to the creation of secondary and preparatory schools, with a heavy focus on the central campus in Mexico City. The board determined that this campus would include a *primaria* (elementary), a *secundaria* (junior high), a *preparatoria* (high school), and a normal (teacher preparation) school. All students would live in homes on campus rather than dormitories, in order to provide a family-like environment, which would allow students to participate with "foster parents" in prayer, scripture study, chores, and other family activities. This environment provides the youth with personal attention and mentoring from active Latter-day Saint couples. All students on campus would be required to work as part of their tuition.

During the next few years, decisions regarding the funding of the schools in Mexico, especially the large campus planned for Mexico City, became topics of concern and even debate among the Brethren and top educational leaders in the Church. With his desire to promote junior colleges in highly LDS-populated areas throughout the United States, Ernest L. Wilkinson pressed firmly for finances to be allocated toward that end. Others including Elder Boyd K. Packer (serving then as Assistant to the Quorum of the Twelve) emphasized putting the money the Church would be spending on junior colleges in privileged areas into places they believed needed it more, such as Mexico. Elder Packer wrote the following in a letter to the First Presidency during a highly inflamed period of debate between Wilkinson and him:

> I confess to a deep yearning concern for the underprivileged youth of the church, particularly those of Lamanite descent, and find myself restlessly hoping that something may be done to provide even a meager education. I have visited in Mexico and know something of our school program there. In Mexico illiteracy is on the increase. . . . Somehow to commit hundreds of millions of dollars to provide the well-privileged youth of the Church with an education they will achieve anyway with less expense and more convenience than if we provide it seems unfortunate stewardship of our educational resources. Is it an error to suggest that the testimony of the Book of Mormon for these underprivileged children in Latin America and elsewhere is predicated upon their ability at least to read?[36]

Eventually, Elder Packer's suggestion for the money to go to those most in need was realized. On November 4, 1963, after years of research and after buying and preparing the land for the proposed, school, Elder Marion G. Romney of the Quorum of the Twelve flew to Mexico City to personally supervise the groundbreaking for the first building.

Following speeches given by local leaders, Agricol Lozano Herrera, a Church attorney and member of the Board of Education, announced the official name of the school: Centro Escolar Benemérito de las Americas (Benefactor of the Americas), referring to Benito Juárez, a well-known national hero in Mexico. Lozano explained that by adopting this name, they were showing appreciation for their great ancestry and common heritage. Furthermore, this name would set this school apart from Catholic schools, which were typically named after Saints.

Elder Marion G. Romney then spoke. He recalled his own childhood education in the Mexican Mormon colonies, he spoke of his love for Mexico, and he encouraged the children to learn every word of the Mexican national anthem and to love not only the song but "to love Mexico." He then prophesied, "This school for which we are breaking ground today is destined to become a great Spanish-speaking cultural

Groundbreaking ceremony at Benemérito de las Americas, November 4, 1963. Left to right: Joseph T. Bentley, Ernest LeRoy Hatch, Agricol Lozano Herrera, and Elder Marion G. Romney with children, parents, and teachers in background. (Photo from record book kept by staff of Benemérito and in possession of author.)

center. Its influence will reach far beyond the valley of Mexico. . . . It will be felt in all of Latin America, including South America. Hundreds of thousands of people will come here. Going out from here, they will help the Nation build up its education, its culture, and its spirituality."[37]

Benemérito student dance performers. (Photo by Esli Hernandez.)

On February 17, 1964, exactly 125 *secundaria* (junior high) students entered and began their studies at Benemérito. Three years later, the *preparatoria* (high school) was opened. The students came from all over Mexico; the majority were recent converts from the poor economic class. They participated in a variety of extracurricular activities, including music, sports, and academic and civic clubs. They attended seminary daily, and for the first time in Church history, a campus stake was organized for high-school students.

In 1967, following much fasting, much prayer, many incredible instances of communication, and a perceived miracle, the Mexican government granted unheard-of permission to establish a normal school, provided that there were adequate numbers of Church-owned *primaria* schools to employ the teachers upon their graduation. Thus, in 1968, the normal school was also included. The number of total students on campus reached 2,803 during the 1974–75 school year.[38]

Mexico School's Government Assessment and Prophetic Potential

In 1971, Manuel Lopez Davila, an official in the Secretaría de Educación Pública recorded, "The education labor of the Mormon community in Mexico must be considered as an effective help in the development of education in our country. . . . All of the Mormon schools are incorporated with and are recognized by the [Secretaría de Educación Pública]." Continuing the report, he described the educational setting of students and faculty. "The school rooms are magnificent. Its shops, laboratories, library, auditorium, and gymnasium are well equipped." He concluded, "The Mormon community, organized educationally as the Sociedad Educativa y Cultural, . . . has the backing of the top officials of the [Secretaría de Educación Pública] because of the objectives and collaboration that said community has in helping us to resolve [the educational problems in Mexico]."[39]

In February of 1977, the Church held its largest conference ever with over 25,000 people in attendance, many of whom were Church school students and faculty. This conference was held in Mexico City. As prophet of the Church, President Kimball gave a notable address, the impact of which cannot be overestimated. In his talk, he related a dream he had had nearly thirty years prior regarding the "progress and development" of Lehi's children. "I saw the great people of the Lamanites in beautiful houses and having all the comforts that science can afford," he related. "I saw the people of Lehi as engineers and builders. . . . I saw you in great political positions and functioning as administrators of the land. I saw many of you as heads of government . . . [and] in legislative positions where as good legislators and good Latter-day Saints you were able to make the best laws for your brothers and sisters." He saw their children as attorneys and doctors "looking after the health of the people." He saw them as "owners of industries and factories" and "of newspapers with great influence in public affairs." He saw artists and authors whose writings had a "powerful influence on the thoughts of the people of the country." He saw "the church growing in rapid strides" and wards and stakes organized by the hundreds. He saw missionaries, "not only hundreds but thousands," and a temple "filled with men and women."[40]

With the foundation of the Church and Church schools in place, this talk empowered the Saints in Mexico and dramatically enabled their educational pursuits. Paragraphs from President Kimball's talk were made into posters, memorized by students, printed in daily student planners, and discussed in families and at many church functions. In reference to her education at the Church's elementary school in Hidalgo and later at Benemérito, and the impact of President Kimball's talk, one alum reminisced, "From these schools, we not only learned the secular information, but we became united as members of the Church. We realized, as we studied the Book of Mormon, and read, studied, and talked about President Kimball's dream, that we were a chosen people with previously unheard of possibilities."[41]

Representando los Ideales, *by Ignacio M. Beteta and Roberto Cueva del Rio, is prominently placed in the entrance to the Benemérito administration building. It represents the need to reach the ideal in life by gaining intelligence, power, truth, and light.*

A Drastic Change in Church Education

Although the schools, especially Benemérito, were deemed effective, changes were afoot that would eventually transform the Church's school system in Mexico. In 1971, under the direction of newly appointed commissioner of education Neal A. Maxwell, the Church adopted a policy to "not duplicate otherwise available" educational opportunities.[42]

During the late 1970s, possibly as a result of the announced Official Declaration 2 removing "all restrictions with regard to race that once applied to the priesthood,"[43] along with the failing health of President Kimball, emphasis turned from the Lamanites to a worldwide Church. Expansion of the Lamanite programs came to a halt. After a thorough investigation by Church leaders in the early 1980s, they determined that the Mexican government was providing adequate educational opportunities for most elementary and secondary students. Therefore, in 1984, all Mexican Church schools were phased out with the exception of Academia Juárez's secondary and preparatory schools and the preparatory school at Benemérito. Dan Workman, the CES administrator over the Church schools in Mexico, reported:

> These meetings were held simultaneously all over Mexico, in all forty of the schools that were going to be closed. They announced that the First Presidency and the Quorum of the Twelve had met. They had been given the information about the schools, and it was the will of the Lord that these schools would now be phased out and they would utilize the public schools. Then each congregation or group was asked to sustain the Brethren in that decision, and they were given the opportunity to object. There were only two or three in all forty schools who raised hands in objection, and none of them were members of the Church. They were all mothers. It was a great revelation to me about the loyalty of those people in Mexico, because none of them wanted to lose their schools. But if the prophet said they were to be closed, they were to be closed, at whatever sacrifice.[44]

Although there was uniform acceptance of the closing of the schools and overwhelming signs of obedience and faith by the members, many Saints quietly struggled with the decision. Efrain Villalobos Vasquez, who was one of the first students at the Hidalgo School and later a teacher and administrator at Benemérito for nearly thirty years, was the superintendent of the Sociedad Educative y Cultural when the decision and announcement were made. Years later, reflecting on his feelings of the closing of the school, he related: "I didn't understand

Academia Juárez building, completed in 1904. (Photo by author.)

the decision, but I knew there was nothing I could do about it. I had been told that this was what was being done, and felt that my only choice was to fall in line with the leaders. I wished we could have been a part of that decision-making process. I wished that our opinions were taken into consideration."[45] Today, many members say that they can now see the wisdom in closing the schools and putting the funds into the international seminary and institute program, but during the time the loss of their schools was a tough pill to swallow.

Although these times were difficult for many members, growth in Mexican membership did not reflect it. When the Church schools were started among the Mexican natives in 1961, there were approximately 25,000 members. By 1972, this number had quadrupled to

Graduating class of 1939. (Taken from The Juarez Stake Academy, 1897–1997.*)*

over 100,000. Over a period of three days, November 7–9, 1975, Elder Howard W. Hunter of the Quorum of the Twelve Apostles created fifteen stakes in the Mexico City area. Because of these numbers, the Church leaders planned and dedicated the first Mexican temple in 1983, during the sensitive time of the school closures. In 1993, Mexico officially recognized the Church, allowing the Church to have ownership of land in its own name—a controversial topic finally resolved after nearly a decade of debate. By 2004, the Church would reach over one million members in Mexico.[46]

Although the majority of the Church schools were closed during the 1980s, Academia Juárez and Benemérito continued to be influenced by the Church's earlier emphasis on Lamanites. In fact, in front of every student academic notebook, the monumental talk by President Kimball is prominently printed, reminding them of who they are and inviting students to fulfill prophetic vision. Students are constantly reminded of their Lamanite heritage on posters, in dances, in assemblies, and in daily dialogue and instruction.

For nearly a quarter of a century, Benemérito and Academia Juárez have existed as well-known, prestigious sister schools in Mexico. With an enrollment of over four hundred students annually at Academia Juárez and over two thousand annually at Benemérito, these schools have been homes to thousands of students. On January 29, 2013, the paradigm of home and family for these students and faculty on Benemérito campus took an unexpected and dramatic shift. Mexico area president Daniel Johnson, accompanied by Elders Russell M. Nelson and Jeffrey R. Holland and others from both the education and missionary departments of the Church, announced the conversion of Benemérito from a high school into the second-largest Missionary Training Center in the world. Elder Holland declared, "This is a dramatic moment in Church history. You have lived to see your role in one of the most historic moments in the Church."[47] Elder Nelson then prophesied, "This sacred place will help the country of Mexico to become all that God intends it to become. With that sanctification, it will be a blessing to the entire world."[48]

When asked why the Saints in Mexico had received so many blessings throughout the last century, including a number of temples, missions, and schools, Elder Nelson responded, "I believe it relates to who they really are. We know who they really are by reading the Book of Mormon. The Book of Mormon was written for the Lamanites, and the people of Mexico have that tradition and the blessing of being a believing people."[49]

Conclusion

By examining the historical, political, social, and religious underpinnings of over a century of LDS Church existence in Mexico, it is clear that the Church's emphasis on the Lamanites influenced its educational endeavors in Mexico. Now, after nearly 120 years since the school officially commenced, and after being a flagship to over fifty schools in the country, the Juárez Academy is the only Church-owned school left in Mexico. Although this school commenced with the intention of teaching the American Mormon colonist youth, the enrollment is now almost completely native Mexican members. Teachers and leaders of the school and community take pride in the school's academic excellence, bilingual curriculum, and history of creating Church, community, government, and family leaders throughout Mexico and the world. According to Elder Paul V. Johnson, who served until 2015 as commissioner of the Church Educational System, there is no intention at this point in closing the school.[50] Although Benemérito and the other schools have fulfilled their missions in Mexico, as Elder Nelson related, "we are only in the middle of Mexico's history, and we do not know what the future holds."[51]

Notes

1. Milton Lynn Bennion, *Mormonism and Education* (Salt Lake City: The Department of Education of The Church of Jesus Christ of Latter-day Saints, 1939), 6.
2. D&C 88:77–78, 136–38.
3. Bennion, *Mormonism and Education*, 12.
4. Bennion, *Mormonism and Education*, 40–49.
5. Albert Kenyon Wagner and Leona Farnsworth Wagner, *The Juarez Stake Academy, 1897–1997: The First One Hundred Years* (Juárez, Mexico: The Academy, 1997), 5.
6. D&C 3:20.
7. Book of Mormon introduction. For more information regarding DNA and the Lamanites, see Gospel Topics at LDS.org under "DNA and Lamanite Heritage."
8. D&C 28, 32.
9. Parker Pratt Robinson, ed., *Writings of Parley Parker Pratt: One of the First Missionaries and a Member of the First Quorum of the Twelve Apostles of the Church of Jesus Christ of Latter-day Saints* (Salt Lake City: Deseret News, 1952), 5.
10. F. LaMond Tullis, *Mormons in Mexico: The Dynamics of Faith and Culture* (Logan: Utah State University Press, 1987), 14.
11. Leonard J. Arrington, *Brigham Young: American Moses* (New York: Knopf, 1985), 383.
12. Wagner and Wagner, *The Juarez Stake Academy, 1897–1997*, 1–2, 6.
13. Tullis, *Mormons in Mexico*, 60–71.
14. Gerry R. Flake, "Mormons in Mexico: The First 96 Years," *Ensign*, September 1972, 21. Also see Tullis, *Mormons in Mexico*, 137.
15. Enrique Gonzalez, quoted in the "Informe General de la Tercera Convencion," 18, translated by Tullis in *Mormons in Mexico*, 127.
16. D&C 49:24.
17. LeRoy Medico Hatch, unpublished autobiography, in author's possession; Tullis, *Mormons in Mexico*, 142–46, 156.

18. For more information on the Third Convention, see Tullis, *Mormons in Mexico*, 137–68.
19. Tullis, *Mormons in Mexico*, 186.
20. *Historia de la escuela,* "Heroes de Chapultepec," San Marcos, Hidalgo año 1944 Y premero da la escuela, n.p., unpublished, in author's possession.
21. Henry L. Cain, "Report of the Juarez Stake School System," October 1, 1942, cited in Clark V. Johnson, "Mormon Education in Mexico: The Rise of the Sociedad Educativa Cultural" (PhD diss., Brigham Young University, 1977), 51.
22. Francis M. Gibbons, *Spencer W. Kimball: Resolute Disciple, Prophet of God* (Salt Lake City: Deseret Book, 1995), 380.
23. Spencer W. Kimball, "The Lamanites," in Conference Report, October 1947, 15–22.
24. M. Dallas Burnett, "Lamanites and the Church," *Ensign*, July 1971, 13.
25. Mormon News Room, "Facts and Statistics: Mexico," http://www.mormonnewsroom.org/facts-and-statistics/country/mexico.
26. "Correspondence 1959," letter, December 9, 1959, Joseph T. Bentley Papers, container 3, file 5, 20th Century Western & Mormon Manuscripts, MSS 848, L. Tom Perry Special Collections, Harold B. Lee Library, Brigham Young University, Provo, UT.
27. Efrain Villalobos, personal notes given to author, in author's possession.
28. Bentley Papers, box 106, folder 9.
29. See Johnson, "Mormon Education in Mexico," 89–90, in reference to Articles 27 and 130 of the Constitution.
30. Johnson, "Mormon Education in Mexico," 88–89.
31. Harvey L. Taylor, *The Story of L.D.S. Church Schools* (n.p, 1971), 11.
32. Taylor, *L.D.S. Church Schools*, 11.
33. Taylor, *L.D.S. Church Schools*, 12.
34. Spencer W. Kimball, "The Day of the Lamanites," in Conference Report, October 1960, 37.
35. Daniel Taylor interview, February 2013, interviewed by Barbara Morgan, American Fork Utah, transcript in author's possession.
36. Boyd K. Packer to First Presidency, February 18, 1963, J. Willard Marriott Library, University of Utah, MS 668, box 59, folder 1.

37. Groundbreaking ceremony, Benemérito de las Americas, November 4, 1963, MS 2491, Church History Library.
38. Abraham Lopez to Barbara Morgan, email, April 25, 2013, in author's possession.
39. Tullis, *Mormons in Mexico*, 198.
40. Dell Van Orden, "Emotional Farewell in Mexico," *Church News*, February 19, 1977, 3.
41. Maria Parra interview, interviewed by Barbara Morgan, May 2014, San Marcos Hidalgo Mexico, transcript in author's possession.
42. Neal A. Maxwell, "Seek Ye Learning Even by Study and Faith: Report for 1971 from Commissioner of Education of the Church of Jesus Christ of Latter-day Saints," M260 S451, Church History Library, Salt Lake City, 1. See also Casey Paul Griffiths, "The Globalization of Latter-day Saint Education" (PhD diss., Brigham Young University, 2012), 208–219.
43. Doctrine and Covenants, Official Declaration 2.
44. Dan Workman interview, interviewed by Dale LeBaron, June 27, 1991, Utah Valley Community College, transcript in author's possession.
45. Efrain Villalobos interview, interviewed by Barbara Morgan, February 2013, Mexico City, Mexico, transcript in author's possession.
46. "Mexico Milestones: Important Moments of Church History in Mexico," *Church News*, July 10, 2004, 10.
47. Elder Holland, speech to Benemérito students and faculty at Centro Escolar Benemérito de las Americas, January 29, 2013, Mexico City, transcript in author's possession.
48. Russell M. Nelson, speech to Benemérito students and faculty at Centro Escolar Benemérito de las Americas, January 29, 2013, Mexico City, transcript in author's possession.
49. Russell M. Nelson interview, interviewed by Barbara Morgan, September 2013, Salt Lake City, transcript in author's possession.
50. Paul V. Johnson, interview by Barbara Morgan, March 2013, Salt Lake City, transcript in author's possession.
51. Elder Nelson interview.

17

"Good Citizens of Our Adopted Country"

The Juárez Academy and Latter-day Saint Globalization through Education

Scott C. Esplin

As The Church of Jesus Christ of Latter-day Saints has expanded globally, its educational system has followed step for step.[1] At present, the Church Educational System operates in 140 countries, generally in the form of its well-recognized seminary and institute programs and its post-secondary institutions. Additionally, it maintains a handful of elementary and secondary school programs serving nearly 7,000 students in several long-established locations, including Fiji, Kiribati, Samoa, Tonga, and, for the focus of this chapter, Mexico.[2] In Mexico, one of the Church's earliest uses of education in a global context occurred at the Juárez Academy, the Church's longest-operating international school. Originally serving an isolationist purpose for Saints seeking refuge beyond the borders of the United States, the school was established in 1897 to educate Anglo, English-speaking children

---

Scott C. Esplin is an associate professor of Church history and doctrine at Brigham Young University.

The original church building and school house in Colonia Juárez, Mexico. (Used by permission of Utah State Historical Society.)

sequestered in northern Mexico. The history of the school, highlighted by the accounts of those who attended or taught at it, captures the successes and challenges in expanding the Church abroad. This study will examine the Juárez Academy's history in order to explore how the Church has employed education to facilitate international expansion.

Settling the Mormon Colonies and Establishing the Juárez Academy

Mormon educational presence in Mexico is rooted in the early history of the faith and especially its response to the United States government's antipolygamy crusade of the 1880s. "A general attack is being made upon our liberties throughout all the territories where our people reside," Church President John Taylor wrote to community leaders in Arizona in December 1884. Characterizing the Church's isolationist response, President Taylor proposed, "Our counsel has been and is to obtain a place of refuge under a foreign government to which our people can flee when menaced in this land."[3] Within weeks of the announcement, more than three hundred Latter-day Saints from Arizona, New Mexico, and Utah poured across the Mexican border, eventually settling nine communities in the northwestern states of Chihuahua and Sonora, Mexico.[4] Chief among them was the community of Colonia Juárez, which became the headquarters for a stake in the region in 1895.[5] Among the primary reasons for relocating beyond the borders of the United States was the desire to completely live the teachings of the faith, including the practice of plural marriage. Though the practice of plural marriage was discontinued during the community's early years, the motivations behind it influenced all aspects of colony life, including its educational practices.

As Church members were settling along the Sierra Madre Mountains of northern Mexico, Church leaders in Salt Lake City

The modern community of Colonia Juárez, Mexico, with the Juárez Academy at the center. (Photo by Scott C. Esplin.)

responded to the loss of societal control brought about by increasing federal opposition to Church practices. Attempting to protect the Church from encroaching outside influence, Church leaders instituted an educational policy of isolation. In April 1886, President Taylor declared, "The duty of our people under these circumstances is clear; it is to keep their children away from the influence of the sophisms of infidelity and the vagaries of the sects. Let them, though it may possibly be at some pecuniary sacrifice, establish schools taught by those of our faith, where, free from the trammels of State aid, they can unhesitatingly teach the doctrines of true religion combined with the various branches of a general education."[6] Following President Taylor's death, President Wilford Woodruff implemented the vision. "The time has arrived when the proper education of our children should be taken in hand by us as a people," President Woodruff declared in 1888 as he called for each stake to create its own private academy.[7] Within months, dozens of Church academies sprang up across Utah, Idaho, and Arizona.[8] Saints in Mexico followed suit when the community of Colonia Juárez opened the Juárez Stake Academy in September 1897. Patterned after its sister academies in the United States, the Juárez Academy offered traditional academic study bolstered by the study of religion. Enrolling 225 common-school students its first year, and the school graduated fifteen students from the eighth grade in 1898. These students became the first ninth-grade class later that fall.[9] Among the students was Anna Lowrie Ivins, a girl whose story reveals early global perspectives within Mormonism.

Anna's life began in St. George, Utah, where she was born to Anthony Woodward Ivins and Elizabeth Ashby Snow on October 20, 1882. The third in a family that eventually included nine children, Anna recalled her childhood days in St. George as "very happy ones . . . and a source of many pleasant memories."[10] Ivins's reminiscent account is punctuated by details of her studies, recess games of little rounders, one old cat, marbles, hikes to the top of St. George's Sugar Loaf mountain,

Anthony W. Ivins, first stake president of the Juárez Stake. (Used by permission of Utah State Historical Society.)

kissing games, and walks home after parties paired off as couples.[11] Its tone, however, changes with her father's call from the First Presidency on August 18, 1895 to relocate to Mexico, preside over the Mexican Mission, organize the Juárez Stake, and serve as its first stake president.[12] Thirteen-year-old Anna notes the sacrifice on the part of her father, who was, in her words, "a very promising candidate for the governorship of the state," and her mother, who was in poor health and "looked forward with dread to life in a new, strange country." For herself, Anna called the move to Mexico "the greatest tragedy of my life thus far."[13]

After a year of preparation, the Ivins couple, together with their then seven children ranging from sixteen-year-old Antoine to nearly three-year-old Gusta, traveled by train from southern Utah to Salt Lake City and then to El Paso, Texas. Crossing into Mexico in October 1896, Anna recalled her mother's nervousness during the family's first night encamped near Ahumada, Mexico. When her father reassured them that government soldiers were stationed nearby, Ivins's mother revealed the tensions evident in this unfamiliar global foray by replying that she "would feel just as frightened of them as of the local population." Ivins captured the scene by reflecting a nineteenth-century Latter-day Saint girl's vision of an international adventure in the process. "As we traveled through the sparsely settled country, it was quite evident that we were, indeed, in a totally different country," Ivins reported. The "many interesting sights" that "met our eyes" included "Mexican men in their tall sombreros and bright colored sarapes driving their heavily loaded burros before them along the dusty roads, the flat-topped brown adobe huts with just as brown men, women and children hovering about the doorways surrounded by their chickens, dogs and goats; the men working in the fields with their primitive methods and crude machinery consisting of wooden plows, and hoes. . . . All [were] indicative of the new country in which we were to live."[14]

Settling in the community of Colonia Juárez, Ivins quickly made friends and resumed her studies. "Educational facilities being so limited my father at once set all out to improve them," she recalled. A schoolhouse with two large classrooms was quickly erected.[15] With an adequate facility in place, Ivins's father next turned his attention to securing a competent teacher for the isolated Mormon community, engaging Guy C. Wilson, an instructor at the Brigham Young

Academy in Provo, Utah, for the task. Curriculum at the international school paralleled that of the academy system in the United States and included, among other subjects, algebra, geometry, English literature, history, psychology, and accounting. Recognizing that the younger grades needed attention if future students were to be prepared to attend the academy, officials arranged for Ella Larsen to assist Principal Wilson in conducting teacher-training classes to develop future faculty. Additionally, professors from Church schools in Utah regularly visited to conduct training and keep the school on par with its sister institutions. In 1903, ground was broken on a new academy building that would mirror facilities at the other Church schools.[16]

With its traditional academic curriculum, corresponding teacher training division, and matching school building, the early Juárez Academy looked like any other Church academy, but with one significant exception: its location outside the United States. Examining the school, little would indicate it was not located somewhere in rural Utah, Arizona, or Idaho. During its earliest years, names of faculty and students reflect the school's Anglo population and contain some of the faith's most prominent local names. For example, though small, the six members of the school's first graduating class had, in addition to Anna Ivins and her older brother Antoine, the surnames Bailey, Clayson, Harris, and Hatch. Similar northern European surnames like Bentley, Cox, Jones, Redd, Robinson, Romney, Snow, Spilsbury, and Taylor dominated the subsequent five graduating classes. Teacher rolls also reflected the American presence, with names like Cannon, Clark, Eyring, Hatch, Larson, Romney, Smith, Snow, Wilson, and Young prominent during the school's first fifteen years.[17] Additionally, all instruction was done in English, with the exception of a Spanish course, the lone curricular deviation from the Church's other academy offerings.[18]

This Spanish course helped the participants in the Juárez Academy come closest to connecting with their Mexican surroundings during the institution's early years. Manrique Gonzalez, an adult

Hispanic student, appears to be the only native Spanish speaker to have graduated from the school during its first twenty-five years of operation.[19] Originally from the state of Coahuila in northeastern Mexico, Gonzalez moved to Colonia Juárez for work in 1898, joined the Church, and enrolled in a first-grade class as a seventeen-year-old young man. Accelerating his education, he graduated from the eighth grade five years later at the age of twenty-two. Later that year, Principal Wilson approached Gonzalez about teaching Spanish at the Academy while continuing his secondary school studies. Teaching part-time, Gonzalez graduated from the Academy in 1910 at the age of twenty-eight.[20] After graduation, he taught Spanish at the school full-time, becoming the only Hispanic member on an otherwise Anglo faculty during the first several decades of its operation. Gonzalez later recalled the influence he had on the school: "My job was to teach them Spanish. That I tried to do to the best of my ability. . . . I was the first Mexican student that graduated from the [Juárez Academy]. I was instrumental in bringing to school many Mexican students that have made great success: Andres C. Gonzalez, Luis Gonzalez, Manuel Gonzalez W., General Julio Gonzalez, Manuel Quijano, Luis Flores, and others that I cannot think of at this time. . . . They all have confessed to me that the foundation they got at the Juárez Stake Academy has been the greatest help to them in their everyday life."[21]

In spite of these examples, interactions between the American expatriates and local Mexican residents were limited during the community's early years. Anna Ivins's account subtly notes her family's employing Ruperta Hernandez, a young Mexican girl, to assist Anna's mother in the home while a neighbor named Andres assisted with the outdoor farm work. Additionally, her brother, upon graduating, spent several years studying Mexican law in Mexico City, where he "spoke the language like a native and learned to understand the Mexican people."[22]

The wording of Ivins's account, writing that her brother understood "the Mexican people," subtly highlights the way settlers of the Mormon colonies viewed themselves as something other than Mexican. In this way, it reflects the limitations to true globalization in the Church's early international endeavors. In reality, the community of Colonia Juárez kept one foot in the United States and another foot in Mexico. This navigating of cultures was highlighted in Ivins's reminiscence of community gatherings that blended elements of traditional Mormon and American celebrations with those of Mexico. She recalled the Utah connections that persisted in the community. "Holidays were of special interest and we had a number of them. We celebrated the 24th of July with perhaps a parade and a public meeting at which we listened to speeches about our Mormon Utah Pioneers." However, she also noted their adopting of Mexican celebrations. "Then there were the Mexican [holidays], the Cinco de Mayo (5th of May) and the Diez y Seis (16th of September). A gathering in the town park, the singing of the National Anthem, orations about the history of the nation, often a parade, the braiding of the May pole on the Cinco de Mayo, games and contests for all, and always a dance in the evening all helped to make these days memorable ones for us. We thrilled to the exploits of [Miguel Hidalgo,] the poor priest who led his people in their struggle for freedom and [Benito Juárez, who] later became president of the Republic." Explaining the balance these settlers sought in being both Americans by birth and yet exile residents in Mexico, Ivins continued, "We were doing our best to be good citizens of our adopted country, not actual citizens in a legal sense, for few of the Mormon colonists ever became naturalized, but we did endeavor to be loyal to the country and its laws."[23] For his part, Principal Wilson, who married Anna Ivins in May 1903, loved his work in Mexico and the successful school he helped found. "There is nothing to be gained by going out of Mexico for anything that is taught in the Juárez Stake Academy," Wilson counseled the student body in 1911. "On the contrary there is every reason why we should all support our home institution and make it the pride of our people and a credit to Mexico. RESOLVE! WORK! COME!"[24]

Ironically, Wilson's invitation for students to stay in Mexico in 1911 was reversed a year later when in July 1912, the Mexican Revolution made it necessary to abandon the school. Leading up to the conflict, Ivins notes in her account, "The colony people endeavored to remain entirely neutral as we desired to incite no animosity toward us." However, "the revolution continued going from bad to worse as far as our people were concerned." Eventually, "much tension and ill-feeling between the local Mexicans and the 'Americanos,' as they called our colonists" developed, and it was determined to evacuate to El Paso, Texas.[25] Though some returned, Ivins's intimation that she would never see her Mexican home again proved true, as her family relocated to Salt Lake City where her husband became the Church's second seminary teacher and, later, the first full-time religion faculty member at Brigham Young University.[26]

While the colony experience in Mexico ended for many with the evacuation of the community in 1912, the Juárez Academy itself lived on. Some residents returned to Colonia Juárez a year later, solidifying effects of the Mexican Revolution into the Church's global approach to education in the early twentieth century by entrenching ideas of isolationism and protectionism. The community of Colonia Juárez and the Juárez Academy itself served as a refuge for Mormon settlers in Mexico during the turbulent years that followed. For this reason, in part, when the Church divested itself of the other Church academies in the 1920s, the Juárez Academy was preserved.[27] At the time of the decision, Church School Superintendent Adam S. Bennion answered why the Juárez Academy survived: "The Church has no desire whatsoever to operate a system of schools in opposition to those under state control. . . . The academies that it now operates, it operates not in a spirit of rivalry, but having operated them in communities not served by public high schools, it continues to do so to the relief of the treasury of the state and to the very great satisfaction of the people served by them."[28]

Juárez Academy main building, completed in 1904. (Photo by Scott C. Esplin.)

The school survived, not because it was an international school or because the Mormon colonies represented an early Church effort at globalization. Rather, the school persisted because it extended American educational opportunity to expatriate Americans in Mexico. Describing his call to a Spanish-speaking mission, J. LeRoy Hatch, a 1930 graduate of the school, reflected the reality of the era, "In our colonies, isolated as we were, all of our schooling, our church services, our activities were conducted in English. Actually, we came in contact with very few Mexicans, only those who had drifted into our area looking for work in the orchards and fields."[29] Though school administrators and educators worked throughout the 1930s to ensure that all graduates could write, read, and speak Spanish fluently and "develop understanding between the colonists and their adopted countrymen," they fought an uphill battle to blend the American and Mexican cultures.[30]

Eventually isolationism and protectionism, with the underlying thread connecting the community to the United States, became entrenched within Church education in Mexico. An elementary school history from a neighboring community whose graduates attended the Juárez Academy chronicled the tension between the cultures. "One day after a session on patriotism for the colors of the flag, a pupil, Allie Acord, paraded an American flag around the school yard. A little Mexican student snatched the flag to the ground and stamped it as he shouted, 'This must not be carried in Mexico!'" Deescalating the situation but reflecting the community divide, "the teacher, thereafter, continued his lesson on patriotism to include the colors of red, white, and green of the adopted country. Always after that, the two flags flew together on the flagpole."[31] Perpetuating the division, the Juárez school "taught the courses required by the Mexican Department of Education," historian Clark Johnson summarized in his analysis of Church schools in Mexico, "but they did not comply with the requirement that these courses be taught in Spanish. They also continued to celebrate Independence Day on July 4 each year rather than on September 16, Mexican Independence Day. The Juárez school simply did not embrace the Mexican culture," Johnson concluded.[32] One teacher summarized the goal of this instruction, "We are going to make the natives good Americans and not good Mexicans for Mexico."[33]

Changing the Church's View on Global Education

For the Church to truly flourish in a global way in Mexico, perspectives and programs needed to change. A 1942 study of Latter-day Saint schools in Colonia Juárez conducted by Henry L. Cain, director of the American School in Mexico City, summarized the Church's challenge. "Although these schools have been in existence since 1885, a visitor can easily imagine himself in Kansas or Utah. And, while Spanish is taught in all grades, it creates nothing of an atmosphere. Some of the teachers were born in Mexico and they speak the Spanish language perfectly, nevertheless they fail to give the child much more of Mexico than his cousin receives from his Spanish class in Salt Lake City. Of the many cultural values which Mexico has to offer, few are entering into the education program in these schools," Cain opined. "All in all, they are giving a good American education to those who attend them."[34] Mexican public school inspector Manuel Lara Villanueva more bluntly summarized that the residents were still "Americans in their hearts."[35]

Segments of Mexican society took exception to this outsider element in their country. Arguing that Mexico had been dominated by the imitation of foreign ideas, habits, and customs, some Mexican educators proclaimed that the "task of education . . . is to dispel from the mind of the Mexican all shadows of inferiority."[36] By the middle of the twentieth century, Mexican authorities began reacting to Mormon exceptionalism in the Colonies and used the Juárez Academy in particular as a point of contention. In 1950, Moisés T. de la Peña, a respected Mexican sociologist, circulated a scathing critique of the Latter-day Saint settlements in northern Mexico. "In scholastic subjects the Mormons say that they accept the official program and that they maintain their schools only until the Government furnishes them with schools," Peña noted.[37] "The truth of the matter," he continued, "is that their religious prejudices make them look upon the official instruction with repugnancy and fear, and they are in fact absolutely free in their academic program, a situation which ought to be corrected, since this illegal privilege cannot be tolerated at this time." Peña praised colonists for being "zealous about obeying the laws regarding public registrations, in births, marriages, and deaths." Indeed, "their respect for Mexican Law, with the exception of the schooling example mentioned, is inalterable and exemplary," he continued. Culturally however, Peña concluded, "they are a demographic cyst, who disdain the society in which they live, that is, the Mexicans as a group. This undeniable truth makes them undesirable people."

Peña's assessment laid bare the lack of globalization evident in the Mormon communities in Mexico by the middle of the twentieth century. In his opinion, "the colonists appear to be optimistic and satisfied with their rapid progress, and add that they are happy 'in participating in the brilliant picture of progress and improvements of our beloved Mexican Country.'" However, he believed that their commitment to Mexico was "a theoretical problem" because the colonist "considers himself a Mexican and civically his conduct is almost without reproach; but he continues to be a Mormon foreigner 100 percent." As evidence, Peña reported a visit to Colonia Juárez, where he heard academy students walking the streets "giggling in English" and met "a happy and robust old lady, who still speaks no Spanish, after 57 years of residence in Mexico." Even among the Mormon colonists who spoke Spanish and contributed in positive economic ways, Peña decried that "these virtues are cancelled out by the fact that they oblige us to tolerate them as a social cyst." In his words, the colonists operated "within an unbreakable purist barrier which in the end is racial and Nordic." Furthermore, of the two hundred Mexican members living in the region, Peña found them to be "a very poor crop" after nearly six decades of proselytizing efforts. "Generally they are humble folks who are treated in a separate world from the opulent foreign Mormons, who speak very little in favor of [them.]"

As a result of his evaluation, Peña called for dramatic change within the Latter-day Saint Mexican community, including a prohibition against foreign language texts in the schools, an obligation to celebrate Mexican civic festivities, the hiring of Mexican teachers without exception, and the requirement that all men and women over the age of ten demonstrate competency in reading and writing Spanish as well as a basic understanding of geography, national history, and civics of Mexico. If these changes did not occur, Peña recommended the expulsion of American Latter-day Saints from the country.[38]

As the school and community underwent these critiques in the 1950s, its very existence as an outpost was threatened from internal challenges, some of which Peña captured in his report. "These colonists have maintained a constant emigration of their young folks, which has prohibited their growth," Peña summarized. "Since the young people feel an outright passion to educate themselves, upon leaving the Academy, they distribute themselves in American universities (very few go to Mexico), and as is apparent they have no reason for returning."[39] Demographic challenges like these undercut community growth, forcing scholastic change. When only nine students graduated from the Academy in 1954, another author questioned, "Have the Academy and the colonies which it guided served their purpose? Will the Academy, which has had such a rich and thrilling historical background and which has fought adversity so many times to survive, finally wink out?"[40]

To make both the school and the community survive, a change needed to occur within the Church's perspective on globalization. Rather than preserving and transmitting American ideals, the school, like the larger Church in its international approach, needed to embrace local culture. In Salt Lake City, Church Apostle Marion G. Romney, himself a product of the community of Colonia Juárez, acknowledged the need for change. "We have a great work to do in these lands . . . developing our programs around the native cultures," Romney counseled. Using schooling in Mexico as an example, Romney outlined, "Stories and illustrations for Mexico should be taken from Mexican history and from the lives of Mexican heroes such as Benito Juárez and Hidalgo. Our activities should feature Indian and Mexican dances, folk lore, and music." Ideally, he hoped that Church membership could "look to Mexico City rather than to the Juárez Stake Academy or the United States" for their educational model.[41] Complying with these desires, programs at the Juárez Academy were revised to strictly adhere to the Mexican regulations.[42]

Additionally, the Juárez Academy as well as local Church-run elementary schools that fed it increased their participation in local celebrations, parades, and activities.[43]

At the same time, the school sought to better integrate Hispanic students into its program, thereby stabilizing the dwindling enrollment. Children of local residents, including those from some of the most influential families in the state of Chihuahua, were recruited to attend the school.[44] While English continued to be the primary language of instruction at the school, special programs were instituted to help native students continue learning in their own tongue while acquiring proficiency in English.[45] Options were also explored to establish scholarships for Church members from across Mexico to study at the academy. As a result, Church officials reported two positive visits by the governor of the State of Chihuahua to the school as well as the belief that the Mormon colonies were becoming "a show window for progress, farming, and scholastic methods" in the area.[46]

The change in and expansion of the student population did not come about without opposition. Responding to a proposal in 1959 to construct new campus facilities, Mexico North Mission president and Juárez Academy graduate Joseph T. Bentley cautioned against going "completely 'overboard'" with ideas that "would damage rather than help the colonies in Mexico." Reflecting the perceptions of the earlier era, Bentley expressed his opinion that overcrowding came from admitting too many students of other faiths. He questioned if the resources could be put to better use elsewhere. "If this money were used to build a school in Monterrey and perhaps some of the other large cities in Mexico, a great many more members could benefit," Bentley offered.[47] Reflecting sensitivity to needs beyond the colonies, Bentley proposed "planning for all of these young folks" across the country rather than a small few who could attend the Juárez Academy. "By greatly increasing the capacity of the Academy," Bentley cautioned, "the additional students will all come from the Mexican population which will bring a great many racial and other problems such as intermarriage, discipline, standards (church), etc." Unsuccessfully, he urged careful, long-range planning and the adoption of a one-to-one ratio between the Anglo and Mexican student population at the school.[48]

In spite of tensions over the changing makeup of the institution, a noticeable increase in Hispanic-named graduates emerged. During the 1967–68 school year, Hispanic students outnumbered Anglo students for the first time, a trend that has continued to increase.[49] At the same time, enrollment rebounded from its earlier lows, eventually stabilizing near its present levels of approximately 400 students in the seventh through twelfth grades. By the end of the twentieth century, roughly 85 percent of the school population was Latino, with about 25 percent of the student body non-Mormon.[50] Academically, the school became a prominent religiously sponsored bilingual preparatory school.

All of these changes at the Juárez Academy coincided with dramatic Church growth across Mexico. Membership exploded more than twenty-five-fold from 5,646 members in 1950 to 141,211 by 1975.[51] By 2015, the Church reported a membership of more than 1.3 million people in Mexico, the highest total for the faith in any country outside the United States.[52] Educationally, with its 52,180 students, Mexico boasts the highest enrollment of seminary and institute students of any country outside the United States.[53] From a globalization perspective, most importantly, this growth occurred among the nation's native people.

Conclusion

In the earliest years of the Juárez Academy, the school worked to preserve an American national heritage in a Mexican outpost. However, the adherence to the United States' educational practices created a barrier for assimilation into Mexican society. Anna Ivins, the daughter of the community leader, a student in the school's first graduating class, and the eventual spouse of the school's principal captured the worldview that permeated her day when she wrote, "We were doing our best to be good citizens of our adopted country."[54]

Eventually, this preservation of an American type of Mormonism, however well intentioned, had to be set aside if the Church was to flourish in Mexico. Isolation needed to be replaced by acculturation. Stanley A. Peterson, longtime administrator of Church education who directed much of the system's international growth, summarized the shift. "It's critical that we use local people," Peterson said. "I saw areas where we kept sending Americans, and every time you send an American and use him the local people don't grow. Over the years, our philosophy has been to use the local people as soon as you can. Don't keep sending Americans because there's no continuity. There isn't the growth locally. It isn't their program."[55]

In the case of the Juárez Academy, "local people" includes the descendants of the colonists who settled the region more than a century ago. However, as a result of demographic shifts, government pressure, and greater cultural awareness, "local" also includes the Hispanic population of the area. Fostering an educational paradigm that celebrates both groups opens the door for marvelous Church growth in Mexico.

Notes

For an extended academic analysis of Mormon education in Mexico, see an academic study by Scott C. Esplin, E. Vance Randall, Casey P. Griffiths, and Barbara E. Morgan titled "Isolationism, Exceptionalism, and Acculturation: The Internationalisation of Mormon Education in Mexico," *Journal of Educational Administration and History* 46, no. 4 (2014): 387–404.

1. For an account of the Church's international education expansion, see Joe J. Christensen, "The Globalization of the Church Educational System," in *Global Mormonism in the 21st Century*, ed. Reid L. Neilson (Provo, UT: Religious

Studies Center, 2008), 183–201. Christensen was associate commissioner of education for the Church during much of this expansion and believes that there was "no other Church program that moved toward globalization and nationalization so quickly."

2. "Seminaries and Institutes of Religion Annual Report for 2015" (Salt Lake City: The Church of Jesus Christ of Latter-day Saints, 2015), 2, 4.
3. John Taylor and George Q. Cannon to Christopher Layton, December 16, 1884, cited in Thomas Cottam Romney, *The Mormon Colonies in Mexico* (Salt Lake City: University of Utah Press, 1938), 51–52.
4. The six colonies in the state of Chihuahua included Colonia Díaz, Colonia Juárez, Colonia Dublán, Colonia Pacheco, Colonia García, and Colonia Chuichupa. The three colonies in Sonora were Colonia Oaxaca, Colonia Morelos, and Colonia San José. (Colonia San José was a late breakoff formed by residents from Colonia Morelos and is not included in some lists of Mormon Mexican colonies.) Clarence F. Turley and Anna Tenney Turley, *History of the Mormon Colonies in Mexico (The Juárez Stake), 1885–1980* (Salt Lake City: Publishers Press, 1996), 1; Romney, *The Mormon Colonies in Mexico*, 56.
5. Clarence F. Turley and Anna Tenney Turley, *History of the Mormon Colonies in Mexico (The Juárez Stake), 1885–1980* (Salt Lake City: Publishers Press, 1996), 87.
6. John Taylor, in *Messages of the First Presidency of The Church of Jesus Christ of Latter-day Saints*, ed. James R. Clark (Salt Lake City: Bookcraft, 1966), 3:58–59.
7. Wilford Woodruff to the Presidency of St. George Stake, June 8, 1888, cited in *Messages of the First Presidency*, 3:167–68.
8. The Church operated as many as thirty-six stake academies and twenty other schools called seminaries because a corresponding stake academy already existed in the stake. These seminaries are not to be confused with the present Church education endeavor of the same name. Scott C. Esplin and Arnold K. Garr, "Church Academies: 1875–1933," in *Mapping Mormonism: An Atlas of Latter-day Saint History*, ed. Brandon S. Plewe, S. Kent Brown, Donald Q. Cannon, and Richard H. Jackson (Provo, UT: BYU Press, 2012), 126–27.
9. Albert Kenyon Wagner and Leona Farnsworth Wagner, *The Juarez Stake Academy, 1897–1997: The First One Hundred Years* (Juárez, Mexico: The Academy, 1997), 6.

10. Anna Lowrie Ivins Wilson, "Reminiscences, 1967," Church History Library, Salt Lake City, 15.
11. Wilson, "Reminiscences," 18–20.
12. Anthony W. Ivins had previously served as president of the Church's Mexican Mission from 1882 to 1884.
13. Wilson, "Reminiscences," 34–35.
14. Wilson, "Reminiscences," 40.
15. Wilson, "Reminiscences," 46.
16. Nelle Spilsbury Hatch, *Colonia Juarez: An Intimate Account of a Mormon Village* (Salt Lake City: Deseret Book, 1954), 153–55.
17. Wagner and Wagner, *The Juarez Stake Academy*, 149, 195.
18. In her account, Ivins records of her struggles with the Spanish language, "All the high school classes were taught by our principal, except Spanish which was a requirement, though I never became proficient in the language." Wilson, "Reminiscences," 49.
19. *The Juarez Stake Academy, Announcements for the Twelfth Academic Year*, reproduced in Wagner and Wagner, *The Juarez Stake Academy*, 36.
20. Nelle Spilsbury Hatch, "Manrique Gonzalez," in *Stalwarts South of the Border*, ed. Nelle Spilsbury Hatch and B. Carmon Hardy ([California], Ernestine Hatch, 1985), 212–13.
21. Manrique Gonzalez to Nelle S. Hatch, November 26, 1950, http://www.orsonprattbrown.com/Pauly-Brown/Gonzalez/ManriqueGonzalez/manrique-gonzalez1882-.html.
22. Wilson, "Reminiscences," 56.
23. Wilson, "Reminiscences," 52.
24. Guy C. Wilson, cited in Nelle S. Hatch, *Academia Juárez A.C., 1901–1976* (Juárez, Chihuahua, Mexico: Academia Juárez A.C., 1977), 17.
25. Wilson, "Reminiscences," 70.
26. Richard O. Cowan, *Teaching the Word: Religious Education at Brigham Young University* (Provo, UT: Religious Studies Center, 2008), 9–10.
27. For a discussion of the Church's discontinuance of its academies, see Scott C. Esplin and E. Vance Randall, "Living in Two Worlds: The Development and

Transition of Mormon Education in American Society," *History of Education* 43, no. 1 (2014): 3–30.

28. Adam S. Bennion, "The Latter-day Saints and Education," *Improvement Era*, July 1920.
29. E. LeRoy Hatch, *Medico: My Life as a Country Doctor in Mexico* (Mesa, AZ: J. J. Hatch, 1999), 20.
30. Annie R. Johnson, *Heartbeats of Colonia Diaz* (Salt Lake City: Publishers Press, 1972), 223; Hatch, *Colonia Juarez*, 233.
31. Johnson, *Heartbeats of Colonia Diaz*, 223.
32. Clark V. Johnson, "Mormon Education in Mexico: The Rise of the Sociedad Educativa Y Cultural" (PhD diss., Brigham Young University, 1977), 50.
33. Manuscript History of the Juárez Schools, 1–2, cited in Johnson, "Mormon Education in Mexico," 40.
34. Henry L. Cain, "Report of the Juárez Stake School System," October 1, 1942, Mexico, cited in Johnson, "Mormon Education in Mexico," 51.
35. Cited in Johnson, "Mormon Education in Mexico," 51.
36. Cited in Johnson, "Mormon Education in Mexico," 48.
37. At the time of Peña's critique, the only government-sponsored school in the area was an elementary school, known today as the Escuela Primaria Niños Héroes. This school opened in Colonia Juárez in the 1930s. A middle school known as the Telesecundaria opened in the 1980s.
38. Moisés T. de la Peña, "Problemas Agrícolas e Industriales de Mexico," translation cited in letter from Daniel P. Taylor to Joseph T. Bentley, January 7, 1959, 3, 7, in Joseph T. Bentley Papers, L. Tom Perry Special Collections, Harold B. Lee Library, Brigham Young University, Provo, Utah.
39. De la Peña, "Problemas Agrícolas e Industriales de Mexico," 3, 7.
40. Dale M. Valentine, "The Juarez Stake Academy" (master's thesis, Brigham Young University, 1955), 72.
41. Harvey L. Taylor, "The Story of L.D.S. Church Schools," 1971, 2:10–11, L. Tom Perry Special Collections, Harold B. Lee Library, Brigham Young University, Provo, UT.
42. Taylor, "The Story of L.D.S. Church Schools," 2:20.
43. Johnson, "Mormon Education in Mexico," 58.

44. Dale M. Valentine, "The Juarez Stake Academy" (master's thesis, Brigham Young University, 1955), 67.
45. Johnson, "Mormon Education in Mexico," 59.
46. Harvey L. Taylor, "Report: Trip to LDS Colonies in Juarez and Dublan, Mexico, and the University of Chihuahua," in Joseph T. Bentley Papers; Joseph T. Bentley to Daniel P. Taylor, February 3, 1959, in Joseph T. Bentley Papers.
47. The Church did advance its educational system in other parts of Mexico, opening Benemérito de Las Américas in Mexico City in 1964. Barbara E. Morgan, "Benemérito de Las Américas: The Beginning of a Unique Church School in Mexico," *BYU Studies Quarterly* 42, no. 4 (2013): 89–116.
48. Joseph T. Bentley to Ernest L. Wilkinson, August 8, 1957, Joseph T. Bentley Correspondence, L. Tom Perry Special Collections.
49. Johnson, "Mormon Education in Mexico," 59.
50. Shawn Foster, "The Mexican Connection: Mormon Colonies in Mexico Feel, Look Like Central Utah," *Salt Lake Tribune*, May 24, 1998, J1.
51. Efraín Villalobos Vázquez, "Church Schools in Mexico," in *Mormonism: A Faith for All Cultures*, ed. F. LaMond Tullis (Provo, UT: Brigham Young University Press, 1978), 127.
52. The Church of Jesus Christ of Latter-day Saints, "Facts and Statistics: Mexico," Mormon News Room, *http://www.mormonnewsroom.org/facts-and-statistics/country/mexico*.
53. "Seminaries and Institutes of Religion Annual Report for 2015" (Salt Lake City: The Church of Jesus Christ of Latter-day Saints, 2015), 4.
54. Wilson, "Reminiscences," 52.
55. Stanley A. Peterson, oral history, May 1, 1991, cited in Casey P. Griffiths, "The Globalization of Latter-day Saint Education" (PhD diss., Brigham Young University, 2012), 272.

WORLDWIDE

18

Development of LDS Humanitarian Aid

Craig James Ostler and Brady Burns

Today the Church and its people are known in many parts of the world due to humanitarian aid efforts. For Latter-day Saints, helping the poor and needy is a sacred work and has become a symbol of who they are as a people in the world community. This work received sharper focus in 2009. While the Church built on its threefold mission to preach the gospel, perfect the Saints, and save the dead, it also announced a fourth emphasis in its mission—caring for the poor and needy.[1] President Thomas S. Monson explained, "The guiding principles of the Church Welfare program and humanitarian service efforts are based on the teachings and example of Jesus Christ. The holy scriptures leave no doubt concerning the responsibility to care for the poor, the needy, and the downtrodden."[2] This article focuses on the foundations, developments, and contributions of Latter-day Saint

---

Craig James Ostler is a professor of Church history and doctrine at Brigham Young University. Brady Burns is a student at Brigham Young University studying exercise science.

humanitarian efforts. These efforts include: (1) the underpinnings of caring for the poor within the Church, (2) the Benson Agriculture and Food Institute and Corporation, and (3) what has become known as LDS Charities, the humanitarian arm of The Church of Jesus Christ of Latter-day Saints.

Philosophically, the Church's initial efforts to provide temporally for its members are tied to present-day humanitarian efforts. In a revelation given in 1831, the Lord commanded his people to esteem others as themselves and to not be respecters of persons (see D&C 38:24–27). Consequently, efforts were made under the laws of consecration, stewardship, and tithing to provide for the poor.[3] In addition, community organizations, sometimes referred to as cooperatives or united orders, were developed to carry out that command throughout the nineteenth century in settling areas in the Western United States.[4] Later, welfare programs were developed to meet the financial

The Newel K. Whitney store in Kirtland, Ohio, served as the first storehouse for the poor, which provided a foundation for later humanitarian efforts. (All photos courtesy of authors.)

crisis of the mid-twentieth century and focused the hearts and minds of the Saints on caring for one another. In time, the Saints joined in united humanitarian efforts to reach out to the poor and needy not of their faith. The development of the Saints' efforts to care for those in need has grown from a bishop's storehouse in one small room of the Newel K. Whitney store in Kirtland, Ohio, to large storehouses and accumulations of funds to meet welfare and humanitarian needs in many parts of the earth.

1831–1936: Laying the Foundation

Today, Church welfare and worldwide humanitarian programs are administered separately. However, the Church's ability to extend emergency humanitarian aid to populations throughout the world and to prepare individuals to care for their own needs had their genesis in efforts to care for Church members. Indeed, Church efforts to care for the poor and needy in or out of the Church have been twofold: first, to encourage and organize employment opportunities for individuals so they can provide for themselves and their families; and second, to provide emergency relief for those in need. Less than a year after the organization of the Church, the Lord revealed the laws of consecration and stewardship, in which he commanded, "And behold, thou wilt remember the poor, and consecrate of thy properties for their support" (D&C 42:30). Formal establishment of the first storehouse for the poor was located within the Newel K. Whitney store in Kirtland, Ohio. An additional storehouse was added in Independence, Missouri. The storehouses were administered by one Church entity when the Lord commanded Church leaders to organize what became known as the United Firm "in regulating and establishing the affairs of the storehouse for the poor of my people . . . for a permanent and everlasting establishment and order unto my church" (D&C 78:3–4). The Lord gave responsibility to the Church's first bishops, Edward Partridge and Newel K. Whitney, to oversee the specific labors of providing stewardships of property and goods, which gave opportunity for members to provide for themselves and their families, as well as responsibility to care for the poor (see D&C 41:9; 42:31–34; 51:1–8; 72:1–22).

As Saints settled and developed communities, they set up buildings that served as bishops' storehouses to which goods were contributed and later distributed to those in need. For example, in the early pioneer era of Salt Lake City, the site of the Joseph Smith Memorial Building was occupied by the tithing offices, the General Bishops' Storehouse, and stockyards. On a smaller scale, local storehouses were built in Mormon communities to provide for the poor in their respective areas, each overseen by local bishops and Relief Society presidencies.[5] During the 1930s, "Church leaders urged every stake to take steps to ensure that enough food and clothing were available to allow bishops to care for their ward members, and to establish welfare employment and production programs."[6]

Admittedly, these first efforts were intended as the foundation of the Church's welfare program, not humanitarian aid. Today, a fine line between the two programs is that the welfare program is administered through fast-offering donations that provide for the poor among Church members and others as the First Presidency sees fit. On the other hand, humanitarian assistance is from voluntary donations only and is used mainly for those who are not members of the Church. Further, humanitarian assistance is usually given through other charitable agencies, such as the Red Cross or Islamic Relief, and the name LDS Charities is used in those efforts rather than The Church of Jesus Christ of Latter-day Saints. However, in many cases, both Welfare Services and LDS Charities utilize large warehouses to store goods intended for the poor and needy, a foundation that was laid early in Church history.

In addition to establishing storehouses for the poor, the early Saints had opportunities to learn how to organize to meet the challenges of man-made and natural disasters. During the trials and persecutions of the early Saints in New York, Ohio, Missouri, and Illinois, members covenanted to care for the poor among them. For example, in the summer of 1834, following the troubles in Jackson County, Missouri, more than two hundred men organized and marched to the aid of their fellow Saints as part of Zion's Camp. In the winter of 1838–39, members of the Quorum of Twelve guided the Saints in their removal from Missouri across the Mississippi River to Illinois, following mob and military persecutions. During the decades of removal from Illinois and other points of the globe to the Great Basin in the Rocky Mountains, the Saints learned how to better organize and provide for thousands of individuals. Successful emergency humanitarian efforts require effective organization. Gail J. McGovern, president and CEO of the American Red Cross, declared, "The most critical thing about disaster response is moving large groups of people to the site of a disaster; and there is no one that can mobilize groups of people better than the LDS Church."[7]

1936–Present: Church Welfare

Church welfare programs expanded the Saints' ability to care for the poor and needy in later worldwide humanitarian efforts. The crisis of the Great Depression in the United States prepared the Saints to provide work opportunities and to mobilize with much greater efficiency and outreach. Widespread unemployment among Church members led to the establishment of a centrally directed welfare program. The First Presidency called Harold B. Lee, then president of the Pioneer Stake in Salt Lake City, as the managing director of the Church's efforts to help those who were out of employment and had families almost destitute of clothing and suffering from hunger.

World War II caused suffering among the Saints in Europe that could not be relieved by local efforts. Much of the Church's understanding of how to undertake emergency humanitarian efforts today—such as efforts to gather, ship, and distribute aid across the globe—originated in the Church's efforts to provide for needy members following this worldwide conflict. Church President George Albert Smith made a visit to U.S. President Harry S. Truman in 1945 to ascertain his attitude toward the Latter-day Saints shipping food, clothing, and bedding to Europe. With both presidents' willingness to provide help and the readiness of supplies collected by the Church, "many people received warm bedding and food without delay. Just as fast as we could get cars and ships, we had what was necessary to send to Europe."[8] From that initial shipment in October 1945 to the end of 1947, "more than seventy-five carloads of food and clothing and bedding" were shipped overseas to the needy with no cost to them.[9]

To this point, most of the Church's efforts had focused on providing work opportunities and caring for their own. A century earlier, the Prophet Joseph Smith taught, "We are to feed the hungry, to clothe the naked, to provide for the widow, to dry up the tear of the orphan, to comfort the afflicted, whether in this church or any other, or in no church at all, wherever he finds them."[10] With that admonition in mind, the time approached to reach beyond Church membership.

Worldwide Humanitarian Efforts and Initiatives

Benson Agriculture and Food Institute and Corporation. In 1975, the Ezra Taft Benson Agriculture and Food Institute was organized at Brigham Young University as part of the college of Biological and Agricultural Sciences. It was named in honor of Ezra Taft Benson and his service as U.S. secretary of agriculture from 1953 to 1961.[11] "The institute's pioneering research in applied nutritional and agricultural development was aimed at lifting families with small farms in the developing world."[12] Families learned to grow vegetables and

The Benson Agriculture and Food Institute and Corporation helps families in developing nations to establish small farms, such as this one in Ecuador.

fruits while also raising small animals appropriate to their circumstances in order to better provide for themselves. Since 2008, The Benson Institute has helped hundreds of thousands of individuals and families with more than 160 Benson Food Initiative projects in over 36 counties.[13] Elder Ezra Taft Benson spoke at the inauguration of the institute, stating:

> Throughout the world—and I have seen most of it—there are vast resources waiting to be used for the betterment of mankind. The objective of this institute is to use the human, physical, and spiritual resources of BYU to help the people of the world help themselves improve their quality of life. In so doing, it is well to remember what the Lord has said in regard to the way this should be done. These statements are the basis of the Church Welfare Program:
>
> "For the earth is full, and there is enough and to spare; yea, I prepared all things, and have given unto the children of men to be agents unto themselves. Therefore, if every man shall take of the abundance which I

> have made, and impart not his portion, according to the law of my gospel, unto the poor and the needy, he shall, with the wicked, lift up his eyes in hell, being in torment" (D&C 104:17–18).[14]

"The Ezra Taft Benson Agriculture and Food Institute (Benson Institute) integrated into LDS Charities in 2008, expanding its global outreach to better accomplish its mission to help families become more self-reliant."[15] The lessons learned at the Benson Institute have been incorporated into a program that is now used all over the world to help families produce their own food, improve nutrition, and better provide for themselves. In 2014, 24,800 individuals in seventeen countries benefited from the knowledge gained in this program.[16]

LDS humanitarian services organized. The LDS Church began institutionally participating in humanitarian work during the devastating Ethiopia famine in 1985. Patrick Reese, previous manager of Planning and Administration for Humanitarian Services for the Latter-day Saint Charities, explained, "Church leaders asked us to hold a special fast, and the money that was collected during that time period helped to provide goods that relieved suffering in Ethiopia. The amount of money raised was significant. There were actually two collections; one that we did on our own, and then again when Pres. Reagan asked the country to donate. From that point, the church leaders made the decision that they would have an ongoing program to support this kind of work."[17] One year later, the Church officially organized the LDS Humanitarian Services in order to fully bring help to the poor and needy worldwide.

On November 2, 1996, "the First Presidency announced the establishment of Latter-day Saint Charities, a charitable, nonprofit corporation designed to help the Church deliver humanitarian aid to poor and needy people of the world."[18] Before and after that time, many varieties of projects were initiated to provide for needs as they were discovered. For example, projects were initiated to provide hearing aids for hearing-impaired teenagers and tools for hearing-impaired students in vocational schools in Romania.[19] A project was sponsored to provide piglets to needy farmers in Croatia.[20] Full-time service missionaries were called to train and provide technical support at a dental school in Peru, and through Church Humanitarian Services "LDS dentists and hygienists traveled to Peru to offer services to the poor."[21] At a Women's Conference at Brigham Young University in 1999, those participating "helped make, compile or sort 31,000 hygiene kits, 2,500 newborn kits, 2,500 education kits, 2,500 school bags, 31,000 sewing kits, 372,000 buttons, 407 quilts and 1,200 surgical drapes. In addition, women took home materials to crochet 2,000 bandages for leprosy patients."[22] Although many individuals and stake units continue with separate projects and programs,[23] today LDS Charities focuses on six major initiatives: wheelchair projects, neonatal resuscitation training, clean water projects, vision care, immunizations, and humanitarian aid and emergency response. Further, LDS Charities is involved in production and distribution of atmit, a nutritional supplement.

Wheelchair projects. The Church of Jesus Christ of Latter-day Saints began the current wheelchair initiative in a partnership with Kenneth E. Behring's independent Wheelchair Foundation.[24] This partnership began "as the Church was responding in many different ways to the crisis in the Balkans in 1996–97, and one of the requests that had been made was to provide a few wheelchairs in a particular community."[25] In 2001, John Yancey—manager of LDS Church medical projects and production—participated in a twelve-day, seven-nation tour. The tour included Nigeria, Tanzania, Ethiopia, Egypt, Jordan, Romania, and Ukraine. He and Elder Ronald A. Rasband of the First Quorum of the Seventy traveled in a private jet provided by the Wheelchair Foundation. The plane's cargo included sixty wheelchairs for ceremonies performed in the first three countries. After delivering the initial group, wheelchairs were replenished at various locations as Brother Yancey and Elder Rasband continued to the other countries.[26]

LDS Charities first began supplying wheelchairs in partnership with other entities and now operates its own program, which includes developing ways to provide employment training to those restricted by use of wheelchairs.

Chronicling the development of the wheelchair initiative, Glen Rudd stated that by 2005, "the Church began to operate the wheelchair program on its own, focusing on building self-reliance and independence." In 2007, the Church began donating "two new styles of wheelchairs specifically made for outdoor use." Significantly, during this time the Church began "purchasing wheelchairs from smaller regional factories in countries such as [China], Mexico, Vietnam, Kenya, South Africa, and the Philippines." This change had the added benefit of providing jobs for disabled workers and contributing to local economies.[27] The Church wheelchair program now focuses on partnerships with local organizations in the countries where the wheelchairs are provided. In addition to initially providing wheelchairs, training in the fitting, use, and maintenance of wheelchairs is currently a key component of the program.[28] The Church is currently developing ways to provide employment training to those who are confined to wheelchairs.[29]

Neonatal resuscitation training. In the mid-1990s the Church became aware of a lack of knowledge in neonatal resuscitation. In 2002 the Church launched an initiative to train birth attendants in this valuable skill through a train-the-trainer method. Patrick Reese explained, "Our volunteers are doctors and nurses who have the certification to do this. About five of these volunteers, will go to a place like Mozambique or the DRC [Democratic Republic of the Congo] and train 80–100 people, and certify that they understand and can train others to learn those techniques. These 80–100 professionals each commit to train 6–8 others who are in a hospital or nurses association."[30]

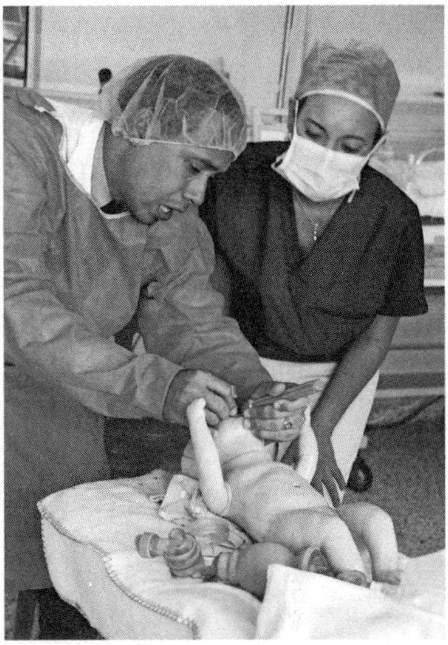

LDS Charities provides training for neonatal resuscitation such as shown in this photo from the Dominican Republic.

Since the inception of this program, LDS Humanitarian Services has partnered with the American Academy of Pediatrics, the Helping Babies Breathe Global Development Alliance, and local health organizations to develop effective training materials and methods for teaching midwives and doctors the skills needed to help newborns.[31] The Church has been instrumental in distributing equipment and training in this field. In 2013, Church efforts resulted in over 27,000 birth attendants trained in neonatal resuscitation skills.[32] Through 2010, in a little over eight years, "almost 200,000 medical professionals [were] trained to save the lives of newborns" in over seventy-four countries, saving more than a million lives each year.[33]

Clean water projects. Another project that the Church established in 2002 was to provide for the approximately one billion people worldwide suffering thirst and disease because of the lack of clean water. This initiative started as a small project in Laos in order to expand and refurbish their existing water system. A unique aspect of this particular project is that it can only be accomplished with the help of the local communities and villages. They are able to locate potential water holes, help dig trenches for needed pipes, establish water committees, arrange a fee-paying system, and take the responsibility for maintaining the water system. The largest project that has been implemented thus far is in the Democratic Republic of the Congo. The eighteen-mile pipeline installed in trenches hand dug by the community has now benefited over 200,000 individuals. In 2006, the Church began providing sanitation facilities such as toilets, showers, and clothes-washing stations. This eventually gave rise to hygiene training in order to help ensure that health improvements are sustained. Consequently, the Church developed the three pillars of health: clean water, sanitation facilities, and hygiene training, which provided clean water to 7,551,312 people between 2002 and 2010.[34] In 2014, "Humanitarian Services provided clean water to 1,100,000 people in 33 countries."[35]

Vision care. The services involving vision care began as a request from local Church leaders who saw the need to address preventable blindness in Indonesia.[36] Their purpose was to create a means to help the 300 million individuals who suffer poor vision quality. Other goals included preventing avoidable blindness and visual impairment and helping to strengthen organizations providing eye-care services for the poor. From 2003 to 2010, roughly 550,000 individuals received improved sight from the help provided by the Church, which includes "surgical training, surgical equipment, supplies, eye screening training, and eyeglasses."[37] Patrick Reese reported that "the Vision Care Initiative has since developed into a program in which

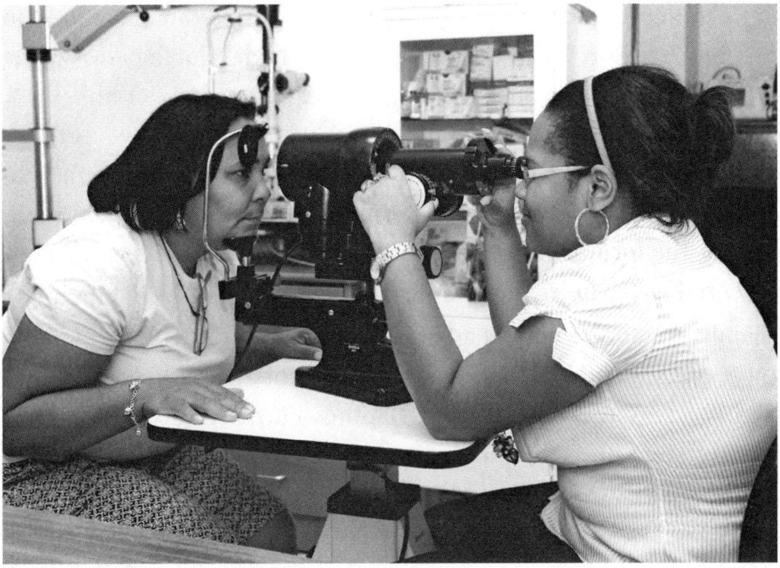

More than half a million individuals have benefited from vision care provided through LDS Charities.

U.S. doctors and local eye care professionals collaborate to alleviate specific and most-needed eye care problems in a community. 88,000 people benefited from equipment donation and collaboration efforts of the Church in 2013 alone."[38]

Atmit. An additional response to the Ethiopian famine of 1985 was the development of atmit, an Ethiopian porridge mix based on a centuries-old recipe. The porridge is made up of a base of powdered milk and oat flour, and also contains "sugar, salt and supplemental vitamins and minerals."[39] It helps malnourished children and the elderly who cannot digest whole grains and food made with coarse flour. In March 2003, the Church sent its first shipment of atmit to Ethiopia to help relieve the starvation that more than 11 million people were facing. The first shipment comprised 80,000 pounds of the mixture. An additional 120 tons of atmit, produced at Welfare Square, was shipped to Ethiopia in ocean-bound containers.[40] From

2003 to 2007, more than 2,000 tons of atmit were manufactured in Salt Lake City on Welfare Square and "sent to developing areas of the world plagued by malnourishment and starvation."[41]

Immunizations. The Church's other 2003 initiative was an immunizations campaign. It has been reported that from 2003 to 2012, more than 766,000 hours of service were donated by Church volunteers to provide immunizations and educate people of their importance.[42] The amount of interest generated by the Church was mainly due to the many partnerships that the Church entered into, most notably the Red Cross, led by the Centers for Disease Control and Prevention and the United Nations. Furthermore, the Church's commitment of one million dollars a year and continued support of the Measles and Rubella Initiative of the United Nations and GAVI (the Global Alliance for Vaccines and Immunizations) has helped provide vaccines for rotavirus (diarrhea), pneumonia, and polio—contributing to 9.9 million people being immunized in 2013 alone.[43] LDS Charities may be the only organization worldwide that can do social mobilization in such a significant way. Because of their affiliation with The Church of Jesus Christ of Latter-day Saints, they have Church units in nearly all nations in which members speak the local language. In many political and government areas in which the Church is not officially recognized, they have representatives that can help carry out humanitarian efforts. Thus they can send people in an organized manner into local communities and dispel myths about immunizations, etc.

Humanitarian aid and emergency response. Perhaps the best-known aspect of humanitarian aid is emergency response to natural disasters, civil unrest, or famine. Neil K. Newell, welfare media representative for the Church, described the scene following Hurricane Katrina in late August 2005:

> Immediately afterward, people from all over the United States arrived and rolled up their sleeves. Among them were thousands of members

As part of the emergency response of LDS charities, over 22,000 Church-sponsored volunteers participated in providing relief following the 2011 earthquake and tsunami in Japan and more than 250 tons of supplies were distribute during the first few months following the disaster.

> of The Church of Jesus Christ of Latter-day Saints. . . . This army of Mormons descended upon the hardest hit areas—sometimes driving for more than six hours to get there. And armed with chain saws, shovels, and pruning shears, they worked 14 hour days, giving their help free of charge to any and all who needed it.
>
> One woman, who had been desperately trying to organize a relief effort in her community center, watched as several vans drove up spilling out dozens of men and women dressed in their distinctive yellow shirts.
>
> "Everybody! Everybody!" the woman exclaimed, her cheeks wet with tears, "The Mormons are here!"[44]

Such response is not accomplished through a haphazard group providentially arriving to provide needed aid. Rather, this example demonstrates a well-coordinated effort by an efficient organization of resources and man power. LDS Charities has organized the world into fifteen international areas, each with an area welfare manager appointed to oversee humanitarian aid. In addition, there are ten areas within the United States whose managers are located in Salt Lake City and help respond to humanitarian needs. Each area welfare manager receives direction and resources from the Area Seventy or Presidency of the Seventy, who are under the direction of the First Presidency. Working under the direction of the area welfare managers are 80–85 humanitarian missionary couples serving throughout the world.[45]

"When local resources are strained or nonexistent, LDS Charities provides short-term, life-sustaining resources such as food, water, shelter, and clothing, as well as medical, school, and hygiene supplies. This response is accomplished in partnership with local relief organizations and sometimes with other major international organizations. Under the direction of local leadership, LDS Charities volunteers distribute supplies and participate in clean-up efforts to help disaster victims recover."[46]

In addition to the formal world organization and administration of humanitarian aid, most, if not all, full-time proselyting missionaries are encouraged to provide service to those among whom they live, at least on a weekly basis. Further, they, along with members in worldwide congregations, are called upon in time of need. This provides a type of minuteman response to needs across the globe wherever LDS missionaries or congregations are located.

Conclusion

Today, comments from those that are helped through LDS humanitarian aid focus on the fact that "even though we are not members of the Mormon Church, we always receive their support."[47] In Church humanitarian work, LDS Charities gives to those in need regardless of nationality, political standing, race, or religion. There is an emerging emphasis not to ship goods from Church headquarters in Salt Lake City, Utah, but instead to purchase needed supplies near the disaster site. This ensures that the supplies are familiar to the people, helps build up local (and sometimes shattered) communities, and allows LDS Charities to build bridges with people of influence that can assure future opportunities to reach those in need.[48] Through humanitarian efforts, the Church's influence for good is not restricted to areas in which it is officially recognized. Due to initiatives and emergency-relief efforts that are offered through LDS Charities, help is welcomed into areas of the world across the globe that might have been closed to Christian church organizations.

Recently, LDS Charities has garnered more attention internationally. On February 27, 2014, the Church's humanitarian efforts were the focus of a United Nations meeting titled "Discovering Mormonism and Its Role in Humanitarian Assistance."[49]

Along with missionaries serving in many parts of the world, humanitarian programs have provided opportunities for members of the Church to become better acquainted with other peoples and cultures and their needs. Similarly, people in many nations have been able to see the Church in additional light beyond missionary efforts or reports of strange beliefs and practices. Indeed, proselyting missionaries often temporarily forgo their work of teaching the gospel to serve those that are in need of humanitarian assistance. It is not unusual to hear returned missionaries declare that some of the most fulfilling experiences of their missionary service were at times of providing humanitarian aid. Further, joining in efforts with other individuals, programs, and institutions to provide care for the needy increases the opportunities for cooperation and goodwill between Church members and those of other faiths or no faith.[50] Church leaders and members have voiced sentiments such as, "This was an opportunity to show we are a caring people and desire to fit into the community."[51]

Efforts to provide for the poor and needy that began with an 1831 revelation and establishment of a storehouse have continued since that time. The most recent data regarding the amount of cash and materials that have been provided report that through 2011 over $1.4 billion have been donated through LDS humanitarian assistance. Quantifying the volunteer hours involved in the worldwide humanitarian efforts is beyond human abilities. Contributions have come from countless individuals to save lives and improve living conditions. Those that received and those that gave both rejoiced in the effort. However, it is worthwhile to note that this effort reflects more than generosity; it demonstrates faith of the Latter-day Saint people. President Gordon B. Hinckley explained, "From the beginning this Church has moved forward with faith. Faith was the strength of the Prophet Joseph. . . . And so it has been with each of the Presidents of the Church. In the face of terrible opposition, they have moved forward with faith. . . . More recently, whether it was an urgent need to extend humanitarian aid to victims of the tsunami, or earthquakes, or floods in divers places, it has all been the same. Welfare shelves have been emptied. Cash by the millions has been dispatched to those in need, regardless of Church membership—all in faith."[52]

Notes

1. "Mormon Church to Emphasize Care for Poor and Needy," KSL.com, December 10, 2009; *Handbook 2: Administering the Church* (Salt Lake City: The Church of Jesus Christ of Latter-day Saints, 2010), 9.
2. Julie Dockstader, "Six Decades Later, Welfare Program Still Restores Hope," *Church News*, February 27, 1999.
3. Craig James Ostler, "The Laws of Consecration, Stewardship, and Tithing," *Sperry Symposium Classics: The Doctrine and Covenants* (Provo, UT: Religious Studies Center, 2004), 155–75; Craig James Ostler, "Consecration," *Doctrine and Covenants Reference Companion*, ed. Dennis L. Largey (Salt Lake City: Deseret Book, 2012), 106–12.
4. *Church History in the Fulness of Times* (Salt Lake City: The Church of Jesus Christ of Latter-day Saints, 1989), 402–5.
5. "Before 1936 there were at least 135 bishops' storehouses throughout the Church." Glen L. Rudd, *Pure Religion: The Story of Church Welfare Since 1930* (Salt Lake City: The Church of Jesus Christ of Latter-day Saints, 1995), 4.
6. Mike Cannon and Frank Richardson, "Roots of the Modern Church Welfare System Tap Into Early Stakes," *Church News*, May 26, 1990.

7. "Humanitarian Visitor Center Film," LDS Media Library, LDS.org.
8. George Albert Smith, in Conference Report, October 1947, 5–6.
9. George Albert Smith, in Conference Report, October 1947, 6.
10. Joseph Smith, *Times and Seasons,* March 15, 1842. See also Alma 1:30, in which all that were in need were succored: "Whether out of the church or in the church, having no respect to persons as to those that stood in need."
11. "Benson Institute Integrated into LDS Charities," LDS Charities Updates, ldscharities.org. http://ldscharities.org/news/benson-institute-integrated-into-lds-charities?lang=eng.
12. Glen Rudd, *Pure Religion Epilogue: The Story of Church Welfare from 1995 to 2010* (Salt Lake City: The Church of Jesus Christ of Latter-day Saints, 2011), 65.
13. "Benson Institute Integrated," ldscharities.org.
14. Copy of Elder Ezra Taft Benson's inaugural address in author's possession, courtesy of Benson Institute.
15. "Benson Institute Integrated," ldscharities.org.
16. http://ldscharities.org/what-we-do?lang=eng#bensonfood.
17. "A Discussion with Patrick Reese, Manager, Humanitarian Services, Church of Jesus Christ of Latter-day Saints," interview on June 18, 2009, Berkley Center for Religion, Peace, and World Affairs, Georgetown University, http://berkleycenter.georgetown.edu/interviews/a-discussion-with-patrick-reese-manager-humanitarian-services-church-of-jesus-christ-of-latter-day-saints.
18. R. Scott Lloyd, "1996: Year in Review," *Church News*, December 26, 1996.
19. Gerry Avant, "LDS Humanitarian Relief in Romania," *Church News*, August 18, 1990.
20. Shawn Stahle, "Pig Project in Croatia Restore Hope, Dignity," *Church News*, June 1999.
21. Sarah Jane Weaver, "LDS Dentists Are 'Teaching the Teachers,'" *Church News*, December 23, 2000.
22. Julie Dockstader, "'Sky's the Limit' Massive Project Called 'Largest Humanitarian Event the Church Has Ever Been Involved with in One Setting,'" *Church News*, May 8, 1999.

23. Latter-day Saints are motivated by the Lord's instructions: "Verily I say, men should be engaged in a good cause, and do many things of their own free will" (D&C 58:27).
24. Jason Swenson, "Hundreds Receive Gift of Mobility, Independence," *Church News*, December 21, 2002. Behring is a philanthropist and former owner of the Seattle Seahawks, a National Football League team.
25. Reese, Berkley Center interview.
26. John H. Yancey, manager of LDS Medical Projects and Production, interview by the authors, February 27, 2014.
27. Rudd, *Pure Religion Epilogue*, 56.
28. Patrick Reese, personal correspondence, March 3, 2014.
29. Correspondence with LDS Charities in the peer review process.
30. Reese, Berkley Center interview.
31. Efforts and successes of the LDS Charities neonatal resuscitation program have been reported to Church members via the *Church News* and *Liahona* and *Ensign* magazines; see Eric James, "LDS Charities Project Rescues Infants," *Ensign*, October 2008; "Church Teaching Life-Saving Techniques to Health Professionals around World," *Ensign*, July 2007; "Church Helping to Save Infants around World," *Liahona*, August 2007; Heather Stock and Larry Hiller, "The Church's Humanitarian Efforts: Disciples in Action," *Liahona*, September 2010.
32. Reese, personal correspondence.
33. Marianne Holman, "'What Love Is'—Emulate Savior's Example," *Church News*, April 16, 2011; Reese, personal correspondence; http://ldscharities.org/initiatives/neonatal-resuscitation-training?lang=eng.
34. Reese, personal correspondence; Rudd, *Pure Religion Epilogue*, 61–62; http://www.ldsphilanthropies.org/humanitarian-services/funds/clean-water.html.
35. http://www.ldsphilanthropies.org/humanitarian-services/funds/clean-water.html.
36. Reese, personal correspondence; Sarah Jane Weaver, "Blessing Lives for Generations," *Church News*, January 10, 2004.
37. Rudd, *Pure Religion Epilogue*, 57.

38. Reese, personal correspondence. In 2014, 81,600 individuals were helped, http://ldscharities.org/what-we-do?lang=eng#vision.
39. Howard Collett, "Providing Atmit, Hope," *Church News*, October 15, 2011.
40. Sarah Jane Weaver, "Ethiopian aid: 'Will literally save thousands of lives,'" *Church News*, March 29, 2003.
41. Jason Swensen, "Helping Others Yields Rich Blessings," *Church News*, January 27, 2007.
42. R. Scott Lloyd, "'Shot@Life' for children through immunizations," *Church News*, July 14, 2012.
43. Patrick Reese, personal correspondence. In recent years, the Church has donated more than one million dollars per year solely for measles vaccinations. In addition, The Church has provided additional money for other kinds of vaccinations (and NGOs that specialize in vaccination, GAVI in particular). It would be accurate to say that since 2003, the Church has given more than twenty million dollars to support immunization efforts worldwide.
44. Neil K. Newell, "Reaching Out to Those in Need," in *The Mormons: An Illustrated History of the Church of Jesus Christ of Latter-day Saints*, ed. Roy A. Prete (London: Merrell Publishers, 2013), 99.
45. John H. Yancey, interview, February 27, 2014.
46. http://ldscharities.org/initiatives/emergency-response?lang=eng).
47. https://www.lds.org/media-library/video/2014-01-100-humanitarian-visitor-center-film?lang=eng.
48. Correspondence with LDS Charities in the peer review process.
49. United Nations Webcast: webtv.un.org (organized by the NGO Relations Section, Outreach Division, Department of Public Information (DPI)), http://webtv.un.org/search/dpingo-briefing-focus-on-faith-mormonism/3267145282001?term=mormonism.
50. "Head of Health Organization Suggests Partnership," *Church News*, August 30, 1997; Sarah Jane Weaver, "Ambassador Calls Church a Friend, Gives Thanks for Aid," *Church News*, July 27, 1996; Sarah Jane Weaver, "Strong Partnership Shared By Church, Red Cross," *Church News*, June 6, 1998.

51. President Gerald J. Cardon of the Fargo North Dakota Stake, "Help Came from the Mormon Church," *Church News*, June 3, 1989.
52. Gordon B. Hinckley, "Faith to Move Mountains," *Ensign*, November 2006, 82–83.

19

The Global Church

Terryl L. Givens

The Great Commission, which the resurrected Christ gave to his Apostles before his ascension, ran into challenges from the very start. Some of these challenges are still with us and have particular relevance as the LDS Church strives to fulfill its promise of becoming a global church—namely, how do you export and disseminate the gospel in all its purity and goodness to myriad peoples, nationalities, ethnic groups, and societies, without the cultural trappings and accretions it has acquired? This problem is as old as Christianity. In the first century AD, the first great controversies in the Church in Palestine were rooted in this very dilemma: what parts of the Jewish context and heritage properly pertain to Christianity's eternal gospel, and which features are expendable, culturally variable, or prophetically fulfilled and no longer essential? In the book of Acts we read

---

Terryl L. Givens is a professor of literature and religion at the University of Richmond, where he holds the James A. Bostwick Chair in English.

of a "great dissension" that broke out on this question as the small Galilean sect first began its long progress to becoming a global religion (see Acts 23:10). Some of the old crowd protested regarding foreign converts, that they were not circumcised "after the manner of Moses" (Acts 15:1). Peter's admonition to his fellow Apostles and elders still rings with relevance today: "Now therefore why . . . put a yoke upon the neck of the disciples, which neither our fathers nor we were able to bear?" (Acts 15:10).

That is the motif I want to highlight. How does one avoid encumbering new converts, as groups and as individuals, with unnecessary yokes, in the effort to render access to the gospel and its fruits universal? The verdict decided upon in this early Church council in response to the urgent question is a model of wisdom and charity: "It seemed good to the Holy Ghost, and to us, to lay upon you no greater burden than [the] necessary things" (Acts 15:28). The project of disentangling the necessary from the peripheral and expendable must be an ongoing one. It requires vigilance, compassion, and deepest humility. Given our profound entanglement in language, habits of thought, inherited traditions, cultural vocabulary, and a consciousness born of a particular time and place and history, the ideal requires struggle. Our ideas of what it means to be Saints, to worship God, and to live the life of discipleship are shaped by myriad factors, conscious and unconscious. Forms of address, rhetorical habits, music and instrumentation, the language of prayer, etiquette and interaction, how we treat the sacred, and how we express love—these and a million other constituents of the religious life are not eternal verities or immutable truths, but shifting modes of pursuing and living by truth.

A certain decentering of one's privileged perspective is a task to which the gospel, the eternal and universal gospel, calls us, for reasons that are moral as well as pragmatic. To the Corinthians, Paul wrote of his fear that he might "hinder the gospel of Christ" (1 Corinthians 9:12). One way to avoid that, he said, was through a particular kind of humility: "I made myself servant unto all" (1 Corinthians 9:19). What he meant by that, it turns out, was that he stepped outside his privileged cultural identity and perspective. "Unto the Jews I became as a Jew. . . . To them that are without law, as without law. . . . I am made all things to all men, that I might by all means save some. And this I do for the gospel's sake," he concluded, "that I might be partaker thereof with you" (1 Corinthians 9:20–23).

Americans, born in the country where the Restoration began and the gathering centered, face particular challenges in this regard. In my remarks to follow, I wish merely to present some scriptural approaches to those challenges that may be useful.

I will begin with a few observations as to why the obstacles to an evangelizing effort freed from cultural baggage are rooted in Mormonism's history and not in cultural arrogance alone or American exceptionalism per se. Then I want to discuss some ways we might move beyond the narrowness and provincialism to which we as humans are prone—ways that are indicated in both the Book of Mormon and in Joseph Smith's revelations.

A Church Grounded in the Americas

First, history. The problems could be said to begin with the Book of Mormon. But that's OK, because the Book of Mormon also gives us the solution to the problems it conjures.

I will use three examples here to illustrate the intensely American geographical flavor the book originally exhibited. First, Book of Mormon witness David Whitmer related to a *Chicago Times* reporter that "three times has he been at the hill Cumorah and seen the casket that contained the tablets, and the seer-stone. Eventually the casket had been washed down to the foot of the hill, but it was to be seen when he last visited the historic place."[1] Try to consider, for a moment, the radical rupture with our own worldview that is implicit in those lines, and more particularly,

Hill Cumorah. Photo by George Edward Anderson.

between those lines. If I can digress to make this point: one of the most incredible moments in the Old Testament is not when Moses parts the Red Sea or when the ass of Balaam speaks to its master. It is when Balaam speaks back to the ass. More remarkable than the eruption of miracles into a past world is a past world in which the miraculous is not an eruption but commonplace. And for the first generation of Mormons, the stage on which so much ancient history transpired was the American ground they trod every day.

I find the casual nature of Whitmer's three visits to the Hill Cumorah astonishing: an ancient stone casket, a physical, tactile remnant of a sacred past, slowly washing down a ravine, still visible to the casual visitor on his third trip there. Even among the committed Latter-day Saints, Nephites and Lamanites and Liahonas and gold plates are objects that call forth an effort of faith. They people the stages of our minds in the same way as the resurrected Christ or the heavenly home—as things hoped for but unseen, elements of a faith story that we espouse on tenuous grounds, assertions that are spiritual in nature and unlikely to find empirical corroboration. But this was not so with David Whitmer, the other witnesses, and presumably a larger circle hearing firsthand not only stories of the miraculous, but of the miraculous rendered commonplace. More to my point, the roots of the Restoration—roots that reached back into ancient history—persisted into the present day and were a part of the physical landscape for early Mormons—not as impersonal landscape, but as visible, tactile artifacts, so familiar that it never occurred to them to guard or preserve or cherish these slowly vanishing relics of sacred history. (Just as in 1900 Joseph F. Smith declined an offer to purchase the printer's manuscript to the Book of Mormon. It was simply a copy, he reasoned, and the book was readily available![2])

As a second example, the Book of Mormon resonates with themes that Americans have claimed as part of their national identity. Wars fought in the name of liberty, a land of refuge for the religiously oppressed, the democratization of revelation, hostility to priestcraft—all these have suggested to generations of New World Mormons that the Book of Mormon civilizations are the spiritual ancestors of American democracy. Historian Richard L. Bushman has shown why Thomas O'Dea's assessment in *The Mormons* is inaccurate, but it is a reasonable reaction to a casual reading of the Book of Mormon. O'Dea wrote, "In [the Book of Mormon] are found the democratic, the republican, the anti-monarchial, and the egalitarian doctrines that pervade the climate of opinion in which it was conceived and that . . . later come from the mouths of Mormon leaders preaching to the people in Utah."[3]

Now third, perhaps the most-quoted Book of Mormon passage in early Church publications was Ether 13:4, 8: "Behold, Ether saw the days of Christ, and he spake concerning a New Jerusalem upon this land. . . . Wherefore, the remnant of the house of Joseph shall be built upon this land; and it shall be a land of their inheritance; and they shall build up a holy city unto the Lord, like unto the Jerusalem of old."

What this means, of course, is that the Book of Mormon was physically connected as an actual artifact, in the minds and in the tactile experience of early Saints, with America. And the history in the Book of Mormon was explicated in terms of that very physical terrain over which the Saints themselves trekked and camped. In addition, the future of this American continent was the most salient subject in the minds of first-generation Mormons who read and consulted the Book of Mormon. My point in all the foregoing is to demonstrate that the equivalence—in the minds of early Mormons—of the restored gospel with an American setting was virtually inevitable, given the way in which the principal Restoration scripture constructed that equivalence. No wonder the fittedness of the first recorded Mormon missionary approach, Samuel Smith's, seemed self-evident—but only within an American culture: "Do you wish to purchase a history of the origins of the Indians?"[4] Not very effective in Hungary or Hong Kong, but reasonable enough in the setting and mental world of early Mormonism. All of the above goes to show the virtual inevitability of the conclusion drawn by Harold Bloom: Mormonism is, prototypically, "*the* American Religion."[5]

But Harold Bloom is wrong. Let me now attempt to put these ethnocentrizing ramifications of the Book of Mormon into conversation with a competing function the Book of Mormon serves, one which overwhelms the historical and temporal delineations with a gesture toward something much more expansive, much more universal.

As illustration, I choose a passage from Mosiah: "And now it came to pass that Alma, who had fled from the servants of king Noah, repented of his sins and iniquities, and . . . began to teach . . . concerning that which was to come, and also concerning the resurrection of the dead, and the redemption of the people, which was to be brought to pass through the power, and sufferings, and death of Christ" (Mosiah 18:1–2).

Now my question: How did Alma obtain this knowledge of Christ? He heard Abinadi preach, we are told, and he "did write all the words which Abinadi had spoken" (Mosiah 17:4). Where did Abinadi get that knowledge? In chapters 13 and 14 of Mosiah, we find Abinadi reading the words of Moses and of Isaiah to Noah's court, and finding in these words clear foreshadowing of a "God [who should] himself . . . come down among the children of men, and . . . redeem his people" (Mosiah 15:1). Where did Abinadi obtain those scriptures? Well, he was a member of Zeniff's colony, and the narrative would apparently have us understand that they took copies of the Nephite records with them when they departed Zarahemla and resettled Lehi-Nephi. And those Nephite records? As we learn early in the Book of Mormon, Nephi and his brothers abscond with Laban's brass plates that contain the writings of Moses, Isaiah, and several other Hebrew prophets. So we have a clear line of transmission from prophetic utterance to brass plates to Nephi's small plates to Zeniff's copy to Abinadi's gloss to Alma's transcription. And that is only half the story. From Alma, we learn that those teachings become a part of his written record. When he and his band of exiles arrive in Zarahemla, King Mosiah reads to the assembled people "the account of Alma and his brethren" (Mosiah 25:6). King Mosiah, as guardian of the large plates, presumably incorporates the record into his own record. Those plates are of course subsequently abridged by Mormon, then translated by Joseph Smith, and finally quoted to you just now by me.

What strikes me about this transmission history is not just its convoluted twists and turns—the wonderful complexity of the Book of Mormon and the way scripture is constructed, transformed, incorporated, and transmitted. What strikes me even more is the greater lesson it holds for the Church in our day. Please note the fact that every successive incarnation of the Christ story—and remember that is the subject of Alma's sermon we tracked above—is unfolded in the context of a new settlement—a new church center, actually. Jerusalem; the wilderness outside Jerusalem; the promised land of the New World; a reoccupied Lehi-Nephi; Alma's church in the wilderness; the land of Zarahemla; the lands where Mormon wandered; Harmony, Pennsylvania—the Book of Mormon is in large measure the story of the unending transmission of the gospel into new contexts, new settings and conditions. It is a chronicle of the volatility and fragility of lands of refuge, a testament to the portability and ceaseless transmutations of Zion, with the only constant being the eternally present promise of spiritual autonomy and direct access to God's power and truth. Joseph Smith himself reenacted the same pattern. Zion is in Ohio, then Missouri, then the gathering shifts to Nauvoo, then Utah. And most significantly for the outlook of the international Church, neither Lehi nor Alma nor the Mulekites nor Joseph Smith thought the Zion they were erecting in the wilderness was provisional. They always thought it was *the* promised land, the end of the exodus, the fixed point after years in the spiritual desert. Each displacement was a disappointment; each renewed exodus a dream deferred and a hope shattered. Parley Pratt said of the Saints exiled from Jackson County that "the idea of being driven away from the land of Zion pained their very souls, and they desired of God, by earnest prayer, to return with songs of everlasting joy."[6] Joseph responded to their pleas for direction by writing, "I take the pen to address you but I know not what to—say. . . . My heart faints within me and I feel to exclaim O Lord let the desire of my heart be felt and realized this moment. . . . I verily know that [Christ] will spedily [*sic*] deliver Zion for I have his immutable covenant that this shall be the case but god is pleased to keep it hid from mine eyes."[7]

As the great theologian Reinhold Niebuhr wrote, man "is constantly tempted to forget the finiteness of his cultures and civilization and to pretend a finality for them which they do not have."[8] Even in Utah, the Saints prepared once again to burn their Zion to the ground and relinquish yet another fixed abode and move south. In modern Church history, beginning with the dawn of the twentieth century, Zion has once again become increasingly decentered—and rather than a map coordinate in America, the ideal of a pure heart governs most of our dreams of replicating Enoch's city in the present time. But the Book of Mormon modeled that all along, just as it models the fluidity of the concept of God's people. Covenant identity begins

The Tabernacle in the Wilderness.

as a family grouping—the Nephites were particularly concerned about the survival of their line, but by the time of Christ's coming, Nephites are a group defined by their faith, not their ancestry, just as the Old Testament taught us not to rely on our place in a bloodline by describing the blessings diverted successively from Ishmael the firstborn to Isaac, from Esau the eldest to Jacob, from Reuben to Joseph, and from Manasseh to Ephraim. The Book of Mormon's treatment of God's people as those "who will have him to be their God" (1 Nephi 17:40)—and of Zion as a portable, figurative tent in the wilderness—seems a prescient warning against the tendency to associate Zion with a particular place, nationality, or historical moment.

There is no holy land, only a holy people. These repeated dislocations, and the efflorescence of prophets, scripture, spiritual epiphanies, and blessedness in the midst of such endlessly fragmented communities cannot, it seems to me, help but speak powerfully to present and coming generations of the Church who may never know what it is to step foot inside the Tabernacle or attend a Boy Scout Jamboree in Mesa or EFY in Provo. If we are to imbibe the lessons of the Book of Mormon, then we need to incorporate the histories of a hundred and more permutations and translocations of Zion in Samoa and Germany and Mongolia—and see them all as part of the same pilgrimage on which we have all embarked.

Expanding into a Global Church

Now, what I have set forth so far is my reading of what the Book of Mormon teaches us about how we might become less insular, more one in Christ, and a more truly international church. But I want to speak now to the topic of the global Church, with a different meaning of *global* in mind than mere internationalism. And here I want to present a different kind of generosity and expansiveness to which I think the Restoration scriptures beckon us.

I want to talk about inclusiveness and exclusiveness in the Lord's conception of his Church. One meaning of a global church might be The Church of Jesus Christ of Latter-day Saints in its international dimensions as it has existed from the first Canadian mission in fall 1830 to the present day. It is another meaning I now have in mind, and this one I am taking to be what the scriptures refer to as the Church of the Lamb of God as it has existed inside and outside institutional forms from the days of Adam to the present.

Christian writers have long thought in terms of two churches: the visible and the invisible. John Calvin contrasted the invisible church, consisting of "the elect who have existed from the beginning of the world" with "the whole body of mankind scattered throughout the world, who *profess* to worship one God and Christ."[9] The great mystic Jacob Boehme spoke of the *Kirche ohne Mauer* (church without walls) as a place where "all rejoice to have the one mother [Sophia or Wisdom]" and live in mutual love and support, as distinct

Jacob Boehme.

from the tainted and unstable institutional church.[10] Successive churchmen and reformers recognized, in the words of one eighteenth-century writer, that when any church becomes "visible as a society, she shall not be safe," but is liable to be "corrupted more or less by the same artifices which overwhelmed the [first] great body of professed Christians."[11] A Methodist contemporary of Joseph Smith gave an equally dour prognosis. "Whenever a people become organized into a visible body," he agreed, "they are no longer the true church of Christ but fall in with the grand apostasy."[12]

Latter-day Saints believe that in this, the dispensation of the fulness of times, the cycle of apostasy and restoration has come to a decisive end, with the present incarnation being a church that shall not fall into the familiar pattern. What makes this Church distinctive, with a unique mission, is the priesthood keys it holds to administer the ordinances of salvation for the living and the dead, ordinances without which, Joseph taught, we cannot access the powers of godliness. I have said before that this makes us the Sadducees, in a sense. According to the *Encyclopedia Judaica*, in ancient Israel the Sadducees were the guardians of the temple, "cherishing the highest regard" for the Lord's house and the things of eternal meaning that transpired therein.[13]

Nevertheless, it is striking to me that in Joseph Smith's revelations, we find recurrent hints, intimations, and outright directives to remember that the institutional church is not the exhaustive repository of the chosen, the blessed, or the eventually saved. The idea of a spiritual church that exists alongside the institutional church, to encompass and eventually transcend it, is persistently reaffirmed. The scriptural examples seem to me striking enough and frequent enough that I can read them only as an orientation that was important to the Lord and that found self-conscious expression in his Prophet Joseph. I will review just five of them and then reflect on how they might bear on contemporary LDS thinking about the global Church.

Section 10 of the Doctrine and Covenants contains a rather remarkable reassurance of the Lord. The date—and this is terribly important—is April 1829, a year *before* the Church is restored. And yet in this revelation the Lord is referring to a church, *his* Church, as something that already exists. And he speaks to reassure its members that the Restoration does not represent a condemnation of all Christian forms already present on the earth. The new church's organization, he says, will not "destroy that which they"—*my people*—"have [already] received. . . . Therefore," he continues—and remember, this is in 1829—"whosoever belongeth to my church need not fear, for such shall inherit the kingdom of heaven." So those who belong to his Church, he tells us, are to receive more light. In his words, a new "part of my gospel" will be theirs. But he repeats reassuringly, this will not "destroy my church, but I say this to build up my church" (see D&C 10:52–54).

Just a month earlier, Joseph had first learned that the Lord's Church was to receive a new incarnation. "I will establish my church, like unto the church which was taught by my disciples," came the words canonized in the 1833 Book of Commandments.[14] But those words do not appear in the Doctrine and Covenants, in part, I would suggest, because the April revelation I described above urged caution in how Joseph was to understand this new church and its relationship to God's invisible church, or what the Lord was calling "my people" and "my church" in those same months. In addition, those words were not canonized because evidence suggests that Joseph was reflecting upon an allegory in the Book of Revelation that further shaped his understanding of what Restoration did and did not entail.

The biblical prophecy in chapter 12 of the Book of Revelation is as follows:

> There appeared a great wonder in heaven; a woman clothed with the sun, and the moon under her feet, and upon her head a crown of twelve stars. . . .
>
> And there appeared another wonder in heaven; and behold a great red dragon. . . .
>
> And the dragon stood before the woman which was ready to be delivered, for to devour her child as soon as it was born. . . .
>
> And the woman fled into the wilderness, where she hath a place prepared of God, that they should feed her there a thousand two hundred and threescore days. (Revelation 12:1, 3–4, 6)

In the King James Version of the Bible, the heading identifies the woman in this allegory, as have virtually all Protestant commentators, as a representation of the church, whose flight before the forces of Satan portends the Great Apostasy. But Joseph seems to have noticed the crucial fact that this woman is not banished from the earth—she retreats into the wilderness. There she does not perish. On the contrary, she is nourished for a prolonged period of time. She survives, nurtured by the Lord.

Albrecht Durer's Woman Clothed with the Sun and the Seven-Headed Dragon.

When Joseph revised the Book of Commandments for republication, he altered considerably the wording referring to the Restoration. He adopted the language of the prophecy in John's revelation. This is how it now reads in our Doctrine and Covenants: "the beginning of the rising up and the coming forth of my church out of the wilderness—clear as the moon, and fair as the sun, and terrible as an army with banners" (D&C 5:14).

Smith's predecessors and contemporaries believed the church in the wilderness symbolized the reality of something that endured even when priesthood authority was lost, a continuing if scattered body of righteous individuals, with whom spiritual gifts and godly principles and practices persisted. And Joseph's deliberate invocation of the language of this allegory suggests an appreciation for vestiges of truth, edifying insights, and inspiring manifestations of beauty, love, and devotion that mark a discipleship that has endured through time. As President Spencer W. Kimball once remarked, it would seem that when God has no prophets, he speaks through poets—and musicians, writers, artists, and many others who enjoy the influence of the Holy Spirit, "the gift of God unto all those who diligently seek him" (1 Nephi 10:19). This allegory of the woman and her return from the wilderness suggests a view of Church history in which many teachings and principles of the original Church survived more or less intact, though clearly in retreat from the mainstream—underground, or on the peripheries of orthodoxy. As his subsequent work was to prove, Joseph came to envision the Christian Church as in retreat, not in oblivion. Strikingly, the Nauvoo Temple exterior, in which Joseph's work found its fullest expression, was ornamented like the wilderness woman in John's vision: with sun, moon, and stars. And Joseph had said that the temple, broken down at Jerusalem's destruction to be rebuilt later, was a "type of the church."[15]

But of course, it is not just teachings and practices that constitute a church—it is, more importantly, people. And the Lord reminded Joseph that the Lord honored "his people" more than those who had formal membership in his institutional church. Some of these people, of course, predated the Restoration. Brigham Young once told a congregation, "I never passed John Wesley's church in London without stopping to look at it. Was he a good man? Yes; I suppose him to have been, by all accounts, as good as ever walked on this earth, according to his knowledge. Has he obtained a rest? Yes, and greater than ever entered into his mind to expect; and so have thousands of others of the various religious denominations."[16] More surprising are the indications from the Lord that "his people" included many of the righteous who have coesisted and coexist *alongside* the restored Church.

One such affirmation came as the Lord directed Joseph and three others relative to an early missionary assignment, in May 1831. "All people are under sin," the revelation declared, "except those which I have reserved unto myself, holy men that ye know not of" (D&C 49:8). Here we have a declaration, in unmistakable language, that even after the Restoration, the invisible church is alive and well. As with the Lord's reminder that in the last days his work would be "first temporal and secondly spiritual" (D&C 29:32), we hear echoes of the principal that spiritual realities and ideals must not be confused with temporal forms. This expansive vision of that church was laid out elsewhere, in an 1830 revelation where God promised to one day "drink of the fruit of the vine" with figures from Adam to Abraham to Elijah to Moroni to Peter—in fact, with "all those whom my Father hath given me out of the world" (D&C 27:5–14).

As I said earlier, the restored Church holds the keys of salvation for the living and the dead. At the same time, God loves, and considers to be his people, all those who honor him and will have him to be their God. The implications for how Latter-day Saints engage the rest of the world are there for the faithful to plumb. My task has been to try to reconstruct, from Joseph Smith's own revelatory pronouncements, what I take to be his way of balancing his certainty of the divine foundations and mission of the restored Church, with both a humility of language and self-conception, with a generosity of vision appropriate to its destiny. As the gospel settles into an increasing number of cultural environments, the kingdom will continue to unfold as a beautiful tapestry of many threads if we do not hinder its progress. Zion will continue to be found, and to be built up, in an array of settings. And like the wind that "bloweth where it listeth" (John 3:8), with its invisible comings and goings, the Church of the Lamb of God will reach further than we may know.

Many prophesied functions are part of the Church's destiny: to be a *leaven* in the world, suggesting an impact far out of proportion to size; to be an *ensign* to the world, setting a standard and point of holy reference; and through its temples and priesthood keys, the Restoration will continue to serve as a *portal*—not as a comprehensive reservoir—leading to salvation for the world's teeming billions living and dead.

Notes

1. *Chicago Times*, August 7, 1875, in Lyndon W. Cook, ed., *David Whitmer Interviews: A Restoration Witness* (Orem, UT: Grandin, 1991), 7.
2. Introduction, in Royal Skousen and Robin Scott Jensen, eds., *Revelations and Translations, Vol. 3: Printer's Manuscript of the Book of Mormon*, vol. 3 of the Revelations and Translations series of *The Joseph Smith Papers*, ed. Dean C. Jessee, Ronald K. Esplin, and Richard Lyman Bushman (Salt Lake City: Church Historian's Press, 2015).
3. Thomas F. O'Dea, *The Mormons* (Chicago: University of Chicago Press, 1957), 32. Bushman's response is in "The Book of Mormon and the American Revolution," in *Book of Mormon Authorship: New Light on Ancient Origins* (Provo, UT: Religious Studies Center, 1982), 189–212.
4. Lucy Mack Smith, *History of Joseph Smith by His Mother* (Salt Lake City: Stevens & Wallis, 1945), 169.

5. See Harold Bloom, *The American Religion: The Emergence of the Post-Christian Nation* (New York: Simon and Schuster, 1992).
6. Terryl L. Givens and Matthew Grow, *Parley P. Pratt: The Apostle Paul of Mormonism* (New York: Oxford University Press, 2011), 67.
7. To Brother William, John, et. al, August 18, 1833, in Gerrit J. Dirkmaat, Brent M. Rogers, Grant Underwood, Robert J. Woodford, and William G. Hartley, eds., *Documents, Vol. 3: February 1833–March 1834*, vol. 3 of the Documents series of *The Joseph Smith Papers* (Salt Lake City: Church Historian's Press, 2014), 263–64.
8. Reinhold Niebuhr, "The Tower of Babel," in *Reinhold Niebuhr: Theologian of Public Life* (Minneapolis: Fortress Press, 1991), 83–84.
9. John Calvin, *Institutes of the Christian Religion* 4.1.7, trans. Henry Beveridge (Peabody, MA: Hendrickson, 2008), 677.
10. Letter 46, in Robin Waterfield, ed., *Jacob Boehme* (Berkeley, CA: North Atlantic Books, 2001), 16.
11. Alexander Fraser, *Key to the Prophecies of the Old and New Testaments, Which Are Not Yet Accomplished* (Philadelphia: John Bioren, 1802), 164. This image of the Church coming out of the wilderness, terrible as an army with banners, combining the language of Solomon and Revelation, appears in Matthew Henry's early eighteenth-century commentary on Joshua's invasion of Canaan. Matthew Henry, *An Exposition of the Old and New Testaments* (London: Joseph Ogle Robinson, 1828), 531.
12. "The Early Degeneracy of the Methodists," *The Telescope*, April 30, 1825, 189.
13. "Sadducees," in *Encyclopaedia Judaica* (Jerusalem: Keter, 1972), 14:621. The analogy with Mormons is hardly fully apt. Sadducees rejected the Resurrection, angels, and the supernatural in general.
14. Book of Commandments 4:5.
15. The architectural parallel was pointed out to me by Joseph Spencer in a personal correspondence. Smith's typology was expressed in Andrew H. Hedges, Alex D. Smith, and Richard Lloyd Anderson, eds., *Journals, Vol. 2: December*

1841–April 1843, vol. 2 of the Journals series of *The Joseph Smith Papers*, ed. Dean C. Jessee, Ronald K. Esplin, and Richard Lyman Bushman (Salt Lake City: Church Historian's Press, 2011), 208.

16. Brigham Young, in *Journal of Discourses*, 26 vols. (Liverpool: F. D. and S. W. Richards et al., 1851–86; repr., Salt Lake City, 1974), 7:5.

Index

Italicized page numbers refer to images.

C

D

E